Language,
Culture,
and Society

FIFTH EDITION

Language, Culture, and Society

An Introduction to Linguistic Anthropology

ZDENEK SALZMANN,
JAMES M. STANLAW,
NOBUKO ADACHI

WESTVIEW PRESS

A Member of the Perseus Books Group

Published by Westview Press,
A Member of the Perseus Books Group

Every effort has been made to secure required permissions for all text, images, maps, and other art reprinted in this volume.

Westview Press books are available at special discounts for bulk purchases in the United States by corporations, institutions, and other organizations. For more information, please contact the Special Markets Department at the Perseus Books Group, 2300 Chestnut Street, Suite 200, Philadelphia, PA 19103, or call (800) 810-4145, ext. 5000, or e-mail special.markets@perseusbooks.com.

Library of Congress Cataloging-in-Publication Data
Salzmann, Zdenek.
Language, culture, and society : an introduction to linguistic anthropology / Zdenek Salzmann, James M. Stanlaw, Nobuko Adachi.—5th ed.
    p.   cm.
Includes bibliographical references and index.
ISBN 978-0-8133-4540-6 (alk. paper)—ISBN 978-0-8133-4541-3 (e-book)
1. Anthropological linguistics.   I. Stanlaw, James.   II. Adachi, Nobuko.   III. Title.
P35.S18 2012
306.44—dc23
                                                                  2011029300

10 9 8 7 6 5 4 3 2

CONTENTS

PREFACE TO THE FIFTH EDITION

It gives us great pleasure to write the preface to the fifth edition of *Language, Culture, and Society*. To a large extent, this edition represents a new book because it contains the contributions of two coauthors, James Stanlaw and Nobuko Adachi. Thanks to them the book now incorporates some of the most recent material reflecting changes in information technology and digital communication, felt even in such fields as linguistic anthropology. The changes in the text are also reflected in the expanded Resource Manual and Study Guide as well as in the Notes and Suggestions for Further Reading, which supplement the text of all fourteen chapters.

We are indebted to the editorial staff at Westview Press who have seen this edition through the process of editing and production, in particular editor Evan Carver and Sandra Beris, whose patience and support have been very valuable. We hope that the readers and users of this new edition will gain as much from using the book as we, the authors, did from preparing it.

Zdenek Salzmann,
James M. Stanlaw, and
Nobuko Adachi

1

Introducing Linguistic Anthropology

The first thing that someone reads in any introductory textbook is the authors' capsule definition of the subject matter at hand. In this book, we have two disciplines that, at first glance, might appear to be very different. Stereotypically, people think of anthropologists in pith helmets out in a jungle someplace uncovering bizarre tribal customs. Likewise, they imagine a linguist as someone who can speak a dozen languages fluently, or else as a scholar poring over ancient texts deciphering secret hieroglyphic messages. In reality, these two fields are hardly like that, but that does not make them any less exciting. This book is about how those people who call themselves linguistic anthropologists study the universal phenomenon of human language. But before we go into the specifics of how they do that, we should ask ourselves an even more basic question:

Why Should We Study Language? Language in Daily Life

"Why should I study language?" is hardly a rhetorical question. Most people never formally study language and they seem to get along fine. But do they? For example, have you ever arranged to meet someone "next Tuesday" only to find that your friend was planning to show up a week later than you had anticipated? Or why do we need lawyers to translate a contract for us when the document is written in a language that all parties share? David Crystal (1971:15) points out that communication between patients and physicians can be extremely difficult given the differences in training and perspective of the persons involved. The doctor often has to take a general phrase, such as "a dull ache in my side," and formulate a diagnosis and treatment based solely on this description. And when responding to what the patient has said, the doctor must choose her words carefully. What a doctor calls a "benign growth" might be heard as "cancer" by the patient.

At school we are confronted with language problems the minute we walk in the door. Some are obvious: "I can't understand Shakespeare. I thought he spoke English. Why is he so difficult?" Other problems are not so obvious: "What is the difference between who and whom? Doesn't one make me sound British?" "Why do I have to say 'you and I' instead of 'me and you?'" Some problems, such as the subtle sexism found in some textbooks, may be beyond our everyday psychological threshold. Problems of ethnicity and community-identity can be seen in such controversial issues as bilingual education or the teaching of **Ebonics.**

Language is involved in a wide variety of human situations, perhaps *every* situation. If something permeates every aspect of human life, and is so complex that we cannot fathom its influence, we should study it. The scientific study of language is one of the keys to understanding much of human behavior.

The study of language will not in itself solve all the world's problems. It is useful enough to make people aware that these problems of language exist and that they are widespread and complex. Besides being of intellectual interest, then, the study of language offers a special vantage point of "linguistic sensitization" (Crystal 1971:35) to problems that are of concern to everyone, regardless of discipline and background.

Some of the questions we will address in the book, then, are broad but fundamental—for example:

1. How can language and culture be adequately described?
2. Do other animals, such as chimpanzees using American sign language, show linguistic capacities?
3. How did language originate? How did it contribute to human evolution and the development of culture?
4. How are languages acquired?
5. How can languages be classified in order to show the relationships among them?
6. What is the relationship between language and thought?

7. What is meaning? How is it bestowed? How is it learned?

8. What does it mean to be human?

Modern Myths Concerning Languages

This may be a good place to provide information about languages in general in order to set some basic matters straight. Every human being speaks a language, but what people think about languages—particularly those about which they know little or nothing—is quite another matter. Consider the following statements. Which ones do you think are true?

Most everywhere in the world everyone is monolingual or monodialectal, just like in America.

Spelling in English is basically phonetic, and governed by clear rules.

Most writing systems in the world are based on some kind of alphabet.

If you really want to learn Spanish, don't take a class in school. It is better to just go, say, to Mexico for a month or two.

Some languages are naturally harder to learn than others.

Some languages are naturally more "primitive" than others.

Language itself is not ambiguous; it is people who misinterpret things that cause problems.

Some dialects are, well . . . stupid, demonstrating that a person is uneducated.

The use of language somehow reflects one's intelligence.

People who are fluent in another language may not have complete mastery of their native language.

The ability to learn a foreign language is a special kind of skill that some of us have, and others don't.

As our grade school teachers taught us, if you want to get it right, go to the dictionary!

People who use double negatives ("I don't need no anthropology classes") are really not thinking logically.

It is easier to learn Chinese if you come from a Chinese family background than from a European family.

Languages seem to have special characteristics or personalities, e.g., French is romantic, German is scientific, Russian is soulful, Spanish is hot-blooded, Italian is emotional, Chinese is simple and straightforward,

Japanese is mysterious, spiritual, and Zen-like, English is logical, Greek is philosophical, etc.

All Native Americans generally speak the same language; that's why they could communicate with each other using sign language (like in the movies).

The more words you know, the better you know your language.

Most anthropologists and linguists would say that all of the above statements are suspect, if not outright wrong. Let us briefly consider a few of these misconceptions concerning languages in more detail, because they appear to be widespread, even among those who are otherwise well educated and knowledgeable. These misconceptions we can refer to as myths, in the sense of being unfounded, fictitious, and false beliefs or ideas.

The most common misconception is the belief that unwritten languages are "primitive," whatever that may mean. Those who think that "primitive" languages still exist invariably associate them with societies that lay people refer to as "primitive"—especially the very few remaining bands of hunter-gatherers. There are of course differences in cultural complexity between hunting-and-collecting bands and small tribal societies on the one hand and modern industrial societies on the other, but no human beings today are "primitive" in the sense of being less biologically evolved than others. One would be justified in talking about a primitive language only if referring to the language of, for example, the extinct forerunner of *Homo sapiens* of a half million years ago. Even though we do not know on direct evidence the nature of the system of oral communication of *Homo erectus*, it is safe to assume that it must have been much simpler than languages of the past several thousand years and therefore primitive in that it was rudimentary, or represented an earlier stage of development.

Why are certain languages mistakenly thought to be primitive? There are several reasons. Some people consider other languages ugly or "primitive sounding" if the languages make use of sounds or sound combinations they find indistinct or "inarticulate" because the sounds are greatly different from those of the languages they themselves speak. Such a view is based on the ethnocentric attitude that the characteristics of one's own language are obviously superior. But words that seem unpronounceable to speakers of one language—and are therefore considered obscure, indistinct, or even grotesque—are easily acquired by even the youngest native speakers of the language in which they occur. To a native speaker of English, the Czech word *scvrnkls* 'you flicked off (something) with your finger' looks quite strange, and its pronunciation may sound odd and even impossible because there is no vowel among the eight consonants; for native speakers of Czech, of course, *scvrnkls* is just another word. Which speech sounds are used and how they are combined to form words and utterances vary from one language to the next, and speakers of no language can claim that their language has done the selecting and combining better than another.

Another myth has to do with grammar. Some think that languages of peoples whose societies are not urbanized and industrialized have "little grammar," meaning that such languages have few, if any, of the sort of grammar rules students learn in school. According to this misconception, members of simple societies use language in rather random fashion, without definite pattern. To put it differently, grammar in the sense of rules governing the proper use of cases, tenses, moods, aspects, and other grammatical categories is erroneously thought to be characteristic of "civilized" languages only. Once again, nothing could be further from the truth. Some languages have less "grammar" than others, but the degree of grammatical complexity is not a measure of how effective a particular language is.

What sorts of grammars, then, characterize languages spoken by members of tribal societies? Some of these languages have a fairly large and complicated grammatical apparatus, whereas others are less grammatically complex—a diversity similar to that found in Indo-European languages. Edward Sapir's description of the morphology of Takelma, based on material collected in 1906, takes up 238 pages (Sapir 1922). In Takelma, the now extinct language spoken at one time in southwestern Oregon, verbs were particularly highly inflected, making use of prefixes, suffixes, infixes, vowel changes, consonant changes, and reduplication (functional repetition of a part of a word). Every verb had forms for six tense-modes, including potential ('I can . . . ' or 'I could . . .'), inferential ('it seems that . . .' or 'I presume that . . .'), and present and future imperatives (the future imperative expressing a command to be carried out at some stated or implied time in the future). Among the other grammatical categories and forms marked in verbs were person, number, voice (active or passive), conditional, locative, instrumental, aspect (denoting repeated, continuing, and other types of temporal activity), and active and passive participles. Sapir's description of verb morphology fills more than 147 pages—yet is not to be taken as exhaustive.

Although the brief characterization here is far from representative of Takelma verb morphology, it clearly indicates that Takelma grammar was anything but simple. A similar and more detailed demonstration of morphological complexity could easily be provided for hundreds of other so-called primitive languages.

When it comes to the vocabulary of languages, is it true, as some suppose, that the vocabularies of so-called primitive languages are too small and inadequate to account for the nuances of the physical and social universes of their speakers? Here the answer is somewhat more complicated. Because the vocabulary of a language serves only the members of the society who speak it, the question to be asked should be, Is a particular vocabulary sufficient to serve the sociocultural needs of those who use the language? When put like this, it follows that the language associated with a relatively simple culture would have a smaller vocabulary than the language of a complex society (see Box 1.1). Why, for example, should the Eskimo have words for chlorofluoromethane, dune buggy, lambda particle, or tae kwon do when these substances, objects, concepts, and activities play no part in their culture? By the same token, however, the language of a tribal society would have elaborate lexical domains for prominent aspects of the culture even though these do not exist in complex societies. The Agta of the Philippines, for example, are reported to have no fewer than thirty-one verbs referring to types of fishing (Harris 1989:72).

For Aguaruna, the language serving a manioc-cultivating people of northwestern Peru, Brent Berlin (1976) isolated some 566 names referring to the genera of plants in the tropical rain forest area in which they live. Many of these genera are further subdivided to distinguish among species and varieties—for example, the generic term *ipák* 'achiote or annatto tree (*Bixa orellana*)' encompasses *baén ipák, čamíŋ ipák, hémpe ipák,* and *šíŋ ipák,* referring respectively to 'kidney-achiote,' 'yellow achiote,' 'hummingbird achiote,' and 'genuine achiote.' Very few Americans, unless they are botanists, farmers, or nature lovers, know the names of more than about forty plants.

Lexical specialization in nonscientific domains is of course to be found in complex societies as well. The Germans who live in Munich are known to enjoy their beer, and accordingly, the terminology for the local varieties of beer is quite extensive. Per Hage (1972) defined ten "core" terms for Munich beers according to strength, color, fizziness, and aging. But when local connoisseurs also wish to account for the degree of clarity (clear as against cloudy) and the Munich brewery that produced a particular beer, the full list now exceeds seventy terms. Such a discriminating classification of local beers is likely to impress even the most experienced and enthusiastic American beer drinker.

However, even though no languages spoken today may be labeled primitive, this does not mean that all languages are the same, do all things in the same way, or are equally influential in the modern transnational world. The linguistic anthropologist Dell Hymes claims that languages are not functionally equivalent because the role of speech varies from one society to the next. One of his examples is the language of the Mezquital Otomi, who live in poverty in one of the arid areas of Mexico. At the time of Hymes's writing, most of these people were monolingual, speaking only Otomi, their native language. Even though they accepted the outside judgment of their language as inferior to Spanish, they maintained Otomi and consequently were able to preserve their culture, but at a price. Lack of proficiency in Spanish, or knowledge of Otomi only, isolated the people from the national society and kept them from improving their lot. According to Hymes, no known languages are primitive, and all "have achieved the middle status [of full languages but not] the advanced status [of] world languages and some others. . . . [But though] all languages are potentially equal . . . and hence capable of adaptation to the needs of a complex industrial civilization," only certain languages have actually done so (Hymes 1961:77). These languages are more successful than others not because they are structurally more advanced but because they happen to be associated with societies in which language is the basis of literature, education, science, and commerce.

The Otomi example is not an isolated case in Mexico. An important factor that contributes to the success of a language is the literacy of its speakers. In countries where many languages are spoken, the language or languages that people learn to read and write are associated with knowledge and therefore also with political and economic power. In Mexico, whose official language is Spanish, more than 250 indigenous languages or regional dialects are spoken (Lewis 2009). These include Nahuatl (several dialects of a Uto-Aztecan language) and Yucatec (a Mayan language), each spoken by more than a million speakers, and about fourteen others that are used by more than a 100,000 speakers each. During the last seventy years, however, the percentage of monolingual and bilingual Mexican Indians has been steadily declining in favor of Spanish (from 16 percent in 1930 to about 7 percent in 2005). Although speakers of Indian languages use them in family life, in the fields, at traditional ritual gatherings and curing ceremonies, and in village markets and other local settings, an increasing number use Spanish in schools, agricultural or other training, hospitals and clinics, and political and administrative meetings organized by representatives of the state or federal government. Speaking knowledge and literacy in Spanish have come to be viewed as a mark of "cultural advancement" and self-confidence; the use of only an indigenous language is viewed as a sign of ignorance, backwardness, and a passive attitude. (Although the absence of writing in no way implies inferiority of a language, it is particularly ironic that in pre-Columbian times a number of Mesoamerican peoples did have writing systems.) Today, "Spanish is . . . exerting a tremendous pressure, particularly among the young, and the rejection of the Indian language has been a first step toward assuming a mestizo [mixed European and American Indian ancestry] identity, 'passing over' from one ethnic group to another" (King 1994:170). But can one talk about unsuccessful languages when their subordinate status is being assigned to them by outsiders and accepted by their own speakers?

To say, however, that some languages may be considered more successful than others must not be taken as justifying linguistic profiling, that is, judging the worth of persons on the basis of their speech. This may happen (and is happening) whenever one of two (or several) languages spoken in a particular area of the world is thought to have more prestige than another. Such valuation may easily lead to language prejudice and result in an irrational attitude of superiority toward an individual, a group, or a population using that language. And strange as it may seem, language prejudice can exist even in situations where two (or more) languages in question have equally long histories and distinguished literary traditions. A case in point may be the attitude in the eastern United States of some white Americans toward Puerto Ricans. The use of "good" English (whatever "good" may mean in this context) is associated by these white Americans with political and economic prestige, but Spanish (or English, the second language of the Puerto Ricans, if spoken with decided accent and grammatical mistakes) is equated with poverty, a lower-class status, lower intelligence, and the like. In other words, languages, dialects, choice of words, and accents become the means by which people are classified and then treated accordingly. Linguistic prejudice and racial prejudice are close relatives.

BOX 1.1 SAPIR ON LINGUISTIC AND CULTURAL COMPLEXITY

All attempts to connect particular types of linguistic morphology with certain correlated stages of cultural development are vain. Rightly understood, such correlations are rubbish. . . . Both simple and complex types of language of an indefinite number of varieties may be found spoken at any desired level of cultural advance. When it comes to linguistic form, Plato walks with the Macedonian swineherd, Confucius with the headhunting savage of Assam.

It goes without saying that the mere content of language is intimately related to culture. A society that has no knowledge of theosophy need have no name for it; aborigines that had never seen or heard of a horse were compelled to invent or borrow a word for the animal when they made his acquaintance. In the sense that the vocabulary of a language more or less faithfully reflects the culture whose purposes it serves it is perfectly true that the history of language and the history of culture move along parallel lines. But this superficial . . . kind of parallelism is of no real interest to the linguist except in so far as the growth or borrowing of new words incidentally throws light on the formal trends of the language. The linguistic student should never make the mistake of identifying a language with its dictionary.

from Edward Sapir, Language (1921), 234

Brief History of Anthropology

This book is a text on linguistic anthropology, so let us now discuss what these two disciplines—anthropology and linguistics—entail. We will begin with anthropology. A very simple definition of anthropology is "the holistic study of humankind," but this may not be especially enlightening. More insightful might be these propositions, which summarize the overall scope of anthropology (Pi-Sunyer and Salzmann 1978:3):

1. Because members of the species *Homo sapiens* are biological organisms, the study of human beings must try to understand their origin and nature in the appropriate context.

2. As hominids (that is, recent humans and their extinct ancestors) strove to adapt to a great variety of natural and self-made conditions, they engaged in a long series of innovations referred to by the term *culture*.

3. In the course of their cultural evolution during the past million years, humans were immeasurably aided by the development of an effective means of communication, the most remarkable and crucial component of which is human language.

Many other fields, of course, are also concerned with aspects of the human condition. Among these fields are anatomy, physiology, history, political science, economics, art history, literature, and sociology. With all these specialized areas focusing on the human experience, why would there be a need for such a broad discipline as anthropology?

When Herodotus, a Greek historian of the fifth century B.C., wrote briefly about the ethnic origin of the Carians and Caunians of southwestern Asia Minor and took into consideration the dialects they spoke, he engaged in (stretching the point a bit) what could be called linguistic anthropology. During the Age of Discovery, European scholars became intrigued by the many different peoples of the American continents and the languages they spoke. Nevertheless, linguistic anthropology in the modern sense is a relatively recent field of study that developed in the United States and has been practiced predominantly by North American academics.

The stimulation for the earliest phases of what was to become linguistic anthropology came from the exposure of European immigrants to Native Americans. The cultures and languages of these peoples were studied by educated Americans of varying professions—physicians, naturalists, lawyers, clerics, and political leaders. Among these amateur linguists, for example, was Thomas Jefferson (1743–1826), who collected the vocabularies of Native American languages. In his *Notes on the State of Virginia* (1787), Jefferson wrote, "Great question has arisen from whence came those aboriginals of America" and then offered the following suggestion: "Were vocabularies formed of all the languages spoken in North and South America . . . and deposited in all the public libraries, it would furnish opportunities to those skilled in the languages of the old world to compare them with these, now, or at any future time, and hence to construct the best evidence of the derivation of this part of the human race" (Jefferson 1944:225–226). In this passage Jefferson referred to more than just the comparative study of languages;

he must have had in mind using linguistic evidence to address questions concerning the cultural prehistory of humankind.

By the middle of the nineteenth century, the world was basically a well-known place, both geographically and culturally. The details certainly remained to be filled in, but no one expected to find a new hemisphere or uncover an unknown civilization. What puzzled scholars, however, was why we found so much human variety. Peoples looked vastly different, they spoke different languages, and their religions, marriage practices, and other customs also seemed very different. One of the main intellectual and scientific tasks of the day was to try to explain this diversity of race, language, and culture, past and present.

Modern anthropology began as the study of subjects that were not already claimed by scholars in other fields. But to say that anthropology just gathered these intellectual leftovers is not quite accurate. It was thought that the study of human biological and cultural development would shed light on the pressing "race, language, and culture" question. Because at that time "primitives" were thought to be the remnants of an evolutionary ancestral past, the study of preindustrial societies naturally became anthropology's main domain. Early anthropologists, then, focused especially on the nonliterate tribal peoples others considered "primitive" or "savage." These humble beginnings are still reflected in the present in the popular conception of anthropologists as people who supply museums with exotic specimens from societies in remote parts of the world or who dig up the remains of past human life and cultures. Many modern anthropologists, however, study their own cultures as well, and some of their findings and comments on them are illuminating.

During the nineteenth century, the study of Native Americans and their languages occupied both distinguished Americans and a number of European explorers who traveled in the western part of the United States. Some of them collected and published valuable data on Native Americans and their languages that would otherwise have been lost. Serious and purposeful study of Native American languages and cultures, however, did not begin until after the establishment of the Bureau of (American) Ethnology of the Smithsonian Institution in 1879. John Wesley Powell (1834–1902), perhaps better known as the first person to run the Colorado River throughout the entire length of the Grand Canyon, became its first director. It was Powell who in 1891 published a still-respected classification of American Indian languages north of Mexico.

Because the early anthropologists were interested in peoples other than specialists neglected, they concerned themselves with all aspects of a society. The German-born Franz Boas (1858–1942) was a dominant figure in the early days of American anthropology and held the first academic position in anthropology in the United States (at Clark University in Worcester, Massachusetts, from 1888 to 1892). He authored, coauthored, or edited more than seven hundred publications ranging from articles on Native American music, art, folklore, and languages to studies in culture theory, human biology, and archaeology. As early as 1911, Boas edited the first volume of *Handbook of American Indian Languages*, followed by two other volumes (1922 and 1933–1938) and part of a fourth (1941). Even though Boas emphasized the writing of grammars, the compiling of dictionaries, and the collecting of texts, research concerning the place of languages in Native American societies and the relation of languages to cultures began to be undertaken with increasing frequency. After World War II, the study of the relationship between language, culture, and society was fully recognized as important enough to be considered one of the four subfields of anthropology. Boas's direct influence was felt until his death at the age of eighty-four, and the course of American anthropology after him was shaped to a great extent by his students at Columbia University.

By World War II, anthropology was well established as an academic field and taught at major U.S. universities. The four main subfields then recognized—in large part a legacy of Boas—were **biological** (or physical) **anthropology, cultural anthropology, archaeology,** and **linguistic anthropology.** More specialized areas of concern and research have developed within the subfields, among them political, economic, urban, feminist, medical, legal, nutritional, visual, and psychological anthropology; and the anthropology of area studies such of Latin America, Asia, Africa, and Europe, to mention a few.

The one commitment that anthropologists profess regardless of their specialization is the holistic approach. The term **holistic** refers to concern with a system as a whole rather than with only some of its parts. Because studying an entire culture in full detail could easily become a lifetime project, anthropologists focusing on only certain of its aspects invariably study and discuss them in full cultural context. In the study of humanity, applying the holistic approach means emphasizing the connections among the many different facets of the human condition so that humankind can be understood in its full complexity—cultural, social, and biological.

One characteristic that sets anthropology apart from the other social sciences is a strong fieldwork component, sometimes augmented (especially in archaeology and biological anthropology) by work in the laboratory. Archaeologists survey land for sites and excavate and analyze the remains of past cultures. Biological anthropologists study such topics as the relationship between culture and disease, the behavior of nonhuman primates (such as chimpanzees and gorillas), gene pool frequencies, and nutritional patterns. They also search in particular locations of the world for skeletal remains relating to human evolution. For some time now, cultural anthropologists have not limited themselves to the study of tribal societies, peasant villages, or bands of hunter-gatherers in remote parts of the world. Many today work in postindustrial modern societies such as Japan and the United States, or those found in Europe. This is certainly as it should be: If anthropology is truly the study of humankind, then it must concern itself with all of humankind.

Anthropology, Linguistics, and Linguistic Anthropology

Another discipline that also focuses on uniquely human attributes is linguistics, the scientific study of language. *Linguistics* does not refer to the study of a particular language for the purpose of learning to speak it; rather, it refers to the analytical study of language, any language, to reveal its structure—the different kinds of language units (its sounds, smallest meaningful parts of words, and so on)—and the rules according to which these units are put together to produce stretches of speech. There is a division of labor, then, between linguists and linguistic anthropologists: The interest of the linguist is primarily in language structure; the interest of the linguistic anthropologist is in speech use and the relations that exist between language on the one hand and society and culture on the other (as seen in Box 1.2). As for the prerequisite training, the linguist does not need to study anthropology to become fully proficient in linguistics; a linguistic anthropologist, in contrast, must have some linguistic sophistication and acquire the basic skills of linguistic analysis to be able to do significant research in linguistic anthropology.

A terminological note is appropriate here. Although *anthropological linguistics* has frequently been employed to refer to the subfield of anthropology otherwise known as linguistic anthropology, and a respected journal

BOX 1.2 LINGUISTICS CONTRASTED WITH LINGUISTIC ANTHROPOLOGY

Unlike linguists, [linguistic] anthropologists have never considered language in isolation from social life but have insisted on its interdependence with cultural and social structures. In this sense, their technical linguistic analyses are a means to an end, data from which it is possible to make inferences about larger anthropological issues. Hence, under the . . . label "language and culture," anthropologists study topics such as the relations between world views, grammatical categories and semantic fields, the influence of speech on socialization and personal relationships, and the interaction of linguistic and social communities. . . . As Hymes has aptly remarked, "language is not everywhere equivalent in communicative role and social value . . . [and] no normal person, and no normal community is limited in repertoire to a single variety of [style], to an unchanging monotony which would preclude the possibility of indicating respect, insolence, mock-seriousness, humor, role-distance, etc., by switching from one code variety to another." Consequently, the relation between languages and social groups cannot be taken for granted, but is a problem which must be ethnographically investigated.

from Pier Paolo Giglioli, ed., Language and Social Context (1972), 9–10

exists under that name (*Anthropological Linguistics*), the term linguistic anthropology is to be preferred, as Karl V. Teeter argued some years ago (1964). Briefly, if anthropology is the study of humanity, and language is one of the most characteristic features of humankind, then the study of language is an obvious and necessary aspect of anthropology as a whole. To modify the noun *linguistics* by the adjective *anthropological* is clearly redundant because, even though members of all animal species communicate, so far as is known no other species uses anything comparable to human language. Only if, say, members of the cat family (Felidae) or of the class of birds (Aves) had something like human speech (not just some system of communication, no matter how intricate) would it make sense to speak of anthropological linguistics to distinguish it from some such field of study as felid or avian linguistics (that is, the study of the language of cats or birds). As we have already seen, there are several subfields of anthropology; just as the subfield concerned with culture is referred to as *cultural anthropology*, the one concerned with language is aptly referred to as *linguistic anthropology*. This is the term used throughout this book: It states exactly what the subfield is about—the study of language (or speech) within the framework of anthropology.

Summary and Conclusions

In its modern form, linguistic anthropology was the last subfield of anthropology to be developed and recognized and was practiced primarily by North American anthropologists. Its beginnings go back to the interest of nineteenth-century scholars in the great variety of Native American societies and the languages they spoke. Linguistic anthropologists view language in its cultural framework and are concerned with the rules for its social use; the analysis of its structure is therefore only a means to an end. By contrast, linguists in their study of languages emphasize linguistic structure and the historical development of languages.

Just as in the rest of anthropology, the data for linguistic anthropology are for the most part obtained in the field. Over the decades, field-workers have developed techniques and methods to the point that anthropology departments with a sizable program in linguistic anthropology now offer courses in linguistic field methods.

2

Methods of Linguistic Anthropology

What linguistic anthropology is concerned with are the consequences of the process that led to language. Because linguistic anthropologists try to view language from the very broad base of anthropology, their research interests are correspondingly comprehensive: from communication among the primates to language origins to structural characteristics of language to nonverbal types of communication to language in social context, and so on—too many to fully enumerate here. If the study of language is the main concern of linguistic anthropologists, then how does linguistic anthropology differ from linguistics?

Contrasting Linguistics with Linguistic Anthropology

Linguistics is the scientific study of language. The term does not refer to the study of a particular language or languages for the purpose of learning to speak them; rather, it refers to the analytical study of language, any language, to reveal its structure—the different kinds of language units (its sounds, smallest meaningful parts of words, and so on)—and the rules according to which these units are put together to produce stretches of speech.

The subject matter of linguistic anthropology, which can be briefly defined as the study of language in its biological and sociocultural contexts, is best illustrated by the table of contents of this book. Perhaps only the term **sociocultural** needs a comment. The term **society** is frequently used almost interchangeably with the term **culture**, and the compound "sociocultural" points out their interconnection. There is a fine distinction, though, between society and culture, and linguistic anthropologists deal with aspects of both concepts: when they study and describe the communicative links between individual members of a group and between groups within a society, and when they study and describe traditional learned behavior (culture) and how it relates to the values of the members of a group, their linkages with language are sociocultural.

The two linguistic statements:

To give concrete examples of the difference between linguistics and linguistic anthropology, consider the following four statements: the first two illustrate statements made by a linguist, the last two statements by a linguistic anthropologist.

1. In English, the nasal consonant *n* as in *sin*, and *ŋ* (written as *ng*) as in *sing*, are in contrast because they differentiate the meanings of two English words.
2. The Modern English word *woman* developed over the centuries from the Old English *wīfman*.

One will notice that there is no reference in these statements as to the speakers, or the circumstances under which the words have been used. Statements from linguistic anthropology:

1. In Javanese, the choice of words is determined by such characteristics of the speaker and the addressee as their age, gender, wealth, education, and occupation; and the more refined the level of speech, the slower, softer, and more even the presentation will be.
2. The remarkable cave-wall paintings and carvings of the Upper Paleolithic Cro-Magnons serve as an indirect proof that these prehistoric people had a full-fledged language.

To sum up, then, a division of labor exists between linguistics and linguistic anthropologists. The interest of the linguist is primarily in language structure and less often in language changes over time; the interest of the linguistic anthropologist is in speech use and the relations that exist between language on the one hand and its users on the other.

The Fieldwork Component

Research concerning the cultures and languages of contemporary societies is for the most part conducted in the field. Exposure of anthropologists to the societies or communities they wish to study is usually not only prolonged (lasting at least several months, and frequently a full year) but also repeated (once accepted by a group, anthropologists tend to return for follow-up research). The immersion of anthropological field-workers for an extended period in the day-to-day activities of the people whom they study is referred to as **participant observation.** To be able to communicate in their own language with the people under study is very helpful to the anthropologist. Lacking such skills, the anthropologist must rely on interpreters who, no matter how eager they are to help, may unwittingly simplify or distort what is being said by those who supply cultural or linguistic data. Because members of a society who are fluent in two languages are sometimes culturally marginal people, they should be selected with care: Individuals who have adapted to or borrowed many traits from another culture could have lost a substantial number of traits from their own. To be sure, studies of how and to what extent individuals or whole groups may have modified their culture by prolonged or vigorous contact with another society are of great importance and interest, but these studies cannot be carried out satisfactorily unless the traditional base of the culture undergoing change is well understood.

The availability of someone who can communicate with the anthropologist does not excuse the researcher from needing to become acquainted with the language of the group. The knowledge of a language serves the anthropologist as an invaluable tool for gaining an informed understanding of the many aspects of a culture—for example, enabling the researcher to judge the relative standing of members of a community on the basis of how they address one another. As early as 1911, Boas emphasized this point in his introduction to the first volume of *Handbook of American Indian Languages* when he insisted that "a command of the language is an indispensable means of obtaining accurate and thorough knowledge [of the culture that is being studied], because much information can be gained by listening to conversations of the natives and by taking part in their daily life, which, to the observer who has no command of the language, will remain entirely inaccessible" (Boas 1911:60).

What Boas insisted on was underscored by Bronislaw Malinowski (1884–1942), the Polish-born anthropologist who pioneered participant observation during his **fieldwork** in Melanesia and New Guinea between 1914 and 1920. In discussing the advantage of being able to speak one of the local languages, he wrote: "Over and over again, I was led on to the track of some extremely important item in native sociology or folklore by listening to the conversation of . . . Igua [his young helper] with his . . . friends, who used to come from the village to see him" (Malinowski 1915:501). And seven years later, in his introduction to *Argonauts of the Western Pacific*, Malinowski offered additional reasons why the command of the native language is useful: "In working in the Kiriwinian language [spoken on the island of Kiriwina in the Trobriand Islands], I found still some difficulty in writing down . . . [a] statement directly in translation . . . [which] often robbed the text of all its significant characteristics—rubbed off all its points—so that gradually I was led to note down certain important phrases just as they were spoken, in the native tongue" (Malinowski 1922:23). Decades later, Malinowski was still being cited for his emphasis on participant observation (Box 2.1).

For linguistic anthropologists, reasonably good speaking knowledge of the language of the society being studied is indeed indispensable. ("Reasonably good" speakers are those who can express themselves comfortably on nontechnical subjects; fluency, if it refers to nativelike command of a language, is very difficult to attain even after an extended period of fieldwork.) It is also necessary for linguistic anthropologists to learn a great deal about the culture of a foreign society, for much of what they study concerns the sociocultural functions of linguistic behavior. In short, both a knowledge of the language and a fair acquaintance with the culture are called for if inquiries made in the field are to be relevant and statements about the relationship between language and culture or society accurate and valid.

The native speaker from whom the researcher collects linguistic (or cultural) information is referred to as an informant. In recent years, the term *consultant* has been used with increasing frequency, in part because some members of the public confuse *informant* with the uncomplimentary term *informer*. More important, though, the term *consultant* gives recognition to the intellectual contribution made to linguistic and anthropological studies by those native speakers who work with anthropologists or linguists. The collaboration between members of a society and outsiders who study various aspects of that society is reflected in the growing number of coauthored articles. Another way of using to advantage the native speakers' insights into their own language is to enable interested individuals to receive training in linguistics and anthropology and then encourage them to use the acquired skills and knowledge not only for the benefit of linguistic anthropology in general but for the benefit of their own societies as well. Perhaps the most prominent among those who have urged that language informants be brought fully into collaboration was Kenneth L. Hale (1934–2001). He pioneered this approach for more than a quarter of a century. As early as 1969, Hale made the points that "for some linguistic problems [it is doubtful] whether the traditional arrangement, in which the linguistic problem is formulated in one mind and the crucial linguistic intuitions reside in another, can work at all—or, where it appears to work, whether it can be said that the native speaker is not, in fact, functioning as a linguist," and, a little further, that

the distribution of linguistic talent and interest which is to be found [for example] in an American Indian community does not necessarily correspond in any way to the distribution of formal education in the Western sense. If this talent is to flourish and be brought to bear in helping determine the particular relevance of the study of language to the communities in which it is located, then ways must be found to enable individuals who fit such descriptions . . . to receive training and accreditation which will enable them to devote their energies to the study of their own languages. (Hale 1974:387, 393)

Data for the analysis of a language or of language use can of course be collected away from the area where the language is spoken if an informant lives within reach of the linguistic anthropologist. Linguistic data obtained in such a manner can be quite useful if the informant's native language skills have remained good and the goal of the research is to make a preliminary analysis of the language. Determining how a language functions in a society, though, cannot be accomplished with the help of only one native speaker removed from those with whom he or she would normally communicate. (Special circumstances may merit exceptions. The description of the grammar of Tunica, a Native American language formerly spoken in northern Louisiana, was based on the speech of the only individual who could still speak the language "with any degree of fluency." The author of the grammar,

Mary R. Haas [1910–1996], who did most of her fieldwork in 1933, noted that her informant "has had no occasion to converse in Tunica since the death of his mother in 1915" [Haas 1941:9]. In this case, the only available informant was clearly preferable to none at all.)

In the early twenty-first century there are likely to remain only a few languages in the world about which nothing is known. However, there are still hundreds of languages about which linguists and anthropologists know relatively little. For the most part these languages are in Irian Jaya (West Irian) and Papua New Guinea (the western, Indonesian, and eastern, independent, halves of New Guinea, respectively) and the basin of the Amazon. According to recent estimates, some 850 languages are reported for Papua New Guinea, some 670 for Indonesia, and about 210 for Brazil—a total of nearly three-tenths of the world's languages (Krauss 1992:6). As a result of the great amount of fieldwork done the world over following World War II, it is now increasingly common for anthropologists to study communities or societies whose languages have already been described at least to some extent (and for which a system of writing may even have been devised, although speakers of such languages may have little, if any, need for writing). Such scholars are fortunate to be able to prepare in advance for their fieldwork by reading the relevant publications or unpublished manuscripts, listening to tape recordings made in the field by others, or even studying the language from native speakers if they are readily available. But occasions still arise in which the linguistic anthropologist must, or does, start from scratch. The following description, then, has two functions: first, to indicate very briefly how potential field-workers who lack any knowledge of the field language should proceed and, second, to indicate how linguists and anthropologists have coped with unknown languages in the past.

Besides being fluent in their native language, informants should be active participants in their culture. In most instances, ideal informants are older men and women not significantly affected by other languages and outside cultural influences. Such people almost always know their language better than the younger members of the society, who are likely also to use the language of whatever dominant culture may surround them. The situation of course varies from one part of the world to another. In many Native American societies in the United States, for example, young parents are no longer able to speak to their children in the language that was native to their own parents or grandparents. Not only do older members of a society tend to remember traditional narratives, which invariably preserve grammatical forms, words, and phrases that do not occur in everyday conversation, but they also are knowledgeable about the traditional aspects of their culture—ceremonies, rules of kinship, artifacts, foods, and the like—and therefore have a good command of the corresponding vocabulary.

Informants should be able to enunciate clearly. The speech of men and women missing most or all of their front teeth may be distorted to the point that a description of the sounds of their speech would not be representative of the typical pronunciation of the society's members. Most commonly, male anthropologists use male informants in the initial stages of their fieldwork; female anthropologists use women simply because individuals of the same gender usually work more comfortably with each other, especially in traditional societies. At some point during the field research, however, it is essential to obtain data from informants of the opposite gender as well, because in some societies the language of women contains certain sounds or words that differ from those heard in men's speech. All such differences should be accounted for and described. It is also important to include younger members of a society among the informants in order to find out whether and how linguistic variation is related to age, and to what extent speakers may be influenced by other languages or dialects used in the area or by the official language of the country in which the group is located. For example, even though typical American teenagers and their grandparents speak the same language, their dialects differ somewhat, especially as far as vocabulary is concerned; older speakers are not likely to be acquainted with teenager slang and, even if they are, may not want to use it. Speakers of Badaga (a Dravidian language of southern India) who learned to speak the language prior to the 1930s make use of twenty distinctive vowel sounds, whereas the younger Badaga use only thirteen (Samarin 1967:61). The result of this simplification of the Badaga vowel system is an increased number of homonyms, words pronounced alike but different in meaning (like the English words spelled *meet* and *meat*, *rode* and *rowed*, and *soul* and *sole*). In general, variations in speech may be influenced by differences in age, gender, socioeconomic class, caste, religion, and various other factors.

In eliciting data—that is, in obtaining from informants words, utterances, texts, and judgments concerning their language—the field-worker should strive to collect material that is dialectally uniform and spoken in a natural tone of voice and at a normal rate of speech. Unnaturally slow speech used by an informant to enable the linguist to transcribe utterances more easily tends to distort sounds, stress, and the length of vowels; when sentences are spoken too rapidly, there is a tendency to leave out sounds, or even to change them (consider the English *Gotcha!* 'I got you!' and *Betcha!* 'I bet you!'). Because dialects of a language may have somewhat different repertoires of sounds and words, using informants who speak different dialects could prove confusing for the field-worker in the initial stages of research. Eventually, of course, dialectal variation is worth noting, as are the sound modifications that words undergo when they are pronounced rapidly.

During the initial stages of fieldwork, eliciting is accomplished by asking the informant relatively simple questions such as "How do you say 'I am hungry' in your language?" "What does _____ mean in your language?" "Am I repeating correctly the word you have just said?" and the like. Once the linguistic anthropologist has become accustomed to hearing the language and working with it, more spontaneous and richer data can be obtained. Informants are then asked to talk, unprompted, about topics of personal interest to them—for example, "Please tell me how your father taught you to hunt when you were young," or "When you were a child, what was your favorite way of helping your mother?"—or to give an eyewitness account of some memorable experience, narrate a traditional tale, or engage in a conversation with another native speaker. Utterances longer than just a few sentences are best recorded on tape. The recordings can later be replayed as many times as needed to ensure accurate transcription. When first used, the tape recorder may inhibit informants somewhat; but if it is used often enough, informants become accustomed to it and their speech should not be appreciably affected.

If field-workers wish to include in their studies so-called body language (eye movements, gestures, and shrugs), which may be a very important component of communicative behavior, video cassette recorders are useful. They record not only the sounds of speech and the body motions of the individuals speaking but also the reactions of the audience and the overall setting, making it possible for the linguistic anthropologist to arrive at an accurate and comprehensive description of the communicative behavior characteristic of ceremonies, conversations, and encounters of other kinds.

What should be the size of a corpus, the collection of language data available to the linguist? A corpus is adequate for studying the sounds and grammar of a language once several days of recording and analysis have passed with no new sounds or grammatical forms noted. As for vocabulary, it would be impractical or impossible to collect every word that members of a society know or use. Quite commonly, words heard in everyday conversation among the members of a group do not include words heard in such traditional contexts as the telling of myths, praying, conducting ceremonies, and the like. A comprehensive description of a language (its sound system, grammar, and sentence formation) should therefore be based on data drawn from both casual and noncasual speech; that is, speech of different styles—everyday conversations, speech of young and old and women and men, speech of traditional storytelling, language used in formal affairs, and so on.

Linguistic anthropologists are of course interested in much more than just the sounds, grammar, and vocabulary of a language, as the following chapters of this book show. However, practical speaking skills and knowledge of a language's structure are prerequisite for the full understanding of the relations between a language on the one hand and the society and its culture on the other.

From what has just been said, it would appear that doing anthropological fieldwork is a challenging but interesting undertaking: The anthropologist makes many friends in an environment that is usually—at least in the initial stages—exciting, even mysterious, and becomes caught up in a discovery procedure that builds from the first day until the project is completed. The overwhelming majority of anthropologists engage in fieldwork repeatedly because they enjoy being away from the paperwork and routine of teaching and being among those whom they are eager to learn about and learn from.

Many demands that require adjusting to, however, are placed upon fieldworkers. The common response to exposure to unfamiliar cultural surroundings and people who speak a different language is culture shock. It manifests itself, at least initially, in disorientation and some degree of anxiety on the part of the field-worker, particularly if he or she is the only outsider in an otherwise close-knit community, and a conspicuous outsider at that. There are many things to adjust or conform to: different foods, almost invariably the absence of personal privacy, poor hygiene, and the lack of physical comfort. There can also be a variety of threats to a field-worker's well-being: excessive heat, humidity, or cold; ever-present insects (some alarming in size or number); larger animals to beware of (snakes, for example); and bacteria and viruses to which the visitor is not immune, with no physician to consult if the need arises. Then, too, it can be frustrating to have no one with whom to discuss the puzzling issues that frequently develop in the course of research. But even if the picture is somewhat mixed, most anthropologists—students and colleagues alike—usually consider their times in the field to be among the most memorable experiences of their lives.

BOX 2.1 PARTICIPANT OBSERVATION

During [Malinowski's] trip to do his first fieldwork, World War I broke out. When he landed in Australia, he learned that he was now the enemy, and the Australians informed him that he was stuck for the duration. But he convinced them that they should let him go and wander the territories, do a little ethno-exploring. He spent two extensive periods of time on a little string of atolls called the Trobriand Islands.

Malinowski became the patron saint of ethnography. He dived right in, lived with the "natives," and learned their language as they spoke it while they went about their everyday business. He talked about the goal of it all in romantic tones—"to grasp the native's point of view, his relation to life, to realize *his* vision of *his* world," or, as he sometimes put it, "to get inside the native's skin."

The name for this approach to fieldwork, a name that is now enshrined in the jargon, is participant observation. You don't just stand around and *watch* like a parody of a lab technician; you jump in and *do* everyday life with people to get a firsthand feel for how things go. At the same time, you keep a third eye at an altitude of several feet above the action and watch what's going on in a more distant way.

Never mind that this is difficult, to passionately commit to the flow of experience and keep your distance at the same time. The concept expresses the right contradiction. Besides, participant observation hides Malinowski's secret about culture. Like Boas and Whorf, he wrote about culture as what "those people" have. But participant observation carries with it a commitment to connect, to put your body and mind on the line, to engage what "those people" are doing and figure out why, at first, you didn't understand. Participant observation signals that culture *has* to get personal.

Given the gregarious nature in general and his devotion to participant observation in particular, it's no surprise that Malinowski's . . .] first love was the real situations that made up the daily life of the Trobriand Islanders. Language wasn't an isolated object that consisted of words and the rules for stringing them together into sentences. Language was the way that people came together in those situations and got things done.

from Michael Agar, Language Shock (1994), 92

A Checklist for Research in the Field

Books have been written about methods on fieldwork in anthropology, but one must realize that each field research experience is unique, even when the linguistic anthropologist revisits a group he or she has previously studied. Cultures of all societies (groups, villages) now experience change even more rapidly than in the past, and an anthropologist's earlier visit could even have introduced changes he or she may not have been aware of.

Practical advice to potential field-workers, however, can be of some use, and this is why included in this edition of the book is a checklist for research in the field (presumably in a foreign country). The checklist cannot be exhaustive, of course, or fit every particular field situation, but it may remind the anthropologist as to what needs to be thought about before beginning the fieldwork, while in the field, and after returning home.

A. Preparatory stage (when the location and the subject of the study have
   been decided upon)
   search for existing related publications
   drafting of a concrete project plan
   preparation of a budget
   write-up of an application for a research grant, to include:
      applicant's curriculum vitae
      title and description of project
         justification
         methodology
         expected contribution when finished
      (be specific; poorly or vaguely described projects are not acceptable)
      anticipated cost
         travel expenses
         maintenance in the field (food and "housing")
         informants' services (money or gifts)
         equipment (computer, camera, etc.)
         minor incidentals
      related academic work
         prior to departure for the field
         upon return
         publication plans

concrete preparation for travel to a foreign country:

valid passport

necessary visa(s)

relevant inoculations

small dictionaries of the languages of the area

information about the local fauna, flora, climate, etc.

glasses (two pairs)

personal medicines

first-aid kit

antibiotic

antihistamine

medicinal preparations used in treating:

    dysentery

    malaria

    general body pain

aspirin

tablets to disinfect water for drinking

bandaging for wounds

camera and accessories

paper, pencils

mosquito net, etc.

B. field-research stage

acclimatization to the environment (people, climate, hygienic conditions, etc.)

overcoming culture shock

efforts to gain confidence of members of the group

cultivating friendly personal relations

finding a local patron (an older and distinguished member of the group)

finding reliable interpreters (if any)

finding good informants (men and women)

stabilizing daily routine

applying implicit and explicit rules for behaving in a foreign culture

C. field-research methods

talk little, listen carefully

record data as soon as possible after receiving information

avoid questions answerable by "yes" or "no"

ask simple to-the-point questions

obtain dialogs between native people

obtain traditional narratives

be a participant observer

collect data using both the emic approach (information elicited from informants) and the etic approach (obtained by "objective" observation)

carry out interviews:

    spontaneous

    with questions prepared beforehand

produce a small-scale demographic survey

map the territory (for example, the village and its surroundings)

conduct case studies

explore the lexicons of native cultural domains

D. possible sources of tension and stress

lack of privacy

strikingly different living conditions:

    food

    beverages

    hygiene

    parasites

    insects

    diseases

(be careful not to become the local physician: lack of success could pose danger)

E. the post-field-trip stage

organizing and indexing of field notes

analysis of data

writing up of results

preparing publications

ethical aspects of publications (could some published information pose risk to members of the group or the informants?)

reporting on the use of grant funds to the funding organization maintaining friendly contacts (if possible) with the members of the group studied

Summary and Conclusions

Linguistic anthropologists view language in its cultural framework and are concerned with the rules for its social use; the analysis of its structure is therefore only a means to an end. By contrast, linguists in their study of languages emphasize linguistic structure and the historical development of languages.

Just as in the rest of anthropology, the data for linguistic anthropology are for the most part obtained in the field. Over the decades, field-workers have developed techniques and methods to the point that some anthropology departments with a sizable program in linguistic anthropology now offer courses in linguistic field methods. For the benefit of those who do not have access to such programs, a checklist for research in the field has been included in this chapter.

3

Language Is Sound: Phonology

The nature of ethnographic fieldwork makes it essential for anthropologists to acquire a working knowledge of the language of those whom they study, to learn something about its structure, and to be able to write it down to record words, utterances, or traditional narratives. American anthropologists have long been concerned with language, in large part because of the great number and variety of Native American languages spoken in their own linguistic backyard.

Each language represents a particular variety of the general language code—in other words, no two languages are alike, although some are structurally similar whereas others are quite different. Understanding the workings of a foreign language rather than simply learning to speak it requires some acquaintance with the plan according to which a particular language code is constructed. Such acquaintance cannot be gained by using the traditional grammar of English, or some other language taught in schools, as a framework. There are several important reasons for a more systematic and specialized approach.

One major reason has to do with converting to written form a language that previously has only been spoken. To accomplish this task, one must learn the principles of phonetic transcription. The use of the conventional spelling system of the anthropologist's own language is invariably out of the question: Not only should one expect the sounds of one language to differ from those of another, but the sounds and the orthographic conventions that represent them in the written language are not likely to correspond to each other on a one-to-one basis. English spelling is notorious for its lack of correlation with spoken English. For example, the sound *sh* of *shy* is written in

English in twelve additional ways, as in *chef, conscience, fuchsia, issue, mansion, nauseous, ocean, potion, pshaw, schist, sugar,* and *suspicion.* The two sentences "The sun's rays meet" and "The sons raise meat" sound exactly alike despite their different meanings and orthographic representations, and in "Where do these lead pipes lead?" the two words written as *lead* are pronounced differently depending on their meaning. It should be obvious that the writing systems of languages with a literary tradition, English in particular, are not suitable for careful linguistic work.

The second major reason for a specialized approach has to do with grammatical structure. Each language has a structure of its own that cannot be analyzed or grasped in terms of the investigator's own language. Many languages, for example, do not possess the definite and indefinite articles corresponding to the English *the* and *a(n)*. And English does not distinguish in the first person of the plural between the exclusive and inclusive forms that are common in other languages, for example, the Algonquian languages of Native North Americans. Where in English one would simply say *we, us,* or *our,* speakers of these languages must specify whether both the addressee (hearer) and perhaps others are included (as when a boy talks to his sister about "our mother"), or whether others are included but the addressee (hearer) is excluded (as when a mother talks to a visitor about "our children," referring to those belonging to her and her husband). In sum, each language has its own distinctive structural characteristics, and these are likely to be overlooked if its structure is accounted for through the grammatical categories of the investigator's mother tongue or some other language serving as a model. Many grammars of American Indian languages compiled in earlier centuries by well-meaning missionaries strongly resembled Latin or Greek, even though the Native American languages could not have been more different; the descriptions betrayed their authors' thorough grounding in the classical languages and the resulting dependence on their structures.

There are many benefits to understanding the structure of a system, not only with respect to becoming acquainted with a foreign language but in regard to other learning situations as well. One practical benefit is that if we are able to understand how the parts of a system function and what kinds of relationships exist among them, we are then spared having to memorize, or at least pay undue attention to, details that may well be trivial. To illustrate this point, let us use a simple example.

Bontok is a language spoken by a people in the mountains of northern Luzon in the Philippines. Among the many words corresponding to English nouns and adjectives are the following four stems: *fikas* 'strong,' *kilad* 'red,' *bato* 'stone,' and *fusul* 'enemy.' To express the idea that someone is becoming what the noun or adjective refers to, the Bontok would use the following words derived from the four stems above: *fumikas* 'he is becoming strong,' *kumilad* 'he is becoming red,' *bumato* 'he is becoming stone' (as in a myth), and *fumusul* 'he is becoming an enemy.' Those not trained in linguistics may find these forms a bit confusing, perhaps expecting, as a result of being native speakers of English, that in each example several words would be needed to indicate that an individual is undergoing some sort of change—becoming strong, red, stone, or an enemy. An examination of the Bontok data reveals a simple rule that accounts for the meaning 'he is becoming _____' (in stating the rule, we are avoiding terminology that might be unfamiliar to readers): Insert the sounds (written here as *um*) after the initial consonant of the stem. This rule produces *f-um-ikas* from *fikas*, and so on. Now that we know this particular piece of Bontok structure, we can guess at the word that would most likely mean 'he is becoming white' if we are given *pukaw* 'white'—namely *pumukaw*; conversely, we can guess what the stem meaning 'dark' would be from the word *gumitad* 'he is becoming dark'—namely *gitad*.

Focusing on recurring patterns of behavior of members of a society—in other words, trying to discover the structure of a cultural system—helps us become familiar with how the system operates. This is particularly true of the thousands of communicative systems we call languages.

The Anatomy and Physiology of Speech

The capacity for speaking and speech itself are taken so much for granted that few individuals ever stop to wonder how sounds are produced and why they vary as much as they do. Although it is true that speakers use their mother tongue automatically, without concentrating, it is equally true that the production of a dozen to a score of speech sounds per second requires extremely well-coordinated and precise movements and positionings of various parts of the speech apparatus located between the diaphragm and the lips (see Figure 3.1).

The extent of these elaborate gymnastics is all the more remarkable when we remind ourselves that the primary functions of the various parts of the speech apparatus are not those associated with producing sounds. For example, the tongue, rich in tactile sensory nerve endings, is the seat of the sense of taste and helps in swallowing food; and the main purpose of teeth is to bite off food (incisors) and then chew it (molars). In short, speech is a secondary function for what we refer to as the vocal tract, or vocal organs.

The production of speech sounds, which is a complex process involving about one hundred muscles as well as other tissues, requires precise coordination. When one speaks, air is taken into the lungs more rapidly than in the normal course of inbreathing and then exhaled in a slow and steady stream. It is forced from the lungs through the trachea (windpipe) and undergoes important modifications in the larynx, located at the upper end of the trachea. The larynx, the position of which is marked externally by the Adam's apple, houses two bands of muscular tissue known as the vocal cords, or vocal folds. The vocal folds stretch from front to back and regulate the size of the elongated opening between them, the glottis. During swallowing, in addition to being protected by the folded epiglottis from above, the vocal cords are drawn together, with the glottis closed, to prevent liquids or food particles from entering the lungs; for the production of **voiced** sounds, such as those making up the word *buzz*, the cords are drawn together and made to vibrate as the airstream forces its way between them; in whispering, they are brought close together, with the glottis narrowed; for the production of **voiceless** sounds, such as those heard at the beginning and end of the word *ship*, they are spread apart but tensed; and during normal breathing, they are relaxed and spread apart. The tension of the vocal cords determines the frequency of their vibration and therefore the pitch, whereas the force of the outgoing air regulates the loudness of sounds.

Having passed through the larynx, the air proceeds out through the pharynx towards the upper rear part of the mouth, just above the uvula, is lowered and the lips are closed, the air is released through the mouth, producing nasal sounds, such as the three different ones in the Spanish word *mañana* 'tomorrow' or the final one in the English word *king*. If the soft palate is lowered but the air allowed to escape simultaneously through both the nose and the mouth, nasalized sounds are the result, as in the French *bon* 'good.' The majority of sounds in the languages of the world are oral, with the air escaping only through the mouth because the soft palate is fully raised, making contact with the back wall of the pharynx and shutting off the entrance to the nasal cavity.

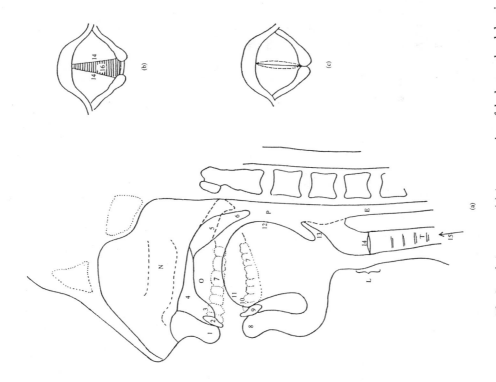

(a)

(b)

(c)

FIGURE 3.1   The Speech Apparatus. (a) A cross-section of the human head showing the principal parts of the vocal tract. The lungs and the diaphragm below them are not shown.

E	esophagus (gullet)	5	velum (soft palate)
L	larynx (voice box)	6	uvula
N	nasal cavity	7	molars
O	oral cavity	8	lower lip
P	pharynx	9	lower teeth (incisors)
T	trachea	10	tongue tip
1	upper lip	11	tongue blade
2	upper teeth (incisors)	12	tongue root
3	alveolar ridge	13	epiglottis
4	(hard) palate	14	vocal cords
		15	direction of outgoing air

(b) A view of the glottis (16), with a vocal cord on each side, during normal breathing. (c) The same view, but with vocal cords vibrating during speech. Adapted from Bohuslav Hála: Uvedení do fonetiky češtiny, Prague, 1962, p. 63.

As the air passes through the upper part of the speech tract, numerous modifications of the vocal **channel**, involving such articulators as the soft palate, tongue, and lips, make possible the tremendous variety of sounds heard in the several thousand of the world's languages. These sounds are customarily classified according to the manner and place of articulation and transcribed by means of phonetic symbols, which are enclosed in square brackets [ ].

Articulation of Speech Sounds

The two main classes of speech sounds are **vowels** and **consonants** (see Notes and Suggestions for Further Reading under Chapter 3 in the Resource Manual and Study Guide). In the production of vowels, the air that escapes through the mouth (for oral vowels) as well as through the nose (for nasalized vowels) is relatively unimpeded. Vowels are classified according to the part of the tongue that is raised, the configuration of the lips, and the extent to which the tongue approaches the palate above it (see Table 3.1). Another variable is the degree of muscular effort and movement that goes into the production of vowel sounds. If the tension in the tongue muscles is prominent, vowels are said to be *tense*, as in *beat* or *boot*; if it is lacking or scarcely noticeable, they are said to be *lax*, as in *bit* or *book*.

Even though an utterance may be viewed as a succession of individual sounds, most speakers tend to subdivide utterances naturally into somewhat larger units: syllables. To be fully serviceable, the term *syllable* needs to be defined separately for each language, but in general one may say that a syllable consists of a nucleus—usually but not always a vowel (V), with or without a consonant (C) or consonants before or after it. The following English words—*a, on, me, pin, spin, drift,* and *strengths*—all consist of one syllable and may be represented as V, VC, CV, CVC, CCVC, CCVCC, and CCCVC(C)CC, respectively. In the word *button,* the nucleus of the second syllable is the nasal [n], because the orthographic vowel *o* is not pronounced. A consonant functioning as the center of a syllable is said to be *syllabic*.

The vowels of American English dialects occur for the most part singly, as in the words *linguistic anthropology* [-ɪ-ɪ-ɪ- æ-ə-ɒ-ə-i]. However, sometimes there is a change in vowel quality within a syllable, as in the words *bite, bout,* and *boy.* What occurs in each of these three words and others like them is a movement from the first, more prominent vocalic part to the second, which

TABLE 3.1   Types of Vowels According to Place and Manner of Articulation

Place and Manner of Articulation	*Vowel Types*					
If the air excapes through the mouth	oral					
If the air escapes *also* through the nose	nasal(ized)					
According to the part of the tongue that is raised		front		central	back	
According to the position of the lips		unrounded (spread)	rounded	unrounded	unrounded	rounded
According to the position of the highest point of the tongue in the mouth (according to the closeness of the tongue to the roof of the mouth)	high (close)	i *beat*	ü German *kühl* 'cool'	ɨ Russian быть 'to be'	ï occurs in Turkish	u *boot*
	lower high	ɪ *bit*		ɨ as in *just* (*you wait*)		ʊ *book*
	mid	e *bait*; German *See* 'sea'	ö German *schön* 'lovely'	ə the second vowel of *sofa*		o *boat*; French *beau* 'beautiful'
	lower mid	ɛ *bet*	ɔ̈ French *peur* 'fear'		ʌ *butt*	ɔ *bought*
	low (open)	æ *bat*		a *body*		ɒ *pot*; in London English, *not*

It is not easy to illustrate various vowel types by examples from English because of wide dialect variation. For example, people native to eastern New England, the central Atlantic seaboard, and the coastal South pronounce the words *Mary, marry,* and *merry* differently, whereas in the rest of the United States, these three words are usually pronounced alike.

is shorter and less distinct. A change in vowel quality within the same syllable is referred to as a *diphthong.*

In the production of consonants, places of articulation range all the way
from the glottis to the lips, the last place in the vocal tract where the outgoing air can be modified (see Table 3.2). The manner of articulation refers to
the several kinds of constriction that may be set up at some point along the
speech tract by the articulators (see Table 3.3).

The vowel and consonant types surveyed here include only the basic ones.
Just as sounds can undergo lengthening or nasalization, they can be modified by secondary articulations. These give rise to labialized, palatalized, ve-
larized, pharyngealized, and otherwise modified sounds. Some consonants
may also be followed by aspiration, that is, accompanied by an audible breath.
Relatively rare are clicks, sharp suction sounds made by the lips or the tongue,
and ingressive sounds, those produced on the inbreath rather than the out-
breath. The most common speech sounds and their modifications are represented by the **phonetic** symbols and diacritics of the International Phonetic
Alphabet (IPA). Its various symbols and diacritics can be used to represent a
great many (but by no means all) sounds occurring in the world's languages.
Because the special characters and diacritical marks used by the IPA are not
always readily available, for the sake of economy and convenience many U.S.
linguists and anthropologists use some symbols that do not correspond to
those of the IPA. One should remember, in this connection, that phonetic
symbols are arbitrary; therefore, in principle one phonetic alphabet used for
transcription is just as acceptable as another so long as each sound is represented by one symbol only and all the symbols are carefully defined.

Articulatory phonetics, the study of the production of speech sounds by
the vocal organs, is not the only way to examine the raw material of language.
It is also possible to examine speech sounds for their physical properties, that
is, from the perspective of **acoustic phonetics.** This approach requires the
sound spectrograph, a device that visually represents acoustic features of
speech sounds in the form of spectrograms, or voiceprints. Spectrograms show
three dimensions of sounds: Duration (time) is displayed horizontally, frequency vertically, and intensity by the degree of darkness. For example, each
vowel is characterized by several resonance bands, referred to as formants,
which represent the overtone structure of a vowel produced by the shape of
the vocal tract. Because the position of the tongue changes with the production
of different vowels, the formants vary correspondingly (see Box 3.1).

TABLE 3.2 Types of Consonants According to Place of Articulation

Place of Articulation	General Description	Consonant Type	Example(s)
Lips	Both lower and upper lips articulate.	Bilabial	the initial and final sound of *bob*
Lower lip and upper teeth	Lower lip articulates with the upper teeth.	Labiodental	the initial sounds of *fan* and *van*
Teeth	Tongue tip is positioned between the upper and lower teeth.	Interdental	the initial sounds of *thin* and *this*
Teeth	Tongue tip articulates with the upper teeth.	Dental	*t* and *d* sounds of Irish English
Alveolar ridge	Front of the tongue articulates with the alveolar ridge.	Alveolar	the initial sound of *sit*
Area where the palate and the alveolar ridge meet	Tip of the tongue, curled back, articulates with the palato-alveolar area.	Retroflex	typically, *t* and *d* sounds in English as spoken by East Indians
	Blade of the tongue (and sometimes the tip) articulates with the palato-alveolar area.	Palato-alveolar	initial sound of *ship*
(Hard) palate	Front of the tongue articulates with the hard palate.	Palatal	the final sound of the German *ich* 'I'
Velum, or soft palate	Back of the tongue articulates with the soft palate.	Velar	initial sound of *calf*
Uvula	Back of the tongue articulates with the uvula.	Uvular	the *r* sound frequently heard in German (voiced variety) or French (voiceless)
Pharynx	Back wall of the pharynx articulates with the root of the tongue.	Pharyngeal	common in Arabic
Glottis	Vocal folds are positioned so as to cause a closure or friction.	Glottal	glottal stop that in some dialects of English replaces the *t* sound (-*tt*-) in such words as *bottle*

TABLE 3.3   Types of Consonants According to Manner of Articulation

Type of Constriction	Subtype of Constriction	General Description	Consonant Type	Examples with Description
Closure	Total	complete closure at some point in the vocal tract, with soft palate raised; sudden release of air pressure	Plosive, or stop	the initial sound of *pick*; closure at the lips
	Total	complete closure at some point in the mouth, with soft palate lowered and air escaping through the nose	Nasal	the initial and final sound of *mom*; closure at the lips
	Total	complete closure at some point in the mouth, with soft palate raised; gradual release of air pressure	Affricate	the initial and final sound of *judge*; the tongue blade forms closure with the front of the hard palate
	Intermittent	an articulator flapping loose or one articulator tapping against another	Trill	the *r* sound in Scottish pronunciation or in the Spanish *perro* 'dog'; the tongue vibrates against the alveolar ridge
	Intermittent	a single tap by one articulator against the roof of the mouth	Flap	the *r* sound in British English pronunciation of *very* or in the Spanish *pero* 'but'; the tongue taps the alveolar ridge
	Partial	partial closure in the mouth allowing the air to escape around one or both sides of the closure	Lateral	the initial sound of *law*; the middle part of the tongue touches the top of the mouth
Narrowing		at some point in the vocal tract the opening is narrowed so as to produce audible friction	Fricative	the initial and final sounds of *fuss*; air is forced between the lower lip and upper teeth, and between the front of the tongue and the alveolar ridge, respectively

BOX 3.1 ACROBATICS OF SPEAKING

The sounds that we hear when spoken to and that we emit when speaking are produced by complex gymnastics executed by our lips, tongue, velum, larynx, and lungs. The activities of these independent anatomical structures are coordinated with a precision that should be the envy of the most highly trained ballet dancer; yet this truly remarkable exercise is performed at the drop of a hat by even the clumsiest person. In contrast, even the most adroit primates have never been able to master it, despite intensive training. These facts suggest that the ability to speak is linked to our genetic endowment, that it is one of the aspects in which humans differ from all other mammals.

The gymnastic feats involved in speaking are clearly not the whole story. Speech is not just some noise that humans are capable of emitting; it is a noise that is produced to convey meaning. And how speech conveys meaning is surely one of the great puzzles that has intrigued thinkers for centuries.

from Morris Halle, The Rules of Language (1980), 54

From Phones to Phonemes

The smallest perceptible discrete segment of speech is a **phone,** a speech sound considered a physical event. A succession of phones in a particular language makes up a stretch of speech, or an utterance. Each utterance is unique, occurring if not under different circumstances at least at a different time. Yet people do not respond to each instance of speech as though it were different from all others. Such utterances as "Where have you been?" or "I have no time just now" are treated as if they were much the same every time they are said regardless of whether the voice belongs to a woman, man, or child, or happens to be clear or hoarse. Because there is so much likeness in what is objectively different, it is possible to represent speech sounds, phones, through the written symbols of a suitable phonetic alphabet. Linguistic anthropologists make phonetic transcriptions of words or utterances whenever they wish to obtain a sample of speech for subsequent analysis.

Let us now consider the English words written as *papaya, pepper, pin, spin, up,* and *upon.* The *p* sound of *pin* is followed by a distinct puff of air, which is completely absent in *spin*. The difference between the two *p* sounds can be easily demonstrated if one holds a sheet of paper vertically between thumb and finger about two inches from one's lips and says the two words. The puff of air, or aspiration, following the *p* sound of *pin* sends a ripple through the sheet, whereas the word *spin* leaves the sheet motionless. We find that the same difference obtains between the *p*'s of *pair, peck, peer,* and *pike* on the one hand and those of *spare, speck, spear,* and *spike* on the other.

In the word *upon*, the *p* sound is about as distinctly aspirated as in *pin*. In *papaya*, however, it is only the second *p* that is strongly aspirated, the first one aspirated only slightly, if at all; in *pepper*, it is the other way around. In the word *up*, especially if it stands at the end of a sentence, as in "Let's go up!," the *p* sound may remain unreleased, that is, the lips simply stay closed in anticipation of the silence that follows.

To generalize about the occurrence of these phonetically similar segments, we may say that in English there are at least four varieties of the *p* sound: an aspirated [pʰ] before a stressed vowel unless preceded by an *s* (as the second *p* in *papaya*, the first in *pepper*, and in *pin* and *upon*); a very slightly aspirated [p] before a weakly stressed vowel (the first in *papaya*, the second in *pepper*); an unaspirated [P] with a relatively small degree of muscular effort and breath force, after an *s* of the same syllable and before a vowel (*spin*); and an unreleased [p̚] in the sentence-final position, where [pʰ] or [p] may also occur. (To illustrate a principle rather than account for numerous other details, the description of the varieties of the English *p* sound and their occurrence has been simplified.)

Let us next consider the words *pin, spin,* and *bin*, which we may transcribe phonetically as [pʰɪn], [sPɪn], and [bɪn]. The difference between the *p* of *pin* and *b* of *bin* is clearly of another kind than that between [pʰ] and [p] or [pʰ] and [P]. By choosing either *b* or *p* for the initial sound, the speaker is distinguishing between two meaningful items of the English vocabulary; *bin* and *pin*. Even if one were to interchange the pronunciation of the *p* sounds in *pin* and *spin* and say [Pɪn] and [spʰɪn] instead, one would no doubt be understood, though the listener would probably suspect that either English is not the speaker's native language or the speaker is trying to imitate a foreign accent. As a matter of fact, native speakers of English never have to choose consciously between [P] and [pʰ]. They employ automatically the former before a vowel whenever the sound *s* precedes within the same syllable, and the latter if it occurs before a strongly stressed vowel.

With specific reference to English—because all languages must be examined and analyzed only on their own terms—linguists establish the *b* sound of *bin* and the *p* sound of *pin* as two contrastive sound units, or **phonemes**, and they classify the several varieties of the p sound—[pʰ], [P], [p], and[p˺]—as **allophones** of the phoneme /p/. (Note the use of slant lines around the symbol to indicate its phonemic status.) To put it differently, when *p* is used to represent the English phoneme /p/, it serves as a cover symbol for a class of phonetically similar sounds that are in complementary distribution or free variation. Phones are in complementary distribution if they never occur in the same phonetic environment—for example, simplified, [P] is found always after *s*, where [pʰ] never occurs. Phones are in free variation if substituting one for another does not cause a change in meaning. But if two phones contrast, as does [b] in *bin* with [pʰ] in *pin*—that is, if substituting one for another causes a change in meaning—they are assignable to two different phonemes (or, phrased differently, they are allophones of two different phonemes).

The simplest way to establish phonemic contrasts in a language is by means of minimal sets, in which each word has a different meaning but varies from the rest in one sound only. From the foursome of words *bit, bet, bat,* and *butt,* we establish phonemic contrast among all four vowels. As for consonants, all the initial sounds (not letters!) of the following set of words contrast with one another and are therefore assignable to different English phonemes: *by, die, fie, guy, high, lie, my, nigh, pie, rye, shy, sigh, thigh, thy, tie, vie,* and *why,* yielding /b, d, f, g, h, l, m, n, p, r, s, š, θ, ð, t, v, w/.

To demonstrate the fundamental principles underlying phonemic analysis, we have, for obvious reasons, used English. But linguistic anthropologists typically face a different situation when they study peoples whose languages have never before been written. A thorough phonemic analysis of a language involves more than just compiling minimal sets; it takes weeks of painstaking listening for contrasting sounds, repeating words and utterances and recording them on tape, and phonetically transcribing a good deal in the initial stages of work. The following need to be established: the distinctive sounds, or phonemes, of a language; the prosodic features that characterize its utterances; the main allophones of each phoneme and the phonetic environment in which they occur; the pattern of phonemes—vowels, consonants, and their subclasses; and the rules for their combinations among each other and in higher-level units. Next, the practical task for the linguistic anthropologist is to devise an appropriate alphabet so that the language can be transcribed phonemically, without the many phonetic details of the initial transcription that have now become easily retrievable: When we write /p/ in English, we know under what circumstances this phoneme is physically realized as one of its four allophones, [pʰ], [p], [P], and [pˀ].

It is important to remember that the same phonemes do not necessarily characterize every speaker of English. It is common knowledge that British, Australian, and other forms of English differ from American English, and that each of these exists in several dialectal varieties, particularly as far as vowels are concerned. In general, though, each language contains its own particular overall system of distinctive sounds. In Spanish, for example, a certain vowel sound approximates that heard in the English word *beat*, but there is no Spanish parallel to the English vowel sound of *bit*. This and similar differences are the source of the "natural" mispronunciations of native speakers of Spanish learning English, as when they pronounce the word *mill* as though it were *meal*. Their Spanish speech habits carry over into a language they are learning or are not familiar with.

The study of the phonetics and phonemics of a language and of the sound changes that take place over time in a language or in several related languages is referred to as **phonology.**

And one more remark about writing—this time about developing a writing system for languages that are spoken but not written, which means primarily for languages of small tribal societies. Today most members of such societies inevitably also speak the language of the larger society that surrounds them, and many are no longer sufficiently proficient in their native language to speak it. One may ask, Why give a written form to a language that is destined to become extinct in a generation or two? One reason would be to enable the linguistic anthropologist (or linguist) to record the society's tales, prayers, ritual speeches, and everyday language in the original form while it is still possible. But then, too, the availability of a written form helps to bolster the viability of a threatened language by giving it prestige in the outside world. It may be possible, for example, to include lessons in the native language in the elementary school system serving the group. One of the authors of this text (Salzmann), for example, compiled in 1983 a *Dictionary of Contemporary Arapaho Usage* to help Arapaho teachers remember and use the language of their grandparents. But then a problem arose—namely, how to represent some of the sounds of the language, which in linguistic literature would be done by means of phonetic symbols. (To use English spelling would be very confusing for reasons explained elsewhere in this book.) Here the advice of informants could be very valuable. An example: One of Salzmann's informants suggested that the sound usually represented by the Greek letter *theta*, that is by θ, could be represented by a graphic symbol found on the keyboard of American typewriters, thereby enabling a teacher to type Arapaho lessons for students. This same informant suggested using the numeric symbol 3 because the English word *three* begins with this particular sound (written in English as *th*). Salzmann accepted this practical and ingenious suggestion, and so the Arapaho word for dog in the dictionary is written as *he3* rather than phonetically (phonemically) as *hεθ*.

Phonemes of English

The dialects of English vary somewhat with respect to vowels, even within the United States. The repertory of vowel phonemes in Table 3.4 is representative of a great many speakers of American English, though not all. The list is supplemented by three diphthongs.

The list of consonant phonemes in American English is shown in Table 3.5 (whenever possible, the occurrence of each phoneme is exemplified for the word-initial, word-medial, and word-final positions).

How does the phonemic system of English compare with the systems of other languages? In the number of segments, it belongs to the middle range, along with the large majority of the world's languages. According to a survey based on the phonemic inventories of a sample of 317 languages (Maddieson 1984), some languages contain no more than a dozen segmental phonemes (for the most part they are members of the Indo-Pacific and Austronesian language families), while a few languages are reported to have in excess of one hundred (members of the Khoisan family in southern Africa). The mean number of consonants per phonemic inventory is in the low twenties (22.8), that of vowels close to nine (8.7). In most languages, the total number of consonants is more than twice as large as the number of vowels. The most common consonantal subsystem includes from five to eleven plosives (stops), including affricates; one to four fricatives; two to four nasals; and four consonants of other types. The most common vowels are those classified as high front unrounded, high back rounded, mid front unrounded, mid

TABLE 3.4 Typical Vowel Phonemes in American English

Phonemic Symbol	Example
Single vowels	
/i/	bead
/ɪ/	bid
/e/	bade (rhyming with *made*)
/ɛ/	bed
/æ/	bad
/ʌ/ (unstressed = /ə/)	bud
/a/	body
/u/	boot
/ʊ/	book
/o/	bode
/ɔ/	bought
Diphthongs	
/aɪ/	bite
/aʊ/	bout
/ɔɪ/	boy

TABLE 3.5 Consonant Phonemes in American English

Phonemic Symbol	Examples
/p/	pit, supper, rip
/b/	bit, fiber, rib
/t/	tip, meaty, kit
/d/	dip, odor, kid
/k/	cap, locker, pick
/g/	gap, soggy, pig
/č/	chin, itchy, rich
/j/	gin, pudgy, ridge
/f/	fat, gopher, belief
/v/	vat, ivy, believe
/θ/	thin, ether, breath
/ð/	then, either, breathe
/s/	seal, icy, hiss
/z/	zeal, cozy, his
/š/	show, potion, rush
/ž/	—, leisure, rouge
/h/	hasp, ahoy, —
/m/	moon, simmer, loom
/n/	noon, sinner, loon
/ŋ/	—, singer, king
/l/	limb, miller, reel
/r/	rim, mirror, rear
/w/	wet, lower, —
/y/	yet, layer, —

back rounded, and low central unrounded. The inventory of segmental phonemes in English appears to be much like the systems characteristic of the bulk of the world's languages. This is not to say, however, that English is a typical language. Although all natural languages are indeed distinct variations on a common theme—human language—each has its own peculiar features of structure that make it unique.

Prosodic Features

Vowels and consonants that combine into words and sentences may be thought of as segments, or segmental units, that is, as discrete units that can be identified in the stream of speech and separated from other such units (as in *part = p-a-r-t* and *slept = s-l-e-p-t*). But there is more to speech than just ordering these segments according to the rules of a particular language. Additional features are essential for an utterance to sound natural and to be fully meaningful, especially stress and pitch, these two sometimes lumped together under the term **accent**. These other features are called **prosodic features**. It is important to note that prosodic features can be distinctive in some languages.

Stress refers to the degree of force, or prominence, associated with a syllable. In the word *under*, the prominent stress is on the first syllable, whereas in *below*, it is on the second. In the sentence "Will you permit me to use your permit?" the word *permit* functioning as a verb is stressed differently from *permit* used as a noun. Some linguists claim that to describe English adequately, as many as four degrees of stress are needed, ranging from primary (1) to weak (4), as in *dictionary* (1-4-3-4) and *elevator operator* (1-4-3-4 2-4-3-4). In English the placing of stress is not completely predictable, as it is in Czech, where as a rule the main stress falls on the first syllable, or in Polish, where it falls on the penultimate, or next to the last, syllable.

A distinctive **pitch** level associated with a syllable is referred to as tone. Among the several dialect groups in China, Mandarin Chinese provides a good example of a tone system. Simpler than the systems of other Chinese tone languages or dialects, Mandarin employs four relative pitch contours, or tones, to distinguish among normally stressed syllables that are otherwise identical (see Table 3.6).

By contrast, the use of pitch in English is not associated with individual syllables but with utterances in a variety of intonation patterns. The intonation

TABLE 3.6   The Four Distinctive Tones of Mandarin Chinese

Syllable	Tone Number	Description	Tone Letter	Pitch Contour	Pinyin Transcription	Meaning
ma	1	high and level	⌐	5–5	—	mother
ma	2	rising	⌐	3–5	ˊ	hemp
ma	3	falling, then rising	⌄	2-1-4	ˇ	horse
ma	4	high falling	⌐	5-1	ˋ	to scold

The tone letter provides a simplified time-pitch graph of each syllable under normal stress. The time-pitch graph is drawn from left to right, with the vertical line serving as a reference scale for pitch range. Similarly, the pitch contour represents pitches by numbers from 1 to 5, with 5 being the highest.

that accompanies the question "Who ran off, Mother?" addressed to the speaker's mother, may elicit some such answer as "Your sister." With the appropriately different intonation, the question "Who ran off—Mother?" addressed to some other member of the family may elicit some such answer as "Yes, without even leaving a note."

The physical duration of a sound is referred to as its quantity, or **length**. In English the difference between the short vowel in *bit* and the longer one in *beat* is not strictly or primarily a difference in length because the two vowels vary in other respects. Yet the consonant written as -*tt*- in *cattle* is somewhat longer than that written as -*tt*- in *cattail* is sometimes contrastive; such word pairs as *lak* 'varnish' and *lák* 'pickle (brine)' or *dal* 'he gave' and *dál* 'farther' are alike except for the considerable lengthening of the vowel in the second word of each pair (marked in conventional Czech spelling by the diacritic ´ over the vowel).

Some linguists also distinguish phonetic features that mark the joining of one grammatical unit to another: so-called *junctures*. English examples include the audible difference between the members of such pairs as *nitrate* and *night rate*, *I scream* and *ice cream*, and *an aim* and *a name*.

Etics and Emics

Let us first briefly review the distinction between phonetics and phonemics. A phonetic transcription (or description) of a particular language is an attempt to account for all the audible or perceivable differences among the sounds of that language. For example, the phonetic transcription of English words would register the difference between the *p* sounds of *pike* and *spike* (the first, [pʰ], is aspirated whereas the second, [p], is not) or between the initial consonants of *shoot* and *sheet*, both conventionally written as *sh* (the first, [šᵂ], is pronounced with the lips rounded in anticipation of a rounded vowel; the second, [š], is pronounced with the lips spread in anticipation of an unrounded vowel). By contrast, the phonemic transcription of these four sounds in the two pairs of words would be simply /p/ and /s/ because in English neither [pʰ] and [p] nor [šᵂ] and [š] distinguish meaning in the way /n/ and /ŋ/ do, for example, in *sin* and *sing*, words given different meaning by virtue of /n/ versus /ŋ/. The terms **etic** and **emic** (and the corresponding nouns *etics* and *emics*) were derived from *phonetic(s)* and *phonemic(s)* and coined by the linguist Kenneth L. Pike (1912–2000) in a work in which he attempted to relate the study of language to a unified theory of the structure of human behavior (1954). According to Pike (1967), there are several important differences between the etic and emic approaches to language and culture. For example, social scientists who study behavior (including language) from outside a particular system are following the etic approach because the units they use are available in advance (as are the numerous phonetic symbols representing the great variety of sounds occurring in the many languages of the world).

By contrast, the emic approach involves a study from within: The emic units must be discovered by subjecting a particular system to analysis (a linguist arrives at the phonemes of a language only as a result of an analysis). Moreover, the etic approach is potentially cross-cultural and comparative in that it may be applied to several languages or cultures at a time; the emic approach is language– or culture-specific because it can be applied only to one at a time. Furthermore, etic criteria are directly measurable and may be considered absolute: For example, both English and Czech include sounds that are phonetically represented as [m], [n], and [ŋ]. Emic criteria, however, are relative to one particular system: In English /m/, /n/, and /ŋ/ are phonemically distinct, as in *sum*, *sun*, and *sung*, but in Czech only /m/ and /n/ are,

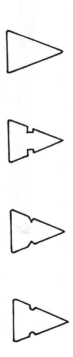

FIGURE 3.2 Deetz's "Facteme" and "Allofacts" Illustrated on Arrowheads

because [ŋ] in Czech is an allophone of /n/ (it occurs before velar consonants). Native speakers of a language, of course, do not know and do not have to know the phonemic system of their mother tongue; they internalize it when they learn their language in early childhood.

Another way to exemplify the difference between etics and emics is to point out that native speakers of English encode their messages etically—although unaware that they aspirate some *p*'s strongly, others weakly, and still others (after an *s* of the same syllable) not at all—but unconsciously decode them emically, paying attention only to distinctive features (such as the voicing that distinguishes /b/ from /p/ in *bunch* and *punch*, *best* and *pest*, and other such pairs).

Pike's extension of the concepts of etics and emics to the study of culture stimulated other scholars to apply these concepts to the fields of their own specialization. James F. Deetz (1930–2000), an archaeologist, suggested (1967:83–93) that in archaeology one may wish to distinguish among facts, factemes, and allofacts (and among forms, formemes, and alloforms). To illustrate what Deetz meant by these terms, let us use his example concerning arrowheads (see Figure 3.2). Some have straight sides, whereas others have notches near the base. Because the notches are used to attach the arrowhead to the shaft, they have a functional significance and may be said to constitute a facteme (by analogy to phoneme). But the notches vary in form: Some are squarish, others triangular, still others rounded, and so on. These variations in notchings constitute allofacts (by analogy to allophones), and any individual notching, regardless of shape, can be termed a fact (by analogy to phone). In this terminology, fact is an etic unit, facteme is an emic unit, and allofact represents a group whose etic members constitute an emic unit.

In similar fashion, the folklorist Alan Dundes (1934–2005) coined the terms **motifeme** and **allomotif** to supplement the established term *motif*.

For example, folk narratives from all parts of the world contain a motifeme that could be described as "the hero is subjected to a difficult or dangerous test." The test can take a great many forms, each of which would be an allomotif of the motifeme—for example, swallowing red-hot stones, tricking a woman who kills her husbands and lovers by means of her toothed vagina, hatching boiled eggs, carrying water in a sieve, and hundreds of other means of testing the hero. Each actual telling of a hero's test would represent the occurrence of a motif in the narrative (Dundes 1962).

How is the study of nonverbal behavior to be approached—etically, emically, or both—and which of these possible approaches is most appropriate for describing culture? That these and related questions are far from having been settled among anthropologists is evident from a controversy that has persisted for more than a quarter of a century. A debate on the subject took place during the annual meeting of the American Anthropological Association in 1988, when eight scholars representing several fields contributed to an etics-emics symposium (their papers were later published; see Headland, Pike, and Harris 1990).

The crux of the controversy has to do with the status of etics. Is etic description no more than a prerequisite for discovering an emic system, or are the etic and emic analyses of equal importance? From the cultural materialist research strategy in anthropology, of which Marvin Harris (1927–2001) was the foremost proponent, "etic analysis is . . . a steppingstone . . . [only] to the discovery of etic structures. The intent is neither to convert etics to emics nor emics to etics, but rather to describe both and if possible to explain one in terms of the other" (Harris 1979:36). And further, "etics for Pike, even at the phonetic level, is in part the observer's emics incorrectly applied to a foreign system. . . . If Pike had meant by etics nothing but the emics of the observer, why did he bother to introduce the term etics? Why not simply be content with the opposition: 'emics of the observer' versus 'emics of the native participant'?" (Harris 1990:49). A good anthropological report, according to Harris, should distinguish between, on the one hand, what the observer has seen and heard to the best of his or her objective ability (and which can therefore be independently verified) and, on the other hand, what is in the heads of the native informants when they comment on their own culture. Etic analysis is therefore to be considered an end in itself.

The finer points of the etics-emics debate are quite technical and therefore outside the scope of an introduction to linguistic anthropology. On the whole, it seems that the distinction between the etic and emic approaches is more easily applicable to linguistic data than to nonverbal cultural behavior.

Summary and Conclusions

For ethnographic research to be conducted as participant observation, anthropologists should have a working knowledge of the language spoken by the people they study. For a linguistic anthropologist, acquaintance with the methods of linguistic analysis and appreciation of structural differences among languages are essential.

Speech sounds are produced by various modifications of the vocal channel as the outgoing airstream passes between the vocal cords and the lips. The two main classes of speech sounds are vowels and consonants, each consisting of various types according to the place and manner of articulation. Vowels are usually associated with accent, which may take the form of stress, pitch, or a combination of both. Languages that make use of distinctive pitch levels are referred to as tone languages, some of those spoken in China being the best-known examples.

Analysis of the sounds of a language involves determining which phonetic differences are contrastive (distinctive, significant), that is, phonemic (for example, [b] and [pʰ] in English, differentiating between *bull* and *pull*), and which are predictable, or allophonic (for example, [P] and [pʰ] of *span* and *pan*). Each language has a characteristic phonemic system: Sounds that are assignable to two or more distinct phonemes in one language may be allophones of a single phoneme in another. Although phonemes have been defined traditionally as the minimal units in the sound system of a language, they can be further analyzed into distinctive features, of which each phoneme is a bundle. The number of segmental phonemes per language varies from a mere dozen to as many as one hundred or more, but the inventories of the great majority of languages (70 percent) range between twenty and thirty-seven segments.

The phonetic and phonemic analytical approaches have been extended from the study of language to nonlinguistic aspects of culture under the terms *etic* and *emic*. Although the techniques of etics and emics have been employed for several decades, not all scholars agree on their status and mutual relationship.

4

Structure of Words
and Sentences

Because many of the languages they encounter have only been spoken, never written, anthropologists must adequately identify all the sounds before they can transcribe and later analyze what speakers of these languages have said. Since accurate transcription cannot be made at the speed at which people talk, magnetic tape recorders have been of great help in modern fieldwork. When ethnographic reports are published in which native words or texts are to be cited, a reliable method of writing down the language must be devised. Phonemic transcription is the most economic and at the same time accurate way of recording utterances ranging from short comments to long ceremonial speeches.

A good transcription is essential for an analysis because only with a reliable text in hand can the linguistic anthropologist determine a language's grammatical structure and exact meaning. Full understanding requires the identification of even the smallest meaningful segments (**morphemes**) that make up the text. Every language has its own stock of morphemes and arranges them into words, phrases, and sentences in a particular way, and every language has its own grammatical categories that vary from one language to the next.

In what units do people communicate? The answer depends on the approach one takes to the study of speech. An important unit of linguistic analysis is the sentence, which is in turn subdividable into smaller constituents—for example, noun phrases and verb phrases or the subject, verb, and object. The principal analytical unit of communicative behavior in linguistic anthropology is **discourse.** The concept of discourse is not easy to define because individual scholars use it differently. Discourse may be as short in duration as a greeting or as long as a protracted argument or the telling of a traditional narrative; it can be oral or written, planned or unplanned, poetic or businesslike, and it can be exemplified by any one of the genres characteristic of the speech behavior of a particular culture. A great deal of any culture is transmitted by means of discourse, and discourse may be said to constitute a significant part of any culture. As Joel Sherzer put it:

> Discourse is the broadest and most comprehensive level of linguistic form, content, and use . . . [and] the process of discourse structuring is the locus of the language-culture relationship. . . . It is in certain kinds of discourse, in which speech play and verbal art are heightened, as central moments in poetry, magic, politics, religion, respect, insult, and bargaining, that the language-culture-discourse relationship comes into sharpest focus and the organizing role of discourse in this relationship is highlighted. (Sherzer 1987:305–306)

Linguistic theories and methods underwent great changes during the twentieth century, the transformational-generative approach of recent decades rapidly gaining followers. And although linguistic anthropologists are more concerned with the relationship between language and culture and society than with linguistic structure in and of itself, they nevertheless follow current linguistic research with interest and when applicable use its results in their own work.

Morphemes and Allomorphs

An overview of phonetics and the fundamental principles of phonemic analysis was presented in the previous chapter. Let us now shift to the level of analysis conventionally referred to as grammar. Consider the phrase *shockingly disgraceful acts*, which can be subdivided into the following meaningful segments (to simplify matters, conventional spelling instead of phonemic transcription is used below):

shock, meaning "to startle, offend, distress,"
-ing, an adjectival segment meaning "causing to . . . ,"

-ly, an adverbial segment meaning "in a . . . manner,"

dis-, meaning "not, opposite of,"

grace, meaning "propriety, decency,"

-ful, meaning "characterized by,"

act, meaning "deed," and

-s, meaning "more than one," that is, marking the plural.

It appears that the three-word phrase consists of eight meaningful segments of English, none of which can be further subdivided without the loss of the original meaning (it cannot be claimed, for example, that the word *grace* is made up of *g-* plus *race*). Linguistic units that have a meaning but contain no smaller meaningful parts are termed **morphemes.** To put it differently, a morpheme is the smallest contrastive unit of grammar. The search for such units in a particular language is called morphemic analysis. And the study of word structure, including classification of and interrelationships among morphemes, is referred to as **morphology.**

There are many thousands of morphemes in any language. The large majority are commonly **free morphemes** because they may occur unattached to other morphemes, that is, they can stand alone as independent words—in the example above, *grace, shock,* and *act.* Some morphemes, but usually relatively few, are bound morphemes because they normally do not occur on their own but only in combination with another morpheme—for example, *dis-, -ing, -ly,* and *-s.* The stem is that part of the word to which inflectional affixes (such as the plural) are attached.

In English and other languages, bound morphemes occur in limited numbers. There are languages, though, in which most morphemes are bound; Eskimo is usually cited as an example of such a language. In still other languages, those noun stems that stand for objects which are typically possessed do not occur as free morphemes. This is true, for example, of Arapaho nouns referring to body parts, kinship relationships, and a few other referents. (In Arapaho, the acute accent ['] marks stressed vowels with higher pitch; long vowels are written doubly.) Examples of dependent nouns are *bétee* '(someone's) heart,' *wonotóno?* '(someone's) ear,' *notóóne* 'my daughter,' *béteh?éi* '(someone's) friend,' and *betéi* 'louse, flea,' because there is no such thing as a heart or an ear apart from a human or an animal, a daughter without a mother or father, a friend unattached to another by affection, or a louse or flea that could survive without deriving benefits from a host. The forms *bétee, wonotóno?, notóóne, bétteh?éi,* and *betéi* consist of either the first-person possessive morpheme *n-* in *notóóne* or the indefinite personal possessor morpheme *b-* or *w-* in the other four nouns. None of these four or some two hundred other nouns ever occurs as a free (unpossessed) stem.

Some but not all bound morphemes in a language are affixes; attached to other morphemes, they modify meaning in some way and make more complex words. If an affix is attached before a stem, it is called a **prefix**; if it follows a stem, it is a **suffix**; and if it is placed within another morpheme, it is called an **infix**. In English only the first two types of affixes occur: Examples of prefixes are *be-, de-, in-, pre-, re-,* and *un-* as in *befriend, debug, inlay, prewash, rewrite,* and *undo;* examples of suffixes are *-en, -er, -hood, -ish, -ize,* and *-ward* as in *oxen, smaller, childhood, bookish, equalize,* and *skyward.* An example of an infix may be taken from Chontal, a language spoken by a people in southern Oaxaca, Mexico: *akán'ó?* 'woman,' *kón'í?* 'grandchild,' *sewí?* 'magpie,' and several other stems form the plural by inserting an infix in the form of *-ł-* (a voiceless lateral continuant) before the second consonant, yielding *akáłn'ó?* 'women,' *kółn'í?* 'grandchildren,' and *sełwí?* 'magpies.' Infixation is fairly common in Native American, Southeast Asian, and African languages.

What about such "irregular" plurals in English as *feet, geese, men,* and *mice?* Rather than by adding a suffix to the stems *foot, goose, man,* and *mouse,* the plural is formed by changing the stem vowel—for example, in *foot → feet* and *goose → geese*—by fronting and unrounding it (see Box 4.1). Pluralization in such words is effected by what is sometimes referred to as a process morpheme and is quite different from the addition of a suffix after the stem (as in *cat* plus *-s*).

A particular morpheme does not have to have the same shape every time it occurs. The plural of English nouns offers an excellent example of the considerable variation in the phonemic shape of a morpheme. Noun stems ending in a so-called sibilant (an *s*-like or *sh*-like fricative) form their plural by adding a vowel plus a *z* sound, very commonly [əz], as in *box-es, pass-es, buzz-es, bush-es, garage-s, patch-es,* and *judge-s.* The great majority of noun stems ending in voiced nonsibilant sounds add a voiced [z], whereas those ending in voiceless nonsibilant sounds add a voiceless [s], as in *bear-s, can-s, comma-s, lathe-s, pad-s, pill-s, rib-s, rig-s,* and *song-s* on the one hand, and *cat-s, laugh-s, lip-s,* and *tick-s* on the other. But a number of noun stems form

BOX 4.1 WHY ENGLISH IS SO HARD

Compared to other Indo-European languages, English has few grammatical affixes. But as in all natural languages, there are some "irregular" forms, as this anonymous poem points out. All the italicized words were used in English before the twelfth century except *vow* and *booth* (thirteenth century), *boot* (fourteenth century), and *moose* (earliest recorded date of use is 1603). They are old words, not likely to become regularized.

We'll begin with a *box*, and the plural is *boxes*,
But the plural of *ox* should be *oxen*, not *oxes*.
Then one fowl is *goose*, but two are called *geese*,
Yet the plural of *moose* should never be *meese*.

You may find a lone *mouse* or a whole lot of *mice*,
But the plural of *house* is *houses*, not *hice*.
If the plural of *man* is always called *men*,
Why shouldn't the plural of *pan* be called *pen*?

The cow in the plural may be *cows* or *kine*,
But the plural of *vow* is *vows*, not *vine*.
And I speak of a *foot*, and you show me your *feet*,
But I give you a *boot*—would a pair be called *beet*?

If one is a *tooth* and a whole set are *teeth*,
Why shouldn't the plural of *booth* be called *beeth*?
Then one may be *that*, and three may be *those*,
Yet the plural of *hat* would never be *hose*.

We speak of a *brother* and also of *brethren*,
But though we say *mother*, we never say *methren*.
So our English, I think you will agree,
Is the trickiest language you ever did see.

the plural differently—among them *alumna, alumnus, child, crisis, criterion, datum, kibbutz,* and *ox*; their plurals are, respectively, *alumnae, alumni, children, crises, criteria, data, kibbutzim,* and *oxen*. And then there are a relatively few noun stems the plurals of which are not overtly marked, for example, *sheep* and *swine*. These and other such nouns are said to have their plurals marked by a *zero* (written as Ø), that is, by the absence of an overt linguistic feature. The variant forms of a particular morpheme are referred to as its **allomorphs** (just as the varieties of a phoneme are called allophones), or morpheme alternates. Allomorphs of a given morpheme, then, are different forms of the morpheme, depending on the context in which they occur.

In summary, then, one may say that the plural morpheme in English has a number of allomorphs, ranging from the most common ones of /-z/, /-s/, and /-əz/, through several others associated especially with loanwords, to zero. And in the case of pluralizing the noun *man* to *men*, one would represent the plural allomorph as /æ/ → /ɛ/. The plural morpheme in English is by no means an exception in that it has morpheme alternants. For example, the stem *child* has a different phonemic shape in its plural form (*children*) from when it occurs by itself or when it is suffixed by -*hood*, -*ish*, and -*like* (in *childhood, childish,* and *childlike*).

Morphemes also vary considerably in length. Some consist of a single phoneme: For example, the three English morphemes marking the plural, the possessive, and the third-person singular (as in *apes, apes', apes,* and [*he*] *apes* [*someone*]) have /s/ as one of their several allomorphs. Others, like *caterpillar* or *hippopotamus,* consist of several syllables. Words, too, in English vary in length: *a* is the shortest, but it is impossible to list the longest. Suppose you wish to refer to a lineal paternal male relative from the sixteenth century: He would be your great-great-......... great-grandfather.

Morphological Processes

Just as languages differ in their phonemic systems, they differ in their morphologies. Some morphological processes, however, are quite common throughout the world even though they may be applied differently in specific languages. One such process is **derivation**, by means of which new words are formed from existing ones, frequently by changing them from one word class to another. In English this process of word formation is frequently accomplished by the use of derivational affixes. For example, affixes change the adjective *modern* to the verb *modernize,* the noun *friend* to the adjective *friendly,* the verb *speak* to the noun *speaker,* and the adjective *abrupt* to the adverb *abruptly.* They also produce such words as *kingdom, outbid,* and *despite.*

The other common morphological process is inflection, the use of affixes to indicate grammatical relationships (number, case, person, tense, and others). In English all inflectional affixes are suffixes and are limited to the plural and possessive markers in nouns (as in *mothers* and *mother's*), comparative and superlative markers in adjectives (as in *taller* and *tallest*), and the third-person singular present-tense marker and the past-tense, progressive, and past-participle markers in verbs (as in *waits*, *waited*, [is] *singing*, and *beaten*).

Derivational and inflectional morphemes may have the same phonemic shape: One *-ing* in English serves as the derivational suffix changing a verb into a noun as in "Excessive eating is harmful," whereas another *-ing* is an inflectional suffix marking the progressive verb form as in "They were eating voraciously." In English inflectional suffixes always follow derivational suffixes, as in *reader's*, *organizers*, and *friendliest* (*read-er-'s*, *organ-iz(e)-er-s*, and *friend-li-est*).

As languages go, English has very few inflectional affixes compared with, for example, Latin. As against the handful of different forms of an English verb (*speak*, *speaks*, *speaking*, *spoke*, and *spoken*), a Latin verb has scores. Regarding number, English distinguishes formally only between the singular and the plural, whereas some languages have special forms also for the dual to refer to two of a kind, and even forms to refer to three and four of a kind. Old English marked the dual number in its personal pronouns: Besides *ic* 'I' and *wē* 'we', there was *wit* 'we two'; besides *mē* '(to) me' and *ūs* '(to) us', there was *unc* '(to) the two of us'; and so on. These dual forms gradually disappeared during the second part of the thirteenth century, halfway through the Middle English period. However, derivational suffixes in English are plentiful: *-able* (as in *reasonable*), *-ade* (*blockade*), *-age* (*breakage*), *-al* (*coastal*), *-ance* (*assistance*), *-ant* (*servant*), *-ar* (*linear*), *-ard* (*drunkard*), *-ary* (*budgetary*), *-ate* (*activate*), *-atic* (*problematic*), and scores of others.

Some languages distinguish nouns according to several genders, each of which may require corresponding forms in pronouns, adjectives, and even verbs. Frequently there is no correlation between grammatical and natural gender. In English all inanimate objects are referred to by the pronoun *it*; in German, however, *der Löffel* 'spoon' is masculine, *die Gabel* 'fork' is feminine, and *das Messer* 'knife' is neuter, as are also *das Weib* 'woman' and *das Mädchen* 'girl'. In Old English, *stān* 'stone' and *wīfman* 'woman' were masculine, *duru* 'door' and *sunne* 'sun' feminine, and *word* 'word' and *wīf* 'woman, wife' neuter. The substitution of natural for grammatical gender also took place during the Middle English period.

Another grammatical category that may serve as an example is **case**. Although Old English had three case forms for, say, *stān* 'stone' in the singular (nominative and accusative *stān*, genitive *stānes*, and dative *stāne*) and three in the plural (*stānas*, *stāna*, and *stānum*, respectively), Modern English manages quite well with only two forms, namely *stone* and *stones*. It has retained case forms only in the interrogative pronoun *who* (that is *whom*) and in several personal pronouns: *me*, the objective case form of *I*, and *him*, *her*, *us*, and *them*. In other languages, however, cases are an important and elaborate grammatical feature. For example, the Czech language has seven cases in both singular and plural applied not only to nouns but also to pronouns, adjectives, and numerals.

Finnish has a particularly rich case system. What in English is usually expressed by means of prepositions, Finnish does with cases. Among these cases modifying, for example, the noun *talo* 'house', is the adessive (case), meaning 'at, near (a place)', as in *talolla* 'at the house', elative, meaning 'out of (a place)', as in *talosta* 'from (inside) the house', inessive 'in, within (a place)', as in *talossa* 'in the house', illative 'into (a place)', as in *taloon* 'into the house', allative 'to(wards) (a place)', as in *talolle* 'to(wards) the house', and several others.

Aspect is a grammatical category expressing how activities denoted by verbs are related to time. This category is particularly well developed in Slavic languages, as some of the following examples from Czech will show. Czech verbs are perfective, expressing action as complete or concluded, as in the suppletive *přišel* "he has come, arrived" from the infinitive *přijít*, or imperfective, expressing action as incomplete or repeated, as in *šel* 'he went' from *jít* 'to go.' The multiplicity of verbal action is expressed in the iterative form *nosil* 'he carried' and the more intensive frequentative form *nosíval* 'he used to carry.' A particular phase of a verbal action may be specified as an initiatory one, as in *vyběhl* 'he ran out,' a completed one, as in *doběhl* 'he reached [a place] by running,' and a terminative one, as in *proběhl se* 'he had run.' The extent of a verbal action may be momentary, as in *střelil* 'he took a shot,' or durative, expressive continuity, as in *střílel* 'he fired away,' or the extent is small, as in *usmál se* 'he gave a smile," or large, as in *nasmál se* 'he had a good laugh.'

An interesting morphological process is reduplication, the doubling or repetition of a phoneme or phonemes. In Isthmus Nahuat, a dialect of Nahuat spoken by Native Americans in eastern Mexico, verb stems are derived by reduplication to mark different kinds of repetitive action: -kakalaki- 'enter a house many times' from -kalaki- 'enter'; -pahpano- 'pass by many times' from -pano- 'pass by'; -poposteki- 'break many times' or 'break into many pieces' from -posteki- 'break'; -papaka- 'wash many times' and -pahpaka- 'wash many things' from -paka- 'wash' and the like. The compound goody-goody, helter-skelter, teeny-weeny, and wishy-washy are reduplications of sorts, but the process in English is quite limited.

One could go on illustrating various other grammatical categories found in the thousands of the world's languages (aspect, mood, tense, voice, and so on) and the processes by which they are marked, but the examples already given should suffice. However, one important point must be made. Whether or not a language formally marks a particular grammatical category does not make it superior (or inferior) to others. If it were so, Old English would have to be rated as much superior to Modern English—something no one can seriously maintain. All languages are fully adequate because they enable native speakers to express all that they wish to say about the society and culture in which they live.

Morphophonemics

Sound alternations like the one between /f/ and /v/ in knife and knives, life and lives, loaf and loaves, and wife and wives are common in English and other languages. Alternations of this kind are changes in the phonemic shape of the allomorphs of a morpheme, and as such they represent important processes in the structure of language. The study of the relations between morphology and phonology or, to put it in other words, the study of the phonemic differences among allomorphs of the same morpheme, is referred to as **morphophonemics** or morpho(pho)nology, and the generalizations concerning the occurrence of the various shapes of morphemes are called morphophonemic rules. To formulate such a rule one usually selects a particular allomorph as the base form and then describes the conditions under which other allomorphs of the same morpheme occur. To refer to an example used earlier in this chapter, nouns in English (except for those specifically exempt) form the plural by adding /z/ to their stem (as in leg, legs) but insert /ə/ before the plural suffix if the stem ends in a sibilant (/s/, /z/, /š/, /ž/, /č/, or /ǰ/ (as in kiss, kisses) or change the voiced /z/ to voiceless /s/ if the stem terminates in a voiceless nonsibilant (as in neck, necks).

Morphophonemic rules in any language are stable even if they are fairly complex. For example, in Arapaho, an Algonquian language spoken by Native Americans in Wyoming and Oklahoma, the word *néíʔíbéhe'?* 'my grandmother' is regularly changed to *hiníʔiiwóho'?* to mean 'his/her grandmother.' (The explanation of why this change takes place is fairly complex, but to satisfy the curious, here it is: In addition to the two common word-initial prefixes marking possession ['my' and 'his/her'], the differences between the two forms are also regular. The final *-o'?* in *hiníʔiiwóho'?* is the obviative suffix [a morpheme that marks the so-called fourth person when two third persons are referred to, in this case a grandmother and the person who claims her as grandmother]. The vowel of the obviative, *o*, influences the selection of a like vowel in the diminutive suffix before it, and *b* regularly changes into *w* before a back vowel [in this case *o*]. The word apparently means 'his/her little one [mother]'—a rather gentle way of referring to one's grandmother.)

Another example of a morphophonemic rule is found in Turkish, one of the languages with **vowel harmony,** the requirement that vowels within a word have a certain similarity. With relatively few exceptions, Turkish suffixes containing high vowels have

$$
\left.\begin{array}{l}
\text{/i/} \\
\text{/ü/} \\
\text{/ɨ/} \\
\text{/u/}
\end{array}\right\} \text{ if the preceding syllable has }
\left\{\begin{array}{l}
\text{/i/ or /e/ (front unrounded vowels)} \\
\text{/ü/ or /ö/ (front rounded)} \\
\text{/ɨ/ or /a/ (back unrounded)} \\
\text{/u/ or /o/ (back rounded)}
\end{array}\right.
$$

whereas suffixes containing low vowels have

$$
\left.\begin{array}{l}
\text{/e/} \\
\text{/a/}
\end{array}\right\} \text{ if the preceding syllable has }
\left\{\begin{array}{l}
\text{/i/, /e/, /ü/, or /ö/ (front vowels)} \\
\text{/ɨ/, /a/, /u/, or /o/ (back vowels)}
\end{array}\right.
$$

However, on occasion morphophonemic changes are irregular in the sense that they are limited to one morpheme and are not repeated elsewhere in the language. Examples are the forms *am, are, is* from *(to) be,* the past tense form *went* from *(to) go,* and the comparative form *better* or superlative *best* from *good.* The occurrence of phonemically unrelated allomorphs of a morpheme is referred to as **suppletion** and the specific instances of it **suppletive forms.** Suppletion seems to occur in all natural (as opposed to artificial) languages; however, it is never extensive because irregularity on a large scale would tend to hinder communication.

The Sentence as a Unit of Analysis

Just as speech sounds normally do not occur in isolation, neither do words. As a rule, human utterances are made up of larger units—phrases and sentences. It is not easy to define these two terms rigorously; for our purposes let us say that a sentence is the largest structural unit of the grammar of a language and that a phrase—for example, *tomorrow evening, in the sky, the wicked witch*—is a structural unit larger than a single word but smaller than a clause.

The number of different sentences that can be produced in any language is infinite. For example, it is most unlikely that the sentence "Whenever the moon is full, bats gather to discuss the state of the local economy" has ever been said before. One could easily generate novel sentences by the thousands. How is it possible that speakers of a language can and do produce and understand sentences conforming to the rules of grammar even though they have never been said or heard before? The answer is simple: Native speakers know the **syntax** of their language—the internal structure of sentences and the interrelationships between the various sentence elements.

All speakers have a largely unconscious knowledge of the system of grammatical rules that characterizes their native language or a language in which they are truly fluent. This knowledge is referred to as competence. What language users actually do with this knowledge in speaking or comprehending speech, however, is somewhat different and is referred to as performance. Although an individual's competence may be expected to remain fairly stable for a long time, performance tends to suffer when a speaker is sleepy, tired, ill, preoccupied, or under the influence of alcohol. Sentences that conform to the syntactic rules of a language are grammatical sentences; those that do not are ungrammatical (as when a speaker's performance has noticeably suffered). Grammatical sentences may be meaningless, as in "Jabberwocky," the poem Alice was able to read by using the mirror in Lewis Carroll's *Through the Looking-Glass:*

'Twas brillig, and the slithy toves
Did gyre and gimble in the wabe.

Yet some ungrammatical sentences may be meaningful, as when a foreigner says, *"I not speak English good" (an asterisk is placed before a sentence to show that it is ungrammatical or unacceptable). Then there are sentences that are grammatical but structurally ambiguous, that is, having more than one meaning—for example, "Visiting in-laws can be very trying": Is it very trying to visit in-laws, or are in-laws who visit very trying?

To gain some understanding of English sentence structure we might look at the sentence "The stream carries the boat." This sentence (S) has two major constituents: The first, corresponding to the traditional subject of the sentence, is the noun phrase (NP) "the stream"; the second, corresponding to the traditional predicate, is the verb phrase (VP) "carries the boat." These constituents consist ultimately of lexical categories: an article (Art), a noun (N), and a verb (V). The tree diagram of the sentence (see Figure 4.1) gives three kinds of information: the linear order of words that make up the sentence, the lexical category of each word, and the grouping of the words into structural constituents.

This sentence has the structure typical of simple English declarative sentences (that is, sentences used to express statements). But what of the corresponding interrogative sentence, "Does the stream carry the boat?" The rule that changes the declarative sentence to the corresponding interrogative sen-

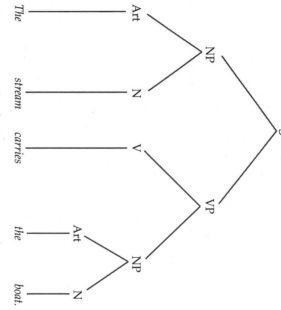

FIGURE 4.1 A Simple Sentence Diagrammed in Tree Form

tence requires certain changes. An operation that adds, deletes, or changes elements in one structure to produce another is referred to as **transformation,** and the general statement describing such an operation as a **transformational rule. In** the sentence above, the appropriate form of the verb *do* is placed at the beginning of the sentence and appropriate changes are made in the main verb, as in "Mother knows best" → "Does Mother know best?"

This is only a very brief illustration of how one approaches the study of sentence structure. A complete description of the great variety of sentence types in English and the processes of their derivation would easily fill a sizable book. Such a description would include transformations having to do with commands, exclamations, complex sentences (consisting of a main clause and at least one subordinate clause), embedding (as in "The man who suddenly appeared in the door was my first cousin," in which "The man suddenly appeared in the door" is embedded in the matrix sentence "The man was my first cousin"), and many other constructions.

As shown in Figure 4.1, analysis is motivated by empirical evidence, that is, it can be verified or rejected on the basis of observation or inquiry. Not only do linguists reject utterances (sentences) native speakers consider ungrammatical, but they may occasionally ask whether two closely similar utterances have the same meaning (for example, "Don't you want some soup?" and "Don't you want any soup?"—many speakers would consider them to be slightly different) or account for structural ambiguities (for example, the phrase "French history professor" may mean "a history professor who is French" or "a professor who teaches French history," and accordingly it would be represented as

or

depending on what the speaker had in mind).

Inflections and Word Order

English is a world language, and for several reasons. It is an official language in some country or countries on every continent: the United Kingdom in Europe, Ghana in Africa, India in Asia, Belize in Central America, Guyana in South America, Fiji in Oceania, and in Australia. But there are also formal linguistic reasons why the use of English is so widespread: Although English has one of the largest vocabularies among the world's languages, its grammar is relatively simple (to put it briefly). What is meant by that? Consider two English sentences and their following translations into Latin and Czech:

English: (1) A hunter tracks a lion   *and*   (2) A lion tracks a hunter.
Latin: (1) Venator leonem vestigat   *and*   (2) Leo venatorem vestigat.
Czech: (1) Lovec stopuje lva   *and*   (2) Lev stopuje lovce.

Although the meanings of the two English sentences are quite different, the five words of each sentence are exactly the same. Whether the hunter or the lion is the grammatical subject or the grammatical object (that is, the goal of the action of the word "tracks"), the same five words are all that are needed. Who is tracking whom is fully indicated by the word order—that is, the arrangement of words.

Of the two other languages, Latin and Czech are richly inflectional, that is, changing the form of the words to mark various grammatical categories. In Latin, the form of the word for the hunter as a grammatical subject is *venator*, and as a grammatical object is *venatorem*. Unlike in English, the word order does not indicate the relationship of the words of a sentence, but instead shows emphasis: If a Roman had said *Venator leonem vestigat*, he would have meant something like *It is the HUNTER who tracks the lion*, but if a Roman had said *Leonem venator vestigat*, he would have meant something like *It is the LION whom the hunter tracks* (rather than, for example, a *DEER* or a *HORSE*).

A similar explanation of the use of inflectional forms holds also for Czech and many other languages. In English, only a few examples of the former inflections still survive—direct object forms *me, him, her, us,* and *them* of the personal pronouns *I, he, she, we,* and *they.*

To show the richness of the inflectional system in Latin, here are the forms (cases) of the noun *venator* in the singular (including the plural would increase the number of forms by three): *venator* (nominative, indicating the subject of a verb); *venatoris* (genitive, indicating possession, like "of" in English); *venatori* (dative, indicating the indirect object of a verb, like "to" as in "throw the ball to him"); *venatorem* (accusative, indicating the direct object of a verb); *venator* (vocative, indicating the person being spoken to; the form is the same as the nominative); and *venatore* (ablative, indicating the instrument or method by which something is done, like "by" or "with" in English). (The description of the function of the six Latin cases has been simplified.)

To return to the claim in the initial paragraph of this section, learners of English as a second language have a tremendous advantage over learners of a highly inflected language as a second language, because learners of English don't have to remember a large number of grammatical forms they would need to know to make themselves fully understood. To carry on a satisfactory general conversation in English, however, a modest vocabulary of English words is all one needs.

Chomsky and Transformational-Generative Grammar

The study of languages and linguistics has been documented for ancient Greece as early as two and a half millennia ago. At about that time, the earliest preserved scientific grammar was compiled in India. The work is Pāṇini's grammar of Sanskrit, written around the fifth century B.C., or even earlier, and described by a distinguished American linguist as "one of the greatest monuments of human intelligence" (Bloomfield 1933:11). Not a great deal is known about the development of linguistics during the Middle Ages, but both pedagogical and philosophical studies of languages continued. In Europe, attention was given almost exclusively to classical Latin rather than to the living languages spoken by the different peoples. By contrast, Arab grammarians furnished excellent descriptions of their own language.

Although the roots of modern linguistics go back to the end of the eighteenth century, most of the revolutionary developments did not come about until the beginning of the twentieth. To simplify matters considerably, one may say that the first half of the 1900s was characterized primarily by structural and descriptive approaches in the study of language: *structural* because language—any language—was considered to be a complex system of elements that were interrelated and could be studied and analyzed only as such; *descriptive* because the aim was to describe actual usage rather than what, according to a traditionalist view, usage ought to be. During the second half of the 1900s, linguistics departed radically from these earlier approaches as a result of the contribution of the American linguist Noam Chomsky, whose theoretical perspective and methodology are referred to as **generative** or **transformational** (or transformational-generative) **grammar.**

Using the descriptivist approach, linguistic analysts would begin by writing down words and phrases of a language phonetically, and when sufficient phonetic data had been collected, proceed to determine the phonemes of the language. Once they had completed phonemic analysis and devised transcription, the analysts would phonemically transcribe words, phrases, sentences, and entire utterances in order to understand the morphology of the language as well as the meanings of its different morphemes. Sentence structure would usually receive only secondary attention.

By contrast, linguists trained in transformational-generative grammar proceed the other way around, from the sentence to its various constituents. Let us consider the following pair of sentences: "Father is eager to please" and "Father is easy to please." The structure of both sentences appears to be the same, and in an analysis concerned with listing morphemes and their arrangements the two would be considered very much alike. Yet they are fundamentally different: In the first one, it is Father who is doing the pleasing and is the subject of the sentence, whereas in the second Father is the person being pleased and therefore the underlying object. If one changes the sentences from active to passive voice, "Father is easily pleased" is acceptable as grammatical and meaningful, but "Father is eagerly pleased" is clearly not. Although the superficial, or surface, structure of the two original sentences is much the same, there is a basic difference between them, and it can only result from differences in their deep structure. It appears, then, that the mere listing of morphemes and their arrangement in sentences is not enough to account for the differences that may obtain between them.

To write the generative grammar of a language, then, is to develop a finite device capable of generating an infinite number of grammatical sentences of the language. That is a very tall order even for professional linguists and it is one reason our coverage of this type of grammar has been so brief. The other, and main, reason is that at this point transformational-generative grammar is not a tool that most linguistic anthropologists are able to use or would profit from using. The semantic component in transformational-generative grammar has not yet been fully charted. However, if lexical semantic structure can be significantly related to the structure of the

BOX 4.2 CONTRASTING THE DESCRIPTIVE AND GENERATIVE APPROACHES

Consider the operation of a gas-powered automobile. Like a language, a car that runs is a complex functioning whole. Like a language, too, it consists of many different parts that make up various systems (the drive train, the electric system, the cooling system, and others), each of which operates according to specific principles. Applying the view of Chomsky and his followers to this example, one can liken the descriptivist approach to the skills and operations of a mechanic who is well acquainted with the various automobile parts and their functions but who is not seriously concerned with *how* and *why* a car runs. Very much like the descriptivist linguist, who restricts his or her analysis to surface structures, the mechanic is familiar with the car only superficially, although capable of maintaining it in good running condition.

According to Chomsky, such an approach is not truly scientific because it makes no effort to explain. A real understanding of what makes a car run comes from the comprehension of such fundamental principles as those of combustion, friction, application of force, and the like. Not until these principles are grasped can one say significant things not only about a particular make of car but about cars in general, and about other conveyances that utilize these principles (for example, snowmobiles). Consequently, the fundamental principles, like the rules of grammar, are prior; and the parts and their arrangements, like the linguistic units and their arrangements, assume secondary importance. . . . Nevertheless, for the anthropological field worker, who is mainly concerned with recording native terms in a service-able phonemic transcription and who rarely possesses intuitive knowledge of the language he or she is dealing with, the descriptivist approach continues to be useful.

from Oriol Pi-Sunyer and Zdenek Salzmann,
Humanity and Culture (1978), 356–357

corresponding culture, then future research in this area will be of special interest to linguistic anthropologists.

How would one compare the merits of descriptive and structural linguistics with those of generative grammar, and in linguistic anthropology to what extent has transformational-generative grammar replaced the earlier approaches? One way of answering the question is presented in Box 4.2.

Summary and Conclusions

Morphology is the study and description of word formation. The principal unit of morphology is the morpheme, the smallest meaningful part of language. There are thousands of morphemes in any language: Those that may be used by themselves are termed free; those that occur only attached to other morphemes are termed bound. Many morphemes have more than one phonemic shape; the variant forms of a morpheme are its allomorphs. Grammar—the various rules that govern the workings of a language and the processes that implement these rules—varies from one language to the next. Some languages are characterized by many inflectional forms (for example, Latin), others by relatively few (for example, English). The complexity of grammar, however, does not add to the prestige of a language. The study of the phonemic differences among allomorphs of the same morpheme is referred to as morphophonemics. The plural morpheme of English nouns has a variety of allomorphs; one may therefore speak of the morphophonemic rules of English noun pluralization.

Sentences are the largest structural units of a language, and their study in the traditional conception is called syntax. In transformational-generative grammar, syntax refers not only to sentence structure but to word structure as well. In this approach, the syntactic component is one of three major organizational units of a grammar, the others being the phonological and the semantic components. Having to do with the structure of meaning, the semantic component has been the last to be studied in modern linguistics and the one worked out in least detail.

The interest of structuralists and descriptivists in linguistic variety the world over has long been shared by linguistic anthropologists, many of whom deal with unwritten languages of little-known peoples. Before the introduction of transformational grammar, the approach to the study of language was somewhat mechanical because it was concerned primarily with items (units) and their arrangement. Chomsky, the founder of transformational-generative grammar, has both posed and attempted to answer new questions concerning language, many of which are of great importance. For example, how is it possible that already at an early age individuals know as much about their native languages as they do without any formal learning? According to Chomsky, one must assume that children are born with a knowledge of what can be termed universal grammar, in other words, that universal grammar is part of our human biological endowment. What the speakers of a particular language must learn, of course, are the specifics of the language they are acquiring (for example, the lexicon).

Linguistic anthropologists are primarily interested in understanding language within the overall matrix of culture, and speech as an inseparable link to social behavior. But even though they are not so much concerned with linguistic structure as such, they are obviously influenced by the latest developments in linguistic theories and methods because of their interest in the speech of those whose cultures they study.

5

Nonverbal Communication

Spoken language—speech—is by far the most common and important means by which humans communicate with one another, but it is not the only one. The many different writing systems used throughout the world are of tremendous importance for communication, having in some respects an advantage over spoken language, especially their relative permanence.

The term *nonverbal communication*, taken literally, refers to the transmission of signals accomplished by means other than spoken or written words. Not everyone agrees on what the term encompasses, and some even question whether nonverbal communication is definable. Used broadly, the term includes bodily gestures, facial expressions, spacing, touch, and smell, as well as whistle, smoke-signal, and drum "languages," and such optional vocal effects as those that accompany spoken utterances and can be considered apart from actual words.

Nonverbal systems of communication may be divided into those that are derived from spoken language and those that are independent of it. With only a few exceptions, writing systems belong to the first category, representing as they do the sounds of speech. In turn, writing systems may serve as the source of other systems. The English word written as *tree* can be transmitted in the International Morse Code by audible or visual signals as – · ·· · ·, with –, · –, and · representing respectively the letters *t*, *r*, and *e*. Similarly, the braille alphabet, a system of writing for the blind, makes use of raised dots within a 2×3 matrix. The different arrangements of raised dots ($\bullet$) represent the letters of the alphabet, as in corresponding to *t*, *r*, *ɛ*, *e*.

Other systems of communication that are based on speech are drum and whistle **"languages,"** which imitate some of the reproducible distinctive features of the spoken languages along with which they are used.

Some sign languages are independent of speech. Because some *are* independent, it was possible for the Plains Indians to use sign language as a means of effective communication among tribes speaking different, and many times even unrelated, languages.

Another way of classifying nonverbal communicative systems is according to channel, or the medium by which signals are conveyed. The channel employed in drum "language" is acoustic, whereas sign language or smoke signals use the optical channel. Individuals who are blind make use of touch when they feel the raised dots of the braille system, and those who are deaf as well as blind may learn to monitor articulatory movements by placing a hand on the speaker's face and neck (Tadoma method). The olfactory channel is not used in the highly structured manner of the channels just mentioned, but it should not be underestimated: As a rule, Americans do not indulge in eating fresh garlic before a social occasion or an important business engagement for fear of sending the wrong signals.

For the most part, human communication is a multichannel affair operating on verbal and nonverbal levels. Regardless of the society, it is not only how people talk and what they say but also how they present themselves to others that seems to make a difference as to how they are perceived. The study of the properties of signs and symbols and their functions in communication is referred to as **semiotics.** Because of the increasing attention given to all modes of communication in humans and other animals, the field of semiotics has been steadily growing in volume and popularity. Among the subfields of semiotics are biosemiotics, the semiotic study of living systems; semiotics of food because the preparation of food transforms its meaning and also because certain foods can be symbolic of specific social codes; and social semiotics, which includes the interpretation of such cultural codes as fashion and advertising.

Paralinguistics

Characteristics of vocal communication considered marginal or optional and therefore excludable from linguistic analysis are referred to as **paralanguage.** The most common paralinguistic features are usually assigned to three categories.

Voice qualifiers have to do with the tone of voice and pacing of speech, and they include variations in volume or intensity (for example, overloud, oversoft), pitch (noticeably high, noticeably low), tempo (overly fast, overly slow), and articulation (for example, drawling, clipping, or rasping).

Besides these and other voice qualifiers, there are various **voice characterizers** that accompany speech or, more precisely, through which one talks. These range from laughing and giggling to crying and sobbing to yelling, moaning, groaning, whimpering, and whining.

And then there are the so-called *vocal segregates,* represented for the most part by such extralinguistic sounds (that is, sounds not part of the phonemic system) as the ones graphically represented in English texts as *uh-huh* to indicate agreement or gratification, *uh-uh* to indicate disagreement, *tsk-tsk* to express mild disapproval, and other graphic approximations of different kinds of snorts and sniffs.

Here are some concrete examples of paralinguistic behavior: Highly controlled articulation produces the crisp, precise pronunciation expected of formal pronouncements addressed to large audiences; by contrast, speech so relaxed as to become slurred is heard from those who are very tired, sleepy, or under the influence of alcohol or other drugs. Speakers of English and other languages tend to associate extreme pitch variation with happiness and surprise; high pitch level or fast tempo with fear, surprise, or anger; and low pitch level or slow tempo with boredom and sadness. The rounding of lips imparts to the voice the cooing quality that is frequently used by adults when talking to a baby.

As an additional example, consider whispering. A person may whisper to avoid waking up others who are napping or sleeping (an example of thoughtful behavior); to avoid being overheard (consideration of privacy); to convey a secret or a conspiracy; or to spread rumors of an intimate nature about someone (hence the phrase "whispering campaign").

In the discussion of speech, one may be tempted to consider silence, or forbearance from speech, not worth mentioning. However, that would be a mistake. Depending on the context, silence can indicate a variety of meanings or feelings. In a tense situation, silence can be threatening if it is used deliberately instead of an appeasing remark; by contrast, it may help to lessen tension by withholding a comment that could worsen a situation. Silence may also express one's uncertainty concerning an issue, or help to avoid an argument. It may be a gentle substitute for saying "no," as when a young man asks "Will you marry me?" and no response is forthcoming. Some of these and other uses of silence are by no means universal; they may vary somewhat, or even quite deeply, from culture to culture.

Kinesics

Just as any speech that is not neutral tends to be accompanied by one or more paralinguistic features, it is also likely to be supplemented by visual gestures. This is the subject of **kinesics**, the study of **body language.**

There is no question that bodily gestures (in the broadest sense) serve as an important means of communication. Comedians are notably adept at slanting, canceling, or completely turning around the meaning of their spoken lines with a well-chosen grimace or gesture of different communicative content, and professional mimes know how to move their audiences to tears or laughter without uttering a single word. But speech-related body motions are by no means limited to performers—they are an integral part of everyone's daily communicative activity.

The basic assumptions that underlie kinesics is that no body movement or facial expression is likely to lack meaning because, just like other aspects of voluntary human behavior, body movements, posture, and facial expressions are patterned and occur together. For example, accidental meetings of good male friends are commonly characterized by a brief raise of hand first, then a firm handshake, a brief rising of eyebrows, and a smile.

Influenced by structural linguistics, Ray L. Birdwhistell (1918–1997) in the 1950s developed a method of studying and describing the body-motion aspects of human communicative behavior by means of units that parallel those employed in linguistic analysis. One such unit, the **kineme** (analogous to the phoneme), has been defined as the smallest discriminable contrastive unit of body motion.

Students of kinesics take note of several basic components, all of which are associated: facial expression, eye contact, body posture, and hand gestures.

Facial expressions signal a wide range of emotions from pleasure, happiness, and pleasant surprise to suspicion, sadness, fear, anger, disapproval, or disgust—to list only the most common feelings.

The nature of eye contact between people in face-to-face interaction varies not only from culture to culture but also within the same society (particularly such a large society as our own) from one individual to the next according to the experience, age, self-confidence, and intentions of the communicator. Eye contacts therefore range all the way from avoidance to the look of a person who is in love.

Types of hand gestures are too many to classify in this brief survey, and two are mentioned to illustrate. One purpose they serve is to emphasize what is being said and, two, handshaking as a greeting can be accomplished in a variety of methods. The hands can be combined together in various ways, and one's second hand can be used to impart emphasis to the handshake with one hand. Handshaking may be elevated to hand clasping, arm clasping, shoulder clasping, or shoulder embracing. All these gestures involve touching behavior, and that is culture-specific.

Body posture conveys the individual's attitude to the face-to-face interaction he or she is participating in: It can signal feelings ranging from interest, concern, or anticipation to boredom, depression, or impatience. During some ritual occasions, of course, specific body postures are expected or required—for example, kneeling, standing, or bowing.

Observant travelers noticed centuries ago that members of societies along the Mediterranean Sea used many more bodily gestures and facial expressions than, say, those living in Scandinavia or Japan. However, not all Italians, for example, use the same "body language," just as they do not all speak the same dialect of Italian. Birdwhistell offered an interesting example in support of the expectation that kinesic behavior is likely to be just as culture-specific as the corresponding language. He reported that even when the sound is removed from films made back in the 1930s and 1940s of the speeches of the late politician and mayor of New York City Fiorello La Guardia, it is possible to tell whether he is speaking English, Yiddish, or Italian, as characteristic body motions are associated with each language (Birdwhistell 1970:102). Although the holistic and contextual approach to communication that Birdwhistell advocated has been uniformly accepted, the extent to which "body language" can be analyzed in terms of his units remains controversial, in part because the detailed transcription he designed is far too complicated and time-consuming.

TABLE 5.1 The Four Distance Zones of Informal Interpersonal Space Among Middle-Class Americans of North European Heritage

Distance Zone	Physical Distance (approx., in feet)	Acoustic-Auditory Channel	Olfactory Channel
Intimate			
Close	0–.5	grunts, groans	
Far	.5–1.5	whispers or very low voice	
Personal			
Close	1.5–2.5	soft voice	almost all odors disapproved of
Far	2.5–4	moderate voice	
Social-consultative			
Close	4–7	normal voice	almost all odors disapproved of
Far	7–12	louder voice	
Public			
Close	12–25	loud voice	almost all odors disapproved of
Far	25+	full-volume voice	

Source: Adapted from *The Hidden Dimension* by Edward T. Hall. Copyright © 1966, 1982 by Edward T. Hall. Used by permission of Doubleday, a division of Bantam Doubleday Dell Publishing Group, Inc.

Proxemics

In the early 1960s, the interdependence between communication and cultural stimulated Edward T. Hall to develop **proxemics**, the study of the cultural patterning of the spatial separation individuals maintain in face-to-face encounters. The term has subsequently come to embrace studies concerned with privacy, crowding, territoriality, and the designing of buildings, private as well as public, with the view of meeting the different cultural expectations of their prospective users.

According to Hall, the distances individuals maintain from one another depend on the nature of their mutual involvement and are culture-specific. For example, under normal circumstances, middle-class American adults of northern European heritage make regular use of four **proxemic zones**, or distances, ranging from intimate to public, each of the zones consisting of a close and a far phase (see Table 5.1).

In the close phase of the intimate distance, the individuals are close enough to be encircled by each other's arms. All senses are engaged: Each individual receives the body heat as well as any odor or scent emanating from the other individual, and the other person's breath is felt; because of the closeness, vision may be blurred or distorted and speaking is at a minimum. As is obvious, this narrowest of all interpersonal distances is suited to love-making, protecting, or comforting.

By contrast, business is transacted at the social-consultative distance: The close phase is characteristic of contact among people who work together or are participants at casual social gatherings; the far phase characterizes more formal business transactions, such as interviews or situations in which two or more people find themselves in the same space and do not want to appear rude by not communicating. For instance, receptionists who are also expected to type and manage a switchboard must have enough space between them and the visitors to permit them to work rather than to feel they must engage in polite conversation with those waiting to be seen.

The manner in which members of different societies space themselves in each other's presence varies along a contact-noncontact continuum. For example, Arabs, other Mediterranean peoples, and Latin Americans prefer spatially close interactions; northern Europeans prefer to keep their distance, literally and figuratively (see Box 5.1).

However, some differences in proxemic and **haptic** behavior (haptic behavior relates to the sense of touch) may be noticeable even among members of societies who live in close proximity. According to a recent study, French and Dutch dyads (two individuals) maintain greater distances than French and English dyads. And one would be justified in undertaking a study to determine whether people born and raised in southern France have the same proxemic and haptic behaviors as those who have grown up and made their homes in northern France.

Without being acquainted with Hall's proxemic matrix, people are aware when someone encroaches into their personal zone, or into the zone of someone for whom they think they have a special claim. An example of the latter would be a young male seeing his girlfriend being spoken to by another young male who is using the close personal zone that touches the intimate zone. The male who feels "threatened" is likely to join the talking couple to alter the proxemic situation.

Finally it should be mentioned that personal space is occasionally modified by the conditions imposed by the physical situation in which people find themselves. For example, the fixed spacing of classroom desks may not be the most proxemically satisfactory for the thousands of foreign students who study in the United States.

BOX 5.1 HALL ON PROXEMICS IN A CROSS-CULTURAL CONTEXT

In Latin America the interaction distance is much less than it is in the United States. Indeed, people cannot talk comfortably with one another unless they are very close to the distance that evokes either sexual or hostile feelings in the North American. The result is that when they move close, we withdraw and back away. As a consequence, they think we are distant or cold, withdrawn and unfriendly. We, on the other hand, are constantly accusing them of breathing down our necks, crowding us, and spraying our faces.

Americans who have spent some time in Latin America without learning these space considerations make other adaptations, like barricading themselves behind their desks, using chairs and typewriter tables to keep the Latin American at what is to us a comfortable distance. The result is that the Latin American may even climb over the obstacles until he has achieved a distance at which he can comfortably talk.

from Edward T. Hall, The Silent Language (1959), 209

Many Americans feel that [older] Germans are overly rigid in their behavior, unbending and formal. Some of this impression is created by differences in the handling of chairs while seated. The American doesn't seem to mind if people hitch their chairs up to adjust the distance to the situation—those that do mind would not think of saying anything, for to comment on the manners of others would be impolite. In Germany, however, it is a violation of the mores to change the position of your chair. An added deterrent for those who don't know better is the weight of most German furniture. . . . To a German, light furniture is anathema, not only because it seems flimsy but because people move it and thereby destroy the order of things, including intrusions on the "private sphere." In one instance reported to me, a German newspaper editor who had moved to the United States had his visitor's chair bolted to the floor "at the proper distance" because he couldn't tolerate the American habit of adjusting the chair to the situation.

from Edward T. Hall, The Hidden Dimension (1966), 129

Whistle "Languages"

Among the various systems of nonverbal communication, of particular interest are those speech surrogates that depend on and are derived directly from spoken language. Some of these "languages" are produced in the vocal tract—the so-called **whistle speech.**

Whistling as a means of serviceable communication is not very common, but it is known to occur in such widely separated areas of the world as Myanmar (formerly Burma), Mexico, the Canary Islands, the French Pyrenees, Cameroon, and New Guinea. One of the better-known instances of whistle speech concerns the Mazateco Indians of northern Oaxaca, Mexico. The language of the Mazateco is a tone language, one in which relative variations in pitch are used to distinguish words of different meanings that would otherwise sound alike. There are four distinctive pitch levels, or tonemes, in Mazateco, ranging from high, 1, to low, 4, with two intermediate tonemes, 2 and 3; when two different tones are associated with one syllabic nucleus, they form a glide. Accordingly, the speakers of Mazateco distinguish between te^1 'he will dance,' te^2 'he dances,' te^{2-3} 'I dance,' te^{4-3} 'wide,' te^3 'ten,' nt^3nto^2 'slippery,' nt^4nto^{3-4} 'pimple,' n^3nto^3 'mountain,' and so on (Pike and Pike 1947:88).

Under special circumstances, as when the distance between two Mazateco men is too great for them to shout, they use whistle speech. By reproducing, with a few modifications, the four tonemes and other whistleable features (glides, different types of syllabic units, and pauses), they are able to carry on an effective conversation concerning a variety of topics. The following exchange was observed by George M. Cowan (1948), to whom we are indebted for the description of Mazateco whistle speech: A Mazateco standing in front of his hut whistled to another man a considerable distance away on a trail below. After several exchanges in whistle talk, the man on the trail turned around and walked up to the hut with the load of corn leaves he had been carrying to market. At the hut, he dumped his load on the ground and received some money from the first man. The entire transaction, including the customary bargaining over price, had been carried on exclusively through whistling.

Although Mazateco women do not whistle, they understand whistle talk. In addition to overcoming distance in the hilly terrain in which these people live, whistling is used to attract the attention of another person by sounding his name or to exchange information without interfering with a simultaneous oral conversation carried on by elders. Even though in principle there are no limitations on what can be signaled by whistling, identical tonal patterns can give rise to ambiguities or confusion. However, the subject that is communicated by whistling is usually easily identifiable from the context.

Whereas Mazateco whistle speech makes use of the prosodic features of the language from which it derives, the whistle speech employed on La Gomera, one of the Canary Islands, is based on articulations. The reason for the development of the *silbo* (Spanish for *whistle*), as it is called, is apparently the island's rugged terrain, which alternates between mountains and gorges. According to André Classe (1957), accomplished users of the *silbo* can be heard and understood over a distance of three miles, and perhaps even more.

The native language of the inhabitants of La Gomera is a dialect of Spanish. Many members of the island's peasant class, men and women, are proficient in the *silbo* by the time they have reached their teen years. The whistled sounds approximate the sounds of the spoken language, making the *silbo* in effect whistled Spanish. Whether or not the whistler uses one or two fingers in the mouth, the dorsal part of the tongue is the only active articulatory organ. Because Spanish is not a tone language, whistled vowels can be differentiated by varying pitches, and most of the consonants of the relatively simple sound system of the spoken language are heard as modifications of the whistled vowels that come before or after them.

Communicative whistling is closer to home than most of us may realize. What we are referring to is the so-called wolf whistle. Typically it was a two-toned whistle, with the second tone a falling guide, sounded by a boy or man to express his appreciation of a girl or woman nearby. Although not as popular as it was a few decades ago, it is still a signal recognizable by most Americans.

That the whistling by the Mazateco and the people of La Gomera is so effective is excellent proof of the high redundancy that characterizes all natural languages: Even when some features are eliminated from the code, there is no appreciable loss of essential information.

Sign Languages

Signing, that is, communicating manually by **sign language** of some kind, is undoubtedly at least as old as speech. From the writings of ancient Greeks and Romans, we know that their deaf made use of signs. It is, however, reasonable to assume that even among the earliest humans those who were not able to communicate orally would have used their hands to make themselves understood. Sign languages used to the exclusion of spoken language—for example, by people born deaf—are referred to as **primary.** Sign languages found in communities of speaker-hearers as regular or occasional substitutes for speech are termed **alternate** sign languages.

For many years, scholars neglected the study of sign languages, considering them as little more than crude substitutes for speech. Serious attention to sign languages dates back to the late 1950s; it was accompanied by renewed interest in the sign language of the Indians of the Great Plains.

In the United States, the hearing-impaired use a combination of two signing systems. One is the manual alphabet, which is made up of signs representing the twenty-six letters of the English alphabet and the ampersand (&). It is fingerspelled, using one hand only, and both the sender and receiver must be acquainted with the orthography of the language. (By contrast, the signs of the manual alphabet used in Great Britain and Northern Ireland are made with both hands.) In the other signing system, sign language proper, a particular sign stands for a concept, or, to put it in terms of spoken language, a word or a morpheme. A number of sign languages are in use in English-speaking countries, most involving some modification of either American Sign Language (ASL or Ameslan) or British Sign Language (BSL). Ameslan offers its users more than 5,000 signs, with new ones coined as needed. It makes use of three-dimensional sign space that forms a "bubble" about the signer extending roughly from the waist to the top of the head and outward from the extreme left to the extreme right as far as the signer can reach. Within the sign space, the user can specify time relationships, distinguish among several persons being signed about, signal questions and embedded clauses, and express a variety of grammatical categories such as plurality and degree (as in *good, better, best*) as well as aspectual differences of a verbal action such as habituality, repetition, intensity, and continuity. Head tilt, eyebrow and lip configuration, and other body motions are frequently used to add to the expressive capacity of manual gestures.

Fluent use of signs can match the speed of an unhurried conversation, as can be seen from television programs in which speech is being translated into ASL for viewers who are hearing-impaired. Finger spelling is considerably slower, but it is indispensable for proper names or concepts for which there are no signs (for example, chemical substances).

There are many different manual alphabets, just as there are many different writing systems; further, sign languages proper vary internally and among themselves, just as do the dialects of a spoken language and as one spoken language differs from another. Regardless of the particular sign language used, the majority of signs are not transparently **iconic,** that is, they cannot be interpreted by those who have not first learned their meanings.

If primary sign languages function much like spoken languages, do they also have duality of patterning, that is, are they analyzable at two levels of structural units comparable to phonemes and morphemes? According to William C. Stokoe Jr. (1960), who devoted many years of study to the sign language of the American deaf, Ameslan grammar has the same general form as the grammars of spoken languages. It is characterized by a small set of contrastive units meaningless in themselves (**cheremes,** on the analogy with phonemes) that combine to form meaningful sign units, the morphemes. Chereme refers to a set of positions, configurations, or motions that function identically in a given sign language. And each morpheme of a sign language may be defined according to hand shape, orientation of the palm and fingers, place of formation, movement and its direction, point of contact, and other spatial and dynamic features. Users of Ameslan and other natural sign languages are no more aware of cheremes than users of spoken English are of phonemes.

To sum up, contrary to popular misconceptions, primary sign languages used by the deaf are highly structured, complete, and independent communicative systems, comparable in complexity to spoken and written languages; otherwise they could not substitute for spoken languages as effectively as they do. Furthermore, they are natural languages in the sense that their acquisition is the automatic result of interaction with others who depend upon signing.

Alternate sign languages take a variety of forms, ranging from occupational sign languages, such as the one developed by sawmill workers in the northwestern United States and western Canada, to the performance sign language employed in the classical Hindu dance tradition to monastic sign languages that make it possible for the members of orders who use them to observe the self-imposed rule of silence. The best-known alternate sign languages, however, are those used by the aboriginal peoples of various parts of Australia, and especially the system of signing developed by the tribes of the North American Plains, the most elaborate in the New World.

For the earliest mention of sign language in North America we are indebted to Pedro de Castañeda de Nájera, the most widely read chronicler of the 1540–1542 Coronado expedition to what is today the U.S. Southwest. His report described an encounter of the Spaniards with what probably was a band of Apaches (he referred to them as Querechos) along the present-day New Mexico-Texas border:

These people were so skillful in the use of signs that it seemed as if they spoke. They made everything so clear that an interpreter was not necessary. They said that by going down in the direction in which the sun rises there was a very large river, that the army could travel along its bank through continuous settlements for ninety days, going from one settlement to another. They said that the first settlement was called Haxa, that the river was more than one league wide, and that there were many canoes. (Hammond and Rey 1940:235–236)

Although frequently mentioned in the travel accounts of the early explorers west of the Mississippi, Plains Indian sign language has not yet received the attention it deserves, particularly as there remain only a very few individuals who are still proficient in it.

For a score of nomadic tribes whose spoken languages were either completely unrelated or related but mutually unintelligible, Plains Indian sign language is known to have been an effective means of intertribal communication in trade and other negotiations. Moreover, it was commonplace for members of a tribe to recount their war exploits or to "narrate" a long traditional tale exclusively by means of manual signs, and it is a matter of record that the Kiowa Indians gave General Hugh Lenox Scott a detailed account of their sun dance ceremony by using signs. Plains Indian sign language consisted of a large repertory of conventionalized gestures performed with one or both hands. The hands were either held stationary in various configurations or moved between the levels of just above the ground to over the signer's head. For example, to sign *snow* or *snowing*, both hands were extended in front of the face, all ten fingers pointing downward, and then lowered in whirling motions. Abstract concepts were conveyed with equal facility. The concept of *cold* or *winter* was conveyed by clenched hands with forearms crossed in front of the chest, accompanied by shivering movements. The idea of *badness* was indicated by a motion suggesting something being thrown away: The right fist held in front of the chest was swung out and down to the right as the hand was opening up.

Although the bulk of the signs must have been shared by the tribes of the north-central Plains, there were no doubt "dialectal" differences similar to those found in widely extended spoken languages. Unlike the whistle "languages," however, sign languages are independent of speech even though they have occasionally been used in combination with it. Only in manual alphabets is there a connection: A manual alphabet represents the elements of a writing system that in turn derives from speech.

Summary and Conclusions

Although spoken language is undoubtedly the oldest and most efficient means of human communication, there are many other ways in which people transmit or exchange information. Information, emotions, and feelings, in addition to writing, can be transmitted nonverbally. Nonverbal systems of communication are based on either spoken or written language, or are independent of it.

The Morse Code and braille derive from the written representation of a language; whistle "languages," by contrast, are based on certain acoustic features of speech. Vocal communication is invariably enhanced or modified by so-called paralinguistic features, such as extra loudness, whispering, or sounds other than those of normal speech. Body language includes facial expressions, hand gestures, and other body motions. Hearing-impaired individuals make use of sign systems that are very nearly as efficient and expressive as spoken languages. The Plains Indians of North America used an elaborate sign language to communicate with members of other Plains tribes whose languages they could not understand; and by means of signs, they were even able to tell very long and elaborate traditional myths.

6

The Development and
Evolution of Language

It is now generally accepted that communication among members of animal species is widespread and that most vertebrates transmit information by acoustic signals. The variety and ingenuity of these communicative systems have stimulated a great deal of research in animal communication and its comparison with human speech. If we accept the single modern human species (*Homo sapiens*) as a very recent result of the evolution living organisms have undergone for more than a billion years, then we may also be likely to assume that human speech is the end result of a long, cumulative evolutionary process that shaped communicative behavior throughout the animal kingdom. But how this happened is not easy to discover. In this chapter we will examine how the evolution of language might have taken place.

Communication and Its Channels

Communication among members of animal species is universal because it is important to their survival; it takes place whenever one organism receives a signal that has originated with another. An early (from the 1940s) but serviceable model of communication uses five components: the sender (or source), the message, the channel, the receiver (or destination), and the effect. These components take into account the entire process of transmitting information, namely, who is transmitting what by what means to whom and with what effect. The model appears to be rather simple and straightforward, but because communication is by no means uniform, some discussion is in order.

Although communication among members of any particular species is to be expected, interspecific communication—that is, transmission of signals between members of different species—is far from rare. An experienced horseback rider transmits commands to a horse and expects them to be received and followed. A dog whining outside its owner's door conveys its wish to be let in. Communication between people on the one hand and their pets or work and farm animals on the other is very common and not limited to sounds. Touching (stroking, patting, holding, and grooming) animals is frequently more effective than talking to them, and the dog that wags its tail and vigorously rubs its muzzle against a human knee leaves no doubt about its feelings of satisfaction and pleasure. The means of sending messages clearly vary and are not limited to sounds (as in speech) or visible signs (as in looks or hand gestures), although these two channels, or media selected for communication, are the means humans most frequently employ.

The most common and effective channel of human communication is the *acoustic channel*, used whenever people speak to each other as well as in so-called whistle speech (discussed in Chapter 5). Writings, gestures, and pictorial signs make use of the *optical channel*, relating to vision. Braille, a writing system for the blind that uses characters consisting of raised dots, is received by the sense of touch, the *tactile channel*. The *olfactory channel* is chosen whenever one wishes to communicate by the sense of smell: People sometimes use room deodorizers before receiving guests and put perfume or deodorant on themselves when they expect to spend time with other individuals at an intimate distance. By the same token, most Americans consider garlicky or oniony breath to be a signal that reflects unfavorably on its senders.

The olfactory channel is especially important among social insects, which do much of their communicating by means of odors in the species-specific substances known as pheromones they secrete. Regardless of the channel used, animals send out messages for a variety of reasons, such as to guide individual organisms of the same species to one another or to help synchronize the behaviors of those who are to breed. In other words, communication enables organisms to maintain certain relationships that are of advantage to them individually as well as to their species as a whole.

Members of any animal species may use several kinds of signaling behavior. The signals familiar to humans are patterns of behavior known as **displays.** They may take the form of birdsongs, croaking (among frogs), chirping (among crickets), spreading fins or changing color (among certain fish), chest beating (among gorillas), and so on. Some signal units are cooperative, involving at least two individuals; others are rather formalized. A male hawfinch touches bills with a female, and during courtship the male bowerbird builds a chamber or passage decorated with colorful objects that will attract a mate. Some animals (for example, dogs and wolves) use urine marking as a chemical signal delimiting territory, whereas others (skunks and bombardier beetles, to mention just two) use chemical signals for defense. Some of the unexpected findings in the field of animal communication have stimulated continued research.

Communication Among Social Insects

Social insects include certain species of bees and wasps and all ants and termites. Among the many species of social insects, the temperate-zone honeybee (*Apis mellifera*) is genetically endowed with fairly elaborate communicative behavior. For our understanding of the so-called bee dance language, we are especially indebted to the Austrian zoologist Karl von Frisch (1886–1982), who spent many years doing painstaking research on the subject and shared with two other scholars the 1973 Nobel Prize in Physiology or Medicine.

One of several pheromones the queen of a honeybee colony secretes is ingested by bees that constantly attend and groom her. These bees subsequently spread the pheromone throughout the beehive to suppress the ovarian development of the worker bees and thus prevent the rearing of new queens. As the distribution of this pheromone begins to lag as a result of the queen's death or the colony's excessive size, new queens are reared and preparations made for swarming. When the developing potential queens communicate from their cells their readiness to assume their duties, their vibrations are received by detectors located in the hollow legs of the beehive population (bees feel rather than hear the vibrations because they have no ears). Swarming itself is triggered by an acoustic signal sent out by a worker bee. As soon as the first new adult queen hatches, she locates the cells containing her potential royal rivals and destroys them. Then she leaves the hive to mate with drones, attracting them by secreting another pheromone.

The most interesting aspect of the communicative behavior of honeybees has to do with foraging for food (see Figure 6.1). A scout bee can communicate the location of an especially abundant source of food by means of a dance inside the hive. The distance of the nectar source from the hive is indicated by the form of the dance the scout bee performs on the vertical surface of the honeycomb. If the source is quite close to the hive, the bee performs a round dance. If the source is farther away, about one hundred yards or so, the scout bee dances in the shape of a figure eight. During this performance, the bee elaborates on its roughly circular dance by adding a tail-wagging walk across the circle, its abdomen moving from side to side. The length of time given the tail-wagging portion communicates the distance of the food source from the hive: the greater the distance, the longer the duration. The angle between the direction of the tail-wagging run and an imaginary line directed to the center of earth's gravity corresponds to the angle between the sun and the nectar source, the hive being a point of reference. If the sun happens to be above the food source and in direct line with it, the tail-wagging portion of the dance is vertical and the bee dances upward; if the sun is in line with the food source but on the opposite side of the hive, the crucial portion of the dance is again vertical but is danced downward. On partly cloudy days, the scout bees are able to infer the position of the sun from the polarization of sky light. In addition to distance and direction from the hive, the richness of the food source is indicated by the amount of liveliness that characterizes the dance. It further appears that the length of the special buzzing sound a bee makes during the tail-wagging portion of the dance contributes to the information concerning distance. Experiments have established that the location of a food source as distant as seven miles from the hive can be accurately communicated through the bee dance.

The honeybee's communication system is innate, that is, young bees do not have to learn how to use it. However, the more experienced the bee, the more precise is its reporting. Then, too, the dance language of the honeybees varies somewhat from one variety to another. For example, black Austrian honeybees perform a somewhat different dance from the honeybees of Italy. These differences are similar to the dialectal variation in human languages, but with one important difference: Dialects of human languages are aspects of a behavior that is learned, whereas the variations in the communicative behavior of honeybees are inherited.

The communicative behavior of ant species may not be as intricate as that of honeybees, but it includes a wide variety of signals. Secreting pheromones from different glands to lay down scent trails that lead other ants to food or to trigger alarm-defense behavior is common to several species. More specif-

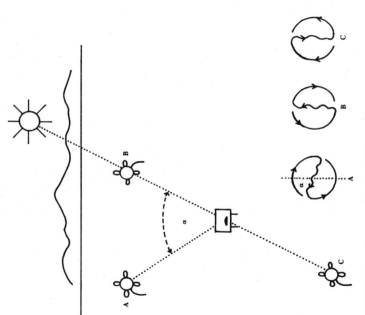

FIGURE 6.1 Communication of Honeybees

The beehive is located at the center, with three sources of nectar (A, B, and C) appearing in various directions from the hive. The three tail-wagging dance diagrams at bottom right show how the direction of the food source from the hive is communicated, using the sun as a point of reference.

ically, a pheromone secreted from the mandibular glands of male carpenter ants synchronizes the nuptial flights of males and females; a female pharaoh ant sexually stimulates a male by a pheromone and by touching him with her antennae or by presenting the enlarged part of her abdomen to him; certain species of ants that conduct slave raids on other ants discharge pheromones for various purposes, among them to disorient the ants under attack; and the workers of several species make tactile signals with their antennae and forelegs so that workers returning to the nest will regurgitate food to share.

Insects are commonly considered to be among the lower organisms of the animal kingdom, but their communicative behavior—especially that of the social insects—is highly specialized and efficient.

Communication Among Nonhuman Primates
and Other Vertebrates

The amount of research concerning communicative behavior of vertebrates other than humans has been considerable; only a few representative examples can be given here, in brief and very general terms.

Of the several channels by means of which birds communicate, the vocal channel is best known to humans. Bird vocalizations are of two major classes: songs and calls. Consisting of several subparts, birdsongs are typically sung only by males and are longer and more complex than calls. Their two main functions are to establish and hold territory by repelling other males and to attract females during the breeding season. Depending on the species, birdsongs are either innate, learned, or in part innate and in part learned. The learning ability of many species of birds is at its maximum during the individual's first few months of life, but birds learn only the song characteristic of their own species. Birdcalls, in contrast, are short (single notes or short sequences of notes) and are used to signal alarm, feeding, distress, imminent takeoff or landing, and the like. For the most part, birdcalls are innate, but in some species a degree of learning is involved. Dialectal differences exist, especially in birdsongs.

For some time, much scholarly and popular attention has been focused on the communication of cetaceans, an order of aquatic mammals that includes dolphins and whales. Despite the number of studies concerning bottle-nosed dolphins, our understanding of their acoustic communicative behavior is still insufficient. Members of this species of dolphins produce clicks, barks, yelps, and moans as well as whistles and squeals. The function of these different vocalizations is not fully understood: Some appear to express emotional states, others may be used for echolocation and navigation, and still others may identify individual dolphins. As yet, however, no evidence suggests that dolphins communicate with each other to a greater extent than do birds, for example.

In addition to various other sounds, humpback whales produce "songs" consisting of several ordered subparts and lasting as long as half an hour. All whales of a particular area sing the same song, although over time these songs may be somewhat modified. Song sessions of whale groups are known to have lasted several hours. Our understanding of whale communication, too, is still far from adequate.

The greatest amount of research on animal communication since World War II has been devoted to nonhuman primates, especially the chimpanzees. In the wild, besides visual and other signals, apes use a variety of vocal sounds, including grunts, pants, barks, whimpers, screams, squeaks, and hoots. Each vocalization is associated with one or several circumstances. The physical similarity between the great apes and humans has long intrigued observers, suggestions that apes could be taught to speak having been made several centuries ago. Of the various experiments to teach chimpanzees to talk, the best documented was the one begun by Keith J. Hayes and Catherine Hayes in the late 1940s. They adopted a newborn female chimpanzee, Viki, and brought her up in their home as if she were a human child. Despite all the Hayeses' efforts to teach Viki to speak, after six years Viki had learned to approximate only four words (*mama, papa, cup,* and *up*), and poorly at that. It appears from the disappointing results of this and similar experiments in home-raising chimpanzees that the ability to speak is unique to humans and that the principal channel of communication for apes is the optical one—postures, facial expressions, and gestures.

In a more recent experiment, Washoe, an infant female chimpanzee, was taught the form of gestural language used by the American deaf. Toward the end of the second year of the project, Washoe was reportedly able to use more than 30 signs spontaneously. After five years of training, she was said to be actively proficient in about 150 hand signs, was able to understand more than twice that many, and could use combinations of several signs. At about the same time, another chimpanzee, Sarah, was taught to write and read by means of plastic tokens of various shapes, sizes, and colors, each token representing a word. According to a report published in 1972, Sarah acquired a vocabulary of about 130 terms that she used with a reliability of between 75 and 80 percent. Her performance included the use of a plastic symbol that stood for the conditional relation *if-then,* as in "If Sarah takes a banana, then Mary won't give chocolate to Sarah" (Premack and Premack 1972).

Studies of communicative behavior among the great apes are continuing, and important new findings have been reported. Some of these studies concern the pygmy chimpanzees (*Pan paniscus*), whose habitat is the dense equatorial forest south of the Congo (Zaire) River in Zaire. Because their population is relatively small, the species may be considered endangered. The behavior of the pygmy chimpanzee is noticeably different from that of the common chimpanzee (*Pan troglodytes*). Pygmy chimpanzees appear to be more intelligent and more sociable and are faster learners; there is also evidence that they are more bipedal, less aggressive, and more willing to share food. Adult males and females associate more closely, and those in captivity seem to enjoy contact with humans. Of interest is a study by E. S. Savage-Rumbaugh (1984) based on two pygmy chimpanzees observed at the Language Research Center of the Yerkes Regional Primate Research Center in Atlanta, Georgia. When the study was conducted, the center had two pygmy chimpanzees, a twelve-year-old female born in the wild and her "adopted" son, Kanzi, then one and a half years old. When Kanzi wanted something, he intentionally used a combination of gestures and vocal sounds to draw the attention of a staff member. His wishes included being taken from one area to another, being helped with a task he could not perform alone (for example, opening a bottle), and the like. He would point to strange objects with an extended index finger, sometimes accompanying such pointings with vocal signals and visual checking; he would also lead his teachers by the hand to where he wanted them to go, pulling on their hands if he wanted them to sit down. On occasion, Kanzi expressed frustration by fussing and whining. If we judge from the behavior of the small sample of pygmy chimpanzees at the center and elsewhere, they appear to be better able to comprehend social situations than are common chimpanzees, and communicate correspondingly. In other words, their behavior is more reminiscent of human behavior than is the behavior of other species of apes.

In another project, research assistants were requested to teach signs for objects to the young chimpanzee Nim; they were to reward him for correct responses but not treat him like a human child. In contrast to a human child, Nim preferred to act upon his social environment physically rather than communicatively and was little interested in making signs simply for the sake of contact. Several years later, an experiment was performed to test the hypothesis that social context can influence the communicative performance of a sign-using chimpanzee. The results of the experiment established that Nim adjusted his conversational style according to whether the interaction with humans was social or instructional (as in drill sessions). For example, in a social context, Nim made more than four times as many spontaneous contributions in sign language than he did when he was being trained. Apparently chimpanzees, just like children, tend to interact spontaneously when the situation is relaxed; in testing situations they are repetitive, imitative, and do not elaborate their contributions. If the communicative behavior of chimpanzees does indeed vary according to context, earlier reports on the cognitive capacities of signing chimpanzees may not tell the whole story.

Another noteworthy finding, made at the Institute for Primate Studies at the University of Oklahoma, involved Loulis, the young male that Washoe adopted when he was ten months old. Although staff members were requested to refrain from signing to Loulis, or even to other chimpanzees when Loulis was present, Washoe and several chimpanzees in contact with Loulis freely used signs they had learned earlier from their human teachers. Five years and three months later, when Loulis's "vocabulary" consisted of fifty-one signs, the restriction on human signing was lifted. During the subsequent two years, Loulis learned to use an additional nineteen signs. Independent observers acquainted with American Sign Language (ASL) were able to recognize the signs Loulis had learned from the other chimpanzees and could identify more than 90 percent of them (Fouts, Fouts, and Van Cantford 1989; Fouts and Fouts 1989).

Some of the great apes also have been observed to indulge in generalization, that is, they made a response to a stimulus similar but not the same as a reference stimulus. To give a few examples: Washoe extended the sign for "dirty" from feces and dirt to a monkey who threatened her and also to Roger Fouts, who had raised her, when he refused to accede to a request. The female gorilla named Koko generalized "straw" from drinking straws to hoses, plastic tubing, cigarettes, and other objects of similar shape. And Lucy, a chimpanzee, signed "cry hurt food" to mean radishes (Hill 1978).

These and other experimental results are naturally of considerable interest, but one must keep in mind that the chimpanzees were learning to communicate in an artificial setting and for the most part were carefully directed by humans. It would have been of greater significance if some of the human-trained chimpanzees had subsequently been able, on their own, to add new signs to their "vocabulary" and to understand conversational turn-taking. Scholars have argued that at least some of the reported animal responses may have been due to unconscious nonverbal cueing by those who studied them. Although this may be true, there is little doubt that apes can learn the communicative behavior researchers have described. But even at that, the nearly sexually mature chimpanzee is quite limited in what it can sign compared to a human child of six, who is capable of communicating verbally about a large variety of subjects. In short, the proficient use of the repertory of gestural signs of which chimpanzees are highly capable is a far cry from the conscious linguistic processing common to all humans from childhood on.

When Does a Communication System Become Language?

The question, When did language originate? is altogether too vague unless one first specifies what is meant by the term *language*. If it stands for a set of discrete vocal sounds, meaningless by themselves, that can be strung together to produce higher-order units ("words") endowed with conventional but arbitrary meanings, and, further, if such a system makes it possible for its users to generate an unlimited number of unprecedented comments about events removed in time as well as space, then most of the several million years of hominid existence would have been languageless.

Members of all animal species have a way of transmitting information among themselves, and before the **hominids** branched off from other hominoids—the gorillas and chimpanzees in particular—from 5 to 8 million years ago, they undoubtedly possessed a means of communicating similar to that of their closest primate relatives. Judging from what is now known about the behavior of the great apes in the wild, the communication system of the earliest hominids likely employed signals that were both visual and acoustic (or auditory) as well as olfactory (connected with the sense of smell) and tactile (especially grooming).

The visual signals, or gestures, would have been made by various parts of the body, including the face; the auditory signals no doubt consisted of a variety of vocalizations—grunts, roars, barks, moans, hoots, howls, and the like—but also of such nonvocal sounds as chest beating or ground stamping. The overall repertory, however, must have been rather modest, with the signals employed only when the stimuli that provoked them were present. The significance, or meaning, of these signals would have been limited to very basic "comments" concerning the immediate environment (for example, sudden danger or the discovery of food) or the individual's emotional state (annoyance, surprise, distress, assertion of dominance, fear, and the like).

It is clear that a vast distance had to be bridged between some such limited means of communication—a mere call system—and full-blown language that modern humans have been making use of for thousands of years. One may refer to the communication system that preceded full-fledged language as **prelanguage**. But even this differentiation into language and prelanguage is extremely rough because it suggests an evolutionary leap from one stage to the next rather than a long series of countless incremental changes that would have been imperceptible to the evolving hominids as they were occurring. Some anthropologists have attempted to reconstruct the evolution of human communication in some detail. For example, Roger W. Wescott (1974) postulated hand waving and vocal synchronization among the members of a group for the australopithecines, finger-pointing and vocal imitation for *Homo erectus*, and manual signing and unintelligible "speech" involving the use of meaningless syllables for the Neanderthals; writing and fully developed language he reserved for later *Homo sapiens*. Most anthropologists would probably find this scheme too conservative; its virtue is in its attempt to correlate the development of two communicative channels, the visual and the acoustic.

Milestones in Human Evolution

The emergence of the order of primates, to which humans belong, dates to some 60–70 million years ago, only a small fraction of the 3–4 billion years since life on earth began. Most of the early primates were arboreal, but in the course of time, as a result of changes in the natural environment, some of them became adapted to existence on the ground (see Figure 6.2).

One of the subdivisions of primates is the superfamily of **hominoids** (Hominoidea), which in turn comprises three families: the lesser apes (siamangs and gibbons), the great apes (gorillas, orangutans, and chimpanzees), and the hominids (Hominidae) (humans and their immediate ancestors). Current evidence suggests that the earliest hominids came from East African sites in Tanzania, Kenya, and Ethiopia and go back about 3–4 million years. The best-known specimen among them, referred to as Lucy, and fossil bones of a similar type have been assigned to the genus *Australopithecus* (southern [African] ape) and the species *afarensis*, named for the Afar badlands in Ethiopia, where the discovery was made in 1974. Small-brained, with cranial capacity estimated at about one pint (473 cubic centimeters), these early hominids were bipedal, that is, they used only their lower limbs for locomotion.

There is not complete agreement on the intermediate link between *Australopithecus afarensis* and the first representatives of the human genus, although most experts would probably choose another **australopithecine**

FIGURE 6.2 Presumed Stages of Human Evolution

A simplified time chart linking the hypothetical stages in the evolution of language with stages of hominid evolution, prehistoric periods, and landmarks in cultural evolution. The reader is reminded that the stages of language evolution and their time assignments are conjectural but reasonable, given the present state of our knowledge. Note that in order to accommodate the chart to a single page, the time scale changes several times (at dotted lines).

Years Before the Present	Stages of Hominid Evolution	Prehistoric Periods	Landmarks in Cultural Evolution	Presumed Stages in the Evolution of Language
10,000		Neolithic	Farming	(Proto-Indo-European)
40,000	Cro-Magnons (*H. s. sapiens*)	Mesolithic / Upper	Spectacular portable and cave-wall art	Earliest stage of full-fledged language
100,000	Neanderthals *Homo sapiens neanderthalensis*	Middle	Stone tools from prepared cores; Belief in afterlife?; Organized hunting; Ritual activities	Duality of patterning; Beginnings of articulate speech
500,000	Archaic *Homo sapiens*	Lower (Paleolithic)	Control and use of fire	Early stage of prelanguage
1 million	*Homo erectus*		Hunting	Blending
2 million	*Homo habilis*		First tools made and used	Adaptations for prelanguage
3 million	*Several species of the genus Australopithecus*			Simple multimodal communication
4 million				
5 million	Hominids branch off from other hominoids			
50 million	Monkeys and apes diverge			
100 million	Primates emerge			

species, *Australopithecus africanus*. This man ape, whose fossil remains in South Africa date to about 3 million years ago, was quite likely an ancestral form of *Homo habilis*, with whom it may have shared parts of Africa for several hundred thousand years. As the term suggests, *Homo habilis* is considered to be the first human, though still far removed from the modern species. The remains of *Homo habilis*, found in Tanzania and Kenya and dated between 1.9 million and 1.6 million years old, came from individuals with a braincase capacity equal to about one half that of modern humans. These early humans were correspondingly shorter in stature but more capable of making and using simple tools than the australopithecines may have been before them. Members of this species undoubtedly began to depend to an ever-increasing degree on group activity and a culturally patterned means of subsistence rather than on behavior governed solely by instinct.

With the appearance of *Homo habilis*, the pace of human evolution accelerated, producing a new species, *Homo erectus*, close to 2 million years ago. Members of this species spread from Africa to Asia and Europe, enduring for more than 1 million years until some 400,000 to 300,000 years ago. The tool kit of *Homo erectus*, best known for the multipurpose hand ax, included a variety of other implements used for cutting, piercing, chopping, and scraping. Evidence indicates that these ancestors of modern humans possessed the skills needed to become proficient large-game hunters. They also learned to use fire to keep warm, to prepare food, and to drive animals to locations where they could more easily be dispatched. The greater complexity of their culture was associated with an increased size of the brain, the average volume of which in *Homo erectus* approached about one quart (1,000 cubic centimeters).

The last major stage in human evolution took place about 300,000 years ago with the transition from *Homo erectus* to *Homo sapiens*, the species to which all contemporary humans belong. It is not yet possible to determine with assurance what course the transition took from one species to the next. One hypothesis is that *Homo erectus* in Africa evolved first into an archaic form of *Homo sapiens* and subsequently into the fully modern subspecies *Homo sapiens sapiens*. In Europe, these modern humans replaced the Neanderthals (*Homo sapiens neanderthalensis*), who, according to some anthropologists, did not complete the full transition. On the basis of some recent tests of mitochondrial DNA from Neanderthal fossil specimens, some anthropologists have suggested that Neanderthals should be assigned to a separate species, *Homo neanderthalensis*.

At this point, a cautionary note is in order. The use of taxons (formal names referring to taxonomic groups), particularly in such an abbreviated account of hominid evolution as that presented above, may be mistakenly taken to suggest a straightforward unilinear process toward anatomically modern forms. Nothing could be further from what the bulk of evidence indicates. At each stage of human evolution there must have existed considerable variation, with generalized hominid forms changing to more specialized ones as a result of adaptation—a process known as adaptive radiation. In other words, the branches of the "tree" of human evolution must have been tangled indeed. Amid all the differentiation, however, a relatively narrow thread of continuity from population to population has led to contemporary humans, and it is along this line that the various changes resulting in language must have taken place.

The evolution from *Homo erectus* to *Homo sapiens* was marked by a significant increase in cultural complexity. The Neanderthals, who persisted in Europe until the appearance of the Cro-Magnons of the *Homo sapiens sapiens* variety, appear to have been the first to bury at least some of their dead with deliberate care, furnishing them with tools and food, decorating them with red ocher, and even surrounding them with wildflowers. Several finds, taken to represent some sort of bear cult, consist of a number of bear skulls, some neatly arranged in a rock chest, others carefully placed in wall niches. These and other activities of the Neanderthals are considered by some as evidence of ritual behavior and possibly even belief in an afterlife. The material culture of the Neanderthals also became more complex. Their characteristic method of producing a variety of specialized implements made use of flakes struck off stone cores that had been carefully shaped in advance.

The Old Stone Age, referred to technically as the Paleolithic, lasted for more than 2 million years, terminating only about 10,000 to 12,000 years ago. The most recent subdivision of the Paleolithic, extending from about 37,000 to 11,000 years before the present, is referred to as **Upper Paleolithic.** From the Oldowan tradition through to the Mousterian culture, a span of about 2 million years, progress in toolmaking was very slow. But an explosion of creative activity occurred during the Upper Paleolithic, when the Cro-Magnons began to fashion elaborate objects—burins, barbed harpoons, spear-throwers, bone needles, and, above all, exquisite art. Working with paints as well as in stone, clay, bone, ivory, and antler, they created art both delicate and monumental (one frieze portraying animals of the hunt is about forty feet long) in styles ranging from abstract and geometric to naturalistic or daringly stylized. The rather sudden and rapid advances in the manufacture of a large variety of material items no doubt parallel similar advances in cognitive processes and indicate that full-fledged language would have been in place.

Today, no one would question the assumption that language was well established at the time of the relatively brief Mesolithic period that followed the Upper Paleolithic and ushered in the Neolithic. Most certainly, the revolutionary changes that human culture underwent during the Neolithic as a consequence of the domestication of plants and animals are unthinkable without full-fledged language.

Design Features of Language

If human language is unique among the many known systems of communication that exist in the animal kingdom, then it must possess some features of design not to be found elsewhere. In the 1960s, Charles F. Hockett and others proposed a set of "**design features**" **of language**—properties that characterize human speech.

This was a radical shift in thinking in linguistics, and even to certain extent, in anthropology. Though there was general agreement on the biological affinity between humans and other animals, language was thought to be unassailable in that it was assumed to be exclusively human. Even through the 1970s and 1980s many structural linguists refused to entertain the possibility that incipient linguistic behavior might be found, say, in chimpanzees or gorillas. They often defined language at the very beginning as something possessed only by humans (e.g., Trager 1972).

Hockett originally proposed seven design features but soon increased the number to sixteen. (In light of new findings from linguistics and cognitive science we will also propose four more shortly.) The following are the properties that Hockett argued characterized human language:

1. ***Vocal-auditory channel.*** Some sounds produced by animals are not vocal (for example, the chirping of crickets), nor are they received auditorily (as with bees, having no ears). (Writing, of course, is excluded because the channel used for written messages is optical rather than vocal-auditory.) Among mammals, the use of the vocal-auditory channel

for communication is extremely common, though they often use other means of communication (e.g., a dog "marking" its presence against a tree). One important advantage of using the vocal apparatus to communicate is that the rest of the body is left free to carry on simultaneously various other activities.

2. *Broadcast transmission and directional reception.* Speech sounds move out from the source of their origin in all directions, and the sender and the receiver need not see each other to communicate, nor do they have to "aim" their speech in a narrow direction. Binaural reception (involving both ears) makes it possible to determine the location of the source of sounds.

3. *Rapid fading.* Speech signals immediately disappear to clear the channel for new messages to come. This is more important than might appear at first glance. If we communicated olfactorily, as many animals do, we would have to wait for old messages to dissipate. This would be very time-consuming. Human sounds, on the other hand, are heard only at the time they are being produced. After that they are irretrievably lost, and the channel is ready for new messages.

4. *Interchangeability.* Speakers of human languages can be speakers and hearers—that is, speech signals can be transmitted or received interchangeably by all adult members (and most child members) of a community. In theory, at least, human beings are capable of uttering what others say (if, of course, the language used is familiar). This is not true of many animal species in which the nature of messages varies between males and females or according to other natural divisions. For example, in some species of crickets only the males chirp by rubbing together parts of their forewings, and the dance language of worker honeybees is not understood nor can it be performed by a queen or the drones of the same colony.

5. *Complete feedback.* Speakers of any language hear what they themselves are saying and are therefore capable of monitoring their messages and promptly making any corrections they consider necessary or appropriate. By contrast, a male stickleback (a fish) cannot monitor the changing of the color of his eyes and belly that serves to stimulate the female of the species. It also "makes possible the so-called internalization of communicative behavior that constitutes at least a major portion of 'thinking'" (Hockett 1960:90).

6. *Specialization.* Human speech serves no other function than to communicate. By contrast, the primary purpose of, say, the panting of a dog is to effect body cooling through evaporation, even though panting produces sounds that carry information (for example, the location of the dog or the degree of its discomfort). In other words, the communication system of many animals transmits signals only as a by-product of some other biological function.

7. *Semanticity.* Speech has meaning. "Salt" means salt and not sugar or pepper. Some features of honeybee dance language denote the distance of a food source from the beehive, and others give the direction in which the food is to be found. However, in no system other than human language is there such an elaborate correlation between the vast number of words and possible sentences and the widely different topics humans talk about.

8. *Arbitrariness.* There is no intrinsic relationship between the form of a meaningful unit of a language and the concept for which the unit stands. The common domestic animal that barks—*Canis familiaris* by its scientific Latin name—is referred to as *dog* in English, *Hund* in German, *chien* in French, *perro* in Spanish, *pes* in Czech, *câine* in Romanian, *sobaka* in Russian, *köpek* in Turkish, *kutya* in Magyar, *pohko* in Hopi, *heθ* in Arapaho, and *inu* in Japanese. But there is nothing about canines that makes English speakers call them "dogs," and there is nothing inherent in the sounds D-O-G that make them necessarily apply to canines.

9. *Discreteness.* Messages in human languages do not consist of sounds that are continuous (like a siren, for example) but are made up of discrete—that is, individually distinct—segments. The difference between the English questions "Would you care for a piece of toast?" and "Would you care for a piece of roast?" is due solely to two discrete sounds at the same place in each sentence, one written and pronounced as *t* and the other as *r*. By contrast, bee dance language is continuous; it does not make use of discrete elements.

10. *Displacement.* Humans can talk about (or write about, for that matter) something that is far removed in time or space from the setting in which the communication occurs. One may, for instance, describe quite vividly and in some detail the military campaign of the Carthaginian general Hannibal against ancient Rome, even though the Second Punic War took place more than 2,000 years ago on another

11. *Productivity/openness.* Humans can say things that have never been said before, and they can understand things they have never heard before. Thinking up a novel sentence is not difficult (as, for example, "Our two cats argue about approaches to linguistic anthropology whenever they are left at home alone"). Good poets quite regularly use language in innovative ways. When a new thing is invented we make up a new name for it. Other animal communication systems have limited repertoires, which can be used only in limited ways.

12. ***Duality of patterning.*** This is perhaps the most subtle design feature proposed by Hockett. This feature tells us that human language is organized on two distinct levels: (a) a level of *meaningless* sounds and (b) a level of *meaningful* parts of a language. Both have their own largely independent patterns (rules for creating combinations). For example, consider just these three sounds: /t/, /æ/, and /k/. On the phonemic (sound) level, they have no meaning, but they can be combined to form words like "tack," "cat," or "act" (here written in the conventional English orthography). That is, the units on the first level—the level of sound—are used to construct units on the second level—the level of words. The obvious advantage of duality of patterning is that a limited number of linguistic units of one kind make up a vast number of units on another level, much as the atoms of only about ninety naturally occurring elements make up the molecules of millions of different compounds.

13. *Cultural* (or *traditional*) *transmission.* Though there are biological predispositions for humans to acquire language, linguistic information is not passed on genetically, but culturally. One does not inherit a particular language; children learn language from parents or others whom they speak with. Speaking a particular language is therefore a part of one's overall cultural behavior, that is, behavior acquired through learning.

14. *Prevarication.* What a person may say can be completely and knowingly false (as if someone asserts that the moon is made of green cheese or that Washington is an hour's leisurely walk from St. Petersburg). Admittedly, an opossum may feign death (play possum) if surprised on the ground, or a bird may pretend to have a broken wing to lead predators away from her nest, but these behaviors are probably instinctive

and do not reflect a cognitive decision or an intent to deceive. On the whole, attempts at deception are not common among animals.

15. *Reflexiveness.* Humans can use language to talk about language, or communication in general, and indeed do so all the time. Nonhuman animals do not appear to be capable of transmitting information about their own or other systems of communication.

16. *Learnability.* Any human speaker can potentially learn any human language. Speakers of one language can learn a second language, or even several languages, in addition to their mother tongues. Some communicative behavior among nonhuman animals is also the result of learning, either by experience or from humans. No other animals, however, possess the ability to learn one or several systems of communication as complex as language.

Human languages possess all these design features, whereas the communicative systems of other animals possess only some. For example, according to Hockett (1960), calls produced by gibbons are characterized by the presence of design features 1 through 9 but lack displacement, productivity, and duality of patterning (Hockett is unsure about traditional transmission). Knowing that none of these design features is a completely either/or proposition, Hockett and Altmann (1968) called for examining design features using five frameworks: the social setting, the behavioral antecedents and consequences of communicative acts, the channel or channels employed, continuity and change in communication systems, and the structure of messages and their repertoires in specific systems. Accordingly, if one is to study a particular communicative system or transaction, one should include inquiries concerning who the participants are and where and under what circumstances they communicate, what channel or channels they use, what the structure of their messages and of the code as a whole is, and so on.

These and related concerns not only are necessary for a fuller understanding of subhuman communication but are equally important for the study and appreciation of human language in the context of society and culture.

Language as an Evolutionary Product

Like all aspects of the human condition, language also must have been a product of evolution. However, unlike items of material culture, language leaves no physical traces of its evolutionary past. Until recently, many anthropologists, linguists, and biologists believed that there was little that could be said about the origins of language.

Though no definitive answers can be given at present, recent studies in human genetics, behavioral biology, anatomy, and artificial intelligence give us reasons to be optimistic about solving some of the mysteries of the origin and development language. Two sets of related issues must be addressed. The first "big" question is, did language suddenly develop all at once, or was it a gradual process? The second is, did language develop under selective forces directly acting upon it, or was it a secondary by-product of evolutionary processes?

Continuity vs. discontinuity. In his book dealing with the biological foundations of language (1967), Eric H. Lenneberg (1921–1975) included an extended discussion of language in the light of evolution and genetics. Language development, he pointed out, may be viewed from two sharply differing positions. One, which Lenneberg called the *continuity theory*, holds that speech must have ultimately developed from primitive forms of communication used by lower animals and that its study is likely to reveal that language evolved in a straight line over time. According to this view, human language differs from animal "languages" only quantitatively, that is, by virtue of its much greater complexity. Although the proponents of a variant version of this theory argue that differences between human and animal communication are qualitative rather than merely quantitative, they also believe that all communicative behavior in the animal kingdom has come about without interruption, with simpler forms from the past contributing to the development of later, more complex ones.

The second theory, referred to as the **discontinuity theory of language evolution** and favored by Lenneberg, holds that human language must be recognized as unique, without evolutionary antecedents. Its development cannot be illuminated by studying various communicative systems of animal species at random and then comparing them with human language. One statement concerning the antiquity of language, however, can be made with some assurance: Because all humans possess the same biological potential for the acquisition of any language, the capacity for speech must have characterized the common ancestors of all humans before populations adapted to different environments and diversified physically.

Lenneberg rejected the continuity theory of language development for several reasons. Even though the great apes are the animals most closely related to humans, they appear to have few, if any, of the skills or biological prerequisites for speech. Frequently cited examples of animal communication have been drawn from insects, birds, and aquatic mammals, but the evolutionary relationships of these animals to humans vary greatly. That only a few species within large genera or families possess particular innate communicative traits indicates that such species-specific behavioral traits have not become generalized and therefore are likely to be of relatively recent date. In the following discussion, human speech and the several representative communicative systems of other animals should therefore be viewed as having no evolutionary continuity. There is, in short, no evidence to suggest that human speech is an accumulation of separate skills throughout the long course of evolution. If it were so, gibbons, chimpanzees, orangutans, and gorillas would not be as speechless as they are.

Language as emergent vs. language as innate: spandrels or language as an evolutionary by-product. The paleontologist Stephen Jay Gould (1941–2002) argued that evolutionary biology needed a term for features that arose as by-products of, rather than actual, adaptations. He calls such features *spandrels* (Gould and Lewontin 1979, Gould 2002:1249–1253), by analogy with the curved areas of supporting arches found in Renaissance architecture. Though pleasing to the eye, and usually covered with beautiful decorative art, spandrels were necessary to provide needed support to a square frame of the archway. Likewise, for example, the feathers of birds may have originally evolved as a mechanism for regulating heat and body temperature (as seen, say, in modern-day penguins). Over time, however, feathers seem to have taken on another use—flight. If true, this co-opting of feathers for use in flight would be an example of a spandrel.

The question is, did language evolve directly or was it a spandrel? Noam Chomsky and some others who subscribe to the existence of a universal "language faculty" believe that language itself evolved as a by-product (Hauser, Chomsky, and Fitch 2010). Stephen Pinker (Pinker 2009, Pinker and Bloom 1990) argues that natural selection played a more direct role in language evolution. The processes of natural selection designed a "language acquisition device" module in the protohuman mind, and evolutionary forces increasingly made it more sophisticated over time. Givón (2002:123), however, believes that modern neurology supports the claim that "human language processing is an evolutionary outgrowth of the primate visual information processing system." The key question, he argues, is, Does the neurology that supports language processing involve any language-specific mechanisms or is it just a collection of pre-existing modules that have been recruited to do so? To put things in extremes, we could phrase these two positions as:

Language as something that emerges: "All language-processing modules continue to perform their older prelinguistic task and reveal no special language-dedicated adaptations."

or

Language as something that is innate: "All language-processing modules are either entirely novel, or at the very least have been heavily modified to perform their novel linguistic tasks" (Givón 2002:123)

Monogenesis Versus Polygenesis

One other question arises when discussing language origins: Did the potentialities and traits required for the development of language originate in separate places at different or approximately the same times (polygenesis), or did they come into being just once (monogenesis)? Although one can never expect a conclusive answer to this question, a reasoned discussion of the alternatives is in order.

The theory of polygenesis, with its implication that languages spoken today ultimately derive from several unrelated sources in the remote past, is not easy to defend. For one thing, the process leading to prelanguage and language must have consisted of a long chain of transformations, structural and functional. That two or more parallel developments of such complexity took place independently of each other cannot be taken for granted. Derek Bickerton (1990) posited that the transition from "protolanguage" (referred to here as prelanguage) to true language was abrupt and the result of a single crucial mutation. However, it is difficult to accept that a system of communication as unique and complex as human language could have been the consequence of a single mutation. Then, too, the capacity of all normal children, regardless of ethnic background, to acquire any one of the several thousand natural languages with the same degree of mastery and according to approximately the same timetable is a strong indication that speech is innate throughout the human species and that all languages are simply variations on a common basic structural theme.

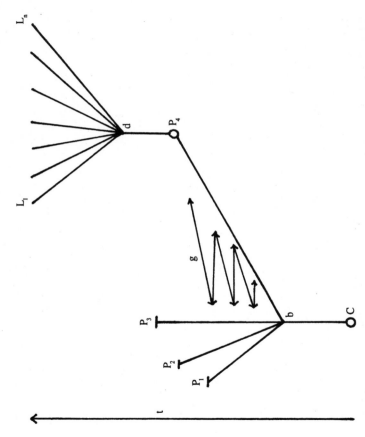

FIGURE 6.3 A Simplified Representation of the "Fuzzy" Version of the Monogenetic Theory.

The time scale (t) is several million years, and the starting point is a closed call system (C). The acquisition of traits essential for the development of language culminates in the introduction of blending (b), which gives rise to several prelanguages ($P_1 \ldots P_4$). Of these, P_1, P_2, and P_3 become extinct; gene flow (g) occurs between the speakers of prelanguages P_3 and P_4, of which P_4 survives in the long run and after the introduction of duality of patterning (d) becomes the source of all extant languages ($L_1 \ldots L_n$).

The theory of monogenesis may take two forms: radical (or straight-line) and, to use Hockett's term, fuzzy. Of the two, the fuzzy version of monogenesis appears more realistic. Although it presupposes a single origin of traits essential for language, it allows for the further development of the incipient capacity for speech to take place in separate groups of hominids within an area. The resulting differentiation could have been bridged by gene flow among the groups or brought to an end by the eventual dominance and survival of that early human population whose communicative system was most efficient (see Figure 6.3). If, instead, several varieties of prelanguage managed to

BOX 6.1 HOCKETT ON BLENDING

Suppose a gibbon finds himself in a situation characterized by both the presence of food and the imminence of danger. The factors, we shall say, are closely balanced. The normal consequence among gibbons is that one or the other factor prevails and just one call is given. This time we imagine our gibbon atypical. Instead of emitting either the food call or the danger call, he utters a cry that has some of the characteristics of each: he produces a *blend* of the two.

This is beyond the experience of the other gibbons in his band. Depending on acoustic conditions, some of them may hear the actual cry as the food call, others as the danger call, and others as nonsense. It is unlikely that any hear it as a new signal, conveying two kinds of information at once. The consequences are thus negligible.

But now suppose that the early hominids had a somewhat richer call system (though closed) functioning in a somewhat more complex social order. Then we may also assume that this type of event occasionally happened, and that sooner or later the other members of a band responded appropriately, thus handling an unusually complex situation more efficiently than otherwise. With this reinforcement, the habit of blending two calls to produce a new one would gain ground.

We have to assume that this is what happened, because blending is the only way in which a closed system can move towards openness of the kind characteristic of language.

from Charles F. Hockett, Man's Place in Nature (1973), 381

Estimating the Age of Language: Linguistic Considerations

Although scholars active in comparative and historical linguistics have developed a reliable method of reconstructing unwritten languages that were spoken in the distant past, evidence from linguistic prehistory can make only a limited contribution. To be sure, reconstructions have revealed, in considerable detail, aspects of language history. But the fact that languages persist, then there would be more than one "dialect" ancestral to all those languages that developed subsequently.

erable detail, many structural features of languages ancestral to present-day language families. The best example is **Proto-Indo-European,** the parent of a large number of languages that first spread throughout Europe and many parts of southern Asia and later, during modern times, to every other part of the world as well. The consensus among linguists is that the speakers of Proto-Indo-European were most likely to be found somewhere in eastern Europe, possibly in the steppes of southern Russia, during the fourth millennium B.C. Despite its early date, Proto-Indo-European matched in grammatical patterns the complexity of its various descendants: It distinguished among three genders (masculine, feminine, and neuter), three numbers (singular, dual, and plural), and perhaps as many as eight cases, and also possessed a comparably rich inflectional verb system. One can take Proto-Indo-European and other such reconstructed parent languages **(protolanguages)**—for example, those of the Uralic and Afro-Asiatic language families—and attempt further reconstructing, as some linguists have in fact done.

In his posthumously published work on the subject, Morris Swadesh (1909–1967) appeared to be convinced that protolanguages of language families were more similar in structure than the languages that descended from them because "human languages were then appreciably closer to their common origin than they are today" (Swadesh 1971:116). But despite the pioneering efforts of Swadesh and others, the majority of those who work in comparative and historical linguistics today have doubts about the effectiveness and reliability of the comparative method beyond a certain time depth. In the words of Paul Kiparsky (1976:97), "the time span over which we can hope to reconstruct anything at all about protolanguages, however generously we set it at, say, 10,000, or even 20,000 years, is still a very small fraction of the period during which language has presumably been spoken by man. Therefore, protolanguages as reconstructed cannot possibly be identified with any original stage of language." That the assumed Proto-Indo-European language was grammatically more complex than many of its modern descendants cannot be taken to mean that the older a language is, the more complex structure it must possess. If this were so, one would have to conclude that the earliest language was the most highly complex, a presumption that runs counter to what we know about long-term evolutionary process. In short, fully developed language must have preceded by many thousands of years any of the protolanguages linguists have been able to reconstruct to date, though, contrary to Kiparsky's estimate, 10,000 to 20,000 years may not have been a "very small fraction" of the period during which true language has been in existence, but a sizable one.

Estimating the Age of Language: The View from Prehistory

Approaching the question of language origins from a different vantage point, some anthropologists look for clues in cultural prehistory. It is generally agreed that the development of the various aspects of culture, both material and nonmaterial, must have been paralleled by developments in communicative behavior, and that a positive feedback must have existed between the two. In other words, the more complex the culture of the early hominids grew, the more elaborate the system of communication had to become to accommodate it; and the more the communication system was able to handle, the more elaborate culture could become. During the initial stages of hominid evolution, advancement was slow. The cultural takeoff dates back to the period of transition from the Neanderthals to the Cro-Magnons. Hockett acknowledged this relatively recent acceleration (1973:413): "True language is such a powerful instrument for technological and social change [that] if our ancestors had it 500,000 or 1 million years ago, why did it take us so long to get where we are?"

Although no one would argue in principle against the linkage between the degree of cultural elaboration and the complexity of a communication system, interpretations of evidence from prehistory vary a great deal. Ashley Montagu argued (1976:270) that some of the stone-tool assemblages found at Olduvai Gorge in Tanzania and dated to be nearly 2 million years old required so much skill and forethought that in all likelihood "speech was already well established among the makers of those tools, so that for the origins of language and speech we shall have to look to earlier horizons, and perhaps to even earlier forms of man [than *Homo habilis*]." Many anthropologists find the reference to "well established speech" in *Homo habilis* overdrawn but would readily agree to the presence of some of the traits that were to contribute to prelanguage.

The possession of prelanguage would, however, probably be granted to the more recent representatives of *Homo erectus*. The first hominid able to adapt successfully to regions of the world having cold winters, *Homo erectus* must have been an efficient hunter of large game. This claim has been particularly well substantiated by excavations at Torralba and Ambrona in northeastern Spain. These two sites revealed large quantities of bones from a variety of animals as well as a large assortment of tools, widely distributed bits of charcoal, and such an intriguing find as the end-to-end arrangement of an elephant tusk and leg bones, probably laid out by those who had butchered the animals. It appears that at one time the site locations lay along a trail between the seasonal grazing areas of animal herds. According to a widely accepted scenario, a band or bands of *Homo erectus* hunters of 200,000 to 400,000 years ago managed by either brandishing torches or setting grass afire to stampede elephants into a swampy area and so render them defenseless for the kill. In the context of our discussion, however, it is not so much the hunting prowess of these people that is important as the planning and coordination that would have been required to bring a potentially dangerous hunt to a successful conclusion—a feat that could not have been accomplished without some sort of prelanguage.

The Neanderthals, far from being the fierce-looking or dim-witted creatures portrayed in earlier reconstructions, adapted the stoneworking techniques of their predecessors to produce far more varied and carefully finished tools and became even more proficient hunters. Of greater importance, however, are the already mentioned archaeological finds that are strongly suggestive of ritual activities. If indeed these early humans believed in life after death, and if their treatment of the remains of cave bears can be associated with mythmaking or taken as an act of worship or the practice of hunting magic, the Neanderthals would have had to make references to other times and places, thus moving a significant distance from prelanguage to language.

The nature of Neanderthal communication continues to be subject to debate, but the presence of language among the Cro-Magnons cannot be disputed. With brains as large as the average for modern humans, they were able to adapt to the climatic and ecological extremes of the Americas, Australia, and even the Arctic regions. The concrete evidence of their imagination and dexterity is no less astounding: Many of the elaborately embellished items of their material culture that they bequeathed to posterity compare favorably with some of the best art that has been created since. Their cultural achievements are unthinkable without the aid of language as fully developed, or very nearly so, as that of recent and contemporary times.

Estimating the Age of Language: Evidence from Anatomy

That all normal humans acquire command of at least one particular language is the result of learning; that all humans possess and make use of the capacity for speech is part and parcel of a biological endowment unique to our species. Any inquiry into language origins should therefore give consideration to the biological foundations of language—in particular those parts of the human anatomy that facilitate it, the brain and the vocal apparatus, and the receiving organ, the ear.

Among the primates, humans have brains that are relatively large in comparison to total body mass. In the course of human physical evolution, the size of the braincase apparently expanded quite rapidly twice: first during the transition between *Homo habilis* and *Homo erectus*, the second time coincidentally with the rise of *Homo sapiens*. These expansions made it possible for the braincase to hold a substantially larger number of brain cells and to achieve a greater density of pathways among them, but it is not certain that, of itself, expansion was the direct result of a selection for greater mental capacity.

Despite much recent research, we still lack adequate knowledge of the structures in that part of the human brain to which the control of speech production is attributed. One variable feature of the neural basis for speech is the lateralization of language functions in the left cerebral hemisphere in nearly 99 percent of right-handed adults. Right-handedness appears to have been prevalent since the times of *Homo erectus* and, according to some scholars, may have been in evidence as far back as the australopithecines. Handedness and the associated lateralization even appear to be established in the great apes, if not also among the other primates, despite their total incapacity for speech.

The general configuration of the brain is similar in hominids, apes, and monkeys except for the more extensive and deeper folding of the outer layer of gray matter, the cortex, and the relatively small size of the limbic region in humans. The limbic system, which in mammals acts as the "emotional brain," is responsible for vocalizations associated with emotional and motivational factors and transmits signals of low informational content, such as cries. The several regions of the brain that appear to be closely associated with speech production (especially **Broca's area**, **Wernicke's area**, and the angular gyrus) are located in the more recent outer part of the human brain, which is developed more fully and complexly than the corresponding structure of our closest primate relatives. It is unfortunate that casts made of fossil cranial cavities showing the approximate shape of the brain do not reveal its internal structure.

In short, the differences in the brain structures between humans and the other primates are sufficiently apparent to indicate why the otherwise highly teachable apes cannot be taught to speak, but prehistoric evidence concerning the internal evolution of the human brain is either spotty or controversial.

The evolution of the vocal apparatus has been studied by Philip Lieberman together with several coworkers. Comparing the skulls of modern human adults with those of newborn infants, the Neanderthals, and contemporary apes, Lieberman and his associates found that the modern adult skull varies from the others in certain important respects. The significant difference seems to be in the position of the larynx and the size of the pharynx that lies directly above it (see Figure 3.1). In modern human adults the larynx is located farther down in the throat, and as a consequence the supralaryngeal area is much larger than in infants, Neanderthals, and apes. Consequently, the sounds emitted from such an area can be modified to a greater degree and encompass the three extreme vowels—[i], [u], and [a] as in *be*, *boo*, and *bah*. The reconstruction of the supralaryngeal vocal tract of the Neanderthals indicates that these hominids were not capable of producing the three critical vowels and certain consonants, at least not very effectively and consistently, and that they therefore lacked the special characteristics of modern human speech, though not by much. As Lieberman concluded (1984:323):

The evidence of Neanderthal culture indicates a highly developed tool-making and using culture, the use of fire, burial rituals, and a social order that cared for the elderly and infirm. . . . I therefore find it hard to believe that Neanderthal hominids did not also have a well-developed language. . . . Though it is . . . impossible to state with certainty all the factors that might have differentiated the linguistic and cognitive ability of classic Neanderthal hominids from their anatomically modern human contemporaries, their speech ability was inferior.

Also during the 1980s, Jeffrey T. Laitman and his colleagues noticed that the shape of the base of the skull is related to the position of the larynx. A detailed analysis of the skull base for many species of mammals revealed that either the skull base is fairly flat and the position of the larynx high or the skull is arched and the position of the larynx low. The first configuration is characteristic of all mammals except humans older than two years. The second configuration is found only in humans past infancy. Laitman's next step was to evaluate the skull bases of various fossil hominid remains and then judge from their shape what the position of the larynx would have been. Laitman reported that "the australopithecines probably had vocal tracts much like those of living monkeys or apes." Furthermore, according to preliminary data on the skulls of *Homo erectus*, Laitman's group discovered "the first examples of incipient basicranial flexion away from the nonflexed apelike condition of the australopithecines and toward that shown by modern humans. This indicates to us that the larynx in *Homo erectus* may have begun to descend into the neck, increasing the area available to modify laryngeal sounds." Fossil data Laitman and his colleagues obtained further suggest that a full arching of the skull base comparable to that in contemporary humans coincides with "the arrival of *Homo sapiens* some 300,000 to 400,000 years ago. It may have been then that a modern vocal tract appeared and our ancestors began to produce fully articulate speech" (Laitman 1984:26–27).

Summary and Conclusions

Speech is only one of several means by which humans communicate, but it is the most common and efficient one. Besides the acoustic channel employed in speaking, people make use of other channels, especially the optical one; they do so whenever they make gestures or facial expressions and, of course, when they write.

Communication is common among animals of all species and in some cases is surprisingly elaborate, as when a worker honeybee signals to other bees in what direction and at what distance from the hive an abundant source of nectar is to be found. To a considerable extent, animals are genetically endowed with communicative behavior, that is, they do not have to learn it. Although the capacity for speech is also a part of human genetic makeup, the particular language or languages an individual happens to speak must be learned. Among the design features that distinguish speech from the communicative behavior of other animals, the most striking are productivity, displacement, and reflexiveness.

Communication among early hominids such as the australopithecines undoubtedly involved several modes, with a combination of the visual channel (manual gestures or facial expressions) and the vocal-auditory channel (simple vocalizations) predominating over touch and smell. Adaptations that made speech possible very likely coincided with the initial stages of hominization—the evolutionary development of human characteristics—some 2 to 3 million years ago. The process was exceedingly slow, but in the course of time the early hominids came to rely primarily on the vocal-auditory channel, probably as a result of the increasing employment of hands for making and using tools. The steadily expanding repertory of calls eventually led to blending, which may have had its beginnings with *Homo habilis* and reached the limits of serviceable complexity (prelanguage) in late *Homo erectus* times. At that point, the stage was set for the development of duality of patterning, which could have been accomplished in principle among the late Neanderthals but did not attain the efficiency of full-fledged language until the complete progression of humans to *sapiens* status some 50,000 to 70,000 years ago.

Of necessity, this has been a very brief and oversimplified account of how language may have come about; the reader should bear in mind the length of time the process took and the countless changes, both behavioral and anatomical (and hence genetic), required for the attainment of full humanness.

7

Acquiring Language(s):
Life with First Languages,
Second Languages, and More

As most students know only too well, learning to speak a foreign language is a demanding undertaking that means coping with unfamiliar sounds and sound combinations, mastering grammatical rules different from those of one's native language, and learning a new vocabulary containing thousands of words. But if for most adults learning a foreign language is a major task, and only relatively few attain fluency in a second language, how is it that small children learn a language, or even two or more, as effortlessly as they do? Is first-language acquisition different from second-language acquisition? Is learning a third language easier than learning a second? Do **polyglots**—people who can speak several languages fluently—possess a special kind of innate intelligence the rest of us lack? Are the brains of **bilingual** and **multilingual** people somehow different from monolingual brains?

The First Steps of Language Acquisition in Childhood

For the most part, children are not taught to speak their native language. They learn it by exposure to people who talk to them. They do not go to language labs, and they are given no pattern drills to memorize. In fact, children seem to pick up the language spoken around them with very little effort, and, indeed, many of the examples they are presented are poor approximations of correct speech, as anyone who has ever heard a grandmother talk "baby talk" to a child knows. Yet by about age two or three, most children are usually communicating well enough for parents and most others to understand them.

The first step for the infant is to find some way to learn the phonological system. To reproduce the speech sounds of any particular language when they begin to talk, infants must learn to discriminate among sounds that may be quite similar. Among the sounds in English considered to be alike or to closely resemble each other are the initial consonants of such pairs of words as *bill* and *pill* or *thin* and *sin*, the final consonants of *sin* and *sing* or *doze* and *dose*, and the vowels of *pet* and *pat*, *pen* and *pin*, or *mill* and *meal*.

How soon and how well do infants discriminate among similar speech sounds? One of the techniques to test infants' acuity of sound perception is high-amplitude sucking. A pacifier connected to a system that generates sounds when a child sucks records the rate of sucking. When infants begin to hear sounds, they suck energetically, but they gradually lose interest if the sound stays the same. When the sound changes, however, vigorous sucking is resumed. Infants only one month old appear to be able to distinguish two synthetic consonant-vowel syllables different only in the initial consonants *p* and *b*. Other tests have established that infants are born with the ability to differentiate between even closely similar sounds, but that this ability diminishes or disappears by the age of about one year in favor of perceiving only the differences crucial to the native language. The acuity of voice perception in newborn babies has also been attested. It has been established that three-day-old infants are able to distinguish their mothers' voices from among other female voices. And it has also been shown that newborn infants prefer to listen to their mother tongue rather than another language.

Although the rate of speech development in normal children varies somewhat, it is possible to generalize about the stages that characterize language acquisition. Only **reflexive** (basic biological) noises such as burping, crying, and coughing are produced during the first eight or ten weeks; these are supplemented by cooing and laughing during the next dozen or so weeks. **Vocal play,** consisting of the production of a fairly wide range of sounds resembling consonants and vowels, becomes noticeable by about the age of six months. The second half of an infant's first year is characterized by **babbling.** According to some observers, sounds made during this stage are less varied and tend to approximate those of the language to be acquired. Babbling appears to be largely instinctive because even children who do not hear go through the babbling stage. In general, even before the onset of babbling, infants show eagerness to communicate and begin to process the information they are receiving through various channels. It also appears that regardless of the language they are acquiring, children learn to use the maximally distinct vowel sounds of their language (usually *a*, *i*, and *u*) before other vowels, and the consonants articulated with the help of the lips and teeth (commonly *p*, *b*, *m*, *t*, and *d*) before those produced farther back in the mouth (Jakobson 1968). Although subsequent research has indicated that the order in which the sounds of languages are acquired is not universal, Roman Jakobson (1896–1982) must be credited with the discovery of significant statistical tendencies.

Intonational contours (such as those characteristic of questions) begin to appear around the end of the first year, at about the same time as the one-word stage (for example, *mama*, *cup*, and *doggie*). This stage is succeeded around the age of two by the multiword stage. At first the child combines two words (for example, *see doggie*, *baby book*, *nice kitty*, and *daddy gone*), but soon expands such phrases to short sentences. On the average, the spoken vocabulary of two-year-olds amounts to two hundred words or more, although they understand several times that many. Initial consonants of words tend to be pronounced more distinctly by this age group than the consonants toward word ends. By the age of five or so, all normal children the world over are able to ask questions, make negative statements, produce complex sentences (consisting of main and subordinate clauses), talk about things removed in time and space, and in general carry on an intelligent conversation on topics they are able to comprehend (but they have yet to learn to tie their shoes). Even though much of the speech to which children are exposed is quite variable and casual, they gain command of the many sounds, forms, and rules so well that they are able to say, and do say, things they have never before heard said—and all of this without the benefit of formal teaching.

Theories of Language Acquisition

Behaviorist Psychology Theory. Behaviorism is a school of psychology popular in the mid-twentieth century; it made a major impact on learning theory. Probably its best-known proponent was B. F. Skinner, who argued for his view of language acquisition in his book *Verbal Behavior* (1957). Behavioral psychology theory is based on the stimulus-response-reward formula, and is not unlike the popular view of language acquisition. According to this theory, the human environment (parents, older peers, and others) provides language stimuli to which the child responds, largely by repetition of what he or she is hearing. If the response is acceptable or commendable, the learner is rewarded (by praise or some other way).

Innatist Theory: Among the most influential approaches to language development is innatism. Where behaviorism argues that all of language is acquired through different types of learning (stimulus-response, classical conditioning, etc.) innatist theory argues that there are at least some aspects of language which must already be present in the child at birth. This point of view received great support when Noam Chomsky (1959) in a lengthy review of Skinner's book convincingly undermined all of its assumptions and claims. For example, some things—like an equilateral triangle—are only products of the imagination, and do not actually exist in the real world. Such things cannot be learned, then, in the behaviorist sense. And it is true that children do imitate, of course, but not as consistently as is generally thought. If children only imitated what they heard, how could we account for such forms they produce as *sheeps, gooses,* and *taked*? There is no way behaviorism, Chomsky argued, could account for such analogical but ungrammatical forms. Such forms as *sheeps, gooses,* and *taked* in fact show that rather than imitating others, children derive these forms on the assumption of grammatical regularity—by extending the "regular" plural and past-tense markers to words to which they do not apply.

In Chomsky's view, children are born with a capacity for language development (see Box 7.1). However, the nature of the innate hypothetical **language acquisition device,** with which all infants are equipped, cannot at present be specified. According to some, it consists only of general procedures helping the child to discover how to learn any natural language; according to others, this device provides children with a knowledge of those features that are common to all languages. Chomsky (1986), for example, speaks of a genetically built-in "core grammar" that besides a number of fixed rules also contains various optional rules; it is up to the child to discover which of these options apply to a particular language. This would help to explain how children manage to overcome what is referred to as "poverty of stimulus"—that is, their ability to learn to speak a language effectively in a relatively short time, regardless of how complex it may be grammatically, even if much of what they hear happens to be largely fragmentary or repetitious.

BOX 7.1 CHOMSKY ON LANGUAGE ACQUISITION

We can think of every normal human's internalized grammar as, in effect, a theory of his language. This theory provides a sound-meaning correlation for an infinite number of sentences. . . .

In formal terms . . . we can describe the child's acquisition of language as a kind of theory construction. The child discovers the theory of his language with only small amounts of data from that language. . . . Normal speech consists, in large part, of fragments, false starts, blends, and other distortions of the underlying idealized forms. Nevertheless, as is evident from a study of the mature use of language, what the child learns is the underlying ideal theory. This is a remarkable fact. We must also bear in mind that the child constructs this ideal theory without explicit instruction, that he acquires this knowledge at a time when he is not capable of complex intellectual achievements in many other domains, and that this achievement is relatively independent of intelligence or the particular course of experience. These are facts that a theory of learning must face. . . .

. . . It is unimaginable that a highly specific, abstract, and tightly organized language comes by accident into the mind of every four-year-old child.

from Noam Chomsky, "Language and the Mind" (1968), 66

It would probably oversimplify the explanation of how young children are able to acquire so rapidly the knowledge of such a complex symbolic system as language if one were to accept any one of these or other theories to the exclusion of the others. There is little doubt that children do imitate, but certainly not to the extent some claim; and it is also quite likely that the earliest phases of language learning are not completely divorced from the child's mental development. However, many of the aspects of the innatist theory are quite convincing, and the theory has received much acceptance. It is indirectly supported by the somewhat controversial critical-period (or **critical-age**) hypothesis that language is acquired with remarkable ease during brain maturation, that is, before puberty. By this time the brain has reached its full development, and the various functions it performs have been localized in one side or the other (**lateralization**). According to recent research, though, lateralization may already be complete by the end of the fifth year, by which age children have acquired the grammatical essentials of their mother tongue.

Sociocultural Theory. Until recently, language acquisition was treated as if it were unaffected by sociocultural factors; correspondingly, the process of children's learning their culture was usually studied without giving attention to the role language plays in the process. Among those linguists and anthropologists who have called for the integration of the two approaches are Elinor Ochs and Bambi B. Schieffelin. In one of their works concerning language acquisition and socialization (1982), their view of the subject was expressed in the following two claims: "The process of acquiring language is deeply affected by the process of becoming a competent member of a society [and] the process of becoming a competent member of society is realized to a large extent through language, through acquiring knowledge of its functions . . . i.e., through exchanges of language in particular social situations" (Ochs and Schieffelin 1982:2–3). In the main body of the article, the authors made use of their fieldwork experiences in Western Samoa and Papua New Guinea (among the Kaluli) and for comparative purposes drew on data pertaining to the communicative development of children of the Anglo-American white middle class. To simplify matters we present only the comparison between the Kaluli and the Anglo-American children.

According to Ochs and Schieffelin and others (e.g., Ochs and Schieffelin 1982, 2006; Ochs and Taylor 2001; Schieffelin 2005), these kinds of acquisition patterns can be found cross-culturally. For example, Anglo-American white middle-class infants interact mainly with their mothers. This dyadic (two-party) interaction is in part the consequence of the typical family form, postmarital residence, and physical setting characteristic of American middle-class apartments or houses—nuclear family, separate home for the young married couple, and a separate bedroom for an infant. Mothers (or caregivers) hold infants face-to-face and treat them as social beings and communicative partners, frequently taking the perspective of the child or displaying interest in what may have been meant by a child's incomplete or unintelligible utterance. To accommodate young children and protect them from injury, the environment is adapted to their needs. Consider the availability of baby food, high chairs, and baby walkers as well as books and toys designed for specific ages, and the parental concern shown for the safety of the child by the cushioning of sharp edges, the placing of protective gates at stairs, and the like. The gap between the caregiver's and the child's verbal competence is reduced by a generous interpretation of the child's utterances or is masked by attempts to elicit stories from the child by posing questions he or she can answer with brief responses. In short, the child is the focus of attention and quite frequently the starting point of social interaction.

Among the Kaluli, a small, nonliterate, egalitarian society, the process of language acquisition and socialization is different. Kaluli babies are considered helpless and unable to comprehend the world around them; their unintelligible utterances tend to be ignored and no attempt is made to interpret them. Infants' needs are of course attended to, and a mother nurses her child even if she is involved in other activities. Nor are infants ever left alone: Mothers carry babies with them in netted bags whenever they happen to be gathering wood, gardening, or simply sitting and talking with others. But despite the physical proximity of a mother and her child, there is little communicative interaction between them. Infants are carried facing others, not their mothers. When infants approaching the age of one year do something they should not, they are reprimanded with such questions as "Who are you?" or "Is it yours?" meaning, respectively, "You are not someone to do that" and "It is not yours." Not until a child begins to use the words *nɔ* 'mother' and *bo* 'breast' is the child considered ready to be "shown how to speak." Because adult men and women are involved in extensive networks of obligation and reciprocity as they organize their work and manipulate social relations, the primary goal of socialization at the time when children begin to talk is to teach them how to talk effectively. Among the conventions of adult speech is avoiding gossip and indicating the source of information by noting whether something has been heard or seen and by quoting others directly. Children are expected to follow these conventions. Very little language is directed to Kaluli children before they begin to talk, but the verbal environment in which they grow up is rich, and children acquire verbal skills from listening to others. Although the one large village longhouse, where all villagers once lived together, is no longer in general use, at least two or more extended family groups share living space. The presence of a dozen or more individuals in one semipartitioned dwelling leads to frequent multiparty interaction. To teach the Kaluli language as spoken by adults, mothers constantly correct children for faulty pronunciation, grammar, and use of words so that they bypass the stage of baby talk.

In evaluating the available information as to how children develop their communicative skills for functioning in different societies or subcultures, the authors were led to assume that "infants and caregivers do not interact with one another according to one particular 'biologically designed choreography' . . . [but] there are many choreographies within and across societies . . . that contribute to their design, frequency and significance" (Ochs and Schieffelin 1982:44). This means, for example, that dyadic exchanges are accorded a varying degree of significance in different societies: Among the Kaluli, children are exposed to multiparty interaction much more frequently than to dyadic interaction. The authors further proposed that the "simplifying features of caregiver speech that have been described for white middle class speakers are not necessary input for young children to acquire language," and on the basis of these two proposals the authors suggested that "a functional account of the speech of both caregiver and child must incorporate information concerning cultural knowledge and expectations . . . [and] generalizations concerning the relations between behavior and goals of caregivers and young children should not presuppose the presence or equivalent significance of particular goals across social groups" (Ochs and Schieffelin 1982:46, 50).

Without language, no child could adequately learn all aspects of the culture and worldview of his or her society. It follows, then, that normal communicative exchanges in which caregivers and small children engage must in some way relate to the behavior patterns expected of adult members of a society. Are situations adapted to the child, or must the child adapt to situations? And if there is a shift from one to the other of these two orientations in any given society, when does it take place?

The authors made clear that their model does not exclude the role biological predisposition may play at the expense of culture and that they did not view socialization as a process that is inflexible over time or during an individual's lifetime. But they insisted that "our understanding of the functional and symbolic interface between language and culture" can be furthered only through studies of "how children are socialized through the use of language as well as how children are socialized to use language" (Schieffelin and Ochs 1986:184).

Language and the Brain

Even though our understanding of how the human brain operates is steadily increasing, our knowledge of its functions is still far from complete. Among the reasons are that the brain is tremendously complex and that experimentation with the brain is still somewhat limited. Some of what is known about its functions has been learned from the location and extent of brain injuries; however, a great deal of information has recently been gained from new experimental techniques (for example, neuroimaging and the stimulation of the cerebral cortex or nerve centers below it by electric current).

Neurolinguistics—the branch of linguistics concerned with the role the brain plays in language and speech processing—explores questions on which parts of the brain control language and speech, how the brain encodes and decodes speech, and whether the controls of such aspects of language as sounds, grammar, and meaning are neuroanatomically distinct or joint.

In relation to body mass, the human brain is not only the largest in the animal kingdom but also the most complexly organized. The largest part is the **cerebrum**, situated at the top of the brain and consisting of two lobes—the left and right cerebral hemispheres—and connecting structures. Each of the two hemispheres fills different functions. For example, the left is specialized for associative thought, calculation and analytical processing, the right visual field, temporal relations, and other functions; the right hemisphere for tactile recognition of material qualities, visuospatial skills, nonlinguistic auditory stimuli (including music), the left visual field, some use of language in social context, and others. In an overwhelming majority of right-handed individuals, the left hemisphere controls language, speech, writing, and reading. In more than one half of left-handed people, it is also the left hemisphere that either controls language or is significantly involved; in other left-handers, language specialization is located in the right hemisphere. Apart from the cerebral cortex—the surface layer of gray matter of the cerebrum—several other parts of the brain contribute to language processing. One such part is the left thalamus, the largest subdivision of the posterior of the forebrain.

Injuries to specific areas of the language-dominant hemisphere from such causes as gunshot wound, tumor, stroke, or infection result in different aphasias or other impairments of linguistic capabilities. To give a few examples, Broca's aphasia, also referred to as expressive or motor aphasia, is caused by a lesion in what is known as **Broca's area** (see Figure 7.1) and is characterized by omission of function words (such as articles, prepositions, demonstratives, and conjunctions) and past-tense and plural endings, as well as by faulty word order and distortions of sounds. Wernicke's aphasia, also known as sensory or receptive aphasia, is due to a lesion in **Wernicke's area;** it is characterized by

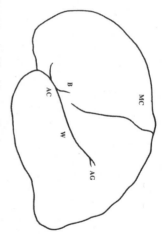

FIGURE 7.1 The Human Brain

Side view of the left hemisphere of the human brain, with its front on the left. The locations of the areas mentioned in the text are indicated as follows: AC = auditory cortex; AG = angular gyrus; B = Broca's area; MC = motor cortex; W = Wernicke's area. The thalamus is not seen from this view.

circumlocutions, impaired ability to understand written and spoken language, and occasional substitutions of inappropriate words, leading in severe cases to nonsensical utterances. Individuals affected by anomic aphasia have difficulty naming objects presented to them. Impairment of this type is associated with lesions in the dominant angular gyrus, one of the characteristic ridges of gray matter at the surfaces of the hemispheres.

Wernicke's area appears to generate the basic structure of sentences, which are then encoded in Broca's area; the articulation of sounds is directed by certain motor areas of the cortex. Comprehension of speech takes place in Wernicke's area after acoustic signals are transferred there from the ear by the auditory cortex. In general, speaking and writing are more likely to be affected by damage to the front part of the brain, listening and reading by damage to the rear part.

From what is now known, lesions in different parts of the language-dominant hemisphere result in different language and speech impairments. But much is yet to be learned about the human brain, both in general and concerning its role in communicative behavior.

Bilingual and Multilingual Brains

In the past, it was often assumed that competence acquired in the first language (**L1**) was qualitatively different from that in a second language (**L2**) or any subsequent language. This privileging the "native language" led to many popular misconceptions, such as believing that children of bilingual parents would never fully acquire either language, remaining somehow linguistically disadvantaged. Such claims are due to the belief that monolingualism is the norm, and they are held by many in the United States and other countries where a single language is politically or socially dominant. That this view must be wrong can easily be seen from the fact that many people in the world are speaking more than one language. In fact, it is bilingualism or trilingualism rather than monolingualism, that is most common. Even in supposedly monolingual nations like the United States, U.S. Census figures show that at least 20 percent of the population regularly speak a language other than English, and 53 percent of these people also speak English.

Another matter which must be considered is definition. "Bilingual" or "multilingual" can mean a variety of things. Some people may learn two languages natively as children, and be equally proficient and comfortable in both. Others may have only full competence in one language, and just get by in the other. Some people may be passive or receptive bilinguals, having the ability to understand a second language but not being able to speak it. There is also the issue of order. Are we dealing with simultaneous bilingualism—where a child learns two languages at the same time—or sequential bilingualism—where a person becomes bilingual by first learning one language and then another? And probably everybody understands at least a little of some other language, whether it is the leftovers from high school Spanish class, the words and phrases from neighbors, or words picked up on a job working with foreign-born employees. Bilingualism, then, should be viewed as a continuum from the relatively monolingual speaker to the highly proficient speaker of two languages.

For our purposes here, speaking in very broad terms, the childhood bilingual acquisition process may be considered as three developmental stages (Crystal 2007:409–415; 2010:374–375). First, the child builds up a set of words from both languages, but usually keep them separate, and not as translations of each other. Second, as sentences begin to appear, words from both languages can be used. This mixing rapidly declines, however, dropping almost completely by the end of the third year. After this, vocabulary in both languages grows, but a single grammatical pattern is used. Usually by the fourth year, however, the syntax of each language becomes distinct as the child becomes more cognizant that the two languages are not the same. It is then that they become aware of the sociolinguistic power of each language—the ways each language is to be used, and for what purposes.

The Social Aspects of Multilingualism

A particular people is as a rule linked with a particular language, and this language more than anything else serves as the people's badge of ethnic identity and uniqueness. As an example, the Plains Indian societies were similar in culture but quite distinct by virtue of the languages they spoke, some of which were as different from each other as English is from Russian or Japanese. And it used to be assumed that peoples who speak different languages have different cultures and therefore the boundaries between different societies coincide with lines separating mutually unintelligible languages. It was also widely accepted that any given language is the medium of communication for members of the corresponding society and that the relationship among language, culture, and communication tends to persist in time. Such assumptions greatly oversimplify matters, as shown by Dell Hymes (1968). According to Hymes, the world of human societies is divisible not so much according to the languages their members speak but rather according to communicative units "composed of repertoires of codes and rules of code-use," and it must further be recognized that these units overlap, that the criterion of mutual intelligibility is only one of several factors to be taken into account, and that the nature of the association between a particular code and particular cultural features must be considered on a case-by-case basis (Hymes 1968:42).

The following example is taken from an article by Hans Wolff (1967) and concerns the relationship of language, ethnic identity, and social change in southern Nigeria. In one part of the eastern Niger Delta live, from east to west, two coastal peoples—the Kalabari and the Nembe—and three hinterland peoples—the Abua, the Odual, and the Ogbia—five ethnic groups altogether. This five-unit ethnic division does not coincide with the language situation. The two coastal peoples speak closely related dialects of the Ijo branch of the Niger-Congo language family. The hinterland peoples speak related dialects of another language group. The Abua and Odual speak divergent dialects of the same language, with poor mutual intelligibility. However, four ethnically Odual villages speak a closely related but different language, Kugbo. To complicate matters further, the eastern dialects of Ogbia are not mutually intelligible with the western dialects but are intelligible with Kugbo. Although the three hinterland groups are aware of their close linguistic relationship, little communication takes place among them because of long-standing feuds over fishing rights and farmlands and because of different trading contacts in the past. Until recently, a great many of the Abua and Odual, especially the males, spoke Kalabari as their second language, whereas a large percentage of the western Ogbia spoke Nembe as a second language. Coastal languages were used in the interior on such important occasions as village gatherings and during Christian church services conducted by African clergy drawn from the coastal peoples. Yet the bilingualism found among the hinterland peoples was nonreciprocal: The coastal peoples did not learn or use the languages spoken by the Ogbia, Odual, or Abua. At the time of Wolff's visit to the area during the mid-1960s, the linguistic situation was undergoing change. Bilingualism continued to be present, with Igbo becoming the second language among the Abua. Another language increasingly used by those with formal education was English. At the same time, there was a concerted effort on the part of the hinterland peoples to use the local vernacular as the main, if not the only, medium of communication in order to achieve political recognition as distinct ethnic units.

Even from this simplified account of the situation it is evident that the existence of mutual intelligibility among some of the languages or dialects spoken by members of these ethnic groups had little significance with respect to their ethnic affiliation or the nature and volume of communication among them.

The second example is drawn from central Europe. The forefathers of contemporary Czechs and Slovaks were members of one political entity during the Great Moravian Empire. After the empire fell at the beginning of the tenth century, its Czech-speaking western part began a thousand-year-long separate historical development, whereas present-day Slovakia became an integral part of the Hungarian state. The Czechs and Slovaks were not again joined together politically until after World War I, when the Czechoslovak Republic was established in 1918. One of the reasons for assigning these two peoples to a common country was linguistic: Czechs and Slovaks speak mutually intelligible languages. In the new state, however, the attitude of the Czechs toward the much less urbanized Slovaks was patronizing, and the relationship between the two peoples remained asymmetrical until 1969, when the federalization of the republic helped to bring about some measure of balance.

During the course of the twentieth century, nationalist movements in Europe lost much of their force. The subsiding of nationalism was due to the increasing economic interdependence of one region on another; in Eastern Europe it was also the consequence of the internationalist character of Communist rule. After the collapse of Soviet control over Eastern Europe at the end of the 1980s, ethnic tensions in Czechoslovakia resurfaced and the Slovaks began to strive for either autonomy in a joint country with the Czechs or for complete independence. That Czechs and Slovaks are able to converse with one another using their two languages had little if any restraining effect on the desire of the numerically smaller Slovak people to emphasize their different historical experience and distinct ethnicity, more than seventy years of coexistence in a common state notwithstanding. The result was that the two peoples peacefully separated as of January 1, 1993, the former Czechoslovakia becoming two countries—the Czech Republic and Slovakia.

And to the southeast of what was Czechoslovakia, in former Yugoslavia, peoples who for the most part speak the same or mutually intelligible languages or dialects but are of different cultural and religious backgrounds have gone so far as to resort to armed conflict costing many thousands of lives and causing wholesale migration of families from communities in which their ancestors had lived for centuries. (There are only a few minor vocabulary differences between what the Serbs and Croats speak. The major difference is the alphabet: The Serbs use the Cyrillic, the Croats the Latin.)

The identification between a sociopolitical unit and language does not hold for the state, a form of politically centralized society that usually encompasses within its boundaries several or even many ethnic groups, each with its own speech. The multilingual nature of both historical and modern states has been obscured because a state is ordinarily associated with the official or quasi-official language used by the majority of its citizens. In the former Soviet Union, for instance, Russian increasingly served as the common language throughout the country's vast area even though the number of its distinct nationalities was around one hundred and most of their languages were actively used. In India, nearly three times as populous as the former Soviet Union but occupying an area only one-seventh as large, the number of different languages is reported to be almost 200. In the United Kingdom, the number of minority languages presently in routine use exceeds one hundred, and in the United States close to 10 percent of the population regularly speak a language other than English. In several African countries that have a single official language, as many as nine out of every ten people are estimated to make regular use of more than one language.

If members of different ethnic groups live side by side and interact frequently, at least some of them learn to speak a language or languages other than their own mother tongue and thereby become multilingual. The most common instance of multilingualism is bilingualism, characterized by the ability to speak two languages. Not everyone agrees on the definition of this term. Strictly speaking, bilinguals are individuals who have complete and equal command of two languages in all situations—in other words, those who pass for native speakers in either language. In practice, however, the term is applied more loosely, extending to those who can spontaneously produce meaningful utterances in a language other than their first.

Relatively stable bilingualism characterizes the situation in Switzerland, which accords national status to four languages—German, French, Italian, and Romansh—and where bilingualism is common and **trilingualism** far from rare. At the same time, none of the four languages thrives at the expense of the others despite the widely different percentages of their habitual speakers (German with more than 65 percent, Romansh with less than 1 percent). In Canada, which in 1969 granted official status to both French and English, most bilingual Canadians live in the province of Quebec, where a large majority (about 80 percent) consider themselves French Canadians and are on guard against the spread of English at the expense of French, even though a great many of them (about 38 percent) speak both languages. A particularly interesting example of multilingualism exists among the Native Americans of northwestern Brazil and the adjacent part of Colombia (Sorensen 1967). Almost every member of at least twenty different tribes in a culturally homogeneous area is fluent in three, four, or more regional languages. The source of this phenomenon is strict tribal exogamy, a custom requiring marriage partners to be from different tribes, making multilingualism the cultural norm rather than the exception. Children first learn their parents' languages, acquire two or more additional ones during adolescence, and often learn still others in adulthood.

More commonly, though, multilingualism is a transitional and asymmetrical phenomenon. During the latter part of the nineteenth century, few working-class immigrants from continental Europe to the Americas learned to speak the language of their newly adopted country to any extent, if at all. Although many of their children used the language learned at school only as a second language, they nevertheless became bilingual or nearly so. By subsequent generations, however, only a few retained even limited passive acquaintance with the speech of their forebears. Much the same has been true of many Native Americans in the United States: The transition from their native languages to English through the intermediate stage of bilingualism was mostly accomplished during the past century, and only the oldest tribal members still possess today a serviceable knowledge of their original speech. Where the concentration of immigrants maintains itself at a high level, bilingualism tends to persist longer.

Speakers of minority languages in the United States have always been numerous. Twenty percent of Americans speak a language other than English at home. Seven states—Arizona, California, Florida, Illinois, New Jersey, New York, and Texas—have more than 2 million speakers of languages other than English (up from four states in 1982). In half the fifty states, speakers of minority languages equaled or exceeded 10 percent of the population. In most of these states, the largest minority language is Spanish. According to 2008 surveys by the U.S. Census, there are some 35 million speakers of Spanish in the United States (about 12 percent of the total population). In four states, more than one in five residents speak Spanish as a first language: New Mexico (43 percent), California (34.7 percent), Texas (34.6 percent), and Arizona (28 percent). Because many Latinos in the United States speak Spanish in the home and with compatriots, and use English only as the medium for contact with the larger society, Spanish continues to be spoken by millions of people and is the most widely used language in the United States after English.

The demand on the bilinguals to use two different linguistic systems may result in various forms of simplification for one of the two languages. Among Mexican-American bilinguals living in a predominantly Spanish-speaking section of Los Angeles in the 1980s, this simplification affected their Spanish in a variety of ways: For example, their Spanish lost some of its compound tenses; the use of *estar* 'to be' was extended to contexts previously limited to *ser* 'to be'; some words were borrowed from English (e.g., *lonche* 'lunch' and *troca* or *troque* 'truck'; and such loan translations were coined as *días de semana* 'weekdays' instead of the idiomatic *días de trabajo* (Silva-Corvalán 1994).

For some years now, efforts have been made to establish English as the official language of the United States (thus far, about half of the fifty states have done so, but these laws are largely symbolic). It has been suggested that a constitutional amendment be adopted to the effect that English is the official language of the United States, that laws mandating multilingual ballots and voting materials be repealed, and that funding for bilingual education be restricted to short-term transitional programs. Those who favor English as the official language maintain that they are not trying to discourage the use of languages other than English in the homes of recent immigrants or unacculturated adults of other ethnic backgrounds; they simply believe that the bond of a common language helps to promote unity in a country made up of people from every corner of the world.

On the other side of the argument are those who point out that the First Amendment to the Constitution guarantees freedom of speech. They maintain that citizens of the United States should have the right to use the language in which they are most proficient. From an anthropological viewpoint, the value of diversity and gradual voluntary assimilation is preferable to the imposition of inflexible language laws that would try to produce a common culture by decree.

Code-Switching, Code-Mixing, and Diglossia

Probably all speakers of every language have a variety of linguistic resources available to them. For example, the prewar Russian literary theorist Mikhail Bakhtin (1981) wrote of the illiterate peasant who prays to God in Old Church Slavonic, speaks to his family in their local village dialect, sings hymns in Standard Russian, and attempts to petition the local government in what he thinks is the high-class speech of officialdom. In most places in the world, there are not only dialects but several languages present in a community, the speakers possessing varying degrees of facility. In these multilingual situations the codes—that is, language varieties or languages—often become blended. This is so common that linguists have special terms for this blending; **code-switching** and **code-mixing.**

This nomenclature has had a long history in linguistics. Einar Haugen (1956:40), who most likely coined the term *code-switching*, defined it as "when a bilingual introduces a completely unassimilated word from another language into his speech." Carol Myers-Scotton (1993:3) broadened the definition by saying that code-switching "is the selection by bilinguals or multilinguals of forms from an embedded variety (or varieties) in utterances . . . during the same conversation." Eyamba Bokamba (1989:3) distinguishes code-switching and code-mixing: "Code-switching is the mixing of words, phrases and sentences from two distinct grammatical (sub) systems across sentence boundaries within the same speech event . . . [while] code-mixing is the embedding of various linguistic units such as affixes (bound morphemes), words (free morphemes), phrases and clauses from a co-operative activity where the participants, in order to infer what is intended, must reconcile what they hear with what they understand." An example of the former would be the Spanish/English bilingual who says: *Sometimes I'll start a sentence in English y termino en español* ["and finish it in Spanish"] (Poplack 2000:221). An example of the latter would be the Japanese/English bilingual who says *Kawai-sō sono-bug!* ("That *bug* is so pitiful" or "Oh, that poor *bug*"), incorporating the English word for insect into the Japanese sentence.

These distinctions are not always separated by all scholars, and some use code-switching to refer to all types of combined languages. The important thing in these situations is that a person capable of using two languages, A and B, has three systems available for use: A, B, and C (a combination of A or B). Mixing and switching probably occur to some extent in the conversations of all bilinguals. Code-mixing and code-switching can serve a variety of functions, such as building or reinforcing solidarity among speakers who share these languages. For example, two Czechs in the United States conversing in Czech may use English words, phrases, or sentences whenever they feel more comfortable doing so—as in *"Viš co? Popovídáme si pěkně u mě doma u piva. Ale než si vlezeme do subwaye, let's buy some pastrami and potato chips!"* (Here's an idea! Let's talk over beer at my place. But before we get on the subway, let's buy some pastrami and potato chips!).

The use of two distinct varieties of a language for two different sets of functions is called **diglossia**. The common language is the colloquial, or the "low," variety (L). A second, "high" variety (H), is used in formal circumstances: It is taught in schools and assumes administrative, legal, religious, and literary functions. Charles Ferguson (1959) coined this term in reference to the Classical Arabic based on the standards of the *Quran* (Koran) used in formal setting against the local or regional dialects of colloquial Arabic found throughout the Middle East.

Of the two varieties, the colloquial typically is learned first and is used for ordinary conversation with relatives and friends or servants and working persons, in cartoons, popular radio and television programs, jokes, traditional narratives, and the like. The formal variety, which carries prestige, is taught in schools and assumes most of the literary, administrative, legal, and religious functions.

Instances of diglossia are fairly common. Those Swiss who use Standard German as their formal variety are fluent in the Swiss German dialect (Schwyzertütsch), the low variety, in addition to the other national languages they may have learned. Similarly, in Greece colloquial Greek is in use side by side with the literary form derived in large part from its classical ancestor. In actual speech, however, neither the two diglossic varieties nor the languages of a bilingual community are always kept strictly apart.

Summary and Conclusions

Learning to speak a foreign language is a formidable task, and most adults fail to achieve fluency even after many years of trying. Children, however, learn their native language with no apparent effort and without instruction before they reach school age. One widely accepted theory concerning language acquisition holds that infants are born with an abstract language model already programmed into their brains (see Box 7.2). Endowed with such a language acquisition device, they apply it as they learn the particular mother tongue they hear spoken around them. Acquisition of language should not be studied without considering the sociocultural context in which it takes place. Knowing how to use their native language effectively helps individuals cope with their culture, and learning to use it appropriately is an important part of enculturation (the process of learning one's culture).

Among the many activities the human brain controls are speech, writing, and reading. Even though much is still to be learned about the workings of the brain, it has long been known that different parts of the brain contribute to different aspects of language processing. Injuries to these areas result in corresponding language and speech impairments.

Competency in one language only, typical of most Americans with English as their mother tongue, is uncommon in the rest of the world, where hundreds of millions of people are able to speak several languages or language varieties—that is, they are multilingual or diglossic. Even though many people speak only one language, they are actively, or at least passively, acquainted with several dialects and speech styles of that language. Their own speech patterns differ from those of others, even if only slightly. All speakers have their individual idiolects.

BOX 7.2 THE HUMAN BRAIN AND
LANGUAGE ACQUISITION

Why aren't babies born talking? We know that part of the answer is that babies have to listen to themselves to learn how to work their articulators, and have to listen to their elders to learn communal phonemes, words, and phrase orders. Some of these acquisitions depend on other ones, forcing development to proceed in a sequence: phonemes before words, words before sentences. But any mental mechanism powerful enough to learn these things could probably do so with a few weeks or months of input. Why does the sequence have to take three years? Could it be any faster?

Perhaps not. Complicated machines take time to assemble, and human infants may be expelled from the womb before their brains are complete. A human, after all, is an animal with a ludicrously large head, and a woman's pelvis, through which it must pass, can be only so big. If human beings stayed in the womb for the proportion of their life cycle that we would expect based on extrapolation from other primates, they would be born at the age of eighteen months. That is the age at which babies in fact begin to put words together. In one sense, then[,] babies are born talking!

And we know that babies' brains do change considerably after birth. Before birth, virtually all the neurons (nerve cells) are formed, and they migrate into their proper locations in the brain. But head size, brain weight, and thickness of the cerebral cortex (gray matter), where the synapses (junctions) subserving mental computation are found, continue to increase rapidly in the year after birth. Long-distance connections (white matter) are not complete until nine months, and they continue to grow their speed-inducing myelin insulation throughout childhood. Synapses continue to develop, peaking in number between nine months and two years (depending on the brain region), at which point the child has fifty percent more synapses than the adult! Metabolic activity in the brain reaches adult levels by nine to ten months, and soon exceeds it, peaking around the age of four. The brain is sculpted not only by adding neural material but by chipping it away. Massive numbers of neurons die in utero, and the dying continues during the first two years before level-

(continues)

(continued)

ing off at age seven. Synapses wither from the age of two through the rest of childhood and into adolescence, when the brain's metabolic rate falls back to adult levels. Language development, then, could be on a maturational timetable, like teeth. Perhaps linguistic accomplishments like babbling, first words, and grammar require minimum levels of brain size, long-distance connections, and extra synapses, particularly in the language centers of the brain. . . .

So language seems to develop about as quickly as the growing brain can handle it.

from Steven Pinker, The Language Instinct (1994), 288–289

8

Language Through Time

The structure of a language may be analyzed and described as it exists at some point in time, either in the present or the past. The approach that considers a language as though it had been sliced through time, ignoring historical antecedents, is referred to as **synchronic** linguistics. But it is also possible to study the historical development of a language by giving attention to the changes that occurred in the language over a period of time. Such an analysis or approach is **diachronic,** or **historical, linguistics.** This chapter shows some of the ways a diachronic approach can benefit anthropologists.

How Languages Are Classified

Anyone who knows Spanish will tell you that other languages, such as Portuguese or Italian, seem to be related to Spanish. This is due to their common origin from Latin. Traditionally, one of the most common activities in historical linguistics has been to classify languages according to these genetic relationships. It is difficult to give the exact number of languages spoken in the world at present, but the total undoubtedly approaches 6,000 (Krauss 1992:5–6), possibly 7,000. It is impossible to guess how many languages must have become extinct in prehistoric times. We do know that during the historical period for which we have written records, a great many languages have died out.

A **language family** includes all those languages that are related by virtue of having descended from a single ancestral language. The concept of the language family is somewhat conservative: It is generally employed only if the relationship and the correspondences among the languages have been firmly established by careful comparative work and a convincing number of cognates. Subdivisions of a language family are usually referred to as branches. The Indo-European language family, for example, consists of about a dozen branches (some of which have sub-branches). Some branches are Germanic (with about a dozen languages, including German and English), Celtic (with four languages), Romance or Italic (with about a dozen languages, including French and Spanish), and Balto-Slavic (with more than a dozen languages belonging to either the Baltic or Slavic sub-branches—including Russian and Polish). Some branches are represented by a single language, for example, Albanian, Armenian, or Hellenic or Greek. Indo-Iranian, with its Indic and Iranian sub-branches, consists of several hundred languages and dialects spoken mostly in southwestern Asia. Some branches of Indo-European, for example, the Tocharian and Anatolian branches, are no longer represented by spoken languages.

The number of languages that make up a language family varies greatly. The largest African family, Niger-Congo, is estimated to consist of about 1,000 languages and several times as many dialects. Yet some languages do not appear to be related to any other; these are referred to as **language isolates.** The Americas have been more linguistically diversified than other continents; the number of Native American language families in North America has been judged to be more than seventy, including more than thirty isolates. The numbers for South America have been even larger, but they are only estimates because our knowledge of the Indian languages of South America is still incomplete.

Several attempts have been made to simplify the apparent linguistic diversity of the New World. In 1929, Edward Sapir proposed a major reduction in the number of language families, assigning all Native American languages north of Mexico to only six "major linguistic groups" (superfamilies), later referred to as phyla. Consequently, a phylum in linguistic classification is a grouping that encompasses all those languages judged to have more remote relationships than do languages assigned to a family. Except for the Eskimo-Aleut "group," which is considered to be one family, each of the other five groups of Sapir's proposed classification included several families and one or more language isolates. A similar simplification of South American language families was proposed in 1960 by Joseph H. Greenberg (1915–2001), who subsumed the hundreds of native South American languages under three "families" (using the term not in the older conservative sense but more in the sense of superphylum or macrophylum). In another classification Greenberg (1987) assigned all native languages of the New World to only three "families," of which the Amerind "family" covers all native languages of the two continents except for those belonging to the Na-Dene and Eskimo-Aleut groups (spoken for the most part in the northern half of North America). Most specialists in Native American languages are not ready to accept the validity of Greenberg's huge Amerind genetic unit, or family. In any event, a family of this size has little in common with the earlier conservative concept of language family. (Most of the objections to this classification are discussed in the lengthy review of Greenberg's work by Campbell [1988].) In 1964, two comparative linguists in the Soviet Union produced evidence that six major language families of the Old World—Indo-European, Afro-Asiatic, Altaic, Dravidian, Uralic, and Kartvelian (South Caucasian)—were remotely related. To this macrofamily, referred to as Nostratic, some scholars subsequently added other language families and languages, among them Eskimo-Aleut, Nilo-Saharan, and Sumerian (Kaiser and Shevoroshkin 1988). And still another proposed macrofamily links together many languages from both the Old and the New World (one of the names of this macrofamily is Dene-Caucasian).

The ten largest conventional language families, ranging from more than 2 billion speakers to about 60 million, are Indo-European, Sino-Tibetan, Niger-Congo, Afro-Asiatic, Austronesian, Dravidian, Japanese, Altaic, Austroasiatic, and Korean (Japanese and Korean are frequently considered language isolates but may be distantly related to each other and to the Altaic family).

Less frequently used are typological classifications, based on structural similarities of languages regardless of their history—that is, regardless of genetic relationship. Typological classifications take various structural features into consideration. For example, some scholars have classified languages according to their sound systems, basing their grouping on how many and which distinctive vowels and consonants are used and whether tones are employed. Others have classified languages according to word order, that is, the sequence of subject (S), verb (V), and object (O) in simple declarative sentences (in English the typical arrangement is SVO, as in 'I love you'). Recently, semantic typology has been proposed; its proponents compare languages, for example, according to how much specificity relating to meaning a language requires. The best-known language classifications are based on morphological characteristics; the most widely used assigns languages to one of four types—isolating, inflecting, agglutinative, and polysynthetic, although frequently a language combines features of more than one type.

Before we discuss these types, we should note something about syntax first. To indicate grammatical relationships between words in a sentence, languages draw on one of two general strategies: **word order** or **inflections**. Chinese (and to a large extent, English) uses the word-order strategy. For example, the English sentence 'I like Linda' would be *Wǒ xǐhuan Linda* in Beijing Mandarin, and 'Linda likes me' would be *Linda xǐhuan wǒ*. The forms of the words in the two sentences are identical, but the order is different to indicate who likes whom. Notice that in both the English and Chinese examples it is the word order that indicates the grammatical relationships at work. 'John loves Jane' is not the same thing as 'Jane loves John.'

Languages that use **inflections** take a different approach. Here we see grammatical relationships not indicated by where they appear in a sentence, but by inflections: suffixes, prefixes, or other markers. Latin is a example of a typical **inflecting language**—one in which words display grammatical relationships by means of suffixes. How the relationship between the subject and the object of a sentence is conveyed may be illustrated by the Latin sentences *Magister discipulum vocat* ('The teacher calls the pupil') and *Magistrum discipulus vocat* ('The pupil calls the teacher'). The pupil calls the teacher,' or, more exactly, 'It is the teacher whom the pupil calls'). The order of the words in the two sentences is the same, but the adding of the suffix *-um* to one or the other noun makes it clear who is calling whom. Furthermore, Latin endings can express several grammatical meanings at the same time: The *-ō* in *laudō* ('I praise') stands for first-person singular, active voice (where the grammatical subject is typically the actor), present tense, and indicative mood (expressing a statement).

Many languages use inflections, just as many languages indicate relationships through word order. Most languages, however—although generally stressing one approach—will use a little bit of both. For example, in English we say *She left him* and *He left her* with the pronouns changing their form.

In **agglutinative** languages, each component of grammatical meaning is expressed by a separate piece of morphemic structure. For example, in the Turkish word *yazmalıymışım* 'I should have written,' the stem *yaz-* 'write' is followed by three suffixes here taking the forms of *malıy-mǐš-ǐm* meaning, respectively, 'obligative' (expressing obligation), 'perfective' (implying completion), and '1.' Turkish, Finnish, Swahili, and Japanese are among languages that are agglutinative.

The last type, **polysynthetic,** is considered by many linguists to be a combination of agglutinative and inflectional features. The words in these languages are long and morphologically complex, often being little sentences, such as the single Eskimo word *a:wlisa-ut-iss?ar-si-niarpu-ŋa,* which translates 'I am looking for something suitable for a fishing line' (the hyphens in the Eskimo word are used to indicate morpheme boundaries).

Internal and External Changes

Languages change not only internally from within but also as a result of external influences. The reasons for such changes vary; here we will illustrate them by discussing sound changes known as assimilation, dissimilation, and metathesis, and a grammatical change by means of which certain irregular forms become regularized.

Assimilation is the influence of a sound on a neighboring sound so that the two become similar or the same. For example, the Latin prefix *in-* 'not, non-, un-' appears in English as *il-, im-,* and *ir-* in the words *illegal, immoral, impossible* (*m* and *p* are both bilabial consonants), and *irresponsible* as well as the unassimilated original form *in-* in *indecent* and *incompetent.* Although the assimilation of the *n* of *in-* to the following consonant in the preceding examples was inherited from Latin, English examples that would be considered native are also plentiful: In rapid speech native speakers of English tend to pronounce *ten bucks* as though it were written *tembucks,* and in anticipation of the voiceless *s* in *son* the final consonant of *his* in *his son* is not as fully voiced as the *s* in *his daughter,* where it clearly is [z].

Another process of this type is **dissimilation,** which works the other way around: One of two identical or very similar neighboring sounds of a word is changed or omitted because a speaker may find the repetition of the same articulatory movement difficult in rapid speech. This is why it is so common to hear *February* pronounced as if it were written *Febyuary,* with the substitution of [y] for the first [r] in anticipation of the [r] toward the end of the word. People are asked to repeat a tongue twister (for example, "The sixth sheik's sixth sheep's sick") to test their ability to pronounce similar neighboring sounds rapidly without making any errors.

Still another process producing sound change is **metathesis,** the transposition of sounds or larger units; for example, the antecedent of Modern English *bird* is Old English *bridd* 'young bird.' A spoonerism, involving the transposition of the initial sounds of several words, is a slip of the tongue based on metathesis, as when *dear old queen* becomes *queer old dean.*

An example of a grammatical change is the regularization of a number of strong (irregular) Anglo-Saxon verbs: Old English *fealdan* 'to fold' and *hel-pan* 'to help' had the first-person singular past-tense (preterite) forms *feold* and *healp* and the past-participle forms *fealden* and *holpen.* In Modern English, these verbs are regular: *fold, folded* and *help, helped.* As for semantic change, Old English *mete* referred to food in general (usually solid), not just to animal flesh, as does Modern English *meat.*

As long as they are being used, all languages change. Today, no members of any society and no speakers of any language are completely isolated from speakers of other languages and dialects, and these contacts between speakers of different languages cause external language changes. The most common instances of external language change are borrowings, which can be of various types. The letter *b* in the word *debt* apparently has been borrowed for the sake of prestige from Latin (*dēbitum* 'debt') even though the Middle English antecedent of the word was *dette*, without a *b*, from Old French *dette* 'something owed.'

Much more common than orthographic borrowings are lexical borrowings, known as **loanwords.** Not all languages adopt foreign words to the same extent. Even though Icelandic serves a modern industrial society, for two centuries now Icelanders have resisted borrowing words from other languages and instead coin new words from their native linguistic resources for the many things and concepts that come to Iceland from other cultures. In grammar, too, Icelandic is highly conservative, having changed only a very little since the Old Norse period. In contrast, Japanese vocabulary reflects quite clearly the historical contacts between the Japanese and European peoples that began in the middle of the sixteenth century. It has loanwords from Portuguese (for example, *shabon* 'soap' from *sabão*), Dutch (*biiru* 'beer' from *bier*, and *garasu* 'glass' from *glas*), and most recently from English (*masukomi* 'mass communication,' *suupaa* 'supermarket,' *insutanto fuudo* 'instant food,' and *kabā-gāru* 'cover girl').

English has always been very hospitable to words of foreign origin. The vocabularies of the Angles, Jutes, and Saxons were enriched by words from Celtic (for example, the word ancestral to Modern English *bin*), Latin (*pipe* and *angel*), Old Norse of the Vikings (*take*), and Anglo-Norman French (*journey*). From the sixteenth century forward, during the Modern English period, the English lexicon borrowed from a great many of the world's languages, ranging from Afrikaans (for example, *aardvark*) to Czech (*robot*) to Yiddish (*chutzpa[h]*) to Japanese (*kamikaze*) to Dakota (*tepee*) to one of the native Australian languages (*boomerang*) to one of the native languages of Africa, probably related to Twi (*okra*). The many thousands of loanwords that have been incorporated into English since earliest times would not recommend English to misguided purists who think a language should be protected from the use of foreignisms, but such borrowings have certainly made the English vocabulary one of the richest in the world.

Some languages borrow selectively. In one of his studies of Native American languages of California, William Bright investigated the origin of words for those domestic animals introduced by European-American settlers. Borrowing from Spanish was considerable, but there appears to have been a resistance toward borrowing from English. In Bright's opinion, this disparity may well have been due to the benevolent (if condescending) treatment of Native American peoples in California under the Spanish mission system and, by contrast, the inhuman treatment they received from Anglo-Americans (Bright 1960:233–234). In this instance, then, the nature of the sociocultural contact between the native peoples and the newcomers was reflected in the vocabularies of the Native American languages.

In addition to borrowing, languages enrich their vocabularies in two other ways. One way is to coin new words from native resources. Newly coined words are added to English (and many other languages) every year: Among thousands of such coinages are the blend *brunch* (from *breakfast* and *lunch*), for a late-morning meal usually combining menu items from both breakfast and lunch; *vaporware*, for new software that has been announced but is not yet available; and *wannabe* (from the phrase *want to be*), for a person who aspires to be or tries to act or look like someone else.

Vocabularies also adjust to new inventions or ideas and objects introduced through intercultural contact by extending the meaning of existing words to include a new referent. For example, during the 1930s when the Western Apache in east central Arizona began using automobiles and pickup trucks and needed terms in their language for the various parts of these vehicles, they chose to extend many anatomical terms referring to the human body to the "corresponding" parts of the automobile: The meaning of the word *biyedaaʔ* 'chin and jaw' was extended to mean 'front bumper,' *bigan* 'hand and arm' to 'front wheel,' *bizéʔ* 'mouth' to 'gas pipe opening,' *bidááʔ ʔeyé* to 'headlight,' *bíta?* 'forehead' to 'windshield,' *bizíg* 'liver' to 'battery,' *bíjíí* 'heart' to 'distributor,' *bíkee?* 'foot, feet' to 'tires, rear wheels,' *bibid* 'stomach' to 'gas tank,' *bíjíʔízólí* 'lung' to 'radiator,' *bitsʔǫǫs* 'veins' to 'electrical wiring,' *bíchįh* 'nose' to 'hood,' and so on (Basso 1990: 20–21). The sense of the word that applies is invariably clear from the context. Similar extensions of anatomical terms to parts of the automobile have been recorded for other Native American languages.

That no confusion results from the use of words that have several senses—unless one indulges in punning—should be evident from the example of the English word *horse,* which has designated the quadruped *Equus caballus* from Old English (before the twelfth century) to the present, but later gained additional senses: 'trestle' or 'sawhorse,' 'pommel horse' or 'vaulting horse,' 'horsepower,' and 'heroin' (in slang).

How and Why Sound Changes Occur

Characteristically, sound changes are gradual. Only some speakers of a dialect or language adopt a particular speech innovation to begin with; others do so later, and ultimately all or most speakers accept the change. To put it differently, a particular sound change initially affects words that are frequently used, and only later is the change extended to other words. The modern view concerning how sound changes operate—namely, that they gradually spread, or diffuse, through the words (the lexicon) of a language—is referred to as **lexical diffusion.** Pioneered by William Labov and others during the 1960s, this view differs from the **neogrammarian** hypothesis of the 1870s, according to which sound laws admit no real exceptions, operating across the board within any given language.

An example of linguistic change proceeding from speakers enjoying higher prestige was provided by Labov (1966) in his famous study of English used by salespeople in three New York City department stores. According to this study (discussed in more detail in Chapter 13), the use of [r] after a vowel in such words as *car, card, four,* and *fourth* tended to characterize careful lower-class speech once the usage had become associated with higher prestige. For an example of linguistic change proceeding from below, one may refer to Labov's study of the speech in Martha's Vineyard, an island several miles south of Cape Cod, Massachusetts. This study dealt with the progressive change in the quality of the first vowel of the diphthongs /ay/ and

/aw/ in such words as *firefly* and *outhouse*. During the 1930s, when data for the *Linguistic Atlas of New England* were being collected, and for a long time before that, the diphthong /aw/ was not centralized, whereas /ay/ was (that is, its pronunciation resembled [əɪ]). During Labov's fieldwork in the early 1960s, the centralization of both diphthongs was most noticeable in the speech of thirty-one-to forty-five-year-old fishermen in the rural parts of the island, especially the Chilmark area in the west. According to Labov (1963:297, 304–305),

[the] high centralization [of the two diphthongs] is closely correlated with expressions of strong resistance to the incursions of the summer people [who at the time outnumbered the native Vineyarders by a ratio of seven to one]. . . . It is apparent that the immediate meaning of [centralization] is 'Vineyarder.' When a man [uses the centralized diphthongs], he is unconsciously establishing the fact that he belongs to the island. . . . [The] younger members of the English descent group [of Vineyarders] . . . recognize that the Chilmark fishermen are independent, skillful with many kinds of tools and equipment, quick-spoken, courageous and physically strong. Most importantly, they carry with them the ever-present conviction that the island belongs to them. If someone intends to stay on the island, this model will be ever present to his mind.

Sound changes, then, are clearly neither random nor do they operate without exception. Careful studies of the conditions under which sound changes take place reveal not only the direction and rate of linguistic change but the motivation behind it as well.

And why do languages change? One reason is a strong tendency in languages to maintain a definite pattern of organization. *Analogy* is another factor: Regular forms tend to influence less regular forms. Many Latin loanwords, for example, are now made plural almost exclusively by using the suffix -*s* (as in *auditoriums*) rather than their original Latin plural ending (as in *auditoria*). At least in some instances, more easily articulated sound sequences replace those that require greater effort (the principle of least effort). Not only have short words (*prof, exam, dorm, math*, and the like) been coined to supplement the original longer ones, but sometimes the simplification has been phonetic, as in the word *clothes*, which is usually pronounced as if it did not contain the sound represented by *th*.

Changes even occur when a language is passed on from parents to children and when children's speech habits are influenced by those of their peers. Though typically small, especially in phonology and morphology; such changes are cumulative and are noticeable when the speech of grandparents is compared with that of their grandchildren.

As we have already seen, sociocultural factors also promote language change. Some individuals like to imitate the sounds, grammar, and words used by those who have social prestige. When such imitations are overdone, hypercorrection results. Someone who has learned that *it is I* is correct rather than *it is me* may then say *between you and I* instead of the correct *between you and me*. On the phonetic level, **hypercorrection** occurs when *singer* is made to rhyme with *finger* because the two words are orthographically similar. Speakers of any language coin new words continually in order to give names to new inventions or new concepts. By the same token, those words that stand for items or ideas that are going out of use become obsolescent and eventually obsolete. The vocabulary of any living language, then, is constantly changing. For written languages, new editions of dictionaries need to be published every ten years or so to record the changes that have come about.

The comparative method in phonology rests on the assumption that sound changes are regular and predictable (this is why these changes have been referred to as "sound laws"). But their regularity is not absolute because the conditions under which sound changes take place are not identical. For example, Latin *t* corresponds to the sound written as *th* in English words cognate with Latin words (a **cognate** is a word related to another by descent from the same ancestral language): Compare Latin *tenuis* and English *thin*, Latin *tongēre* 'to know' and English *think*, Latin *trēs* and English *three*, and Latin *trāns* 'across' and English *through*. But English words have retained *t* when it is preceded by *s* in the Latin cognate: Latin *stāre* 'to stand' corresponds to English *stand*, Latin *stēlla* 'star' to English *star*, Latin *stīpāre* 'to compress, cram' to English *stiff*, Latin *stringere* 'to clasp, tighten' to English *strain*, and so forth.

Or to give an example of a so-called regular sound correspondence from the historical development of English, consider Old English *ā* (that is, long *a*) as in *bāt, gān, māwan, sāwan, slāw*, and *stān* changing in Modern English to the respective vowel sound in the words *boat*, (to) *go*, (to) *mow*, (to) *sow*, *slow*, and *stone*; but in words in which Old English *ā* occurred after a cluster containing *w*, the sound correspondence was different: Thus *hwā* and *twā* changed in Modern English to *who* and *two*, respectively.

Sometimes an expected correspondence is not found because the words that are being compared are not cognate despite their having similar forms. For example, this is why Latin *d*, which in English cognates corresponds to *t* (as in *two*, *duo* in Latin, and *ten*, *decem* in Latin), does not appear as *t* in *day* because the words *day* and *dies* 'day' are not related. Another example: The first consonant of the word *tooth* shows the expected correspondence to Latin *d* in *dēns* (*dentis*) 'tooth,' but the word *dental* does not because it was borrowed from medieval Latin at the end of the sixteenth century, too late to be subject to the regular change of Latin *d* to English *t*.

The force of analogy may also interfere with the regularity of sound changes. The inflection of the strong Old English verb *helpan* 'to help', which had among its various forms *hilpst* (second-person singular), *healp* (the first- and third-person singular of the preterite), *hulpe* (the second-person singular of the preterite), *hulpon* (the plural form of the preterite), and *holpen* (the past participle), was simplified by analogy with weak verbs to Modern English forms *help* and *helped*.

In short, then, sound changes are regular provided they occur in like circumstances, but given the complexity of languages and the many different influences on them (regional, social, and others) as they are spoken century after century, it seems more appropriate to refer to such so-called laws as tendencies. Concerning the conflict between "phonetic laws" and analogy, one of the most outstanding American comparative linguists, Edgar H. Sturtevant (1875–1952), noted: "Phonetic laws are regular but produce irregularities. Analogic creation is irregular but produces regularity" (1947:109).

Reconstructing Protolanguages

It is generally accepted that the beginning of modern linguistics, historical linguistics in particular, dates back to 1786. It was then that Sir William Jones (1746–1794) observed in his presidential address to the Royal Asiatick Society of Bengal that Sanskrit, Greek, and Latin "have sprung from some common source, which, perhaps, no longer exists [and that] there is a similar reason . . . for supposing that both the *Gothick* and the *Celtick* . . . had the same origin with the *Sanscrit* [and] the old *Persian* might be added to the same family" (Salus 1969). As early as the sixteenth century it had been suspected that many European languages were related and that their parent language might be Sanskrit, an ancient language of India. Jones, however, went still further; according to him, Sanskrit, ancient Greek, Latin, and other European languages were the descendants of a language spoken in prehistoric times. During the first half of the nineteenth century, a number of major works were published to demonstrate in some detail that relationships existed not only among the several ancient languages that were no longer spoken but also between them and Germanic, Slavic, Romance, Baltic, and other languages spoken in Europe and southwestern Asia. During the same period, reconstructions were begun of words of the ancestral language, assumed to have been spoken before the invention of writing and therefore never documented. These reconstructions proceeded so rapidly that in 1868 the German philologist August Schleicher (1821–1868) was able to "translate" into the prehistoric ancestral language a short fable about a sheep and three horses.

What can be reconstructed, and how are such reconstructions accomplished? It is possible to reconstruct the sounds and meanings of words as well as the grammar and syntax of an earlier undocumented state of a language, but usually the ultimate goal of linguistic reconstruction is the assumed ancestral language, or protolanguage, of all those languages derived from the same source. Reconstruction of a protolanguage requires thorough knowledge of historical grammar and good acquaintance with the daughter languages. The procedure is intricate, but the two main assumptions underlying it are not difficult to explain. The first assumption is that recurring similarities between words from different languages or dialects indicate that these languages or dialects are related to each other and must therefore have descended from a common ancestral language. The second assumption is that, as discussed above, sound changes are regular under like circumstances.

For example, we know from written records what the forms of the word meaning *cloud* were in the three ancient languages assumed to be related: *nábhas* in Sanskrit, *néphos* in ancient Greek, and *nebo* in Old Church Slavonic. There is a similarity among the three words, and the sound correspondences may be represented as follows:

Sanskrit	Ancient Greek	Old Church Slavonic
n	n	n
a	e	e
bh	ph	b
a	o	o
s	s	s

If these three words for *cloud* are found in the daughter languages of the protolanguage, in this instance Proto-Indo-European (PIE), what would the PIE word most likely have been? The first sound, the nasal consonant *n*, presents no problem; one would reconstruct a PIE **n* (the asterisk marks a reconstructed form, one that has not been attested or is unattestable). An alternative reconstruction, using the nasal **m*, is much less probable because the presumption would then be that all three daughter languages independently made the same change, from **m* to *n*. The second sound, a vowel, was *a* in Sanskrit and *e* in both ancient Greek and Old Church Slavonic. Here one would reconstruct the PIE sound as **e* because it is more logical to assume that only one of the daughter languages innovated while the other two kept the original sound than to assume that two of the daughter languages independently effected the same change. The medial consonant, which is different in each of the three words, is reconstructed as **bh* because the reconstructed sound has something in common with each of the three sounds derived from the earlier one—bilabial articulation in all three cases, a voiced sound with Sanskrit and Old Church Slavonic, and aspiration (*h*) with Sanskrit and ancient Greek. The second vowel and the final consonant pose no new questions. Consequently, the reconstructed PIE word for cloud is **nebhos*. This is not to assert, however, that this very word must actually have existed in Proto-Indo-European times but rather that there must have been such a word, or a very similar one, to have given rise later to the three words attested for Sanskrit, ancient Greek, and Old Church Slavonic.

Historical linguists have further established that Proto-Indo-European was a highly inflected language. For example, its nouns had three genders (masculine, feminine, and neuter), three numbers (singular, plural, and dual for objects occurring in pairs), and eight cases, and its verbs had three persons, three numbers, and a variety of tenses, moods, and other features. Those who assume that the grammatical systems of prehistoric languages must have been rather simple (primitive) could scarcely be further from the truth. The grammatical system of Modern English is an example of simplicity when compared with that of Proto-Indo-European.

For several Indo-European languages, written records (some on clay tablets) exist from as far back as the second millennium B.C., and for many others the earliest records are on the order of 1,000 years old. Documentation of such time depth provides invaluable information about the changes that occur over time and aids historical linguists in their efforts to make reliable reconstructions. But for most other groups of related languages, such documentation is the rare exception rather than the rule. Some scholars were convinced, in fact, that comparative reconstruction was feasible only in the case of related languages whose history was known at least to some extent.

That the comparative method is just as applicable to unwritten languages, provided that some reliable sketches of their contemporary structures are available, was demonstrated in 1946 by Leonard Bloomfield (1887–1949), a well-known American linguist. His reconstruction of the sounds and grammar of the ancestral language of Native Americans speaking Algonquian languages was based on four of the so-called Central Algonquian languages—Fox, Cree, Menomini, and Ojibwa. Through his fieldwork begun in the early 1920s, Bloomfield was well acquainted with three of them. Basing his judgment on his knowledge of Algonquian languages, Bloomfield believed that the "reconstructions will, in the main, fit all the [Algonquian] languages [including the divergent Blackfoot, Cheyenne, and Arapaho in the West] and can accordingly be viewed as Proto-Algonquian" (1946:85). Research by others during subsequent decades has shown that except for some details, Bloomfield was correct. The reconstruction of protolanguages on the basis of their modern descendants is now a fairly common linguistic undertaking. Some of the protolanguages reconstructed for North and Central America are Proto-Athapaskan, Proto-Mixtecan, Proto-Otomian, Proto-Popolocan, Proto-Salishan, Proto-Siouan, Proto-Uto-Aztecan, and Proto-Zapotecan.

Reconstructing the Ancestral Homeland

People—individuals, families, bands, and still larger groups—have always migrated to new places from localities in which they were born and raised, frequently as far away as to another continent. The main reason for such migrations has been population pressure: Whenever the natural resources of an area have become insufficient to support the local population, some of its members have had little choice but to move away. Moving from one locality to another was already true of early humans, who were hunters and gatherers—foragers for game, wild plants, and water. But once animals and plants were domesticated in the Middle East about 10,000 years ago, the need for hunting and gathering diminished in many parts of the world as permanent settlements became established. In modern times new situations caused people to migrate. The institution of slavery was responsible for the forced removal of large numbers of people not only from region to region but even from one continent to another (by the middle of the nineteenth century, the slave population in America had surpassed 4 million). Others migrated voluntarily, attracted to a particular area or country by the news of better living conditions as reported by acquaintances or relatives who had already resettled there (chain migration). Many of the 17 million or so people from various European countries who entered the United States between 1880 and 1910 were following compatriots who had pioneered the transatlantic migration. During the twentieth century, much migration occurred for political reasons. Immediately following World War II, more than 10 million Germans were either transferred to a reduced German territory from countries that had suffered under the Nazi regime or chose to resettle there on their own initiative. At about the same time (in 1947), the Indian subcontinent was partitioned between India and Pakistan, and a total of more than 15 million Hindus from Pakistan and Muslims from India moved from one of the two new countries to the other in order to live among peoples of the same religion. The United Nations reports that in 2009, there were more than 42 million refugees in the world.

For those time periods and parts of the world long characterized by the use of writing, information is available in more or less detail concerning the historical migrations that took place. However, such information is very shallow where written language has been in use for only several centuries, the Americas and Australia in particular. For example, in North America speakers of more than two dozen languages and major dialects of the Algonquian language family (along with enclaves of other language families, of course) extended from Tennessee and eastern North Carolina in the Southeast, to northeastern Newfoundland and the southern coast of Hudson Bay in the North, and to Colorado, Wyoming, Montana, Saskatchewan, and southeastern Alberta in the West. In the absence of historical records extending several thousand years into the past, is it possible to discover where the speakers of Proto-Algonquian, the language that must have been ancestral to the present Algonquian languages, originally lived? It is, and the method of investigation involves the careful use of linguistic data as well as information pertaining to the natural history of the North American continent. This method of reconstruction was illustrated by Frank T. Siebert Jr. (1912–1998) in his well-known article "The Original Home of the Proto-Algonquian People" (1967).

Let us summarize the working assumptions on which reconstructions of this kind are based. First, the territory occupied at some time in the past by speakers of an ancestral language would have been rather limited in extent when compared with the area in which the daughter languages are (or were) spoken. The fairly large part of North America that the Algonquian-speaking peoples inhabited at the time of their initial contact with the European immigrants was the result of many centuries of movements by their ancestors away from wherever their ancestral home may have been. Second, the vocabulary of the ancestral group must have been rather limited in extent when compared with the area in which the daughter languages are (or were) spoken. The fairly large part of North America that the Algonquian-speaking peoples inhabited at the time of their initial contact with the European immigrants was the result of many centuries of movements by their ancestors away from wherever their ancestral home may have been. Second, the vocabulary of the ancestral group must have included words designating the main features of the surrounding natural environment—among them the words for the various kinds of mammals, fish, birds, trees, and the like. To be able to refer fairly specifically to such features of the environment would have been essential for their survival. The families and groups that wandered off from the population in the ancestral homeland began their independent existence using the speech of the parent group. In the course of time, however, the speech habits of those who moved away began to show the inevitable changes to which all living languages are subject. The method for locating the ancestral homeland of linguistically related peoples is based on the justifiable assumption that one can reconstruct from certain cognates in the descendant languages the portion of the ancestral vocabulary that reveals the original location of the parent population.

Drawing on more than a dozen available vocabularies of modern Algonquian languages and their dialects, Siebert reconstructed fifty-three Proto-Algonquian (PA) words referring to particular features of the natural environment. Of these words, eighteen are bird names, nineteen mammalian names, twelve tree names, and four fish names. All these reconstructed words of the ancestral vocabulary are regularly derivable from the corresponding words of the modern Algonquian languages. For example, PA *a·škikwa 'harbor) seal' (Phoca vitulina concolor), one of the fifty-three words, is reconstructible from the Swampy or Woodland dialect of the Cree word a·hkik, the Lake St. John dialect of Montagnais a·hčok, Ojibwa a·skik, and the Penobscot dialect of Abnaki áhkik^w; PA *a?šikanwa 'smallmouth black bass' (Micropterus dolomieu) is reconstructible from the Fox word a·šikanwa, Menomini word a?sekan, Ojibwa word aššikan, Shawnee word a?šika, and the Penobscot dialect of the Abnaki word ásikan; and PA *a·kema·xkwa 'white ash' (Fraxinus americana), a compound of PA *a·kem-'snowshoe' and PA *-a·xkw- '(hard)wood', from the modern cognates obtained from Swampy or Woodland dialect of Cree, the Lake St. John dialect of Montagnais, Ojibwa, and the Penobscot dialect of Abnaki. (In Ojibwa and Penobscot the original meaning has been preserved, whereas in the Cree and Montagnais dialects the name came to be applied to the black ash after the speakers of these two dialects migrated north of the white-ash range.) Of the approximately fifty reconstructible species terms, about a score contributed significantly to the solution of the problem.

The data Siebert used consist of the reconstructed Proto-Algonquian words designating the following natural features: for mammals, bear, beaver, bison or buffalo, buck (male of moose, deer, elk, caribou), fawn, flying squirrel, fox, lynx or bobcat, mink, moose, muskrat, porcupine, raccoon, (harbor) seal, skunk, squirrel, weasel, woodchuck or groundhog, and woodland caribou; for birds, blue jay, bobwhite or quail, common loon, golden eagle, great horned owl (two terms), greater yellowlegs, gull, hawk, heron or crane, kingfisher, merganser, nighthawk, old-squaw, pileated woodpecker or logcock, raven, ruffed grouse or partridge, and large edible game bird; for fish, brown bullhead, lake trout, northern pike, and smallmouth black bass; and for trees, (speckled) alder, basswood, American beech, conifer or evergreen, elm, quaking aspen, sugar maple, tamarack, white ash, white spruce, willow, and a kind of tree whose species could not be determined.

Because all these animals and trees—the names for which are reconstructible for the Proto-Algonquian language—must have been present in the environment surrounding the speakers of the ancestral language, the task that next confronted Siebert was to locate the corresponding area on this continent. But finding it was not as easy as it might seem. The distribution of individual animal and plant species had changed considerably over the past several centuries as a result of the rapid settlement of the continent by immigrants from the Old World. Some forestlands had been converted to fields and pastures, some species of fish had been eliminated by pollution while other fish species may have been introduced into streams and lakes in which they were not native, and some species of mammals had been greatly reduced or virtually exterminated by indiscriminate hunting (for example, the buffalo) or urbanization. What Siebert therefore had to establish was the earliest possible ranges of the fifty-odd species. He consulted nearly a hundred sources containing information about the natural history of North America, some dating as far back as 1625. Trees served as particularly reliable guides because they are fixed and their ranges are governed by soil, moisture, and long-term climatic patterns. Bird species contributed much less to the investigation because seasonal migrations tend to make their geographic ranges quite extensive. Once the geographic distributions had been established, Siebert plotted the ranges on a map of the continent. The earliest homeland of speakers of Proto-Algonquian would have had to be in the area that all the significant species shared in common, or at least touched. For Siebert's ingenious reconstruction of the location of the original home of the Proto-Algonquian people, we can refer to the author's own discussion and conclusion (here abbreviated in Box 8.1 and supplemented by the map in Figure 8.1).

Reconstructing a Protoculture

Reconstruction of words of a protolanguage and their meanings is likely to throw light on some aspects of the prehistoric culture of those who spoke the protolanguage. A good way to illustrate this statement is to consider those Indo-European kinship terms that are reconstructible for Proto-Indo-European. They include ancestral words (**protowords**) for individuals related by blood, such as *father*, *mother*, *brother*, *sister*, *son*, *daughter*; protowords for a woman's relatives by marriage, such as *husband's brother*, *husband's sister*, *husband's mother*, *husband's father*; and protowords referring to women related by marriage, such as *daughter-in-law*. To give an example, there are cognate words in a number of Indo-European languages for the kinship term *daughter-in-law*; among these words are Sanskrit *snuṣā́*, Greek *nuós*, Latin *nurus*, Russian *snokhá*, Old English *snoru*, German *Schnur*, and others. On the basis of numerous known sound correspondences, it is possible to reconstruct the PIE form *snusós* 'daughter-in-law'. Because the word referring to *son-in-law* is not reconstructible, the assumption can be made that there was no such word in Proto-Indo-European times. The existence of *snusós* 'daughter-in-law' but not of the corresponding male term (son-in-law) strongly indicates that a young wife would have been brought to live with or near her husband's family and then referred to by a special term to distinguish her from the blood-related females of the household. If the custom had been for a young man to live with his wife's parents, one would expect to find cognate terms for son-in-law rather than for daughter-in-law. The linguistic evidence based on the protolanguage points to patrilocal residence among the ancient Indo-Europeans, that is, a young couple

BOX 8.1 SIEBERT ON THE ORIGINAL HOME OF THE PROTO-ALGONQUIAN PEOPLE

The primeval home. . . . lay between the almost strictly coniferous forests to the north and the deciduous woodlands to the south. That the Proto-Algonquians lived in a mixed-forest zone is evident from the frequent use of the two contrasting noun-finals in many tree names, PA *-a·ntakw- 'evergreen tree, conifer' and *-a·xkw- 'wood; hardwood or deciduous tree.' The relatively southern species of deciduous trees, like the white ash, sugar maple, basswood, and beech, extend more or less only slightly farther north than the Algonquian homeland, whereas northern conifers, like the white spruce and tamarack, were found commonly only to the southern borders of the original home or slightly beyond.

The original home lay at the southern limit of the woodland caribou. . . . The harbour seal is the only seal that is common on the eastern coast of the United States . . . [but] in aboriginal times its ascent penetrated . . . into the interior along the upper St. Lawrence River and affluent streams. . . . The distributions of [four species of fish] provide additional reasons for pinpointing the earliest Algonquian residence to southern Ontario rather than to a more western portion of the Great Lakes region. . . .

In order to allow for possible undetermined changes in the distribution of fauna and flora in the prehistoric period . . . the earliest original home is diagrammatically represented as Stage Number 1 . . . and an expanded area of occupancy of slightly later date, which certainly includes the entire Algonquian homeland, is characterized as Stage Number 2. To these the tentative dates of 1200 B.C. and 900 B.C., respectively, are assigned as suppositions to serve as a basis for further discussion. . . .

The earliest residence of the speakers of Proto-Algonquian is ascertained by the multiple intersections of the distributional lines of significant species. The original home of the Algonquian peoples lay in the region between Lake Huron and Georgian Bay and the middle course of the Ottawa River, bounded on the north by Lake Nipissing and the Mattawa River and on the south by the northern shore of Lake Ontario, the headwaters of the Grand River, and the Saugeen River.

from Frank T. Siebert, Jr., "The Original Home of the Proto-Algonquian People" (1967), 36–40

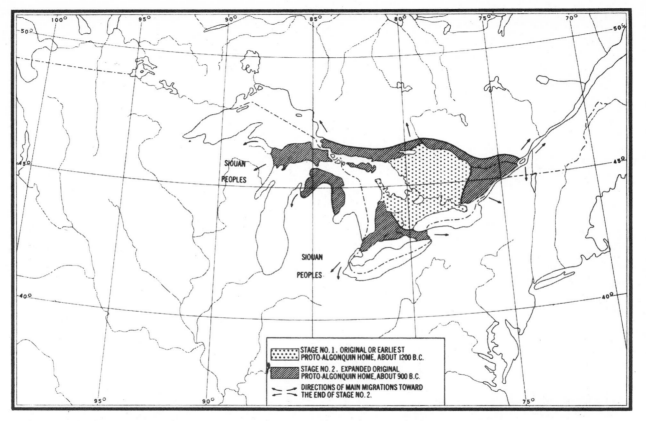

FIGURE 8.1 The Two Assumed Stages of the Proto-Algonquin Home and Their Locations

Source: From Frank T. Siebert, Jr., "The Original Home of the Proto-Algonquin People," National Museum of Canada, bulletin 214 (Ottawa, 1967), 35. Reproduced by permission of the Canadian Museum of Civilization.

habitually living with or near the husband's father's family. Such information could not be obtained from archaeological evidence.

Linguistic reconstructions tell us much more about the ancient Indo-Europeans: that they used yokes and probably wheeled vehicles of some kind and depended on or kept horses, cows, dogs, sheep, pigs, and goats; furthermore, that they lived in an environment in which they encountered wolves, bears, foxes, eagles, salmon (probably a type of trout resembling salmon), otters, beavers, and other animals; as well as alder, aspen, beech, birch, oak, and yew among the flora. They practiced agriculture and cultivated cereals, which they ground into flour. The ancient Indo-Europeans used numerals at least through one hundred and employed a decimal system. They were led by tribal chiefs or kings and, judging from the reconstructible vocabulary, developed rather elaborate religious practices. The wide distribution of words for *snow* and the easy reconstructibility of *sneigwh-'(to) snow'* appear to exclude as the probable ancestral Indo-European homeland those warm southern parts of Europe and southwestern Asia where snow is not seen.

The reconstructions of protoculture have not been limited to prehistoric Indo-European society but have been extended to other parts of the world, for example, sub-Saharan Africa. Some linguistic inferences about early Bantu history are reproduced in Box. 8.2 (the Bantu languages form a large subgroup of the Niger-Congo language family).

Trying to Date the Past: Glottochronology

A modern attempt to determine statistically the length of time during which a language or a group of genetically related languages has been undergoing independent development was made by Morris Swadesh in his article concerning the internal relationships within the Salishan language family of the American Northwest (Swadesh 1950). The method, which Swadesh and others subsequently elaborated, involves lexicostatistics and glottochronology (in that order). *Lexicostatistics* is a method of establishing linguistic relationship on the basis of a quantitative study of lexical items (words); *glottochronology* is a method of determining the time depth of a linguistic relationship. For the sake of brevity, we are combining the use of these two methods under the term **glottochronology.** The method became controversial soon after its introduction, but because it has been repeatedly applied to linguistic data and frequent references to it appear in the literature, it deserves to be briefly examined.

When first introduced, glottochronological analysis yielded relative dates not unlike those archaeologists obtain from the stratigraphic record. The method was later revised so that absolute dates could be determined much like those archaeologists obtain by using carbon 14 to date ancient organic materials recovered from archaeological sites. Glottochronological dating is based on the assumption that in all languages there are certain words that tend to be replaced at a constant rate over long periods of time. This basic core vocabulary consists of words that designate things, qualities, and activities most likely to be named in all languages of the world. Among these words are body parts, natural objects and phenomena, plants and plant parts, animals, colors, numerals, bodily sensations and activities, and words belonging to several other semantic domains, among them positions and movements, persons, and common qualities. On the basis of tests made with two-hundred-word lists from languages whose history is known, the rate of replacement, or loss, of the basic core vocabulary appears to average nearly 20 percent per 1,000 years, amounting to a word retention rate of just over 80 percent. For the smaller and more concentrated one-hundred-word list developed by Swadesh in 1955 (see Table 8.1), the comparable rates are 14 and 86 percent. According to the proponents of glottochronology, the length of time required for two languages to diverge from a single language can be calculated by using the formula $t = (\log C)/(2 \log r)$, where t is the time depth in millennia, C is the percentage of cognates, and r is the constant, that is, the percentage of cognates assumed to remain after 1,000 years of divergence (81 percent for the two-hundred-word list and 86 percent for the one-hundred-word list).

In applying the method, one first translates the basic core vocabulary into the colloquial equivalents of the two related languages and then determines which pairs are cognate by virtue of similarity. For example, the English words *blood, cloud, hair, sand, tree,* and *black* would translate into German as *Blut, Wolke, Haar, Sand, Baum,* and *schwarz*. Of the six pairs, only three would be considered cognate (*blood, hair,* and *sand* and their German equivalents). In contrast, *deer* and German *Tier* 'animal' are cognate but no longer equivalent. Other pairs of words are cognate but may not be recognized as such, for example, the English word *toe* and the German cognate *Zehe* 'toe,' English *beam* and German *Baum* 'tree,' and English *swart(hy)* and German *schwarz* 'black.'

TABLE 8.1   The 100-Word Core Vocabulary

I	dog	nose	die	smoke
you	louse	mouth	kill	fire
we	tree	tooth	swim	ash
this	seed	tongue	fly	burn
that	leaf	claw	walk	path
who	root	foot	come	mountain
what	bark	knee	lie	red
not	skin	hand	sit	green
all	flesh	belly	stand	yellow
many	blood	neck	give	white
one	bone	breasts	say	black
two	grease	heart	sun	night
big	egg	liver	moon	hot
long	horn	drink	star	cold
small	tail	eat	water	full
woman	feather	bite	rain	new
man	hair	see	stone	good
person	head	hear	sand	round
fish	ear	know	earth	dry
bird	eye	sleep	cloud	name

It should be noted that the large majority of these words can be traced to Old English—that is, they are very old English words. Because of the universal nature and occurrence of the referents for which these words stand, equivalents in other languages are available and may also be expected to be old.

Almost since the development of glottochronology, its basic assumptions have been controversial. Some of the problems were aptly summarized by Dwight Bolinger: "We cannot be sure that the social and historical forces of change have not been stronger in one epoch than in another, or that many items of supposedly basic vocabulary have not actually been borrowed rather than inherited." Further, he continued, referring to a study by Labov, "A survey of the speech of the year-round inhabitants of Martha's Vineyard found that their desire to be different from the detested mainlanders is leading them to speed up certain changes in the pronunciation of their vowels. Social pressures create variable rates of change in phonetics as well as in vocabulary" (Bolinger 1968:132–133). It is also known, for example, that the retention of cognates between Old Norse and Modern Icelandic is much higher than the formula would indicate. Another problem is the assumption that the basic core vocabulary list is equally applicable to all cultures, that is, that it has no cultural bias and is truly universal. Harry Hoijer (1904–1976) showed, for example, that one would have to choose from among five Navajo forms for the English *this* and *that*, from among four for *who* and *what*, from among two for *black*, and so on (Hoijer 1956).

To eliminate the objection that the acceptance of absolute time references is untenable, the suggestion was made to adopt a relative unit of time depth that would be less misleading. This unit is referred to as *dip* (for "degree of lexical relationship"). To arrive at dips, the absolute time depth (in millennia) is multiplied by fourteen. Accordingly, two related languages, each of which has gone its own way for 2,000 years, would be separated by twenty-eight dips.

In summary, if applied to related languages whose history is not known and for which written records do not exist, glottochronology may provide some preliminary estimates of their closeness. But careful linguistic anthropologists would look for supporting evidence from archaeology, comparative ethnology, and linguistic reconstruction using the comparative method before accepting glottochronological results as valid.

Time Perspective in Culture

How linguistic data can aid the reconstruction of cultural history was discussed at length and exemplified in one of the early works of Edward Sapir, a brilliant American linguist and anthropologist, and probably the greatest specialist on Native American languages until World War II. *Time Perspective in Aboriginal American Culture: A Study in Method* (1916) was his longest monograph in ethnology and is testimony to his methodological prowess. The few examples that follow illustrate Sapir's discussion of inferential linguistic evidence for time perspective.

The relative age of a culture element can be determined with some reliability from the form of the native (not borrowed) word that refers to the element. Such simple and not further analyzable words as *bow*, *plow*, *spear*, and *wheel* are as a rule much older than words that can be broken down into smaller constituent parts—for example, *airplane*, *battleship*, *railroad*, and *spaceship*. Irregular grammatical forms also indicate the great age of those words with which they are associated and, by implication, of those entities to which they refer; hence the plurals *geese*, *kine* (archaic plural of *cow*), *lice*, *oxen*, and *sheep* on the one hand, but *elephants*, *lions*, *parrots*, and *tigers* on the other.

BOX 8.2 LINGUISTIC INFERENCES
ABOUT EARLY BANTU HISTORY

The oldest Bantu subsistence vocabulary so far reconstructible accords with postulation of a high-rainfall, tropical environment for the proto-Bantu homeland. No grain terms can be reconstructed, but there is instead a word for yam. Two or three possible root words dealing with the oil palm may also date to proto-Bantu, and the reconstructible proto-Bantu name for alcoholic drink apparently referred specifically to palm wine. At least one cucurbit, probably the bottle gourd, a pulse (the cowpea?), and probably the *Voandzeia* groundnut were also known to the proto-Bantu. . . . These three crops would all have been domesticated elsewhere than in the proto-Bantu homeland, but apparently they could be effectively grown in high-rainfall savanna and/or rain forest. . . .

A second indication of a high-rainfall environment is provided by the reconstructibility of fishing and boating vocabulary. . . . Apparently the proto-Bantu made considerable use of riverine resources and lived where large perennial streams were commonplace.

Knowledge of two domestic animals, cattle and goats, can be reconstructed. . . . Whatever the cause of proto-Bantu knowledge of cattle, it was lost by those who expanded into the equatorial rain forest, for the proto-Bantu root *nyaka is found no farther south than some of the forest languages in which it was reapplied, in the absence of cattle, to the buffalo. . . .

Contrary to a widely held view, knowledge of ironworking cannot be linguistically reconstructed for proto-Bantu. . . . By the beginnings, however, of Bantu expansion into eastern Africa, on linguistic grounds most probably during the last millennium B.C., metallurgical terms had come into use among at least the ancestral Eastern Bantu communities.

from Christopher Ehret, "Linguistic Inferences
About Early Bantu History" (1982), 61–62

Loanwords, which usually designate elements of foreign cultures, can frequently be identified by their different phonetic structure (we would now say "phonemic"). Thus, although /z/ and /j/ occur in old words of the native English vocabulary in medial or final position (as in *frozen, rise, bridges,* and *ridge*), initially these two sounds are found only in loanwords, for example, in *zeal* (adapted from Late Latin) or *just* (adapted from Middle

French.) Similarly, some combinations of sounds betray the foreign origin of words in which they occur, as /ps/ does in *apse* and *lapse* (both from Latin) and *rhapsody* (from Greek via Latin). But the final /-ps/ in *lips*, *sleeps*, *ships*, and other such words is not comparable because the /-s/ represents other morphemes—the plural, the third-person singular, or the possessive, respectively. For societies with a long tradition of writing, inferential linguistic evidence may add little if anything to what is already known about their cultural history. This is not the case, however, with nonliterate societies.

The assignment of related languages to a language family implies the earlier existence of an ancestral language from which all modern languages of the family have descended. The more differentiated these descendant languages are, the longer the period of time one must allow for their development to have taken place; the time depth has important consequences for culture history.

Linguistic scholars have known for some time that phonetic (or phonemic) and morphological similarities sometimes exist among unrelated neighboring languages to an extent that could scarcely be due to chance. Such similarities are indicative of an extensive period of cultural contact between the respective societies, a circumstance the ethnologist must take into account.

In the concluding remarks of his monograph, Sapir made the point that although direct evidence is much to be preferred to inferential evidence in the study of culture history and the establishment of culture sequences, anthropologists frequently face situations where direct evidence is either insufficient or completely lacking. In such cases inferential evidence, linguistic in particular, becomes invaluable.

Summary and Conclusions

Living languages change slowly but constantly. The Old English is no longer intelligible to speakers of Modern English, and even words that rhymed in Shakespeare's time do not always rhyme today. The tendency of sound changes to be regular makes it possible to reconstruct the assumed ancestral language of daughter languages. Reconstructible words having to do with the natural environment of a prehistoric society facilitate determining the location of its ancestral homeland. Furthermore, the reconstruction of protowords may also throw light on features of a prehistoric culture not discoverable by other means. For example, the reconstructibility of certain kinship terms, such as those for in-laws, may provide clues to postmarital residence practices of the people who used them. Reconstruction of an ancestral homeland location and other protocultural features on the basis of linguistic data is not always a standard procedure, but when the archaeological record is insufficient or lacking, it may be the only means of probing the prehistoric past.

When languages are classified genetically, those that are related by virtue of a common origin are assigned to one language family. The original concept of a language family was conservative, requiring the relationships among the member languages of a family to be close and well documented. The tendency since the 1960s has been to group together languages that are considered to be much more remotely related. Such languages are said to constitute a phylum or even a superphylum (or macrophylum). The difference between the older conservative unit of language family and the newer phylum can best be illustrated by comparing numbers: The several hundred language families of the New World are said to be reducible to only three superphyla.

Linguistic typology, on the other hand, is based on examining similarities among languages other than those due to a common origin. Scholars engaged in finding common features or attributes in crosslinguistic diversity have taken various approaches as they attempt to assign to a relatively few basic types the many languages of the world.

9

Languages in Variation and Languages in Contact

Strictly speaking, the speech pattern of one individual is somewhat different from the speech pattern of the next, even though the two speak the same language, and regional varieties of language differ from each other by features of vocabulary, grammar, and pronunciation.

Idiolects

This is why it is possible to identify over the telephone people we know well without their having to say who they are; similarly, we recognize familiar television newscasters even when we cannot see the screen. The recognition of individuals by voice alone is possible because of their idiosyncratic combination of voice quality, pronunciation, grammatical usage, and choice of words. Voice quality, or timbre, is determined by the anatomy of the **vocal tract** (the tongue, the nasal and oral cavities, the vocal cords, the larynx, and other parts), over which the speaker has little or no control. Other voice features—for example, tempo, loudness, and to some extent even pitch range—can be controlled fairly simply. But none of these features of an individual's speech pattern is constant. Voice quality changes with age as muscles and tissues deteriorate and the dentition undergoes modification. Over a lifetime, changes tend to occur in the choice of words, grammar, and pronunciation as well.

An individual's speech variety is referred to as an **idiolect**. Almost all speakers make use of several idiolects, depending on the circumstances of communication. For example, when family members talk to each other, their speech habits typically differ from those any one of them would use in, say, an interview with a prospective employer. The concept of idiolect therefore refers to a very specific phenomenon—the speech variety used by a particular individual.

Dialects

Often, people who live in the same geographic area, have similar occupations, or have the same education or economic status speak relatively similar idiolects compared to those from other groups. These shared characteristics may entail similarities in vocabulary, pronunciation, or grammatical features. When all the idiolects of a group of speakers have enough in common to appear at least superficially alike, we say they belong to the same dialect. The term **dialect**, then, is an abstraction: It refers to a form of language or speech used by members of a regional, ethnic, or social group. Dialects that are mutually intelligible belong to the same language. All languages spoken by more than one small homogeneous community are found to consist of two or more dialects.

Mutual intelligibility, of course, can vary as to degree. In the early 1950s, a number of men and women from eight reservations in New York and Ontario were tested in an experiment designed to determine which of their local dialects were mutually intelligible and therefore dialects of one language, and which were not and therefore could be classified as individual languages of the Iroquoian language family. Even though the investigators arrived at percentages of intelligibility between any two of the Iroquoian speech communities, the question of where the boundaries lay between intelligibility and unintelligibility remained unresolved. If the boundaries between language and dialect had been drawn at 25 percent of mutual intelligibility, there would have been four different languages, of which one would have consisted of two dialects and another of three. If set at 75 percent, there would have been five languages, two of which would have consisted of two dialects each.

Because it is spoken in so many different areas the world over, English is particularly diversified dialectally. Speakers' home countries may be guessed from their pronunciation and from the use of certain words that are characteristic of specific varieties of English. For example, included in the vocabulary of Australians is *bludger* 'loafer, shirker'; of Canadians *to book off* 'to notify an employer that one is not reporting for work'; of the Irish *spalpeen* 'rascal'; of the Scots *cutty sark* 'short (under) garment'; and of the British to *knock up* 'to wake up (someone), as by knocking on the window.' A speaker of any dialect of American English is likely to find it quite difficult to understand a cab driver in London who speaks cockney, the dialect of London's East End, even though both speak dialects of the same language.

English was brought to North America during the seventeenth century by colonists from England who settled along the Atlantic coast from Maine to Georgia. The language of these colonists consisted of dialects reflecting the social stratification and geographic division of their former home country. Today, despite regional differences (especially along the East Coast and in the South), American English exhibits a remarkable degree of uniformity. Historically, this uniformity resulted from the mingling of settlers from various parts of the East as they pushed westward; since World War II it has been due to the ever-increasing mobility of Americans. Today, few people live in the communities in which they were born; most move from one place to another when they change jobs, marry, or retire. Nevertheless, certain regional dialects in the United States are well known and readily recognizable when heard—for example, those of Boston, Virginia, or Texas. Vocabulary may be just as helpful in identifying where older speakers from rural areas have come from. For example, the dragonfly is referred to in most of Virginia as *snake doctor*, in southwestern Pennsylvania as *snake feeder*, in eastern North Carolina as *mosquito hawk*, in New England as *(devil's) darning needle*, in coastal New Jersey as *spindle*, in northern California as *ear sewer*, and so on.

The way individuals speak varies not only according to their regional and social dialects but also according to context. The distinctive manner in which people express themselves in a particular situation is referred to as style. Speech styles are thus comparable to styles of dress. One would feel out of place and uncomfortable going on a hiking trip in formal attire or attending a traditional wedding reception in sneakers, jeans, and a sweatshirt. Similarly, a person who might use the vulgar expression "I'm pissed" when talking with former schoolmates would probably substitute the colloquial phrase "I'm mad" under other circumstances and use such words as "angry" or "aggravated" under more formal conditions.

Styles

Stylistic variations are not only lexical, but also phonological (for instance, the casual pronunciation of *butter* with the flap [r] rather than the dental [t]), morphological (as in the casually styled "Who are you taking to lunch?" as against the formal "Whom are you taking to lunch?"), and syntactic (as in "Wanna eat now?" as against "Do you want to eat now?"). A stylistic or dialectal variety of speech that does not call forth negative reaction, is used on formal occasions, and carries social prestige is considered **standard**; varieties that do not measure up to these norms are referred to as nonstandard or substandard. Standard British English, often referred to as Received Standard (and its pronunciation as Received Pronunciation), is used at English public schools (private secondary boarding schools), heard during radio and television newscasts, and used when circumstances call for a serious, formal attitude (sermons, lectures, and the like). In less formal situations, there has been an increasing tendency to use a style that deviates from or falls short of the standard. Informality in dress, behavior, and speech is a sign of the times both in the United States and elsewhere.

How many different styles do speakers of English use? According to Martin Joos (1907–1978), five clearly distinguishable styles were characteristic of his dialect of American English (spoken in the east-central United States); he termed them frozen, formal, consultative, casual, and intimate (Joos 1962). Today, very few speakers of American English ever use the frozen style except perhaps occasionally in formal writing. The assumption that the exact number of speech styles can be determined for a language serving millions of speakers does not seem to be warranted. No two native speakers of English talk alike, and just exactly what use each person makes of the various stylistic features, ranging all the way from a pompous formality to an intimate or even vulgar informality, is up to the individual speaker.

Language Contact

Languages must have been in contact as long as there have been human beings. From what can be ascertained from the current and historical ethnographic record, people have also often been in close proximity with those who spoke languages that were mutually unintelligible. Trade, travel, migration, war, intermarriage, and other nonlinguistic causes have forced different languages to come into contact countless times throughout history. When this occurs, several things can happen over time: languages can die, new languages can develop, or languages in contact can become mixed in various ways. We will now explore some of the consequences of mixing and see how it can sometimes lead to the development of drastically different linguistic structures.

When a new physical item or concept is borrowed from another culture, the name for that new item in the donor language is often just directly taken over. For example, Hawaiian gave English *ukulele*; Bantu, *gumbo*; Czech, *polka*; Cantonese *wok*; Arabic, *algebra*; German, *pretzel*; and Malay, rice *paddy*. Of course, English has contributed hundreds of words to other languages as well, as *weekend* to French, *boyfriend* to Russian, *aerobic classes* to German, and *beefsteak* to many languages.

This exchange can go both ways. As most native English speakers know, many words of French origin have been borrowed into the language. In return for *le weekend*, English received *rendezvous* and *lingerie*. One of the reasons for this was the introduction of Old French during the Norman conquest of England in 1066, which replaced Old English as the language of the ruling classes in England (and which held prominence until well into the fourteenth and fifteenth centuries). During these centuries of French linguistic dominance, a large proportion of English vocabulary drastically changed. Some words disappeared, others acquired different meanings. For example, consider the words in this table:

Modern English	Old English	Modern German	Modern English	Old French	Modern French
cow	*cū*	*Kuh*	**beef**	*boef*	*boeuf*
calf	*cealf*	*Kalb*	**veal**	*veel*	*veau*
swine	*swīn*	*Schwein*	**pork**	*porc*	*porc*
sheep	*scēap*	*Schaf*	**mutton**	*moton*	*mouton*
chicken	*cicen*	*Küken*	**poultry**	*pouletrie*	*volaille*
deer	*dēor*	*Tier*	**venison**	*venesoun*	*venaison*

Here we see two columns of Modern English terms in bold: cow, calf, swine, sheep, chicken, and deer on the left (followed by Old English and German equivalents); and beef, veal, pork, mutton, poultry, and venison (followed by their Old French, and modern French equivalents). In both instances, it is fairly easy to see the relationships (e.g., "cow" and *cū*, etc.). What are the connections between these two sets of Modern English terms? The column on the left names the live animal. The column in the middle labels the food derived from that animal (e.g., "beef" from a "cow"). We might say that the Anglo-Saxon terms became restricted for the names of animals and the more prestigious French terms were applied to the cooked and prepared animal brought inside the house (Jackson and Amvela 2007).

Pidgins

A common way in which individuals and groups interact across language boundaries is by means of a **pidgin.** Typically, a pidgin originates when speakers of two or more mutually unintelligible languages develop a need to communicate with each other for certain limited or specialized purposes, especially trade. Because pidgins have a much narrower range of functions than the languages for which they substitute, they possess a limited vocabulary, and because they need to be learned rapidly for the sake of efficiency, they have a substantially reduced grammatical structure. From a sociocultural perspective, an important characteristic of a pidgin is that it does not serve as the native, or first, language of any particular group.

A pidgin is not the result of the same kind of development true languages are subject to: It tends to come about suddenly, as the need arises, and ceases to exist when no longer called upon to perform its original function. It may last as little as a dozen or so years; only infrequently does it outlast a century. In its phonology and morphology, a pidgin is invariably simpler than the first languages of those who use it, and the bulk of its lexicon is based on, or derived from, one of the languages in contact.

Although customarily associated with European colonialism, pidgins have developed whenever speakers of different languages have been in regular but limited contact. Among the examples that abound are the English-based China Coast Pidgin that may have originated as early as the seventeenth century but became especially widespread during the course of the nineteenth; the English-based Maori Pidgin current during the early years of British colonization of New Zealand; Trader Navajo, the Navajo-based pidgin used by traders in the Southwest; and the various Congo pidgins that facilitate contacts among the speakers of a variety of African languages used in the Congo River basin. Reflecting the impact of European colonialism during the eighteenth and nineteenth centuries, many of the former pidgins as well as those still in existence are English-, French-, Spanish-, Portuguese-, or Dutch-based.

A good illustration of the origin, succession, and demise of pidgins can be drawn from recent Vietnamese history. When Vietnam was ruled by the French as part of Indochina, a French-based pidgin was used by those French and Vietnamese who lacked command of the other's language. After the defeat of the French at Dien Bien Phu in 1954, and the evacuation of French forces from Vietnam two years later, the pidgin was no longer needed and became almost extinct. With the introduction of U.S. combat forces into the Republic of Vietnam in the early 1960s, an English-based pidgin rapidly developed to assume the role of its French-based predecessor. After the U.S. soldiers were withdrawn in 1973, and political events in 1975 brought the influence of the United States in Vietnam to an abrupt end, the new pidgin, too, all but disappeared.

Although it is true that pidgins can be simplified versions of any language, the most common are those based on English. The reason for this is the widespread contact that English-speaking people have had with non-Western nations. The British Empire not only spread the Union Jack, but also its language over much of the world. Thus, English-based pidgins were found from the coasts of Africa to the New World to the South Pacific. For example, here is an example of the first lines of Shakespeare's *Julius Caesar* (Act 3, Scene 2) in Melanesian Tok Pisin compared to the original English (Murphy 1980:20):

Pren, man bolong Rom, Wantok, harim nau.
Mi kam tasol long plantim Kaesar. Mi noken beiten longen.

Friends, Romans, countrymen, lend me your ears;
I come to bury Caesar, not to praise him.

We can see here many of the typical devices pidgins (and later creoles) use that allow them to communicate effectively with a limited set of grammatical and lexical resources. Words such as *pren*, *mi*, and *kam* are simply nativized forms of English "friend," "me," and "come." "Romans" comes out as *man bolong Rom* (lit. "man/men belong(ing) to Rome"). Countrymen is *Wantok*—those of us who all speak "one talk." Though "lend me your ears" loses some of its power when rendered as *harim nau* ("hear 'em now"), it still makes its point; but *plantim* ("plant 'em") meaning "bury" is almost a poetic metaphor. The pidgin *tasol* ("that's all") acts as a conjunction (such as "but") or adverb (such as "only"). The word *noken* ("no can") is a verbal negative auxiliary. There are no inflections, case markers, or tenses in pidgin, therefore certain words must do a multiplicity of tasks. Once such word is *long*. This word serves many uses, as a preposition ("to," "at," "with," "under"), a comparative marker ("than . . ."), indirect object sign, or an indication of duration. For example, *lukluk long* (lit. "look look long") can mean to seek, to watch, to look for, to take care of, or to protect. *Beten* or *beiten* is "prayer," and *beiten longen* ("prayer belong 'em") is a way of saying "praise."

Although they characteristically lack inflection and possess a limited vo- cabulary, pidgins have a structure of their own and readily adapt to changing circumstances. The structural simplicity of pidgins is to their advantage, al- lowing cross-cultural communication with a minimum of effort. The reduc- tion or total elimination of inflectional affixes, the use of morphemic repetition for intensification, and simplified syntactic constructions make ge- ographically separated pidgins look remarkably similar—so much so that some scholars have argued that in their basic structure all modern and recent pidgins may well go back to some such protopidgin as Sabir, the original lin- gua franca, a medieval pidgin based on Romance languages and used in Mediterranean ports until the beginning of the last century. As similar as pid- gins may be structurally, though, they differ according to the languages that have lexified them (that is, supplied them with the bulk of their word-stock).

Finally, it is important to remember that pidgins are not "broken" lan- guages, a kind of "primitive" speech or manifestations of "corrupt" thought processes of simple peoples. They are quite the opposite: "pidgins are demon- strably creative adaptations of natural languages, with a structure and rules of their own. Along with creoles, they are evidence of a fundamental process of linguistic change . . . [and] they provide the clearest evidence of language being created and shaped by society for its own ends, as people adapt to new social circumstances" (Crystal 2010: 344).

From Pidgins to Creoles

The process of grammatical and lexical reduction of a language such as Eng- lish or Navajo to a pidgin, referred to as **pidginization**, reflects a limitation on functions the pidgin is expected to serve. But it would be wrong to as- sume that the role pidgins are destined to play is invariably humble. In many instances, a pidgin has come to be used by a growing number of people over an increasingly large area, especially when none of the native languages can claim priority by virtue of population size or the prestige of a written tradi- tion. In short, a pidgin may become widely recognized and depended upon as an indispensable means of interethnic communication. Under such cir- cumstances, the growing demands placed on the pidgin cause an expansion of its vocabulary and elaboration of its syntax—a process opposite to pidginization. It may be furnished with a writing system and used in the mass media, it may acquire a semiofficial status, and it may even become the mother tongue of those children in whose families it is habitually used. This process of expansion of a pidgin to other language functions is referred to as **creolization,** and the end result is termed a **creole.** A creole, then, is a pidgin that has become the first language of a speech community.

Among the many places in the world where this process has taken place is Papua New Guinea. There what once was an English-based pidgin of limited utility has been elevated over the past several decades to one of the official languages of the now independent country. Known as Neo-Melanesian, or Tok Pisin (from talk pidgin), it has become the lingua franca of about 1 million people who speak some 700 languages native to Papua New Guinea and the first language of some 20,000 households (Mühlhäusler 1987:178). Tok Pisin has acquired such prestige that more parliamentary debates are now conducted in it than in English, and most recently it has been heard even in the country's university lecture halls.

At least three fourths of the Tok Pisin vocabulary derives from English, some 15 percent from indigenous New Guinea languages, especially Tolai (Kuanua), and the remainder from various other languages, including German. For example, in the singular, Tok Pisin personal pronouns *mi* 'I, me,' *yu* 'you,' and *em* 'he, him; she, her; it' remain the same whether they serve as subject or object. In the first-person plural, the distinction is made between the inclusive form *yumi* 'we, us (including the hearer)' and the exclusive form *mipela* 'we, us (excluding the hearer)'; and in all three persons of the plural the exact number (up to three) is usually indicated, as in *yutupela* 'you two' or *yutripela* 'you three'; the form *ol* for the third-person plural occurs in addition to the expected form. Possession is indicated by *bilong,* the predicate is commonly marked by the particle *i,* and transitive verbs have the suffix *-im,* which also converts adjectives into causative verb forms. Accordingly, *Mi kukim kaikai bilong mi* translates as 'I cook my food,' *Wanpela lek bilong mi i bruk* as 'One of my legs is broken,' *Em i krosim mi* as 'He scolded me,' and *Ol i kapsaitim bensin* as 'They spilled the gasoline.'

A New Guinea road safety handbook (*Rot Sefti Long Niugini*), which instructs readers in three languages, contains the following English paragraph and the Tok Pisin equivalent (Crystal 2010:345):

If you have an accident, get the other driver's number, if possible, get his name and address too, and report it to the police. Don't fight or abuse him.

Sapos yu kisim bagarap, kisim namba bilong narapela draiva, sapos yu ken, kisim naim bilong em na adres tu, na tokim polis long em. Noken paitim em o tok nogut long em.

Even though creoles are languages in their own right and have in some in-stances found their way into the mass media as well as into primary school in-struction, they nevertheless tend to carry less prestige than the standard European languages beside which they are used and from which they derive the bulk of their vocabulary. Consequently, some speakers of creoles, espe-cially those who live in cities and hold semiprofessional jobs, try to "improve" their speech by using the standard language as a model. When this happens, creoles undergo a change, moving in the direction of the standard language in a process known as **decreolization.** Such a change is currently taking place, for example, in English-based Jamaican Creole, giving rise to a continuum ranging from the **basilect,** the variety most differentiated from the standard and used by members of the rural working class, to the **acrolect,** an urban variety approaching the standard and therefore seen as more prestigious.

The great majority of pidgins and creoles are found in coastal areas of the equatorial belt where contacts between speakers of different languages, in-cluding those of former European colonialist nations, have been a common occurrence because of trade. Some recent pidgins, however, have been de-veloping under different circumstances—for example, the Gastarbeiter Deutsch spoken in the Federal Republic of Germany by several million guest workers from southern and southeastern Europe.

Pidgins and creoles have received the serious attention they deserve only during the fourth quarter of the last century. Some of the most stimulating (but also controversial) contributions to their study were made by Derek Bickerton. One important concept based on the study of creoles is Bickerton's bioprogram hypothesis (1981), that is, the assumption that the human species must have a biologically innate capacity for language. In support of this hypothesis, Bickerton linked pidgins and creoles with children's language acquisition and language origins. Because the syntax of Hawaiian Creole English, which Bickerton knew well, shares many features in common with other creole languages, the cognitive strategies for deriving creoles from pid-gins are so much alike as to be part of the human species-specific endow-ment. Furthermore, the innate capacities that enable children to learn a native language are also helpful to children as they expand a pidgin into a

BOX 9.1 CREOLIZATION OF TOK PISIN

World War II greatly accelerated the spread of Tok Pisin within New Guinea. New Guinean males who were pressed into service by the various foreign armies had only Tok Pisin as a common language. In addition, there were extensive movements of indigenous populations during the war and Tok Pisin spread with them. Following the war, the traditional state of warfare or hostility between indigenous groups in Papua New Guinea was almost completely eliminated as a result of the continuous efforts of missionaries and the pacification programs of various foreign governments. This has enabled people to leave their native groups without the fear of being killed. Mobility is increasing considerably as transportation improves, and many people are leaving their home villages to seek employment and excitement in urban areas. When groups mix in this way, Tok Pisin is usually the only means of communication, except where Hiri Motu or English is spoken, and thus Tok Pisin is commonly used in public urban life in New Guinea. There are an increasing number of marriages between men and women from different linguistic groups. When such couples live in towns away from the home group of either partner they generally speak only Tok Pisin in the home, and their children acquire Tok Pisin as a native language. Such young native speakers now number in the thousands.

from Ellen B. Woolford, Aspects of Tok Pisin Grammar (1979), 3

creole. According to Bickerton, some basic cognitive distinctions (such as *specific* versus *general* and *state* versus *process*) must have been established prior to the hominization process (development of human characteristics), and these distinctions are evident in the structure of creoles as well as in the earliest stages of language acquisition.

Some of the recent research concerning pidgins and creoles has resulted in the "blurring" of these two types of speech (Jourdan 1991). It is now accepted that pidgin and creole varieties of a particular language can exist side by side and that a creole can become the main language of a speech community without becoming its native language. In other respects, however, our understanding of pidgins and creoles has improved because greater attention is being paid to the historical and socioeconomic contexts in which pidgins and creoles come into being (see Box. 9.1).

Language Contact in the Contemporary World

In spite of the dominance of English, or the effects of electronic mass media and the internet which are supposedly diluting some of the linguistic differences among us, languages are still in contact in very complex ways. As an example of what might happen in current contact situations, we can consider Japanese. English has been very much a presence in the country ever since a Japanese infatuation with English began in the nineteenth century. Almost every Japanese takes some six years of formal English instruction in school, yet Japan is hardly a bilingual nation. In fact, Japanese critics and English language instructors alike often lament the poor English abilities of most Japanese, especially conversational.

Nonetheless, the number of English loanwords is extensive. Estimates of the number of *commonly* used loanwords in modern Japanese range up to five thousand terms, or perhaps as high as five to ten percent of the ordinary daily vocabulary (Stanlaw 2004a, Stanlaw 2010). The presence of some of these loanwords is not surprising: *terebi* for "television," *tabako* ("tobacco") for cigarettes, and many baseball terms (e.g., *battā* for "batter" or *pitchā* for "pitcher") all came as these things were imported. Many words, however, are *wa-sei-eigo* terms, or "made in Japan" English—vocabulary created using English words as building blocks to coin words that have no real correspondents in the United States or England. Examples include *famikon* ("FAMIly COMputer") for a Nintendo Entertainment System, *furaido poteto* ("fried potato") for french fries, *purasu-doraibā* ("plus driver") for a Phillips screwdriver, *sukin-shippu* ("skin-ship") for bonding through physical contact of the skin as with a mother and a child, *uinkā* ("winker") for an automobile turn signal, *handoru* ("handle") for the steering wheel of a car, *romansu-gurē* ("romance gray") for the silver hair of an older virile man who is still sexually attractive, and the ubiguitious *pokemon* ("POCKEt MONster") for the Pokémon game and anime franchise. Probably most of these vocabulary items are not immediately transparent to native English speakers.

Often English loanwords reflect changing Japanese cultural norms. For example, the very productive English loanword possessive pronoun *mai* ("my") apparently is indicative of a new view held in Japan that the values of corporate allegiances or group loyalty which were thought to be the mainstay of Japanese society are now being questioned. Terms such as *mai-hoomu* (owning "my home"), *mai-waifu* (adoring "my wife"), *mai-peesu* (doing things at "my pace"), *mai-puraibashii* (valuing "my privacy"), or being a member of the *mai-kaa-zoku* (the "my own car tribe") suggest that individual interests and goals can compete on equal footing with the traditional priority given to collective group responsibilities. In the mass media this prefix is found on a vast array of products or their advertisements: *my juice, my pack, my summer, my girl calendar* (Stanlaw 2004a: 17–18).

Besides pidginization, mixing, or one language dominating another there are other possibilities that can occur when speakers of different languages come into contact. Speakers of mutually unintelligible languages who wish to communicate with each other have a variety of means available to them. One widespread method of bridging the linguistic gap is to use a **lingua franca,** a language agreed upon as a medium of communication by people who speak different first languages. In present-day India, for example, the English that spread with British imperialism frequently serves as a lingua franca among speakers of the many different languages native to the subcontinent. In the United States the language used for communication with members of the many different Native American tribes has been English, the speech of the dominant society. And in Kupwar, a southern Indian village with speakers of four separate languages—Marathi, Urdu, Kannada, and Telugu—where almost all male villagers are bilingual or multilingual, the speakers of the first three languages have been switching among them for so long that the structures of the local varieties of these languages have been brought very close together, making it easier for their speakers to communicate (Gumperz and Wilson 1971).

We should mention another possibility when discussing how people who speak different languages try to communicate. Besides choosing a lingua franca or a pidgin, some have proposed adopting an **artificial** or **auxiliary language** to facilitate international communication. Although several hundred are known to have been devised over the past several centuries, only a few have achieved any measure of acceptance and use, with Esperanto, already more than 100 years old, the most widespread. Despite efforts to make Esperanto the official international language, however, English, the mother tongue of some 400 million speakers and the official or semiofficial language serving well over a billion people in the world, appears today to have little, if any, serious competition (Crystal 2010:371).

The World of Languages

It may come as a surprise to learn that no one knows exactly how many languages are spoken in the world today. One standard source suggests the total is more than 6,900 (Gordon 2005). This number includes creole languages but excludes pidgins, as well as the thousands of languages in the course of history and prehistory that must have disappeared without a trace. There are several reasons for the lack of precision in gauging the world's linguistic diversity. A few languages are likely to be discovered in those regions of the world still only partly explored, especially the equatorial rain forests of South America, Africa, and New Guinea. Some languages are on the very verge of extinction, currently used by as few as a handful of speakers and not even habitually at that. Then, too, it is not always easy to determine whether two dialects are sufficiently divergent to become mutually unintelligible and therefore merit the status of two separate languages. In this respect, sociocultural considerations sometimes override the linguistic criterion of mutual intelligibility. For example, Czechs and Slovaks communicate with one another in their respective languages without the slightest hindrance, although Czech and Slovak have separate standards and literary traditions as well as dictionaries and textbooks. If these two languages were to be spoken in nearby villages somewhere in New Guinea, they would unquestionably be classified as two dialects of one language. As for the number of dialects of the languages currently spoken in the world, the total would reach tens of thousands if anyone were interested in making such a count.

The figure of some 6,900 languages amounts to an impressive number when one considers that each represents a distinct means of communication with its own elaborate structure and unique way of describing the cultural universe of its speakers. However, in terms of the numbers of speakers, the great bulk of today's world population makes use of relatively few languages. It is obvious that at this point in human history, speakers of some languages have been more successful than speakers of others, whether by conquest, historical accident, or some other circumstance. The greatly uneven distribution of speakers of the world's languages is graphically represented in Figure 9.1.

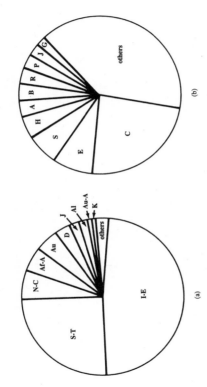

(a)

(b)

FIGURE 9.1 The World's Languages and Their Speakers

The estimated relative numbers of speakers belonging to the top ten language groups (families) are graphically represented in (a). The following abbreviations are used:

I-E Indo-European: most of the languages spoken in Europe, several of which have spread to other parts of the world, as well as some languages spoken in India and southwestern Asia

S-T Sino-Tibetan: various Tibetan, Burmese, and Chinese languages spoken in southeastern Asia

N-C Niger-Congo: most of the languages spoken in western, central, and southern Africa, including the Bantu languages

Af-A Afro-Asiatic: various Semitic, Berber, Cushitic, and Chadic languages spoken in northern Africa and southwestern Asia, as well as extinct (Ancient) Egyptian

Au Austronesian: languages spoken in the vast area extending from Madagascar eastward through the Malay Peninsula to Hawaii and Easter Island

D Dravidian: languages spoken primarily in southern India and parts of Sri Lanka

J Japanese: the language of Japan, considered by some scholars to be distantly related to the Altaic family

Al Altaic: languages spoken from Turkey in the west across central Asia into Siberia

Au-A Austroasiatic: languages spoken for the most part in southeastern Asia (Laos, Vietnam, and Cambodia) but also in some parts of India

K Korean: the language of the two Koreas, considered by some scholars to be distantly related to Japanese or the Altaic family

Others: a great variety of languages belonging to numerous language groups and spoken in Eurasia, Africa, and Australia as well as all native languages of the New World—altogether nearly 3,000 languages, or half of the world's total

The estimated relative numbers of speakers of the top ten mother tongues are graphically represented in descending order in (b). The following abbreviations are used: C = Chinese (languages or dialects); E = English; S = Spanish; H = Hindi; A = Arabic; B = Bengali; R = Russian; P = Portuguese; J = Japanese; G = German; the others include the remaining 6,000 to 7,000 languages of the world.

The top ten official or semiofficial languages serving the largest number of speakers are, in descending order: English, Chinese, Hindi, Spanish, Russian, French, Arabic, Portuguese, Malay (including Indonesian), and Bengali.

Based on data provided in David Crystal, *The Cambridge Encyclopedia of Language* (Cambridge, UK: Cambridge University Press, 2010: 294–297; 465–484).

Summary and Conclusions

Although about 6,900 languages, assignable to several hundred language groups (families), are currently spoken, the overwhelming majority of people speak languages that belong to only a dozen or so language families, with Indo-European at the top of the list for most speakers. The worldwide spread of English and various other European languages dates back to the beginning of the Age of Discovery in the mid-fifteenth century.

Competency in one language only, typical of most Americans with English as their mother tongue, is uncommon in the rest of the world, where hundreds of millions of people are able to speak several languages or language varieties—that is, are multilingual or diglossic. Among the great variety of languages, pidgins occupy a special place: Although structured and efficient as a means of communication, their vocabularies are limited because pidgins are not called upon to perform the broad range of functions that characterize full-fledged languages.

Even though many people speak only one language, they are actively or at least passively acquainted with several dialects and speech styles of that language. Their own speech patterns differ from those of others, even if only slightly. All speakers have their individual idiolects.

The number of languages spoken in the world today is rapidly diminishing. According to one estimate, of the 6,900 languages only 600 can be considered safe from extinction during the twenty-first century. The primary reason for languages of small-sized societies becoming extinct is that in order to survive, small tribal populations must adapt to the economic and cultural influence of the nation-states that encompass them, and one of the vital adaptive processes is the use of the language of the large society.

10

Ethnography of Communication

In an article written in 1966, Hymes observed that it used to be customary to consider languages as different from each other but the uses to which they are put as closely similar if not essentially the same. Hymes then noted that the opposite view was beginning to prevail: Languages are seen as fundamentally very much alike but the social uses of speech as quite different from one culture to the next. In the earlier period, distinct division of labor existed between linguists and cultural anthropologists. With few exceptions, linguists studied languages to discover the structural differences between them and to learn about their historical development, whereas anthropologists studied human societies in order to understand the workings of their cultures. But culture and the use of language are not easily separable. People must use language to accomplish a wide variety of culture-specific goals. If societies are function smoothly, their members must have not only **linguistic competence** (the knowledge of the grammatical rules of their mother tongue, acquired well before adulthood) but also **communicative competence**—the knowledge of what is and what is not appropriate to say in any specific cultural context. As Hymes put it, "A child from whom any and all of the grammatical sentences of a language might come with equal likelihood would be . . . a social monster" (Hymes 1974:75). Some parents occasionally learn this from their own experience when a child who is not yet fully communicatively competent makes an embarrassing comment in front of guests, such as saying to a guest who praises the coffee cake being offered, "My mom said it was lousy, but it was good enough to give to you."

The nature and function of communicative behavior in the context of culture are the subject of **ethnography of communication.** In its modern form, ethnography of communication dates back to Hymes's 1962 article "The Ethnography of Speaking." Inasmuch as this relatively new field focuses on those aspects of human behavior in which communication meets culture, research in ethnography of communication contributes to the interdisciplinary studies that are proving to be of increasing value in modern scholarship. Some scholars consider ethnography of communication as one of the several fields of inquiry within the scope of sociolinguistics. Others argue that ethnography of communication, as the study of communicative behavior in relation to the sociocultural variables associated with human interaction, is broader and more encompassing than sociolinguistics. Be that as it may, sociolinguistics and ethnography of communication are fields of inquiry that have been gaining in importance and attracting significant research.

Speech Community and Related Concepts

The terms *society* and *culture* in anthropology are useful as general concepts, but no society's culture is uniform for all its members. Any complex of learned patterns of behavior and thought that distinguishes various segments of a society (minorities, castes, and the like) is referred to as a subculture. By extension, this term is also used to refer collectively to all those who exhibit the characteristics of a particular subculture (for example, the homeless as well as the so-called beautiful people). Language and speech, too, are characterized by lack of uniformity. In general, any particular society is associated with a specific language, and multinational societies are associated with several. But no language is ever uniform for all speakers of a society (people, community, tribe). As we have already seen, certain ways of speaking the same language may differentiate men from women, the young from the old, the poor from the rich, and the like. All those who share specific rules for speaking and interpreting speech and at least one speech variety belong to a **speech community.** However, it is important to remember that people who speak the same language are not always members of the same speech community. On the one hand, speakers of South Asian English in India and Pakistan share a language with citizens of the United States, but the respective varieties of English and the rules for speaking them are sufficiently distinct to assign the two populations to different speech communities. On the other hand, Muriel Saville-Troike (1982:20) identified even monolingual speakers of either Spanish (the official language) or Guarani (the national language) as belonging to the same speech community in Paraguay because the social roles of the speakers of the two languages are complementary—both groups are mutually dependent for services or employment.

Most members of a society, even if they happen to live in the same town, belong to several speech communities. For example, an elderly person may have considerable difficulty following the monotonous chant of an auctioneer or comprehending what students talk about among themselves. But an auctioneer and a college student can easily make the adjustment necessary to engage in a conversation with the elderly person and be fully understood; all they have to do is to share enough characteristic patterns of pronunciation, grammar, vocabulary, and manner of speaking to belong to the same speech community.

It may also be that peoples live in different countries and speak different languages but share some rules for speaking, as do the Czechs and the Austrians (and for that matter some of the other peoples who until World War I were part of the Austro-Hungarian Empire or lived in adjacent areas). As an example, the commonly used phrase for greeting or taking leave of a woman who is economically and socially well situated was (and to some extent still is) "*Rukulíbám, milostivá paní!*" in Czech and "*Küss' die Hand, gnädige Frau!*" in German. The English translation, "I kiss your hand, gracious lady," clearly indicates how different such rules of speaking are from those used, say, in Britain or the United States. Linguists refer to an area in which speakers of different languages share speaking rules as a **speech area.**

Less frequently employed terms for related concepts include *language field, speech field,* and *speech network* (Hymes 1972:55). The first of these (language field) refers to all those communities in which an individual is able to communicate adequately by virtue of knowing the languages and language varieties serving the communities. The concept of speech field parallels that of language field but involves the knowledge of rules for speaking rather than knowledge of languages. The last term (speech network) refers to linkages between persons from different communities who share language varieties as well as rules for speaking. To give an example, in addition to her mother tongue, a woman knows four languages well enough to read books and newspapers published in them; a total of five languages make up her language field. However, the same woman is able to communicate easily in only one foreign language in addition to her native language; the speech communities within which she functions effectively in the two languages make up her speech field. Within that speech field the woman has special rapport with those persons, regardless of where they may come from, who share with her the two languages, rules for speech, and a professional interest in, say, archaeology; the linkages with these people make up her speech network.

Units of Speech Behavior

To distinguish among different levels of speech activity Hymes made use of three terms for the ethnographic analysis and description of speech behavior—**speech situation**, **speech event**, and **speech act** (Hymes 1972:56–57). (If one were to include nonverbal communication as well, these three terms would need to be broadened and the word *speech* replaced by *communicative*; after all, a hand gesture or the wink of an eye can be just as effective as an entire sentence.)

A **speech situation** is the context within which speaking occurs—that is, any particular set of circumstances typically associated with speech behavior (or absence of it). A speech situation may be a family meal, birthday party, baby shower, seminar meeting, campus beer party, auction, fishing trip, Quaker meeting, or any one of a large number of situations that take place in a society and are definable in terms of participants and goals and are therefore distinguishable from other speech situations.

The minimal unit of speech for purposes of an ethnographic analysis is the **speech act**. A speech act may be a greeting, apology, question, compliment, self-introduction, or the like. Although normally attributable to a single speaker, collective speech acts also exist as, for example, the "Amen" said by a congregation or the reciting of the Pledge of Allegiance by young pupils. In size, a speech act may range from a single word ("Scram!" or "Thanks") to a five-minute shaggy-dog story or a long harangue on conduct. Speech acts that follow each other in a recognized sequence and are governed by social rules for the use of speech combine to form a **speech event**, the basic unit of verbal interaction. Examples of speech events include conversation, confession to a priest, interview, dialogue with a salesperson, telephone inquiry, and so on. Boundaries between successive speech events are marked by a change of major participants, a noticeable silence, or some remark designed to introduce another topic of conversation, for example, "If I can change the subject . . ." or "By the way, have you heard that. . . ." Under special circumstances, a speech act may become a speech event, as when someone shouts "Fire!" in a crowded movie theater.

An alumni reunion can be used to illustrate the three units of speech behavior. The gathering itself is an example of a speech situation: It has a beginning and an end and lasts usually only part of one day; the participants are restricted to former members of a class and their spouses or partners. Within such a speech situation, a number of speech events invariably take place: For example, one group may be reminiscing about favorite teachers and classroom antics; those in another group may be giving brief accounts of what they have been doing since graduation or the last reunion; and still others may be simply swapping jokes and stories. Within these speech events, the telling of a single joke or personal experience is a speech act.

Just as native speakers of any language are expected to produce sentences that are grammatically acceptable and meaningful, speech acts are judged according to how appropriate they are to any specific speech situation or speech event. It would be considered odd if one were to say to a stranger in the street, "My name is John Smith; what time do you have?" Similarly, at a baby shower it would be out of place to bring up the increasing infant mortality rate. When inappropriate speech acts do occur, participants in the speech event or situation are later likely to comment on them: "Did you hear what she said? How inconsiderate!" or "What a crazy thing for Bill to say. Has he lost his mind?"

Components of Communication

Participants and Setting

Describing a language with emphasis on its function as the primary means of communication requires more than simply describing its sounds (phonology) and grammatical structure (morphology and syntax). Careful field research is necessary to discover how members of a society use their language under differing circumstances to satisfy the goals they set for themselves.

Traditionally, speech behavior was said to involve a speaker and a hearer and include the message transmitted between them. Modern ethnographic descriptions and analyses have shown that many more components need to be taken into account if any particular instance of communicative behavior is to be fully understood. Which of these components assume a crucial role depends on a given speech situation and the particular community in which it takes place.

The component termed participants includes not only the sender of a message (also referred to as the speaker or addresser) and the intended receiver (hearer, addressee) but anyone who may be interested in or happens to perceive (hear, see) the message—the audience. The number of participants can vary from only one to many thousands. For example, a person who has a job interview scheduled may practice for it by posing potential questions and then answering them, thus assuming the role of both sender and receiver. But at an outdoor political rally one or more charismatic leaders may not only address several hundred thousand followers but also succeed in mobilizing them.

In some cultures, the ability to communicate is not perceived as limited to ordinary humans. Among the Ashanti, a West African people on the Gulf of Guinea, a midwife may direct a question to a fetus concerning its father's identity, and recently deceased persons are believed to be able to inform their surviving relatives as to who or what was responsible for their deaths. The Ashanti also believe that forest fairies and monsters are able to instruct young men in medicine; these beings are said to communicate in a whistle language but are able to understand Twi, the language in which humans pray to them.

As indicated earlier in the discussion of language in its social context, a thorough ethnographic account of communicative behavior must carefully note the characteristics of the participants. Age, gender, ethnic affiliation, relationship (kinship) among participants, their relative social status, the degree to which they are acquainted, and other factors can influence how communication proceeds. Who talks to whom and in whose presence tends to determine not only how one talks (casually or respectfully) but also whether or not one can interrupt the other participant, how long speech acts should be, what additional channels one should use to enhance the presentation, and so on.

Any communicative act or event happens at a particular time and place and under particular physical circumstances—that is, it is characterized by a particular *setting*. Settings are likely to vary somewhat from one instance to the next even if the events are of the same kind, but the variation has culturally recognized limits. Small college classes normally meet in classrooms, but on warm spring or autumn days they may be conducted in the shade of a tree outside the classroom building; to meet in a nearby tavern or the lobby of the administrative building would be considered inappropriate. On April Fools' Day, practical jokes are accepted by people who would consider them presumptuous on any other day. Hymes distinguished between setting and scene, the latter designating the "psychological setting." It is true that the mood pervading a given setting may invite or inhibit certain communicative acts or events, and in this sense the scene contributes to the definition of setting. One can easily imagine the identical setting and participants but completely different scenes: Compare, for example, the atmosphere surrounding the announcement of across-the-board wage increases with the announcement of the company's going out of business.

Purpose, Channels, Codes, and Message Content and Form

The purpose of speaking is not always to transmit information or to exchange ideas. Sometimes it is to establish an atmosphere of sociability and is the equivalent of a hug or a hearty handshake. Speech behavior with the goal of bringing about such an emotional effect is referred to as *phatic communion*.

The motivation for communicative behavior varies from one occasion to the next: An individual may make an offer or a request, threaten or plead, praise or blame, invite or prohibit some action, reveal or try to conceal something, and so on. One's goal or purpose quite frequently determines the manner in which one speaks or acts. Even an aggressive person may speak meekly and deferentially when stopped for speeding by a police officer, hoping that polite and apologetic speech behavior will influence the officer to issue a warning instead of a ticket.

Although the acoustic channel, best exemplified by spoken words, is the one most commonly employed, other channels of communication should not be overlooked. To do so would be to ignore that communicative behavior that makes primary use of one channel frequently depends on other channels for reinforcement. To hear a play read aloud or to see it professionally performed can mean the difference between experiencing boredom or enjoyment. Quite commonly, too, one channel offers an effective substitute for another: The military salute, using the optical channel, substitutes a visual expression of respect or honor for what could otherwise be orally recited, and photojournalists strive to present news events pictorially because "a picture is worth a thousand words."

The most common form of the acoustic channel is oral, as in singing, whistling, and of course speaking. If human language is to be considered as a general language code, then it is manifested in several thousand specific codes, of which English, Russian, Navajo, and Japanese are examples. Each of these codes subsumes a number of subcodes. English has not only several national varieties, such as American, British, and Australian, but also regional dialects such as those of New England, the English Midlands, and South Australia, and a number of slangs peculiar to particular groups.

Among the Ashanti, the acoustic channel is quite diversified. The principal verbal code is Twi, a language characterized by five distinctive tones. The ceremonial language priests and priestesses use is a subcode; it is identified as an earlier form of Twi that Ashanti laypeople apparently cannot understand. The so-called language of the ghosts, consisting of cooing noises and said to be intelligible only to unborn babies and toothless infants, is an example of an oral but nonverbal form of the acoustic channel. Other nonverbal codes of the Ashanti include the drum code to convey messages and signals; the horn code, used for similar purposes; the gong code, employed for public summonses; and whistling, used not by the Ashanti themselves but by the forest fairies and monsters who instruct their medicine men. Some parts of the ceremony at which ancestral spirits are propitiated are conducted in complete silence; other parts permit the chief to communicate only by gestures.

Message form and message content are closely related, or as Hymes (1972:59) put it, "It is a truism . . . that *how* something is said is part of *what* is said." A paraphrase may be sufficient to indicate the message content, but only the quoting of the exact words can represent adequately the message form of a speech act. To paraphrase the statement "Like hell I'm kidding; I've warned you—now get out, fast!" as "I told him in no uncertain terms that he was no longer welcome" does away with so much color and feeling that the changed form no longer has much in common with the original content.

Here it is appropriate to mention the term *register*, referring to a variety of language that serves a particular social situation. In American linguistics the term is used to differentiate between broad varieties of a language—for example, between the vernacular (everyday, casual spoken form) and the standard (prestige form) in English. In Great Britain *register* is used for any of a number of specifically defined varieties, such as legal, scientific, religious, intimate, and so on.

Genres, Key, Rules of Interaction, and Norms of Interpretation

The term **genre** refers to speech acts or events associated with a particular communicative situation and characterized by a particular style, form, and content. Ritual or religious occasions, for example, regularly call for such special genres as prayers and sermons. Both sermons and prayers make use of a ceremonial style of speech with special attention to form. This is why *thou, thee, thy,* and *thine* for 'you,' 'your,' and 'yours' have survived to the present in prayers and the language of the Friends (Quakers).

A good storyteller of Old World fairy or wonder tales would customarily begin the telling by some such phrase as "Once upon a time" and signal the end of the tale by the formula "And they lived happily ever after" or, more elaborately, "The festivities lasted nine days and nine nights. There were 900 fiddlers, 900 fluters, 900 pipers, and the last day and night of the wedding were better than the first." Important incidents in Old World tales usually take place three times (that is, the formulaic or magic number is three), whereas in Native American tales things happen four times.

Myths represent another genre, one found in the traditions of all of the world's societies. Arapaho stories concerning *nih?óóθoo* 'Whiteman,' a popular character of Arapaho trickster tales, almost invariably have him walking down (or up) the river in the initial sentence of the story. The end is signaled by the formula "This is the end of the story." In Upper Chinook, a Native American language spoken in Oregon, myths are characterized by features not found elsewhere in the language (Hymes 1958). The diagnostic features of Upper Chinook myths are phonological (for example, the doubling of a consonant word-finally to indicate stuttering from fright or excitement), morphological (limiting the use of certain noun prefixes to the speech of characters appearing in myths), lexical (reserving the use of certain names for myths only), and syntactic. Other linguistic features of Upper Chinook are limited to casual speech.

A "war talk" genre was employed among the Navajo (Hill 1936) and other Native Americans. Upon entering enemy territory, the leader of a Navajo war party would instruct the group to use words different from the ones commonly used to refer to the livestock, captives, and whatever else they hoped to bring back; members of the war party spoke this warpath language until they turned toward home.

Perhaps more than genre or other components, key varies widely among cultures. By the term *key,* Hymes referred to the "tone, manner, or spirit in which an act is done" and added that "acts otherwise the same as regards setting, participants, message form, and the like may differ in key, as, e.g., between *mock* [and] *serious or perfunctory* [and] *painstaking*" (Hymes 1972:62). Key may even override another component, as when a speaker who is presumably praising someone becomes slowly but increasingly so sarcastic that the person spoken of feels hurt or ridiculed. A particular key may be used so frequently by members of a group that it loses much of its effect, whereas another key may be so rarely employed that it may require some effort on the part of hearers to identify it and comprehend its social meaning.

Communicative activity is guided by **rules of interaction:** Under normal circumstances, members of a speech community know what is and what is not appropriate. Among members of the middle class in the United States, for example, interruptions are not considered appropriate except among close friends or family members, but if someone monopolizes a conversation, there are acceptable ways of breaking in. A compliment addressed to another person is usually gratefully acknowledged or some remark is made to the effect that the compliment may not be fully deserved. When rules of interaction are broken or completely neglected, embarrassment results, and unless an apology is offered, future contacts between the parties may be strained or even avoided.

The judgment as to what constitutes proper interaction is of course subject to interpretation. The **norms of interpretation** (just as the rules of interaction) vary from culture to culture, sometimes only subtly but usually quite distinctly or even profoundly. And within a single society, if that society is socially or ethnically diversified, not all members are likely to use the same rules of interaction and the same norms of interpretation.

If the norms of interpretation are shared by the interlocutors, their relations are likely to be marked by understanding and harmony. Deborah Tannen (1982:219) gave an example of shared norms of interpretation that differ subtly from those employed by most Americans. (Reference is to a Greek family.) Before marriage, a Greek woman "had to ask her father's permission before doing anything. . . . If she asked, for example, whether she could go to a dance, and he answered, ' *An thes, pas* (If you want, you can go),' she knew that she could not go. If he really meant that she could go, he would say, '*Ne. Na pas* (Yes. You should go).'" In addition to the manner in which the father phrased his answer, his intonation (a rise on the *if* clause) reinforced his meaning of disapproval.

In an interethnic conversation, even though carried on in English between husband and wife, subtle differences in the norms of interpretation may lead to a misunderstanding. The following example is also from Tannen (1982:220–221). The reconstructed conversation between a native New Yorker wife and her Greek husband runs as follows: "Wife: John's having a party. Wanna go? Husband: OK. (Later) Wife: Are you sure you want to go to the party? Husband: OK, let's not go. I'm tired anyway." Tannen's commentary (given here only in part):

In discussing the misunderstanding, the American wife reported she had merely been asking what her husband wanted to do without considering her own preference. Since she was about to go to this party just for him, she tried to make sure that that was his preference by asking him a second time. She was being solicitous and considerate. The Greek husband said that by bringing up the question of the party, his wife was letting him know that she wanted to go, so he agreed to go. Then when she brought it up again, she was letting him know that she didn't want to go; she had obviously changed her mind. So he came up with a reason not to go, to make her feel all right about getting her way. This is precisely the strategy reported by the Greek woman who did what her father . . . wanted without expecting him to tell her directly what that was.

Misunderstandings may be expected when individuals interpret cues generated by others according to rules that are different. U.S. citizens of Mexican origin may well have norms of interpreting communicative behavior that differ from those adhered to by fellow citizens of Japanese ancestry. Awareness of these differences and a need for understanding and adjustment are particularly crucial in intercultural communication. In a study conducted at the University of Colorado among male students from Arabic-speaking countries and male students from the United States, Michael Watson and Theodore Graves (1966:976–979) found, much as they had hypothesized, that "Arabs confronted each other more directly than Americans when conversing. . . They sat closer to each other . . . [and] were more likely to touch each other. . . They looked each other more squarely in the eye . . . and . . . conversed more loudly than Americans. . . Persons from the various Arab countries [appeared to] be more similar to each other than to any regional group of Americans." Interpretation of American communicative behavior by foreign visitors to the United States according to their own norms, and vice versa, can only result in misunderstanding rather than the appreciation of different cultures.

In discussing the various components of speech, Hymes used as a mnemonic device the word S P E A K I N G, whose letters stand for settings, *participants*, ends (discussed previously as "purpose"), *act* sequences (the arrangement of components), *keys*, instrumentalities (discussed previously as "channels," "codes," and "message form"), *norms* (of interaction and interpretation), and *genres*.

A concept frequently used in recent years is termed **frame** (or, to endow it with some dynamic, *framing*). It is closely related to what Hymes called "key" and to what is referred to in modern folklore as performance. A particular performance—that is, what the participants in a face-to-face interaction (or discourse) are doing when they speak—commonly determines the frame of reference in which the exchange is to be interpreted and understood. Authentic frames are culture-specific and vary, somewhat or a great deal, from one society to another. A short list of frames (or framings; the list could be greatly expanded) might include bargaining, complaining, congratulating (someone), consulting, excusing (oneself), insinuating (something), interviewing (someone), joking, mimicking (someone), and reporting (something). These and other speech situations have meanings that participants are familiar with, except in situations of wide difference in age or socioeconomic status. A lack of common frame could be extreme if two (or several) individuals of strikingly different cultural backgrounds were to interact. The purpose of such a discourse might be poorly served, or even a serious misunderstanding could result.

A sample list of means by which discourses are framed includes such stylistic devices as rhyme; prosodic devices—for example, tempo or intonation; such figures of speech as metaphor and metonymy; genre formulas such as conventional openings or closings of fairy tales; special codes—for example, the use of archaic words or obscenities; and a distinctive manner of speech such as a very formal style or an intimate one.

Suwako Watanabe's account of American and Japanese university students' group discussions (Watanabe 1993) addressed the cultural differences in framing. To give an example: Whereas the American students entered and exited the discussion frame immediately and directly, the Japanese students began their participation deliberately and made their points gradually. Moreover, the American students accepted a potential confrontation as a given, whereas the Japanese students tried to avoid confrontation, considering both supportive and opposing arguments. This particular characteristic was perceived by the Americans as too indirect and ambiguous. According to Watanabe (1993:205),

[W]hen Japanese and Americans are to discuss a controversial issue, the Japanese may experience frustration, being unable to participate in the argument because they find the one-at-a-time argumentation of the Americans too fast [the reference here is to the fact that American participants presented one position at a time and drew a conclusion each time]. At the same time, the Americans may perceive the Japanese as illogical and elusive because they give both supportive and contradictory accounts.

Subanun Drinking Talk

A good example of an ethnography-of-speaking account of a speech situation is the paper "How to Ask for a Drink in Subanun" (Frake 1964). The Subanun are swidden agriculturists who live in the mountainous interior of a peninsula on the Philippine island of Mindanao. Frake's article dealt only with the drinking of *gasi*, a fermented beverage usually made of rice, manioc, and maize, that Frake labeled "beer." The drinking of beer is a required activity limited to festive gatherings occasioned by some specific event and characterized by the participation of several families. The beer is drunk with bamboo straws from a Chinese jar containing the fermented mash. Just before the drinking begins, the jar is filled with water. The resulting beer, which contains a fair amount of alcohol, is sucked up by straw from the bottom of the jar by each participant in turn.

The first stage of the drinking encounter consists of tasting. During this stage, the person who provides the jar invites the participant who enjoys the highest respect to drink. This person must then ask each of the other participants to permit him to drink, expressing role distances and authority relations between himself and the others by the order in which he asks their permission and the terms of address he uses. Several rounds of tasting are succeeded by competitive drinking. During this stage, the talk centers on the quality of the beer and the performance of the participants. The drinkers must consume no less than the amount drunk by the person initiating the round. During the competition, the number of participants as a rule is reduced to fewer than a half dozen. Competitive drinking then continues with a discussion—beginning with trivial gossip and proceeding to subjects of current concern. It culminates in what Frake termed "game drinking," which features a display of verbal art. (Frake's description of the last two discourse stages, discussion and display of verbal art, appears in Box 10.1.)

In short, among the Subanun, speaking in the context of festive drinking can be used to extend, define, and manipulate a person's social relationships.

BOX 10.1 FESTIVE DRINKING AND TALKING AMONG THE SUBANUN

As the size and role-structure of the gathering becomes defined, discourse changes in topic to removed referents, usually beginning with relatively trivial gossip, proceeding to more important subjects of current interest, and, finally, in many cases arriving at litigation. . . . Success in effecting legal decisions depends on achieving a commanding role in the encounter and on debating effectively from that position. Since there are no sanctions of force legally applicable to back up a decision, the payment of a fine in compliance with a decision is final testimony to the prowess in verbal combat of the person who made the decision.

. . . If drinking continues long enough, the focus of messages shifts from their topics to play with message forms themselves, following stylized patterns of song and verse composition. Songs and verses are composed on the spot to carry on discussions in an operetta-like setting. Even unsettled litigation may be continued in this manner, the basis for decision being shifted from cogent argument to verbal artistry. The most prestigious kinds of drinking songs require the mastery of an esoteric vocabulary by means of which each line is repeated with a semantically equivalent but formally different line. Game drinking is a frequent accompaniment to these displays of verbal art. Together they help assure that the festivity will end with good feelings among all participants, a goal which is explicitly stated by the Subanun. Participants who had displayed marked hostility toward each other during the course of drinking talk may be singled out for special ritual treatment designed to restore good feelings.

from Charles O. Frake, "How to Ask for a Drink in Subanun" (1964), 130–131

To speak Subanun grammatically and sensibly is not enough. In order to become respected and achieve a position of leadership in Subanun society, a person must have the skill to "talk from the straw," that is, one must know what to say to whom and when, and in addition be able to use the language creatively.

Attitudes Toward the Use of Speech

The bulk of information in all communities is transmitted by speech, but members of some communities engage in speaking more readily than do members of others. In his *Laws*, Plato has an elderly Athenian comment that in Greece it is widely believed that Athenians not only take delight in talking but talk a great deal, Lacedaemonians (Spartans) are inclined to be taciturn, and Cretans have versatile minds but prefer to be concise in speech (Plato 1961:1242:641e). In other societies, talking is encouraged and appreciated by some members but discouraged or negatively valued by others. According to Inez Hilger (1891–1977), among the Araucanians of south-central Chile and neighboring parts of Argentina, men are expected to talk a great deal, and those who do and speak well are highly respected. By contrast, Araucanian women are brought up to say little and speak quietly in public and to keep silent in the company of their husbands (although they speak freely when in the company of women) (Hilger 1957:44–45, 81–83). Among Mongolian nomads, daughters-in-law have such a low status that they are severely restricted in the use of language. For example, they are forbidden to use not only the names of their husbands' male relatives but also any words or syllables that sound like these names.

In the United States almost everyone knows some individuals who talk incessantly, or at least a great deal (talkers, gabbers, chatterboxes, jabberers, chatterers), and others who say very little (they are said to be tight-lipped, close-mouthed, reticent, taciturn, and so on). Those who talk freely are generally preferred because they appear more self-confident and are easier to get to know than those who say very little. The saying "Still waters run deep" suggests that a quiet demeanor may conceal unexpected characteristics. On the whole, keeping silent is not looked upon favorably in the United States: Even ten seconds of no one's saying anything during a party can cause such embarrassment that several people are likely to begin speaking at the same time to break the silence. But under some circumstances speech is virtually proscribed: During the meetings of the Society of Friends (Quakers), for example, communion with God is sought through silent waiting for the Inner Light rather than through praying aloud or singing.

In some societies, refraining from speaking is expected under a variety of circumstances and provides an interesting contrast with the general attitudes toward speech in the United States. For a description of situations in which the Western Apache of Cibecue in east-central Arizona "give up on words," we are indebted to Keith H. Basso (1970, 1990) for his discussion of several types of situations in which Western Apaches are expected to refrain from speaking. One concerns meeting strangers, whether Apaches or others. Such a situation usually takes place at large gatherings such as rodeos but is reported to have occurred even when two strangers happened to work together on a four-man roundup crew. They did not begin to speak to each other until the night of the fourth day. In Western Apache culture a stranger who is quick to talk to others is suspected of wanting something from them or of having had too much to drink. Another situation in which no speaking occurs has to do with the initial stages of courtship. At public gatherings young couples may be holding hands but saying nothing to each other for as much as an hour, and they are generally just as silent when they are alone. Their silence, especially that of the girls, is attributed to shyness, self-consciousness, and modesty.

Complete silence is also maintained for as long as a quarter of an hour when Western Apache parents meet children who are returning from boarding schools. While the children become comfortable enough to talk soon after their arrival, it may take several days before the parents engage in normal conversation with them. The reason for the initial restraint on the part of the parents is their belief that the attitudes and behavior of their children are likely to have changed as a result of exposure to new ideas and that it is therefore wise to wait and see "how they would like . . . being [at] home [again]." "Getting cussed out" (whether interpreted as deserved or not) is also a reason for silence. Those sufficiently enraged to "cuss someone out" are considered temporarily irrational, and answering them is thought likely to add to their loss of self-control. There are still other conditions that call for silence: "being with people who are sad" (it is considered thoughtful not to engage in conversation individuals who have recently lost a spouse or relative because deep grief may cause them to become hostile) and "being with someone for whom they sing" (one does not talk during a curing ceremony, especially while the medicine man is chanting). Basso hypothesized that in Western Apache culture "the absence of verbal communication is associated with social situations in which the status of [the main] participants is ambiguous . . . [and constitutes] a response to uncertainty and unpredictability in social relations" (Basso 1970:227).

There is some evidence that traditional Navajo silence behavior occurs in similar social contexts. Although this could be taken as an indication of a wider distribution of this use of silence, we must remember that the Navajos and Apaches are closely related and therefore at least some of these behavioral traits may be very old.

That speaking is a cultural focus for the Tenejapa Tzeltal, who live in the central highlands of the state of Chiapas in Mexico, is evident from their elaborate terminology for ways of speaking. Among the 416 terms recorded by Brian Stross (1974) are those referring to talk occurring in a grassy area, nighttime talk, speech coming from a person who is lying on his (her) side, the announcement by a woman that she is pregnant, talk among several people who are sitting down, speech of a person who is hungry or fasting, and so on. Malicious gossip, insults, mockery, threats, and ungrammatical or incoherent speech are considered of little worth; songs, prayers, eloquent speech, and deliberate utterances using careful pronunciation are highly valued.

The ability to speak well, especially in public, is valued in all societies. But definition of what "speaking well" means would not be the same in all cultures. The sacred vocabulary of Zuñi prayers, songs, myths, and ceremonial conversations carries prestige and is considered dignified; the rapidly changing slang words of young Zuñis are considered foolish and of little value but are not condemned (Newman 1955). The tendency of the Kwakiutl of Vancouver Island, British Columbia, to go beyond the literal meaning of words was documented by Boas (1940) in his discussion of metaphorical expressions in Kwakiutl. They range (in English translation) from "to nettle" for "to ridicule" to "post of our world" for "chief" to "having a sweet taste" in reference to a good speech. And for the Navajo, words are "things of power. Some words attract good; others drive away evil [and] certain words are dangerous—they may be uttered only by special persons under specially defined conditions" (Kluckhohn and Leighton 1962:260).

As a rule, people consider their native language to be the most natural and efficient means of communication, and one can easily understand why they would think so. But it is also true that many peoples view other languages (and their speakers) with less respect. The Czechs believe their language to be very rich and expressive (which it is), and many Czech writers and poets have celebrated their language in their writings. At the same time, some Czechs tend to view the very closely related and mutually intelligible Slovak language, which is spoken to the east of the Czech Republic, as a caricature of Czech. Slovak expressions that are not identical or nearly identical with Czech ones seem to Czechs to possess a measure of grotesqueness, and Slovak words or phrases they cannot understand at first hearing strike Czechs not simply as foreign but as monstrous. Unintelligible languages fare no better. The Czech word for a German, *Němec*, was derived centuries ago from the adjective *němý* 'mute' because, it was thought, someone who uttered inarticulate and unintelligible foreign sounds might as well be mute.

Recent Trends in the Ethnography of Speaking

The methods of the ethnography of speaking are increasingly applied even in what is essentially linguistic (rather than linguistically anthropological) inquiry. When field-workers so apply these methods, they make use of recorded narratives, monologues, or dialogues to show, for example, how the syntactic patterns of a language are adjusted to principles of culture-specific discourse. Jeffrey Heath discussed this approach in his article about clause structure in Ngandi, a language now spoken by only a very few aborigines in southeastern Arnhem Land (northern Australia). For his analysis, rather than using a text corrected and refined with the help of an informant after a more or less spontaneous first recording had been made, Heath preferred "the original text, warts and all" or at least kept "editorial emendations . . . to a minimum" (Heath 1985:90). Furthermore, he liked to obtain texts that are stylistically diverse rather than uniform. Having such texts made it easier to match different styles with corresponding grammatical (or even "ungrammatical") forms.

To cite (in a simplified form) one of the several examples with which Heath illustrated his discussion: Among many speakers of English, such fillers as *er*, *uh*, *um* used to fill pauses or gaps in discourse carry a stigma. Not so among speakers of Ngandi. The most common of what Heath termed a "whatchamacallit" element in Ngandi, the noun *jara*, is fully acceptable in all styles, and its syntactic prominence is attested by its having derivational forms (as in *man-jara* 'group associated with whatchamacallit' and *bicara whatchamacallit* [place-name]') and a full set of noun-class prefixes and suffixes. The word *jara*, usually heard after a pause, is used while a speaker searches his or her memory for a specific noun, and when a second such element is used in the same utterance, *ŋuri* is added to express impatience and self-irritation, as in *buluki? bicara ba-ga-n-i-, bicara ŋuri* 'they also sat (lived) at whatchamacallit place—what the hell was the name of that place?' (Heath 1985:107). To linguists who would most likely be analyzing unwritten languages spoken by very small out-of-the-way societies, Ngandi discourse structure might well appear as highly fragmented and unpredictable. What struck Heath in particular "about the differences between English and such

Australian languages as Ngandi . . . is that most of them relate closely to 'psycholinguistic' aspects of speech production" and that the underlying clear-cut grammar and the psycholinguistic component concerned with memory limitations, surface ambiguities, and the like "are far more tightly welded to each other than it seems at first" (Heath 1985:108). To make some sort of sense of this connection, the investigator must attach due significance to language as it is used. Here we have a good example of the recognition of the contribution that ethnography of speaking can make to linguistics.

In papers dealing with language use, the term *context* has been commonly employed to denote the interrelated conditions under which speech and other forms of communicative behavior occur. There has recently been a tendency to employ the term *contextualization* instead. Many linguistic anthropologists believe that it is preferable, at least in some instances, to view context as a process—as something that develops and perhaps even changes significantly while two or more individuals are interacting rather than as something that is given, or fixed. Those features of the settings that are used at particular stages of the interaction to aid in the interpretation of the content are signaled by contextualization cues.

To put it differently: When two (or more) individuals interact for even a relatively short period of time, the nature and purpose of their verbal exchange may abruptly change as well as the message content and form, rules of interaction, and so forth. Such a situation is easy to imagine. For example, two neighbors are chatting casually about the weather and their gardens until one happens to make a remark about the other's child and the remark is taken as a criticism of parenting skills. The casual atmosphere surrounding the conversation changes instantly. The tone of the person whose child's behavior has been found wanting may suddenly turn cool, indicating that the conversation is about to end, and on a very different note from the way it began; or the tone may become angry, with a countercharge launched against the child of the one making the original criticism. In the latter case, the contextualization cue could well be some such remark as "My child is fine—why don't you concentrate on your own, who is always leading our boy astray!"

Summary and Conclusions

Ethnography of communication is an important recent development supplementing the already well-established study of cultures by anthropologists and languages by linguists. The goals of this new field are first to give as complete an account as possible of the social uses of speech in different societies and then to produce historical and comparative studies on the subject (ethnology of communication). Thus far the scope of ethnography of communication has been largely descriptive and synchronic, but cross-cultural comparisons of the social uses of speech as well as studies of how speech uses change over time are forthcoming.

Because their purpose is to discover how humans interact under the many different circumstances of the real world, anthropologists who specialize in the ethnography of communication obtain their data from direct observation of communicative performances. The social unit to which studies in ethnography of communication refer is the speech community—that is, all those people who share at least one speech variety as well as specific rules for the social uses of speaking and for interpreting what is being communicated.

An understanding of the diversity in the ways of communicating is of course of great interest to linguistic anthropologists, but we need to look beyond the merely intellectual satisfaction derived from the study of the subject. There is reason to hope that the application of the growing body of information in the field of ethnography of communication may contribute to the solution of some of the social problems of societies in which many peoples live side by side but do not always share the same ways of speaking.

11

Culture as Cognition, Culture
as Categorization: Meaning and
Language in the Conceptual World

We have already seen that minimal units of sound (phonemes) are used to compose morphemes, the smallest units of grammatical or lexical function. These morphemes combine to make up the words of our vocabulary. Words form into sentences, and these sentences make up conversation and discourse. But when does language cease to be self-contained? At some point language must make contact with the outside world. As the noted twentieth-century linguist Dwight Bolinger said, this point of contact is what we call meaning, and the study of meaning is generally referred to as **semantics** (1975:185).

But this connection is hardly foregone or obvious. Probably no two things are more unlike than utterances of sounds and things in the world (though through force of habit, these connections come to seem only natural and unquestionable to us). But what some word or sentence means is hardly transparent (see Box 11.1). For example, one of the first words a child learns is the word for mother, but this is done only in the context of a single case—one's own maternal parent—and it is not easy to see how this meaning can be extended to all the other mothers in the world. Often we call our own biological mother "Mama," but why can't we do this for other "mothers," such as the head of a Catholic convent? It is doubtful that the nun who won the 1979 Nobel Peace Prize would ever be called "Mama Teresa." But sometime "Mamas" can indeed be found in other places, such as the names of blues singers (Big Mama Thorton), or in the popular *Big Momma's House* movie series starring Martin Lawrence. But why do we say that necessity is the mother—not the father—of invention, and that it is not nice to fool Mother—not Father—Nature? (cf. Macnamara 1982, Lyons 1977, Weinreich 1980).

Modern linguistics has begun to study semantics in a rigorous and systematic way only relatively recently. Part of the reason for this has to do with the influence psychological behaviorism had on the social sciences until the 1960s. *Behaviorism* sought to reduce most of human activity to conditioning and reinforcements. The seminal American structural linguist Leonard Bloomfield viewed meaning as a kind of connected series of speakers' and hearers' stimuli (S) and responses (R): A person is hungry and, seeing food (S), tells another to bring it, which he does (R). Presenting the food to the hungry person (S), elicits a "thanks" in return (R). Meaning arises from the events that accompany an action. For structural linguistics through the 1950s such notions were generally sufficient. They relied on these kinds of "differential meaning" to do their phonemic and morphological analysis. For example, to determine phonemes of a language, they would ask informants to differentiate between two words of a minimal pair, say [art] and [ark]. If the two words did not mean the same thing, it would be concluded that [t] and [k] were different phonemes.

Most linguists of the first half of the twentieth century saw little reason to go much further than this. Even the great pioneer Edward Sapir failed to include a chapter on semantics in his influential classic *Language* (1921). But the limitations of this kind of analysis were apparent to linguists, anthropologists, and philosophers even during the height of structuralism's popularity. Such a narrow semantics precluded explanations of figurative language, metaphorical uses of words, or language change—to say nothing of having little to offer about simple concepts such as **synonyms or homonyms.**

Modern linguistics and philosophy now have a more nuanced view of semantics, realizing that meaning is not something isolated from the rest of language, but is intrinsic to it. If Chomsky is right in claiming that we should study linguistic competence—that is, what speakers know of their language—then semantics must be as important to its description as syntax or phonology. Nonetheless, semantics is quite multifaceted and diverse, being influenced by many different disciplines—from modern computer scientists working on artificial intelligence to classical scholars studying Greek rhetoric.

In the rest of this chapter we will examine meaning from the point of view of the linguistic anthropologist. That is, we will seek to see how meaning emerges through the interactions of culture, cognition, and categorization. We start with some issues of nomenclature—how we might formally define words, concepts, and categories—and we will make some remarks on how such terms have been thought about in the past. We will then look in some detail at how language meets the real cultural world by examining the lexical, grammatical, and social nature of concepts.

BOX 11.1 AN EXAMPLE OF HOW MEANING IS DISCOVERED

It is still not definitively clear how we as children learn what words mean. For the most part, words are never explicitly defined for us, even though many times specific examples are pointed out ("Look, there's a 'puppy' coming!"). Still, this process is often equally mysterious, even to adults, when things are explained to them and they have the intellectual maturity to know what to look for and the tools to do so. A case in point is when one of the authors (Stanlaw) was studying Japanese. The first week of language class he learned two important survival words: "eat" (*taberu*) and "drink" (*nomu*). When Japanese people would consume tea, beer, or water they would *nomu*; when they would consume sushi, hamburgers, or pizza they would *taberu*. There were a few oddities, however (as seen below). Japanese people would *nomu* chicken soup or aspirin, while Americans would "eat" the soup or "take" the aspirin. If something was dropped on the floor, a dog could "eat" it—or *taberu* it—in both languages (even if it was an aspirin). Stanlaw chalked this up to just some of the inevitable exceptions to the rules in learning a foreign language and never thought much more about these peculiarities, as about 90% of the time he ate and drank in Japanese just fine.

	ENGLISH	JAPANESE
water, beer	"drink"	*nomu*
hamburger, sushi	"eat"	*taberu*
chicken soup	"eat"	*nomu*
aspirin	"take"	*nomu*
dog's stuff on the floor	"eat"	*taberu*

(continues)

(continued)

On his first trip to Japan, Stanlaw went to the zoo one day to people-watch and noticed a grade school class on one of their ubiquitous field trips getting a guided tour in the reptile house. After being shown a number of snakes, someone asked the zookeeper "What do pythons *nomu?*" Assuming he was smarter than a Japanese fifth grader, Stanlaw thought the answer would be obvious. Even snakes sometime probably had to "drink" water. He was surprised at the zookeeper's reply, "Pythons *nomu* mice and rats." Pondering how pythons could "drink" mice, it finally dawned on him what *nomu* really meant: "to ingest something without chewing." Pythons, of course, swallow their prey whole, so they don't "ingest by moving the jaws," which is what *taberu* refers to. This is why Japanese can *nomu* soups or aspirins, as these are generally not chewed. A dog, however, will chew something he picks up off the floor, even an aspirin, so the right verb is *taberu* in this case.

Stanlaw went to his Japanese teachers with his new insights: First, in English the world of consumables is divided into liquids (which are "drunk") and solids (which are "eaten"). Second, the Japanese divide the world into actions—whether or not something is chewed (*taberu*) or not chewed (*nomu*). His teachers looked at him as if he had just discovered that the sky is blue or dogs have tails. This fact about the cultural universe was so self-evident to the Japanese teachers that they were at a loss to even know that it had to be pointed out (and in fact, at the time, most Japanese-English dictionaries didn't).

Stanlaw also realized a third thing: In the English world, speakers "take" medicines, regardless of whether they are solids or liquids. So there is another distinction English makes—that between consumables and medicines. It is the *intent* behind the ingestion that is as significant as either the act itself or the item ingested. Dogs snatching up the dropped aspirin are not really "taking" it, they are just eating it as they would any stray scrap of food they find. But if a dog were sick and went to the vet, he might be given some baby aspirins that the owner would be instructed to have him "take" at certain times. These were aspects about the meaning of the English words "eat," "drink," and "take" that Stanlaw had never been explicitly taught. Nor had he really noticed their usage before, even though he had been using these words—presumably correctly—for decades.

Jim Stanlaw

Concepts, Words, and Categories

A commonly held view of meaning is that it entails the names of things in the world: "Bill" standing over there, or this "tree" here. These are sometimes called ostensive definitions. But there are many problems with such a view, and we'll mention just three. First, there are many words for which it is hard to see what they refer to in the world (e.g., abstract nouns such as "truth" or "beauty"; properties such as "big," "terrible," or the "redness" of an apple; or verbs such as "thinking" or "doing"). Second, there are some things that are named but do not exist (e.g., "unicorns" or "Godzilla"). Third, when we say the word "tree" we might not be talking about just this particular tree in front of us, but of treeness (the quality or nature of trees).

Some early rhetoricians argued that the things in the world (**referents**) and the words (**symbols**) that refer to them are mediated by concepts in the mind that underlie them (thought). This is reflected in the left diagram below, the famous "semiotic triangle" of Ogden and Richards (1923:99). For example, seeing an actual physical referent, such as a "tree," conjures up thoughts about trees, giving rise to the spoken symbol, that is, the word T-R-E-E. Of course, things can go the other direction: hearing someone say the word "tree" puts all these same processes in reverse motion. There have been dozens of varieties of the semiotic triangle—all emphasizing different aspects of the connections between objects in the world, the words used to symbolize them, and the thoughts these words generate—and we will use the version depicted on the right for our discussion here.

"Concepts" and "words" are often not distinguished, and much of the literature uses the terms interchangeably. By concept we mean a nonlinguistic psychological representation of a category or class of entities in the world (Murphy 2002:385). A word is the linguistic—usually spoken—manifestation of that representation. Concepts, then, are the mental glue (Murphy

2002:1) that ties past experiences—our knowledge of some category or class of objects in the world—with our present experience in labeling them by means of words.

Categories are subtle. We can begin thinking about categories by realizing that no two objects in the real world are exactly the same. No matter how close they may seem, given enough time and attention to detail, we can always find some differences between them. If the differences do not matter, the two items are placed in the same category. If these differences do make a difference, then they are not. Categories, then, are the bridge between the necessity of making generalizations (and ignoring differences that don't matter), and the necessity of making distinctions (and attending to differences that do make a difference). This has some important implications.

First, perception is just as much about ignoring stimuli as it is about responding to them. We have an infinity of stimuli coming into our brains at any given moment. A language or culture's categories allow us to filter out the unimportant from the important. Second, the human brain allows us to react to the world using categories instantaneously. If we had to look at, and uniquely respond to, every desk in the classroom as we walked in, it would take us an hour to take a seat. Classifying them all together as "desks"—where presumably one is the same as any other—allows us to get on with more important things, such as today's quiz or the person sitting next to us.

Both perceptual devices—editing out and taking in stimuli—are necessary to apprehend the world, and presumably most, if not all, of this is conducted through the medium of the categories of one's language. But getting at these categories is not an easy thing to do. How and when we create categories is rather complicated, and will be discussed in more detail in the next sections. For now, we can think of a category as a set of referents that is somehow grouped together.

Sometimes the terms "categories" and "concepts" are used interchangeably, and other authors use them in somewhat different ways. At any rate, there are five points to notice: (1) Categorization by itself is not necessarily useful, but it is our ability to apply our knowledge *about* the category that makes categorization useful. (2) Here we are not talking about a single referent, as in the classic semiotic triangle on the left above, but of classes or kinds of referents. This is analogous to the notion of the phoneme; that is, a group of sounds that are psychologically thought of as being the same (in spite of certain phonetic differences between their allophones). (3) The essential aspect of cognition is the ability to categorize: to judge whether or not a particular thing is an instance of a particular category (*Rover* is a "dog"; *Garfield* is a "cat"). (4) The ability to apply categories successfully is "indispensable in using previous experience to guide the interpretation of new experience: without categorization, memory is virtually useless" (Jackendoff 1983:77). (5) We should remember, however, that although categories are indispensible for living, not all categorization is necessarily linguistic. Animals must do so all the time—this is "eatable," this is "harmful"—without using *linguistic* categories.

Finally, we should note that some semanticists and linguists use the term "lexeme" or "lexical item"—rather than "word"—when they want to distinguish a word as an abstraction from any of its specific forms or parts of speech. For example, there is some underlying notion of "runningness" in the terms "run," "ran," "running," "runs" and so on, that would be missed if we considered them to be different terms entirely. We will now look at how concepts become incorporated into language by way of words, grammar, and discourse.

The Lexical Nature of Concepts

One of the primary ways meaning is demonstrated in language is through its words. Words are basic to all communication, and seem to be the first things children learn when acquiring their language. Indeed, as anyone who has ever been to a foreign country can tell you, knowledge of a few words can sometimes get you a long way, even if your command of the other aspects of the language are limited.

Sense vs. Reference. In our discussions of the semiotic triangle we saw that the term *referent* was used when speaking about concrete real things, such as a tree. Reference, then, deals with the connection between a specific expression and a specific case or individual instance. But we can also look at trees as an abstraction. In short, *reference* deals with things in the real world, but *sense* is concerned with how a word contrasts with, or is related to, other words.

In one way, we might think of sense as the way lexemes are organized in a language. Sense is the set of relations among lexical units, or semantic relations among words. There are many kinds of these relations. Two words are said to be **synonyms** if they have the same sense. For example, *big* and *large, cat* and *feline,* or *to investigate* and *to research* might be examples of pairs of synonyms (or near synonyms) in English. Synonymy is common in every language, as an examination of any dictionary can show. However, it is doubtful that any two synonyms mean exactly the same thing, as is often clearly revealed by usage. A *big brother* and a *large brother*, for example, probably do not sound like the same thing to native English speakers.

Another important relation is inclusion. Here two terms, X and Y, are linked by inclusion if we can say "X is a kind of Y." An *oak* is a kind of *tree*, a *thoroughbred* is a kind of *horse*, and a *Ford* a kind of *car*. The more inclusive and broader terms such as *tree*, *horse*, and *car* are called superordinate terms.

Some lexemes may be related through coextension (MacLaury 1997). Sometimes this appears as overlap, where terms may share some, but not all, semantic properties. For example, *turquoise* may be thought to have elements from both *blue* and *green* colors. At other times, a coextensive relation may indicate that two terms may be synonyms (or near synonyms) in free variation, but have different focuses. For example, "The Sears Tower is very tall" and "The Sears Tower is very high" both suggest that *tall* and *high* are near synonyms, but closer inspection reveals this is not so (e.g., *high ceiling* vs. **tall ceiling*). John Taylor argues (2002:269) that these two terms differ because *high* can designate both "vertical extent" (height measured from the bottom to the top of something) and "vertical position" (height measured from one reference point to another: e.g., the floor up to the ceiling). *Tall* is used only for vertical extent, never for vertical position.

Antonyms are two terms that have the opposite meaning. Some are absolute, such as *right* vs. *left*. Others, such as *hot* and *cold*, are gradable. For example, we can see the continuum of degree of temperature in the following terms: *very hot, hot, warm, lukewarm, tepid, cool, cold, very cold*. Absolute antonyms have been of special interest to structural anthropologists, among them Claude Lévi-Strauss (1963), where they are often termed **binary oppositions**. Binary oppositions abound in all languages of the world, for example, *up-down, male-female, inside-outside, night-day, raw-cooked, good-evil, sacred-profane*. They appear often in word associations protocols (e.g., What first comes to mind when I say the word *"white"*? *"Black"*). Early structural anthropologists believed that binary oppositions were powerful devices that cultures used to form and organize human thought; perhaps they even had a biological or neurological basis, based on visual perception. All people everywhere were said to think about the world in terms of binary opposites, and many aspects of culture could be understood in this way. For example, Lévi-Strauss found that among the Gê of the Amazon rain forest, villages and kinship systems were divided into competing halves. Nonetheless, these rival halves mediated their conflicts, for example, through marriage exchanges. Such practices were said to be universal, and many aspects of culture—from kinship, to mythology, to cooking behavior—demonstrated the cross-cultural importance of binary oppositions.

Graphically, these relationships—synonyms, inclusion, coextension, and antonyms—can be depicted below for two hypothetical lexemes, A and B. Starting at the left, the semantic fields of A and B almost completely overlap as an example of synonymy. Next, B is included in the field of A as an example of inclusion. A and B partly overlap in a relationship of coextension in the third diagram. At the right, A and B do not overlap at all, and if they are antonyms, then they represent completely opposite semantic fields.

Two other notions concerning words should be mentioned before we go on. In **polysemy,** a single lexeme carries more than one meaning. In English, for example, *patch* can mean a small plot of land, a piece of cloth used to repair a hole, an emblem worn on a uniform, a small bandage, or an eye cover, among other things. In **homonymy,** however, two different lexemes have the same appearance. These are the kinds of entries that are typically noted by superscripts in dictionaries (e.g., [1]*sole,* [2]*sole,* [3]*sole,* and [4]*sole*).

Connotation vs. Denotation. The definition of **denotation** is quite close to reference in many ways, and semanticists and linguists generally use the two terms interchangeably. Denotation is the relationship between the lexical item and the thing or class of things it refers to. Denotation might be thought as the explicit dictionary definition of a word, detached from its associations, e.g., *winter* as a particular time of the year, regardless of whether it is pleasant or not, or *dog* apart from his being man's best friend. **Connotation,** in contrast, refers to the emotional feelings that are tied to that lexeme. For Shakespeare, "winter" was not just one of the four seasons but a time "of our discontent." A dog is not just a particular kind of domesticated animal but connotes feelings of loyalty and companionship.

It is obviously very hard to measure connotation, but the cross-cultural psychologist Charles Osgood developed a **semantic differential** scale in the 1970s as one means to quantify the connotative meaning of words and concepts. Basically, using a number of sets of bipolar adjectives ranked on a seven-point scale, informants were asked to rate a presented item. For example, one might ask, as Krus and Ishigaki (1992) did, how someone feels about World War II Japanese kamikaze pilots by checking one of the seven spaces below (kamikaze pilots were assigned to make a suicidal crash on a target):

good——————bad

7 6 5 4 3 2 1

Other pairs of adjectives are also used (e.g., weak-strong or warm-cold). These pairs of adjectives are typically found in all the languages that have been investigated. The advantage of using a numbered scale and a variety of experimental stimuli is that aggregate data can be compiled and compared. For example, Japanese respondents rated the kamikaze pilots an average of 1.7 on the good-bad scale and 2.3 on the warm-cold scale. Americans rated them 1.4 on the good-bad scale and 0.8 on the warm-cold scale. After looking at eight of these kinds of scales, Krus and Ishigaki interpreted them to mean that modern Japanese people (who were the subjects of the test) no longer see the kamikaze pilots of their grandfathers' generation as making a logical and rational choice to defend the country—a claim the overwhelming number of kamikaze survivors and their trainers make, and which was also presumably the conventional wisdom of the time. In these scales, the Japanese respondents differ little from Americans. However, in certain "subtle scales," such as beautiful-ugly and warm-cold, Japanese respondents are much more positive. "[O]n the level of the indirect descriptions using the subtle scales, they describe the Kamikaze pilots in terms that suggest a positive emotional response associated with the Japanese pilots wearing the God's Wind scarf over their foreheads during their final encounter with the enemy" (1992:602).

Osgood and others (e.g., Heise 2010) make two major claims about the use of the semantic differential. First, they argue that ultimately, after collapsing scales, there are three recurring attitudes that people use to appraise items: evaluation, potency, and activity. Evaluation is typified by the good-bad scale. Potency is typified by the strong-weak scale. Activity is typified by the active-passive scale. Second, they claim that the semantic differential is valid cross-culturally. However, the scales can be difficult to interpret. It is hard to know what to make of the fact that 100 Japanese rated the term *kamikaze pilot* as 2.3 on a 1 to 7 warm-cold scale. If next year the results are 4.6, does this mean the pilots are now regarded twice as positively? Such questions are still open. However, for all its limitations the semantic differential is widely used in attitudinal research. Few other techniques have been as extensively used to measure affect and connotation.

The Rise and (Relative) Fall of Ethnoscience

The well-known anthropologist Ward Goodenough claimed (1964:39), "We learn much of a culture when we learn the system of meanings for which its linguistic forms stand. Much descriptive ethnography is inescapably an exercise in descriptive semantics. . . . [However,] relatively little [systematic] attention [has been] devoted . . . to isolating the concepts or forms in terms of which the members of a society deal with one another and the world around them, and many of which are signified lexically in their language." Goodenough was writing at a unique time in the history of anthropology. The Allied victory after World War II made the United States an economic and military superpower. Turning away from its prewar isolationism, American foreign policy became increasingly proactive and internationalist. At universities and colleges, area studies programs proliferated; and anthropology departments, and their students, exponentially increased. Thus, more Americans were becoming professional anthropologists than ever before, and more fieldwork was being conducted.

Several other things happened in the 1950s and 1960s that caused some anthropologists to re-evaluate certain prewar assumptions about the discipline. For one thing, anthropologists rediscovered that culture was not only encoded *in* language, it was encoded very much *like* language. This entailed three points (Stanlaw 2004b): (1) Culture appeared to be rule-bound, as consistent and replicable behaviors were easily found. (2) The natives knew these rules well, as children acquired them very early and most adults made few mistakes. (3) As much as these rules were internalized, the natives were always hard-pressed to explain them adequately.

All these contradictions came together in the 1960s and 1970s into what was called at the time the **new ethnography**, and later **ethnoscience**. The new approaches focused on lexical classification of the social and physical environments of speakers of a language by means of its vocabulary rather than the relationships of grammatical categories. This was definitively an emic rather than an etic approach. But an important motivation was to try and make anthropology more scientific. As more fieldwork was being done, concerns over ethnographic *validity*—that is, how do we know we found out what we thought we were looking for?—and *reliability*—if I did this study again, or if you did it instead of me, would the same conclusions be drawn?—became a nagging problem.

Ethnoscience addressed both the problems of covert rules and reliability (or replicability) directly. The intent was to find a way to extract accurate information from the minds of informants, despite the fact that much of this knowledge was overtly unknown to them. It was thought that finding the appropriate methodology was critical, and several related techniques were proposed. The most influential were the study of folk taxonomies and componential analysis. In both methods, however, the assumption was that in general the words in a language reflect the mental categories and the cultural elements held by the speakers. However, this idea, as we will see, is problematic.

A good example of viewing a domain of another culture with the help of native categories was the work of Charles Frake on how disease is diagnosed among the Eastern Subanun, slash-and-burn farmers of western Mindanao in the Philippines. Sickness is one of the most frequent subjects of conversation among these people, and consequently their language has many terms related to disease. Frake's paper is a partial analysis of 186 disease names, one of the numerically more modest terminological sets in Subanun. (The following English labels briefly explain but do not define Subanun terms.) Among the names of human diseases Frake recorded, some were descriptive phrases such as *meŋe-bag gatay* 'swollen liver,' but most of the disease names were expressed by a single Subanun word. Let us consider the term *nuka* 'skin disease,' which contrasts with, for example, *samad* 'wound,' and *pasu?* 'burn.' There are several varieties of *nuka: pugu* 'rash,' *meŋebag* 'inflammation,' *beldat* 'sore,' *buni* 'ringworm,' and others. A *beldat* 'sore' is further classified according to depth (shallow as against deep), distance from the point of origin or attachment (away from, or distal, as against close to, or proximal), severity (severe as against mild), and spread (single as against multiple), with each of the existing varieties referred to by a Subanun term—for example, *telemaw glai* 'shallow distal ulcer (considered severe),' *selimbunut* 'multiple sore,' and the like. The diagnosis of any particular disease may require advice from different people who judge, among other things, whether a particular *baga?* 'proximal ulcer' is shallow (*baga?*) or deep (*begwak*). But proper diagnosis is not an end in itself, it is a pivotal cognitive step in the selection of culturally appropriate responses to illness by the Subanun [and] bears directly on the selection of ordinary, botanically-derived, medicinal remedies from 724 recorded alternatives. The results of this selection . . . influence efforts to reach prognostic and etiological decisions [decisions having to do with the causes of a disease and the prospect of recovery], which, in their turn, govern the possible therapeutic need for a variant of one of sixty-one basic named types of propitiatory offerings. (Frake 1961:131)

In doing a folk taxonomy, the field-worker tries to uncover how natives conceive of the structure of a particular domain. As a simple example, consider the concept of 'cars' in the United States. Americans love their cars, so it is not so surprising that they have hundreds of names for them. But how is this knowledge of cars structured in their heads? One thing we might do is first elicit as many car terms as possible. We might ask someone, "What are all the different kinds of cars you know?" and write all these words down. We would elicit names like 'Fords,' 'Chevys,' 'hatchbacks,' 'Mitsubishis,' 'Corvettes,' and so on (Stanlaw 2004b). The result of data concerning foreign cars obtained from an informant may then be represented as follows:

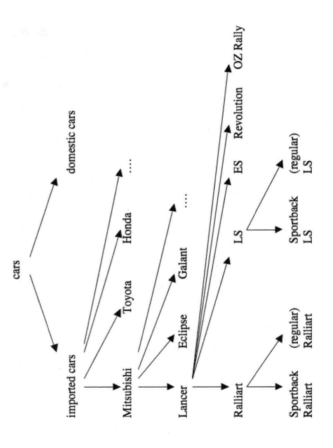

Componential analysis has similar techniques and goals. Here the focus is on the necessary and sufficient features that are used to distinguish all the terms in the domain. For example, in table below (Stanlaw 2004b) we see how the properties of *diet* vs. *non-diet* and *caffeine* vs. *caffeine-free* accounted for all the different kinds of Coca Cola drinks there were, at least a decade ago.

	+caffeine	-caffeine
-diet	COKE	CAFFEINE-FREE COKE
+diet	DIET COKE	CAFFEINE-FREE DIET COKE

Now there are different flavors, such as *cherry* Coke and *vanilla* Coke, so we have to modify our table to account for this third dimension, *flavor*. These new data might be accounted for in a table like that shown below.

		+caffeine	-caffeine
regular	-diet	COKE	CAFFEINE-FREE COKE
	+diet	DIET COKE	CAFFEINE-FREE DIET COKE
cherry	-diet	CHERRY COKE	--------
	+diet	DIET CHERRY COKE	--------
vanilla	-diet	VANILLA COKE	--------
	+diet	DIET VANILLA COKE	--------
lemon	-diet	LEMON COKE	--------
	+diet	DIET LEMON COKE	--------
lime	-diet	LIME COKE	--------
	+diet	DIET LIME COKE	--------

The appealing thing about an analysis in terms of components, as shown in these figures, is that such an analysis is economical and can readily be changed or expanded in light of new information. For example, in 2005 another diet product, Coca-Cola Zero (sweetened with aspartame), was introduced, as was the short-lived Raspberry Coke. In 2007, Diet Coke Plus (supposedly a "healthy soda" containing vitamins B6, B12, magnesium, niacin, and zinc) was also marketed. Had these products lasted, they could have easily been incorporated into the table above by adding new component features.

Initially, using the standard questions (called *elicitation frames*) to uncover the underlying properties of various domains was thought to be productive. It seemed to offer recipes that would insure that anthropologists would get pretty much the same data if they were working on the same topic at the same place. It also seemed to offer a way to get at some of the cognitive patterns used by informants themselves to structure their world, even if they didn't articulate them—or could not articulate them.

Optimism was high, and two special issues of the *American Anthropologist* (Romney and D'Andrade 1964, Hammel 1965) offered legitimacy to what came to be called cognitive anthropology. Important edited volumes (e.g., Tyler 1969, Spradley 1972) saw cognitive anthropology being fruitfully applied to the study of kinship systems, as well as to a number of special domains such as disease terminologies, categories of beer in Germany, and spatial concepts of the homeless. Plant terminologies (e.g., Berlin, Breedlove, and Raven 1974), zoological classifications (e.g., Brown 1984), and ceramics and material culture (Kempton 1981) were also extensively analyzed in this way with good success.

By the 1980s, however, it was clear that ethnoscience as initially conceived was not fulfilling its promises (Stanlaw 2004b). Although the specifics of certain domains were elucidated, many anthropologists began to wonder whether it wasn't just "hocus pocus," as one early critic alleged (Burling 1964), or a "paradigm lost" (Keesing 1972). Part of the problem was that the notion of classification itself needed rethinking (e.g., Kronenfeld 1996). Some argued that the idea that a domain could be defined by just discovering its necessary and sufficient features was proving simplistic or ethnographically inadequate. Such analysis ignored, for example, the fact that cultural knowledge is interlocking, and organized on the basis of principles relevant to, and emergent from, experience (Stanlaw and Yoddumnern

1985:152). And it soon "became evident that there is a problem inherent in determining core meanings in a vastness of meaning-influencing contexts" (Shaul and Furbee 1998:166).

It would be incorrect to think that ethnoscientists were the first cultural anthropologists to insist on the importance of discovering how a culture is seen from the perspective of the society's members. Such a view has had a long tradition in American anthropology. Nevertheless, the practitioners of these recent approaches have made some valuable contributions to the study of culture; they have elicited helpful data by making the language of those they study a rich source of information rather than merely the means of communicating. The main shortcoming of the ethnoscientific method is that its emphasis on understanding culture through language results in the neglect of nonverbal behavior and those aspects of culture that lie outside the domains accessible through terminological sets.

Sound Symbolism and Synesthesia

One of the tenets of modern linguistics, going back to the beginnings of the twentieth century, was the arbitrariness of linguistic symbols (words). If words were arbitrary, then common sense would suggest that the components of words—sounds—should be equally arbitrary, and carry no independent meanings on their own. But things might not be quite that simple.

There are two terms that describe some direct associations often found between form and meaning in language. **Synesthesia** is the stimulation of one sense by another. For example, the famous jazz musician Duke Ellington was said to "hear" colors: "I hear a note by one of the fellows in the band and it's one color. . . . If Harry Carney is playing, D is dark blue burlap. If Johnny Hodges is playing, G becomes light blue satin" (George 1981:226). **Sound symbolism** is the presumed association of sound and meaning found in some cases in many of the world's languages.

One of the first anthropologists and linguists to address sound symbolism was—once more—Edward Sapir (1929b). He invented two words, *mal* and *mil*, and asked English informants to indicate whether these referred to a "large" or "small" table. A majority of this informants said that the word with the high front vowel (*mil*) was the small table, suggesting that phonemes in isolation might hold meaning. However, no real evidence of symbolic representation of magnitude in natural language has been revealed. But when placed in the context of whole words, some intriguing things appear. For example, consider the table below:

fl-	*gl-*	*sn-*	*š-*	*-š*	*θ-*
flash	glisten	snout	sharp	splash	throw
flicker	gleam	sneeze	shear	crash	thrust
fly	glitter	sniff	shred	crush	thump
flow	glow	snore	shard	slash	throttle
flutter	glaze	snort	shave	thrash	thrash

sl-	*pr-*	*-p*	*-rl*	*w-*	*-b*
slug	probe	snap	swirl	wobble	knob
slack	prick	clip	twirl	weave	glob
sloth	prong	zip	curl	wander	lobe
slow	propel	rip	unfurl	waggle	nib
slouch	press	tip	spiral	wave	boob

sw-	*-z*	*-f*	*-l*	*-k*	*-i-/-i*
swat	wheeze	cough	tickle	crack	teeny
swish	ooze	woof	wiggle	creak	tiny
sway	sleeze	puff	rustle	crick	weenie
swirl	sneeze	poof	snuggle	flick	jimmy
swing	breeze	huff	sniffle	kick	baby

Probably most English speakers can sense something that all words in every column share, even if they cannot define it. For example, the words in the first fl- column are associated with things that are flexible, such as a flag fluttering in the breeze. The gl- column refers to shiny or sparkling objects. The sn- words in the third column conjure up connections to the nose or sinus. Next, the initial sh- (š-) words are associated with cutting things with a sharp-edged object. The word-final -sh (-š) words in the next column seem to invoke a feeling of something hitting or coming into contact with something else. The th- (θ-) words in the last column of the top row arouse feeling of some kind of definitive—or even violent—action, perhaps with hands or arms.

There are many other examples. The question now is whether sound symbolism is universal. It seems all languages have some of it. But does sound symbolism operate the same way? Some evidence suggests that it does, at least for some sounds. For example, John Ohala showed that Sapir's intuition that high front vowels are associated with smallness has support from data from numerous other languages. For instance, consider the forms below (adjusted from Ohala 1997:99–100 for our purposes):

Language	"small/diminutive"		"large/largeness/fat"	
English	teeny	[titʃíkítsi]	large	
Ewe		[kitsíkítsi]		[gbàgbàgbà]
Yoruba		[bírí]		[bírí]
Spanish	chico		gordo	
Greek		[mikros]		[makros]
French	petit		grand	

This and other evidence seems to support the contention that "small" is associated cross-linguistically with high front vowels, high tones, and voiceless consonants; and "big" with low vowels, low tones, and voiced consonants. Some have argued that evidence of sound symbolism is found in other domains, for example, proximity and distance (Tanz 1971), but these connections have been less studied.

There also seem to be cross-language universals in paralanguage, such as intonation or stress. Many languages in the world ask questions by using a rising intonation at the end of a sentence. In many languages, including English, pitch becomes lower at the end of normal discourse. Bolinger (1978) found this was true for thirty-eight out fifty-seven languages that do not use tone phonemically. Cruttenden (1986:168) claims that the following tonal patterns are near-universal:

falling intonation in	rising intonation in
neutral statements	tentative statements
ends of sentences	yes/no questions
commands	requests

Studies of Discourse

Many linguistic anthropologists are aware that those native societies in South and Central America that have remained relatively intact are especially suitable for the study of **ethnopoetics.** To be sure, discourse among these peoples is rarely poetic for the sake of aesthetic effect alone; the poetic aspects of discourse are almost invariably integrated with ceremonial, ritual, magical, curative, political, or other functions. Sherzer (1986) illustrated the co-occurrence of the aesthetic and pragmatic functions by analyzing a speech made in 1970 on one of the San Blas islands along the northeast coast of Panama.

The occasion for this particular speech was the homecoming of Olowitinappi, one of the outstanding Kuna curing specialists in the village of Mulatuppu. With the help of a scholarship awarded him by the village, Olowitinappi had gone off to study snakebite medicine with a teacher in another part of Kuna territory. On his return, the village community was eager to hear from him what new curing practices he had learned and how the scholarship money had been spent. Olowitinappi's presentation took place in the centrally located gathering house of the village. His report was very effective, mentioning not only how one can prevent snakebite but also what curing chants should be used and what herbal or other medicines should be applied when someone is bitten. Part of his speech was devoted to a financial accounting for the money he had received. In short, the presentation described in some detail his experiences during the study trip. The speech as transcribed by Sherzer (in 455 numbered lines of text) is followed by a line-by-line English translation and several pages of analytical comments.

The information concerning curing methods and the expenses incurred during the trip was only a part of the presentation. Regardless of what practical goals a Kuna public speaker has in mind, he knows that verbal art is greatly valued among his people and that his presentation will be critically evaluated. An analysis of Olowitinappi's speech must therefore also take into account the poetic and rhetorical devices used in its performance. (In Kuna culture, verbal performers are usually men; women express their artistic talents primarily by making colorful appliquéd blouses.)

To begin with, paralinguistic features need to be considered. Olowitinappi stretched out certain words or phrases to emphasize important points; made use of rising pitch, vibrating voice, and pausing for effect; and on several occasions increased or decreased his volume. Direct quotations of others as well as of oneself are a prominent feature of Kuna discourse. Such quotations, identified by the use of *soke* or *soka* ('I say,' 'he says,' or 'they say') and *takken soke* or *soka* ('see I say,' 'see he says,' or 'see they say'), occurred throughout Olowitinappi's speech. At one point during the speech, Olowitinappi quoted his teacher, who was quoting one of the first great leaders of the

Kuna, who was quoting a member of a neighboring tribe, who was quoting a spirit-world chief, who was quoting God.

Olowitinappi's speech consisted of a series of narrative episodes, embellished by the use of understatement, irony, and humor as well as parallelisms, allusions, and metaphors (for example, "the golden people" refers to the Kuna, and "encountering a vine" refers to being bitten by a snake—a common Kuna euphemism). As Sherzer noted elsewhere, "There is . . . an intimate relationship between Kuna culture and verbal esthetics. Verbal art and . . . verbal play are at the heart of Kuna culture" (Sherzer 1990:6).

Summary and Conclusions

In this chapter we deal with the lexical, grammatical, and social nature of meaning and conceptualization. We find several ways that meaning and concepts appear to be similarly manifested across languages. First, there is a tendency for people to think in terms of linguistic and sociocultural binary oppositions. Second, all languages and cultures classify at least certain aspects of the world through labeled domains which are hierarchical (as in taxonomies) and consist of identifiable components available for formal analysis. These universally demonstrate many of the same properties (e.g., numbers and levels of superordinate terms). Third, there are apparently some direct nonarbitrary associations between form and meaning found in all languages (sound symbolism). Fourth, all languages have rules that govern social discourse and conversation, and these encode the roles of the participants, their points of view, and their presuppositions. Violations of these accepted—though unarticulated—patterns, presumptions, and regulations result not only in miscommunication but also in social sanction.

12

Language, Culture, and Thought

The nature of the relationship between language, thought, and culture was under consideration long before anthropology became recognized as a scholarly field in its own right. Wilhelm von Humboldt (1767–1835), a well-known German diplomat and scholar, was one of those who had very definite ideas on the subject. He wrote, "The spiritual traits and the structure of the language of a people are so intimately blended that, given either of the two, one should be able to derive the other from it to the fullest extent. . . . Language is the outward manifestation of the spirit of people: their language is their spirit, and their spirit is their language; it is difficult to imagine any two things more identical" (1907:42). Not only did the Danish linguist Otto Jespersen declare (1955:17) that language and "nation" (i.e., culture) are synonymous, he even believed that one language—English—was superior to, say, French, because it is a more "methodical, energetic, business-like and sober language, that does not care much for finery and elegance, but cares for logical consistency."

To modern anthropologists these statements are unacceptable in the forms in which they were made. But such quotations show the concern people historically have had about how language reflects the culture of the society it is spoken in, and the thought processes of those who speak it. In this chapter we will look at some of the relationships between language, thought, and culture, in particular, the so-called Sapir-Whorf hypothesis. The **Sapir-Whorf hypothesis** argues, first, that the language one speaks determines how one perceives the world, and, second, that the distinctions encoded in each language are all different from one another. Thus, in its strong form this hypothesis claims that each society and culture lives in it own "linguistic world," perhaps incommensurate with the linguistic worlds of other societies and cultures. If true, this has profound philosophical, social, and even political implications.

The Stimulus of Sapir's Writings

In the past, language, culture, and race were often lumped together as though any one of them automatically implied the other two. One of the tasks and accomplishments of anthropology has been to demonstrate that culture, race, and language are historically separable. Although it is true that human culture in its great complexity could not have developed and is unthinkable without the aid of language, no correlation has yet been established between cultures of a certain type and a certain type of language. In fact, there were and still are areas in the world where societies share a very similar cultural orientation yet speak languages that are not only mutually unintelligible but completely unrelated and structurally different. Such was the case, for example, of the North American Indians of the Great Plains, who possessed many of the same, or very similar, cultural characteristics but whose languages belonged to at least six different language families: Algonquian (for example, Arapaho and Cheyenne), Siouan (for example, Crow and Dakota), Uto-Aztecan (for example, Shoshone and Comanche), Athapaskan (Sarcee and Kiowa Apache), Caddoan (Wichita and Pawnee), and Kiowa-Tanoan (Kiowa). The opposite may also hold true: Estonians and Lapps speak related languages (both belong to the Finnic branch of the Finno-Ugric subfamily of the Uralic family of languages), but their cultures are quite different. The absence of any intrinsic (inherent) relationship among a people's physical type, culture, and language was repeatedly declared by Franz Boas, particularly in his eighty-page introduction to the first volume of *Handbook of American Indian Languages* (1911).

The subject of language-culture relationship was also prominent in the work of Edward Sapir. Although Sapir was convinced, just as Boas had been earlier, that "language and culture are not intrinsically associated," he nevertheless believed that "language and our thought-grooves are inextricably interwoven, [and] are, in a sense, one and the same" (Sapir 1921:228, 232). If the distinction between Boas's view and Sapir's contention, as cited, sounds like hairsplitting, let us try to clarify the difference. Boas and Sapir had no doubt that the association of a particular culture, physical type ("race"), and language was not given by nature but was a historical coincidence. If this were not so, how could it happen that peoples of different physical types speak the same language or closely related languages and that peoples of the same or similar physical type speak a variety of different and completely unrelated languages? The same sort of random association holds true for language and culture as well as for language and physical type. However, Boas and Sapir believed that inasmuch as each particular language serves a particular society and is instrumental in helping the youngest members learn to operate within the society's culture, some relationship between the language and the culture could be expected to develop.

Because Sapir's writings aroused a great deal of interest in the question of how languages influence the culture of their speakers, it is important to take up the recent history of this subject in more detail and also to examine it from the perspective of contemporary anthropology. Sapir, who had come to the United States at the age of five, became acquainted with Boas at Columbia University while doing graduate work. Impressed by Boas's breadth of knowledge and field experience, he switched from Germanic studies to anthropology. From that time on, most of his energies were devoted to the study of Native American languages. He published prolifically, his book *Language* (1921) remaining a classic to the present day.

In *Time Perspective in Aboriginal American Culture* (1916), Sapir discussed various methods that can be employed to develop cultural chronologies for aboriginal America whenever native testimonies and historical or archaeological records are either lacking or of little or no help. Sapir observed that compared with changes in culture, linguistic changes come about more slowly and evenly, and that language is far more compact and self-contained than culture taken as a whole and therefore is largely free of conscious rationalization on the part of its speakers. Major revolutions, whether violent or not, usually change profoundly the structure of the societies in which they occur, yet languages remain unchanged except for relatively minor adjustments in vocabulary.

Two examples from the many given by Sapir illustrate his use of language as a key to the cultural past of a society. Mount Shasta in northern California was visible to a number of Native American groups. Among these, members of the Hupa tribe referred to the mountain by the descriptive term *nin-nis-ʔan ɫak-gai* 'white mountain,' whereas the Yana name for it was *waġalu*, a word no longer translatable or analyzable. According to Sapir, the Yana word is therefore undoubtedly much older, and one may assume that the country dominated by Mount Shasta was home to the Yana long before the Hupa came to the region. For the Northwest Coast, Sapir considered the

Nootka word *tło-kwa-na*, which refers to the wolf ceremonial complex of the tribe. Because Nootka words characteristically consist of one syllable (made up of a consonant-vowel-consonant sequence) rather than three syllables, the form of the term suggests that it, along with the ceremony, may have been borrowed from another tribe. And indeed the neighboring Kwakiutl people have a wolf dance to which they refer by a term that appears to be the source of the Nootka word. Linguistic data in this case indicate not only that at least some aspects of a culture complex may have been borrowed by another tribe but also which tribe was the likely source of the influence.

What caught the imagination of a great many scholars and inspired active research for several decades, however, was a particular paragraph of a paper Sapir read in 1928 at a scholarly meeting in New York attended by linguists and anthropologists:

In a sense, the network of cultural patterns of a civilization is indexed in the language which expresses that civilization. . . . Language is a guide to "social reality." Though language is not ordinarily thought of as of essential interest to the students of social science, it powerfully conditions all our thinking about social problems and processes. Human beings do not live in the objective world alone, nor alone in the world of social activity as ordinarily understood, but are very much at the mercy of the particular language which has become the medium of expression for their society. . . . The fact of the matter is that the "real world" is to a large extent unconsciously built up on the language habits of the group. No two languages are ever sufficiently similar to be considered as representing the same social reality. The worlds in which different societies live are distinct worlds, not merely the same world with different labels attached. (Sapir 1929a:209)

The most provocative statement was the assertion that humans are at the mercy of the language they happen to speak.

The Whorf Hypothesis of Linguistic Relativity
and Linguistic Determinism

Whereas Boas's and Sapir's ideas concerning the relationship between language and culture primarily influenced only their students and other scholars, the writings of Benjamin Lee Whorf (1897–1941) caught the attention of

BOX 12.1 HOW WORDS AFFECT BEHAVIOR

It was in the course of my professional work for a fire insurance company, in which I undertook the task of analyzing many hundreds of reports of circumstances surrounding the start of fires, and in some cases, of explosions. My analysis was directed toward purely physical conditions, such as defective wiring, presence or lack of air spaces between metal flues and woodwork, etc., and the results were presented in these terms. . . . But in due course it became evident that not only a physical situation *qua* physics, but the meaning of that situation to people, was sometimes a factor, through the behavior of the people, in the start of the fire. And this factor of meaning was clearest when it was a LINGUISTIC MEANING, residing in the name or the linguistic description commonly applied to the situation. Thus, around a storage of what are called "gasoline drums," behavior will tend to a certain type, that is, great care will be exercised; while around a storage of what are called "empty gasoline drums," it will tend to be different—careless, with little repression of smoking or of tossing cigarette stubs about. Yet the "empty" drums are perhaps the more dangerous, since they contain explosive vapor. Physically the situation is hazardous, but the linguistic analysis according to regular analogy must employ the word "empty," which inevitably suggests lack of hazard.

from Benjamin Lee Whorf, Language, Thought, and Reality (1956), 135

the educated public. Whorf, a chemical engineer by training, was a fire prevention inspector and later an executive of a New England fire insurance company. Although he continued to work for the company until his untimely death, in 1931 he enrolled in a course at Yale University to do graduate study under Sapir, who had just been awarded a professorship at Yale. Among Whorf's numerous subsequent publications, the best known are those in which he expounded on what some have referred to as the Sapir-Whorf hypothesis (see Box 12.1).

Expanding on Sapir's ideas, Whorf wrote that

the background linguistic system (in other words, the grammar) of each language is not merely a reproducing instrument for voicing ideas but rather is itself the shaper of ideas. . . . We dissect nature along lines laid down by our native languages. . . . We organize it into concepts, and ascribe significances as we do, largely because we are parties to an agreement to organize it in this way—an agreement that holds throughout our speech community and is codified in the patterns of our language. . . . [Not] all observers are . . . led by the same physical evidence to the same picture of the universe, unless their linguistic backgrounds are similar. (Whorf 1940a:231)

He further asserted that "users of markedly different grammars are pointed by their grammars toward different types of observations . . . and hence are not equivalent as observers but must arrive at somewhat different views of the world" (Whorf 1940b:61). In these passages Whorf set forth a double principle: the principle of **linguistic determinism,** namely, that the way one thinks is determined by the language one speaks, and the principle of **linguistic relativity,** that differences among languages must therefore be reflected in the differences in the worldviews of their speakers.

Many of the examples Whorf used to support his contention came from Hopi, a language spoken by Native Americans in the pueblos of northeastern Arizona. Although Whorf briefly visited the Hopi villages in 1938, the data for his grammatical sketch of the language (1946) were obtained from a native speaker of Hopi who lived in New York City. In an article dealing with grammatical aspects of Hopi verbs, Whorf put forth the claim that the Hopi "have a language better equipped to deal with such vibratile phenomena [that is, phenomena characterized by vibration] than is our latest [English] scientific terminology" (1936:131). Among his examples are the verb forms *wa ´la* 'it (a liquid) makes a wave, gives a slosh,' *ti ´ri* 'he gives a sudden start,' and *ʔi´mi* 'it explodes, goes off like a gun.' These and others can be changed from their punctual aspect (a term used to refer to a verb action concentrated into a very short period of time) to the segmentative aspect by repeating (reduplicating) their last two sounds and adding the ending *-ta* to produce the forms *wala´lata* 'it is tossing in waves,' *tiri´rita* 'he is quivering, trembling,' and *ʔimi´mita* 'it is thundering.'

Whereas in English the difference between something happening once briefly and something occurring repeatedly over time may call for different phrases (for example, "it explodes" as against "it is thundering," or "it makes a wave" as against "it is tossing in waves"), the Hopi express it by the use of a simple grammatical device. In Whorf's words, the example illustrates "how the Hopi language maps out a certain terrain of what might be termed primitive physics . . . with very thorough consistency and not a little true scientific precision" and "how language produces an organization of experience" (1936:130–131).

In another article, written in the mid-1930s but not published until nine years after Whorf's death, the author stated that "the Hopi language is seen to contain no words, grammatical forms, constructions or expressions that refer directly to what we call TIME, or to past, present, or future . . . or that even refer to space in such a way as to exclude that element of extension or existence that we call TIME" (1950:67). Instead, the grand coordinates of the universe for the Hopi are manifest, objective experience and the unfolding, subjective realm of human existence.

Whorf illustrated his notion of linguistic relativity by using as an example the Apache equivalent of the English utterance "It is a dripping spring" (referring to a source of water): "Apache erects the statement on a verb *ga*: 'be white (including clear, uncolored, and so on).' With a prefix *nō*- the meaning of downward motion enters: 'whiteness moves downward.' Then *tó*, meaning both 'water' and 'spring,' is prefixed. The result corresponds to our 'dripping spring,' but synthetically it is: 'as water, or springs, whiteness moves downward.' How utterly unlike our way of thinking!" (Whorf 1941a:266, 268).

Following up on the hypothesis that a language and the culture it serves mirror each other, Whorf compared the Hopi language with western European languages (labeled SAE for "Standard Average European"). According to him, the differences in linguistic structure between Hopi and SAE are reflected in "habitual thought" and "habitual behavior." For example, "the Hopi microcosm seems to have analyzed reality largely in terms of *events* (or better[,] 'eventing'), referred to in two ways, objective and subjective" (1941b:84); the emphasis is on being in accord, by means of thoughtful participation, with the unfolding forces of nature. Speakers of SAE, in contrast, conceive of the universe largely in terms of things and of time in terms of schedules. SAE languages use tense to mark the time at which an action takes place (as in the past, present, future, or, even more specifically, as in "I had eaten," to express the completion of an action before a specific past time). No wonder, then, that speakers of western European languages tend to be preoccupied with "records, diaries, book-keeping, accounting . . . calendars, chronology . . . annals, histories . . . [and] budgets" (1941b:88).

The implications of Whorf's ideas concerning linguistic relativity and determinism are quite serious. If the worldview and behavior of a people are significantly affected by the structure of the language they speak, and if languages differ in structure, then cross-cultural communication and understanding are likely to be noticeably impaired, if not impossible to achieve. This is why Whorf's ideas received a great deal of attention and stimulated much discussion for a number of years after World War II.

Whorf's Hypothesis Reconsidered

From a contemporary standpoint, however, it appears that Whorf overstated his case. According to a strong version of this proposition, lexical and grammatical categories of a language completely determine how its speakers perceive the world around them. This is undoubtedly not true. That we can translate from one language to another belies the correctness of the hypothesis in its strongest form: Humans do *not* live in incomparable linguistic worlds. But according to a weaker version, there is some sort of correlation between a language and its speakers' worldview (the philosophical dimension of a society's culture).

Whorf's Views of Lexical Differences in Language. There is no question that the lexicon of any language mirrors whatever the nonverbal culture emphasizes; that is, those aspects of culture that are important for the members of a society are correspondingly highlighted in the vocabulary. For example, words conveying the various characteristics of camels (age, breed, gender, function, condition, and so on) are undoubtedly more plentiful in a language spoken by Bedouins who depend on camels than they are in English; the vocabulary of American English, for its part, is replete with the names of makes and models of automobiles, with new names of models of the various makes being added every year. In Pintupi, one of the aboriginal languages of Australia, there are at least ten words designating various kinds of holes found in nature or in manufactured objects: *mutara* is a special hole in a spear, *pulpa* is a rabbit burrow, *makarnpa* is a burrow of a monitor lizard, *katarta* is the hole left by a monitor lizard after it has broken the surface after hibernation, and so on. This example also shows that even though a language may not have a one-word equivalent for a word of another language, it is possible to provide an adequate translation by a descriptive phrase (for *katarta* this may take as many as fifteen English words). To avoid wordiness or the use of borrowed words, many languages coin new words. Some years ago, an American anthropologist thought a kinship term was needed to include the meanings of *nephew* and *niece* and coined the word *nibling*, using the word *sibling* (brother or sister) as a model. However, to conclude that the absence of equivalent terms between different vocabularies must always be associated with a different perception of the world would be far-fetched.

Whorf's examples from Hopi also call for comment. According to Voegelin, Voegelin, and Jeanne (1979), the relationship between the punctual and segmentative aspects is not as straightforward as Whorf described it: For example, not all nonreduplicated (not doubled) stems without the ending *-ta* can be said to express the punctual aspect. Furthermore, although speakers of Hopi make little of the division between future and nonfuture, they do indicate tense by temporal adverbs, the suffix *-ni* (future), and the gnomic suffix *-ŋʷɨ* (meaning that something is generally true).

Whorf claimed that the Apache way of thinking is "utterly unlike" that of speakers of English because the utterance "It is a dripping spring" translates literally from Apache into English as "As water, or springs, whiteness moves downward." But suppose that speakers of a foreign language were to interpret literally *breakfast* as "breaking the fast (abstinence from food)," *bonfire* as "a fire of bones, bone fire," and *spinster* as "a woman whose occupation is spinning" and as a result saw a profound difference between their own way of thinking and that of English-speaking people. But some lexical differences between languages may have some consequences as to how speakers view the corresponding parts of their environment. Pronominal usage and kinship will serve as examples.

Pronouns. Speakers of English use the personal pronoun *you* whether they are addressing one or several children, adults, old persons, subordinates, or individuals much superior to themselves in rank. Only when addressing God in prayer or in certain very limited contexts—for example, in the language of the Friends (the Quakers) or in poetry—does one use the pronoun *thou* (which is singular only). The typical situation in other languages, including most of those spoken in Europe, is more complex. When addressing someone, speakers of Dutch, French, German, Italian, Russian, Spanish, and other languages must choose between the "familiar" personal pronoun (T form) and the "polite" personal pronoun (V form) and/or the corresponding verb form. (The symbols T and V are derived from the French *tu* and *vous*, the familiar and polite second-person pronouns, respectively.) In Czech, for example, to address an individual who is closely related, someone socially close and of long acquaintance, or a child below the age of puberty, one commonly uses the personal pronoun *ty*. But in addressing a casual acquaintance, a stranger, or a person deserving respect, one uses the pronoun *vy*, which also serves as the plural of *ty*. A speaker may occasionally wonder, for example, which of the two forms to use when addressing an adult whom the speaker knew as a child and referred to repeatedly as *ty*. A translation from Czech into English, or vice versa, that involves these pronouns (and/or the corresponding verb forms) is therefore not equivalent. The Czech phrases *"ty a já"* and *"vy a já"* both translate into English as "you and I," even though the first one makes use of the informal, familiar—even intimate—pronoun and would not be used in situations in which the formal, polite pronoun of the second phrase would be appropriate. The English translation, then, can only be approximate, as it cannot fully convey the nature of the relationship between the speaker and the addressee.

Pronoun usage in Japanese is more complex than in the Indo-European languages, as other dimensions beside familiarity must be considered. Pronouns must be selected depending on differing levels of intended formality and the gender of the speaker. For example, consider some of the various ways of saying "we" in Japanese:

for female speakers	for male speakers
watakushi-domo	watakushi-domo
watakushi-tachi	watakushi-tachi
watashi-tachi	watashi-tachi
watashi-ra	watashi-ra
atashi-tachi	—
—	boku-tachi
atashi-ra	boku-ra
—	ore-tachi
—	ore-ra

From top to bottom, the terms become less formal. Though there are no exact rules, the levels depicted above probably correspond to intuitions most Japanese native speakers have of how these pronouns should be used. Some of the factors affecting levels of politeness and use of **honorifics** include:

- familiarity (e.g., stranger, family member, friend)
- age (older or younger than speaker)

- professional relations (e.g., boss, salesperson, customer)
- gender (same or different from speaker)
- in-group/out-group (e.g., same family, school, department, company)
- context (e.g., request, command, greeting)

Other Lexical Differences: Kinship Terminology. The Japanese kinship and pronominal systems reflect fine nuances of meaning or social distance. Japanese social structure—a least linguistically—follows what anthropologists call an "Eskimo" kinship terminology. What this means is that the kinship system in Japanese is similar in many ways to the American one, but with three important exceptions:

- terms of address are different from terms of reference
- older siblings are distinguished from younger siblings
- terms for relatives of the speaker are different from terms for others' relatives.

For example, if I were talking to my older brother, I would call him by the kinship term *o-nii-san* ("elder brother" with the honorific *-san* suffix attached)—rather than using his name. If I were talking about my older brother, I would use the term *ani*. If I were addressing someone else's older brother, I would use the family name (with the *san* suffix being obligatory) or a title. To talk about him, I would use *o-nii-san*. When talking to my younger brother, I would use his first name (without the *-san* suffix, or possibly adding the diminutive suffix *-chan*). I would refer to him as my *otōto*. When introducing my wife I would use the term *tsuma* (neutral), *nyōbō* (colloquial) or *kanai* (polite), but would need to use *oku-san* (polite) or *oku-sama* (very polite) for someone else's wife. There are some two dozen terms for wife in Japanese, each reflecting different emotional connotations, social attitudes, and levels of respect. Common these days is even the English loanword *waifu*, which some have claimed entered the Japanese language precisely to *avoid* some of the cultural baggage carried by these other terms.

Let us consider another example, one with even more significant consequences. Among the Arapaho, a Native American tribe of the Great Plains, the term for "my mother" is *néinoo* (Salzmann 1959, 1983). This Arapaho term for "my mother" also applies to ego's mother's sister, a person referred to in the American kinship system as "my aunt" (**ego** is the person of reference to whom others are shown to be related). However, the term by which ego calls his mother's brother is *nési*, roughly equivalent to "my uncle." Similarly, the term for "my father," *neisónoo*, also refers to ego's father's brother, whereas father's sister is referred to as *nehéi*, roughly equivalent to "my aunt." Now if ego's father's brother is termed *neisónoo*, as is also ego's father, it follows that father's brother's wife would be referred to by the same term as ego's father's wife, that is, *nétnoo*. And by the same token, ego's mother's sister's husband is referred to in Arapaho as *neisónoo* 'my father.' Whereas in the American kinship terminology biological parents are distinguished from uncles and aunts, the Arapaho and many other peoples lump together lineal relatives with some of their **collateral relatives**—the biological mother, her sister, and father's brother's wife on the one hand, and the biological father, his brother, and mother's sister's husband on the other (see Figure 12.1). It follows, then, that anyone who calls some relatives of the parental generation by terms that apply to the biological mother and father is in turn called by all these relatives by terms that apply to biological sons and daughters.

Is one to conclude from the Arapaho kinship terminology that the Arapaho are unaware of the difference between a biological mother (or father) and her sister (or his brother)? Of course not. What it means is that the extension of the Arapaho kinship terms *neisónoo* and *nétnoo* from ego's biological parents to additional relatives is paralleled by an extension of ego's behavior toward his or her biological father and mother to all those relatives who are referred to by the same kinship terms. All Arapaho terminological "fathers" and "mothers" have the same obligations toward their terminological "sons" and "daughters," and vice versa, even though opportunities to fulfill them may sometimes be limited by circumstances. Among those "parents" and "children" whose interaction is limited by distance, the emphasis is on extending the relevant attitudes rather than behavior. It is clear that the kinship terminology by which one classifies relatives also governs the type of behavior patterns and attitudes applied to them.

Shape, Color, Space. Several studies indicate that grammatical features may indeed have some influence on memory and nonverbal behavior. Among the best-known studies of this type is the report on an experiment administered to Navajo and white American children by John B. Carroll and Joseph B. Casagrande (1915–1982) in the late 1950s. A speaker of Navajo must choose from among several forms of Navajo verbs of handling according to the

FIGURE 12.1 Partial Comparison of the American and Arapaho Kinship Systems

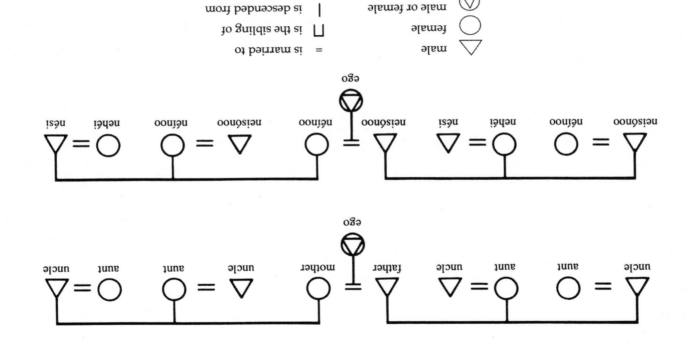

△ male   = is married to

○ female   ⌐ is the sibling of

▽̄ male or female | is descended from

shape or some other characteristic of the object being handled—for example, solid roundish (rock), slender and flexible (rope), flat and flexible (cloth), slender and stiff (stick), noncompact (wool), and so on. Even though the use of the appropriate forms is obligatory, the selection operates below the level of conscious awareness on the part of the speakers, and even children as young as three or four make no errors. (In a somewhat similar fashion, in English one *shrugs* one's shoulders and *nods* one's head, and no native speaker would ever use one term for the other.) One of the hypotheses of the investigators was that this feature of Navajo affects the perception of objects and consequently the behavior of speakers.

Ten pairs of objects were used, each pair significantly differing in two characteristics. The 135 Navajo children who took part in the experiment included some who spoke only Navajo, some who were more proficient in Navajo than in English, some who were balanced bilinguals, some who spoke predominantly English, and some who spoke only English. Each of these children was presented with one of the pairs of objects, shown a third object similar to each member of the pair in one characteristic only (for example, a pair represented by a yellow stick and a piece of blue rope of comparable length, with a yellow rope as the third object), and then asked to match one of the paired objects with the third. The matching on the part of the Navajo-dominant children was predominantly on the basis of shape rather than color, this tendency increasing with the age of the child. Among the English-dominant Navajo children, color appeared to be more important among the youngest, but by the age of ten the two groups had almost converged, with the selection dominated by shape.

The performance of white children in the Boston area was more similar to that of the Navajo-dominant than the English-dominant Navajo children. According to the two investigators, this result may be due at least in part to the early and continued play of white children with toys of the form-board variety, stressing form and size rather than color. On the basis of the difference between the Navajo-dominant and English-dominant groups of Navajo children, the investigators concluded:

The tendency of a child to match objects on the basis of form or material rather than size or color increases with age and may be enhanced by . . . learning to speak a language, like Navajo, which because of the central role played by form and material in its grammatical structure, requires the learner to make certain discriminations of form and material in the earlier stages of language learning in order to make himself understood at all. (Carroll and Casagrande 1958:31)

In general, those examining the relationship between language and culture in recent years have advocated more experimental rigor. They have argued that research concerning this relationship must be comparative, that is, contrast two or more languages, preferably widely differing; that it must use some "external nonlinguistic reality" (stimulus) as a standard for determining by comparison the content of linguistic and cognitive categories; that it must contrast the languages of the respective speech communities to determine how they differ in understanding a common stimulus; and that it must make plain the implication of differences in language for differences in thought between the members of these speech communities (summarized from Lucy 1992a).

For example, some assumptions that notions of space (that is, a three-dimensional area in which events and objects occur and have relative direction and position) are universal—are being reexamined. Stephen Levinson (1996:353) showed that "systems of spatial reckoning and description can in fact be quite divergent across cultures, linguistic differences correlating with distinct cognitive tendencies." More specifically, languages vary in their use of spatial concepts and, in some instances, determine the cognitive categories relating to space concepts; also, the speakers of a number of languages do not use spatial terms corresponding to the bodily coordinates of left-right and front-back. One example comes from the Tenejapa Tzeltal of Mexico: Their language uses no relative frame of reference and therefore has no terms for spatial reference that would correspond to *left*, *right*, *front*, and *back*. Although terms exist for *left hand* and *right hand*, they do not extend to other parts of the body or to areas external to it (Levinson 1996).

Color Nomenclature and Other Challenges to Linguistic Relativity

As intriguing as the linguistic relativity hypothesis is, it is difficult to test objectively. After all, its claims lie in the realm of subjective experience and it is hard to get inside people's heads. Early on, it was thought that one of the areas where linguistic relativity might be empirically examined was color. Around the turn of the twentieth century Franz Boas anticipated much of this later work by stating that

Differences of principles of classification are found in the domain of sensations. For instance: it has been observed that colors are classified in quite distinct groups according to their similarities, without any accompanying difference in the ability to distinguish shades of color. What we call green and blue is often combined under a term like "gall-color," or yellow and green are combined into one concept which may be named "color of young leaves." In course of time we have been adding names for additional hues which in earlier times, in part also now in daily life, are not distinguished. The importance of the fact that in speech and thought the word calls forth a different picture, according to the classification of green and yellow or green and blue as one group can hardly be exaggerated" (Boas 1938:210).

Color terminologies, then, have been a source of fascination for anthropologists ever since early ethnographers noticed that "non-Western" peoples often have very different ways of dividing up the color spectrum. For instance, some languages, it was found, would blend the colors blue and green under a single term (as Boas noted above); others would break up the English reds using three or four separate names. It was puzzling to find that so natural and neutral a stimulus as the color spectrum could be divided up in hundreds of different ways. Such findings supported the notions of the linguistic relativity hypothesis that the distinctions a language makes are arbitrary, and that there is no *a priori* way to predict what distinctions a language might, or might not, make.

Aspects of Formal Color Nomenclature Theory. One of the most important—though also somewhat neglected—studies in color was conducted by Eric Lenneberg and John Roberts (Lenneberg and Roberts 1956). Their idea was to use an array of 320 scientifically calibrated color chips—similar to those you might see on display at a hardware store—from *The Munsell Book of Color,* varying in the dimensions of hue and brightness, and put them together in a physical chart. A more modern version, including ten shades of gray on the left, is shown below (Stanlaw, Arrigo, and Anderson 2006). You can find the full color version at the Virtual Anthropology Color Lab (http://www.mind.ilstu.edu/curriculum/modoverview.php?modGUI=207).

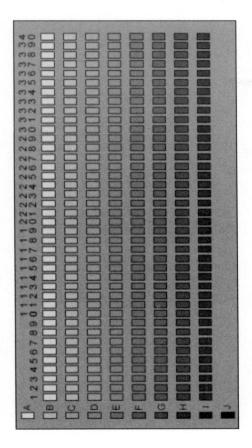

Lenneberg and Roberts worked with the Zuni from the American Southwest and native English speakers, and asked them to circle on this chart all the chips of some color category (e.g., "please circle all the *red* colors").

Lenneberg and Roberts immediately found significant differences between the Zuni and English speakers, both in the number of color terms found in each language and in the ranges informants marked off for these color terms. For example, they found that while English speakers distinguished *yellow* and *orange* colors—and circled them on the chart as two separate groups—Zuni informants circled all the yellows and oranges together as one group (and gave it a single name). Also, they discovered that for speakers of English the color categories varied greatly in size (e.g., *red* being very small and *green* being very large). For Zuni speakers, the categories were generally about the same size. Though the main intention of Lenneberg and Roberts was to provide a tool, and a comparable methodology, that could be used for further research, most anthropologists and linguists through the 1960s felt this was sufficient evidence to provide support for the linguistic relativity hypothesis.

However, Brent Berlin and Paul Kay (1969, 1991), two linguistic anthropologists, expanded the Lenneberg and Roberts experiments for twenty languages, and examined written materials on seventy-eight others. Both studies revealed several similar findings. For example, although Lenneberg and Roberts found that not every language uses the same color terms—and their number was apparently arbitrary—Berlin and Kay concluded that languages tend to use less than a dozen basic color terms. They also found that the chips chosen by informants to represent the ideal example of a color category (e.g., "Which is the best *red*?") were often quite similar across languages.

The critical theoretical insight made by Berlin and Kay was that color terms need to be operationalized. Many local colors in every language mostly depend on the particulars of the environment, for example, "the color of the so-and-so plant" or this or that animal. Such color terms are useful if everyone in the area is familiar with the particular referent. Every language has thousands of these "secondary color terms" as well, including English (*denim blue, fire-engine red,* or *olive green*). But are there some more general abstract colors that all cultures seem to have? It was this question that Berlin and Kay realized needed to be addressed before any real cross-cultural comparisons of color nomenclature could be attempted. They decided to define abstract "basic" terms using the following criteria (1969:5–7):

1. A basic color term should be *monolexemic* and *unanalyzable.* Compounds and terms that are lexically or morphologically modified will not be basic. Thus, "red" and "blue" are basic colors in English, but "reddish," "blue-green," or "light red" are not. Also, a term's meaning should not be predictable from the meaning of its parts (thus excluding such words as "olive green" as basic in English).

2. The meaning of a basic color term should *not be included* in the range of any other term. Thus, because "khaki" is "a kind of brown" it would not be an English basic color term. This means that subsets of colors are not basic colors. "Navy blue" is a kind of blue and therefore not a basic color term in English.

3. The term in question must have *wide applicability,* and not be restricted to any single—or just a few—referents but should exist as an abstract label widely applicable to all objects. Using this criterion, a term such as "blonde" is not basic in English because it usually only refers to hair color. The same applies to "peach," which generally refers only to the light pink of peaches.

4. The term in question must be *psychologically salient* with respect to the number of speakers who use the term, and the number of occasions it is used. That is, the term must be conspicuous either in terms of frequency of usage or extensive occurrence and acceptability in a speech

community. Thus, "sepia" in English would not qualify as a basic color term because it is not well known to all speakers. Common terms such as "white," "red," "blue," and "black" would be.

5. Basic color terms are *consistently productive* using various morphemes in the language. Thus, "red-*ish*" and "green-*ish*" substantiate the status of "red" and "green" as basic color terms in English because it makes sense to use them. However, the problematic status of "crimson-*ish*" confirms that "crimson" is not a basic term.

6. Terms for basic colors should *not name objects*. Thus, terms such as "gold" or "ash" are not basic color terms in English.

7. Recent foreign *loanwords* are suspect, and probably not basic color terms.

8. *Morphological complexity* can be given some weight in determining a lexeme's status, particularly in questionable instances. Basic color terms are the less morphologically complex terms.

A common methodology was now established, as researchers knew what they were looking for to compare: salient abstract colors that had no specific ties to any referent. A list of basic colors would be elicited, and informants then asked, on the Munsell color array, to pick out the one chip that best corresponded to a term (focal color). They would then be asked for the range of each term (e.g., "circle all the chips that you think are *color X*"). Though later work altered the steps somewhat, this general idea has been used for investigating color terms in many studies for the past four decades.

The results of Berlin and Kay's carefully designed experiments were quite surprising, and they stimulated new types of research. In brief, they concluded that:

1. In all languages, there were at least two, but no more than eleven or twelve, color terms that could be considered as basic. Not every language has the same number of basic color terms, though all languages have many sets of culture-specific secondary color terms.

2. These basic color terms label universal perceptual categories ("psychological referents") of which there are probably no more than eleven.

3. These basic color categories are historically encoded in a given language in one of two possible orderings, as given on the next page.

This last finding is most intriguing and very important. Languages seem to develop color categories in strictly limited ways—in seven steps or stages (as labeled in Roman numerals above). All languages in the world have at least the terms for *white* and *black* (Stage I). If a language has only three basic color terms (Stage II), these color categories would always cover *white*, *black*, and *red*. Next is *green* followed by *yellow* or *yellow* followed by *green* (Stages III and IV). The next terms to appear are *blue*, and then *brown* (Stages V and VI, respectively). At Stage VII, *pink*, *orange*, or *purple* could appear in any order or combination. *Grey* was thought to be a wild card that could appear any time after Stage III.

In the decades since the original Berlin and Kay work (1969), many studies have generally supported their original findings, albeit with some modifications. Today, their account is considered to be the standard model of color nomenclature against which all data and other models are evaluated. Though modified and refined, the universalist arguments of Berlin and Kay have remained principally substantiated for the past forty years.

Linguistic Relativity and Gender. Do grammatical features have any influence on how speakers of a language perceive and categorize the world around them? In some instances they do, at least to some extent, but often the influence is negligible, if any at all. To give just one example, consider grammatical gender. In English the word *teacher* refers to a person who teaches, whether it is a woman or a man. From a pupil's remark "Our teacher is too strict," there is no indication of the teacher's gender, though in subsequent conversation gender may be disclosed by the use of the teacher's name or the gender-specific personal pronoun (*she* or *he*). Such ambiguity is not so likely to occur, for example, in German, which distinguishes between the mascu-

```
white            green -->   yellow                              pink
 and   --> red -->      or          --> blue --> brown -->      and/or
black            yellow -->  green                              orange
                                                                and/or
                                                                purple

  I       II      III      IV         V      VI        VII
```

line form of *teacher* (*Lehrer*) and the feminine form (*Lehrerin*). Similarly, the suffix *-in* in German changes *Arzt* 'male physician' to *Ärztin* 'female physician' and *Professor* 'male professor' to *Professorin* 'female professor.' English clearly differs from German in that what is optional in the former is obligatory in the latter. But the claim that this and similar distinctions between the two languages have an influence on the outlook of their speakers would be hard to prove: No one would argue, for example, that sexism is more or less common in countries that speak German, in which the marking of gender is more common (but in these and most other languages, the feminine form is derived from the masculine, as in *lioness* from *lion*, and *Löwin* 'lioness' from *Löwe* 'lion' in German).

Like some other Indo-European languages, German has three genders—masculine, feminine, and neuter—that for the most part have nothing to do with maleness, femaleness, or absence of sexual characteristics. In German, for example, window (*das Fenster*) is of neuter gender; as are girl (*das Mädchen*) and woman (*das Weib*); blackboard (*die Tafel*) is feminine, as is crowbar (*die Brechstange*); and bosom (*der Busen*) is masculine, as are the season of spring (*der Frühling*) and skirt (*der Rock*). Do German-speaking people believe that crowbars and blackboards are feminine in the same way as mother (*die Mutter*) or a woman with whom someone is in love (*die Geliebte*) is? The answer is no.

Theoretical and Philosophical Counterarguments. It was not only the Berlin and Kay work that discredited various forms of the linguistic relativity and determinism; other experiments, and examples such as grammatical gender above, contribute as well. There are also serious theoretical and philosophical challenges. We mention here eight of the more persuasive counterarguments:

1. *Translatability.* Simply put, translation across languages is possible and occurs every day, even between quite diverse languages. This should not be possible if we are experiencing different "realities." Thus, at least a strong Whorfian position—that speaking different languages cause us to live in different perceptual worlds—is questionable.

2. *Mutual linguistic comprehension.* Likewise, even if we grant the possibility that translations can never completely capture what was said in the original, we can still usually get at least the general idea. And even if we cannot know what it is like to be a Navajo or a Japanese—or to

think their thoughts or have their experiences—we can at least entertain the possibility of guessing what another cultural system might be
like.

3. *Language and thought.* It is not clear that all thinking is linguistic in
nature. For example, Keller and Keller (1998) demonstrated that creating a physical artifact is a very different process from verbally describing it to someone. If this is true, how can Whorfian effects
manifest themselves in a nonlinguistic realm?

4. *Multilingualism.* What does the Sapir-Whorf hypothesis say about a
person who grows up learning to speak several different languages at
the same time? In which "linguistic world" does such a person live? A
strong Sapir-Whorfian position does not seem to allow for the possibility of a person being able to go back and forth between two different "realities" depending on the language being spoken. Nor does it
seem to allow for some sort of mixed mental structure combining these
two or more linguistic worlds.

5. *Language change.* One of the problems of the extreme linguistic determinism of the Sapir-Whorf hypothesis is that of change. Languages
and cultures change over time. Both the English and the physics of
Newton's day are different from today. How did the replacement of
Newtonian physics with the theory of relativity occur? Or did the
change come about because of the change in language? Unfortunately
the Sapir-Whorf hypothesis is hard-pressed to answer these questions.

6. *Untestability.* One of the main criticisms leveled against the Sapir-
Whorf hypothesis is that it is untestable, and therefore vacuous no matter how intriguing it may sound (Black 1962). Many philosophers of
science require that a useful theory be falsifiable—that is, one should be
able to state what kinds of evidence would be needed to either support
or refute it. Until recently, the possibility of finding experimental evidence for the Sapir-Whorf hypothesis was rare.

7. *Language and perception.* It appears that at least some aspects of perception are beyond the reach of language-influence or interpretation.
For example, cross-cultural psychologists found certain basic colors—
such as pure "fire engine" red—are easier to remember and recall than
other colors, even if a language has no name for them. It is not yet clear
if such findings are due to anatomical universals (for example, neurology) or other factors. Whatever the cause, it seems that at least some

concepts are not perceptually arbitrary, and some categories—for example, certain vowels and consonants—are more "natural" than others

8. *Language universals.* Since the 1970s linguists have—with great success—become increasingly absorbed in the search for those aspects all languages have in common. For example, all languages are spoken in sentences, and seem to have some notion of subject versus predicate. Most languages have many sounds in common. The existence of these linguistic universals seems to suggest that languages, and the construction of linguistic categories, may not be as totally arbitrary as Sapir and Whorf have implied. In fact, it was the strength of the universalist arguments by linguists such as Noam Chomsky that led to a gradual decline in interest in linguistic relativity.

Theoretical Alternatives to Linguistic Relativity

In the last section we saw that linguistic relativity, at least in unmodified form, is facing some serious challenges. In this section we will look at two theoretical alternatives to linguistic relativity—the commonly accepted universalism of Noam Chomsky, and the approach of cultural determinism (such as proposed by Gary Witherspoon and Daniel Everett).

Chomsky and Universalism. In the mid-twentieth century the intellectual climate underwent a substantial change in attitude towards languages and their structures. Until the 1950s, scholars were relativists. They were most fascinated by the tremendous linguistic diversity found throughout the world. Non-Western languages had some features that the Indo-European languages did not: time was counted in different ways, and words were found for concepts that Europeans hadn't an inkling of. And in many ways this was a holdover from the days of Franz Boas, who made passionate arguments for relativism, mostly in a valiant attempt to undermine some of the racist claims popular even until World War II. To Boas, a belief in universalism usually led to comparisons that left the non-Western world wanting. And such beliefs were only one small step away from dangerous biological reductionism: peoples and their languages are the way they are due to their biology (that is, their race).

But in the 1960s, a brilliant young linguist, Noam Chomsky, wrote a series of books and monographs showing that grammar across all the world's languages is very much the same if you examine them thoroughly. Chomsky has made a compelling case that there is much more linguistic similarity in the world than previously thought. But, more important, his so-called transformational grammar movement has swayed the court of scholarly opinion to a rejection of relativism in favor of universalism. Simply put, universalism is the current standard model in many of the social sciences:

> The dominant view among contemporary linguists is that language is primarily an instinct; in other words, that the fundamentals of language are coded in our genes and are the same across the human race. Noam Chomsky has famously argued that a Martian scientist would conclude that all earthlings speak dialects of the same language. Deep down . . . all languages share the same universal grammar, the same underlying concepts. . . . The only important aspects of language, therefore, or at least the only ones worth investigating, are those that reveal language as an expression of innate human nature (Deutscher 2010:6).

Chomsky turned around some of the questions asked by the early structural linguists. Instead of trying to descriptively analyze sentences that an informant had uttered, Chomsky argued that we needed to find the mental rules that would generate these sentences. Over the course of several decades, Chomsky's formal approaches have gone through several revisions, each refining universalist arguments in more subtle ways. Perhaps Chomsky's most compelling claim for universalism was what he calls the "poverty of stimulus" argument" (1980). According to him, there is simply no way for a child to infer all the complex rules of grammar from mere exposure to its speakers. There must be some knowledge or predispositions already present in the child's brain to enable it to make sense of what it is exposed to. Children, after all, are never really *taught* their native language.

The Claims of Cultural Determinism. There are several ways to view the relationships between language, thought, and culture. As we have seen, linguistic relativists such as Whorf and Sapir claim that languages influence culture, thought, and perception. Universalists such as Chomsky argue that language is an innate human property and that language, culture, and thought have no connections (except insofar as dictated by the limitations and psychobiological structure of the human mind). We might ask if there are those who argue for **cultural determinism**—where culture determines to a large degree grammatical patterns and modes of thinking. Such claims have been made, and we will examine two cases, the Navajo in the southwestern United States and the Pirahã in South America.

Controlling the World Through Language Among the Navajo. The Navajo are among the most extensively studied Native American peoples, and the depth of our understanding of Navajo culture is due in large measure to those individuals who were exposed to the culture for an extended period of time. One such person is the anthropologist Gary Witherspoon, who made the Navajo country his home for more than ten years. Prior to his academic career, he worked for Navajo communities and local boards of education and became an interested and concerned participant in the life of the local communities. He learned the Navajo language by listening to Navajos and talking with them.

In *Language and Art in the Navajo Universe* (1977), Witherspoon shared some of the results of his unique experience with the Navajo language and culture. "In the Navajo view of the world," noted Witherspoon (1977:34), "language is not a mirror of reality; reality is a mirror of language." Ritual language in Navajo culture is powerful, its primary purpose being to maintain or restore *hózhǫ́* (the symbol ['] marks high tone; *ǫ* is nasalized *o*). Although this word refers to the central theme of Navajo worldview and religious thinking, its use is not restricted to ritual contexts—the word is heard frequently in everyday speech. What is *hózhǫ́?* The stem *-zhǫ́* refers to a state characterized by goodness, peace, order, happiness, blessedness, health, beauty (of the natural surroundings), satisfaction, perfection, well-being, deliberation, care, success, and harmony in one's relations with others (the list is not exhaustive but should serve). The form therefore refers not only to aesthetic but also to moral, emotional, and intellectual qualities, and it is difficult to translate into English by a single word or even a phrase. The verbal prefix *hó-*, which is part of *hózhǫ́*, adds to the meaning of the stem the idea of "total environment"—the whole, the general, the abstract, the indefinite, the infinite. As Witherspoon put it, "Navajo life and culture are based on a unity of experience, and the goal of Navajo life—the creation, maintenance, and restoration of *hózhǫ́*—expresses that unity of experience" (Witherspoon 1977:154).

The Immediacy of Experience Among the Pirahã. Linguistic anthropologist Daniel Everett (2005, 2008) has offered some serious formal challenges to Chomskian universalist grammar. A much-discussed article in *Current Anthropology* that captured the attention of many linguists and anthropologists soon after it appeared was called a "bomb thrown into the party" by the noted psycholinguist Steve Pinker (Colapinto 2007:120).

The Pirahã—as described by Everett (2005)—are one of the most interesting peoples in the linguistic and ethnographic literature. Their language supposedly has no concept of counting or ordinal numbers, few, if any, terms for color, a poverty of kinship terms, no tradition of art or drawing to speak of, and one of the simplest pronoun inventories ever documented. For example, for counting, there appear to be only three terms: *hói* ("small size or amount"), *hoí* ("somewhat larger size or amount"), and *ba-a-gi-so* ("cause to come to together"). A single term, *baíxi*, is applied to both one's biological mother and father, and generally there are no gender distinctions in the Pirahã kinship system.

But it is perhaps culturally that the Pirahã are especially intriguing. They have no tales or creation myths, and their discourse almost always consists of descriptions of immediate experience or interpretations of experience. Stories of the past go back only a few generations. Also, the Pirahã continue to be monolingual in spite of more than two centuries of regular contact with Brazilians and other peoples. In fact, Everett argues that there is striking evidence for the influence of culture on major grammatical features of the Pirahã language. Everett hypothesized that the Pirahã embody a living-in-the-present cultural ethos—an "immediacy of experience" principle (2008:15)—that affects every aspect of the language. For example, consider the cultural notion *xibipíío*. As a mere gloss, it might translate as "just now," as in someone arriving, but it really encapsulates a condition whereby an entity comes into sight or goes out of sight (2008:128). It delimits a boundary of direct experience: "When someone walks around the bend in the river, the Pirahã say that the person has not simply gone away, but *xibipíío*—'gone out of experience.' They use the same phrase when a candle flickers. The light 'goes in and out of experience'" (quoted in Colapinto 2007:130). Thus, "The Pirahã language and culture are connected by a culture constraint on talking about anything beyond immediate experience. The constraint, as I have developed my conception of it, can be stated as follows: *Declarative Pirahã utterances contain only assertions related directly to the moment of speech, either experienced by the speaker or witnessed by someone alive during the lifetime of the speaker*" (emphasis in the original; Everett 2008:132).

To be sure, Everett has his detractors, as noted in the commentary to the *Current Anthropology* article itself and other places. Everett questions many of the tenets of the supposed innate structure of universal grammar proposed by Chomsky and in addition, he also questions a Whorfian approach, arguing in essence that it is culture that dictates how language and thought become manifested rather than saying that language determines thought, perception, and culture. His work therefore offers different perspectives that universalists and relativists alike might wish to take into account.

Future Tests of Linguistic Relativity and Linguistic Determinism

In this section we examine a few of the latest experimental findings concerning the Sapir-Whorf hypothesis. We saw that the Berlin and Kay color experiments seemed to cast doubt on the whole enterprise of linguistic relativity. We will see this time, however, that there is also some experimental evidence for the claims of the Sapir-Whorf hypothesis, at least in somewhat weakened forms.

Yucatec Mayan and English Number. John Lucy has examined the Sapir-Whorf hypothesis in several domains other than color. For example, he compared Yucatec (a Mayan language) and American English. The focus of his study has been on the marking of the grammatical category of number (for example, the pluralization of nouns): Is there any correspondence between the grammatical treatment of number and the habitual thought (cognition) of the speakers of Yucatec on the one hand and those of American English on the other?

For example, in English, the marking of the plural is obligatory for numerous "thing" nouns, or countables, such as *child, horse,* or *chair;* the only exceptions in nontechnical contexts are mass and abstract nouns, or uncountables, such as *sand, water, butter,* and *honesty.* By contrast, speakers of Yucatec mark plural optionally and for a relatively small number of nouns. The two languages also differ fundamentally in the use of numerals. In English, numerals modify a noun, as in *one candle* and *two baskets.* In Yucatec, numerals must be accompanied by a special piece of structure, a classifier, that identifies the counted object as to its material properties, as in *un-tz'íit kib'* one long thin wax', referring to a candle.

In nonverbal experimental tasks, speakers of English and Yucatec were responsive to the number of objects presented to them according to how the objects were treated grammatically in the respective language. Speakers of English were aware of the number of animate entities and objects but not of the substances represented by mass nouns; speakers of Yucatec were sensitive to number only for animate entities. In classifying three test objects as to which two of the three were more similar (a small cardboard box, a plastic box similar in form, and a piece of cardboard), speakers of English preferred to classify them according to shape (selecting the cardboard box and the plastic box), whereas the speakers of Yucatec preferred to classify them according to material (selecting the cardboard box and the small piece of cardboard). Although Lucy considered his study exploratory in nature, his findings suggest that "language patterns do affect cognitive performance" or, in other words, that "there is good preliminary evidence that diverse language forms bear a relationship to characteristic cognitive responses in speakers" (Lucy 1992b:156, 158).

Theoretical Considerations. We have looked at three ways to describe the relationships between language, culture, and thought. At the risk of oversimplifying, we might summarize them as follows (with the arrow sign meaning "determines," "affects," "predisposes," or "influences," depending on how strong a claim one wants to make):

Label	Proponents	Claim
linguistic determinism	Whorf, Sapir, Lucy	language → culture, thought, perception
universalism	Chomsky, Pinker	"thought" → language, culture, thought
cultural determinism	Witherspoon, Everett	culture → language, thought

Here, under "thought" for the universalism row, we are actually referring to the psychobiological structures of the human mind. And we should note, too, that probably some of these individuals might not be comfortable being placed in the same pigeonhole on a table. For example, while both Chomsky and Pinker believe that language is innate—a biological instinct—each differs in their view on how this came about. For Pinker (2009), language was an evolutionary adaptation, and was selected for by itself. For Chomsky (2010), language was a biological by-product of other evolutionary adaptations, and was not necessarily selected for on its own.

Are all these positions irreconcilable? Perhaps not, if we view Sapir and Whorf's position in a more nuanced way. Sapir suggested that the lexicon and syntax of a language might compel a speaker to attend to certain environmental features and presumably pay less attention to others. For example, when using pronouns in English we must know something about the sex of the referent we are talking about, as we have to choose among "he," "she," or "it" when speaking. Another way of stating the Sapir-Whorf hypothesis is this:

- Languages have categories.
- These categories are encoded in linguistic features.
- These linguistic features affect cognition and behavior.

However, what Sapir and Whorf believed was that the most important part of these compulsory linguistic choices was not the particular syntactic feature itself but the categorization that was the underpinning of this feature. But where did these categories come from? Categories are not given to a language out of thin air. They must be motivated, and come from somewhere. It is most likely that this underpinning or conceptual framework is largely culturally dependent.

Thus, there is another way of looking at the Sapir-Whorf hypothesis that is often neglected, namely, the cognitive or mental schema that underlie the categories, and ultimately the language itself. Instead of viewing language as modifying perception by way of grammar or vocabulary, another way is to look at the conceptual system that must be underlying it. We see this not as turning the Sapir-Whorf hypothesis around but as extending it. This extended version of the Sapir-Whorf hypothesis, then, might look something like this:

- Culture, society, and environment interact to produce physical-psychological reality.
- People handle this reality through mental models and cultural schemas.
- These mental models and cultural schemas are instrumental in the creation of categories.
- Languages obtain these categories from the above models and schemas.
- Therefore languages have categories.
- These categories are encoded in linguistic features.
- These linguistic features affect cognition and behavior.

The reason why we pay attention to an object's sex when speaking English, therefore, is not because we use the word "he," "she," or "it" when choosing a pronoun, but because we know ahead of time that we must be making a gender-based pronoun choice that we will be looking at the sex of things as we speak. What this means is that we must a have a mental construct or schema in our heads for how reality works—in this case, a world where gender is important, indeed so important that it is encoded in our particular language.

Noting that speakers of a particular language might neglect objects or events that speakers of another language normally take into account, John Carroll also restated the hypothesis of linguistic relativity and determinism in a more modest but more acceptable form: "Insofar as languages differ in the ways they encode objective experience, language users tend to sort out and distinguish experiences differently according to the categories provided by their respective languages. These cognitions will tend to have certain effects on behavior" (Carroll 1963:12; for his examples, see Box 12.2).

Summary and Conclusions

Today, people from a variety of disciplines are coming together to study some of the most basic problems of humanity: What is the nature of knowledge? What is the nature of thought? How is the mind structured? What, if anything, is innate or biological? What is cultural or environmental? Just what *can* we think about—or can *not* think about? Linguistic anthropology has much to contribute to these discussions.

There is no question that languages differ—if only superficially, as contemporary universalist linguists would add. But linguists would agree that any nontechnical utterance can be expressed with reasonable accuracy in any language, although usually not on a word-by-word basis. When it comes to technical subjects, some languages have highly specialized terminologies that may be lacking in others—one could hardly expect to give a report on quantum chromodynamics in, say, Hopi. Yet Hopi has specialized areas in its lexicon that are not matched in English. In general, the aspects of any culture that are worked out in some detail receive corresponding attention in the vocabulary of the language so that the speakers of the language can discuss them with ease and accuracy.

Whorf concerned himself with the important question of language-culture dependency, but he overstated his case. Some of his evidence is anecdotal, that is, short and amusing but not necessarily representative of a specific language taken as a whole. One may also wonder how reliable for the purposes of Whorf's illustrations was his Hopi informant, who resided in New York City and must have been nearly or fully bilingual: If the perception of one's environment is affected by the particular language one speaks, then fluency

BOX 12.2 CARROLL ON LINGUISTIC RELATIVITY

The speakers of one language . . . may tend to ignore differences which are regularly noticed by the speakers of another language. This is not to say that they *always* ignore them, for these differences can indeed be recognized and talked about in any language, but they are differences which are not always salient in their experiences. The effect of any one language category is to lead language users to assume, perhaps mistakenly, that there is uniformity of some sort within the category. . . . For example, historians have pointed out that the use of the term "the Middle Ages" may lead to the false impression that the period between the fall of Rome and the Italian Renaissance was in truth a distinct historical period which had uniform characteristics, throughout its length, which set it apart from other periods. . . .

Let us now analyze a simple cross-linguistic example. In English, it is possible to report about someone, "He went to town." Nothing is said about his mode of travel: he might have walked, run, rode a horse, driven a car, or taken a bus or even a boat or a helicopter. It is well known that in German one would have to specify at least a minimum of information about the mode of travel. Use of the verb *gehen* (as a cognate of *go*, apparently the most direct translation) would imply walking or some other form of self-propelled movement; use of *fahren* would imply going in a vehicle; of *reiten*, going on horseback; etc. Russian, and, it so happens, Navaho, could use an even longer list of verbs to distinguish modes of transportation. Thus, in English, it is possible to focus attention on the mere fact of someone's having departed in the direction of town, even though the speaker of English can be more specific if he wants to: *walked, ran, drove, rode, flew, bicycled, rowed, helicoptered* could be substituted for *went* in the sentence indicated. . . . As compared with German speakers, English speakers are sometimes benefited, sometimes disadvantaged by the possible lack of specificity in the meaning of the English term *go*.

from John B. Carroll, "Linguistic Relativity,
Contrastive Linguistics, and Language Learning" (1963), 12–13

in Hopi and English alike might obscure the contrast between the two. According to Whorf, "the Hopi language contains no reference to TIME, either explicit or implicit" (Whorf 1950:67). Hopi may indeed not have tenses in the same sense that English has (as in *I go, I went, I will go, I had gone,* and so on), but speakers of Hopi are able to refer to the time at or during which an action takes place by using morphemes or words that pertain to such time references as "today, late morning, noon, last night, towards evening, yesterday, tomorrow, day after day, once in a while, from tomorrow on until the next day" and "next year" (Voegelin and Voegelin 1957:24).

We have seen that the breakthroughs of the Berlin and Kay color research established some important universal constraints on the way color categories can operate in a language system and culture. These universal constraints seemed to be so strong—and the evidence presented so overwhelming—that many believed positions such as the Sapir-Whorf hypothesis could be discarded. But we have also found in the experiments discussed in this chapter that there still seems to be much life left in the linguistic relativity hypothesis. Can the two extremes be united, without contradiction? It might be possible.

Sapir was not only a linguist and psychologist but also an anthropologist and poet. He asked questions about the relationships between language, culture, and thought that in many ways were years ahead of their time. The "cognitive anthropology" revolution in America, which began in the mid-1960s, would have disappointed him several ways. First, many anthropologists simply equated cognitive categories with linguistic categories. The assumption was that if we were looking at language, we were looking at the mind. Second, many anthropologists believed that formal devices such as "elicitation procedures" would ensure cross-informant, cross-researcher, and cross-cultural replicability. Sapir understood that things were not that easy.

Today, linguistic anthropologists are more sophisticated, and most are quite sensitive to such philosophically naive assumptions. So a more nuanced way of viewing the Sapir-Whorf hypothesis does not make the claim that language determines behavior or thought in a simple or reductionist way. What we must consider is where the categories and schema that underlie language come from. That is, there is room for culture in the explanation as well, as Witherspoon and Everett remind us. And we must always remember that "language, culture, and meaning have inextricably contaminated each other" (Hill and Mannheim 1992:382–383).

13

Language and Ideology: Variations in Class, Gender, Ethnicity, and Nationality

It is obvious people speak quite differently, even those who share the same native language. But there are other reasons why people speak the same language in different ways. For example—to speak in broad generalizations—a presidential speech sounds different from two young men joking in a locker room, and a retired women's garden party has little in common with the lyrics of a hip-hop artist's song. In this chapter we will discuss some of the sources of language variation.

As we saw in Chapter 1, during the nineteenth century most people thought that physical difference and language were closely connected. That is, people were thought to speak differently because of race. In the early twentieth century, Franz Boas vehemently argued that there is no relationship between race, language, and culture, though this often fell on deaf ears. That children of immigrants learn to speak the language of the new country should be the obvious proof of this statement. However, even today, this is forgotten at times. For example, Chinese Americans are sometimes complimented on their excellent English, even though they (and perhaps even their grandparents) were born in the United States and never learned to speak Chinese. Likewise, language ability is separate from religion, occupation, financial status, or other aspects of culture. Unlike many physical attributes, language and culture are subject to change from generation to generation. In one sense, then, one's language and culture is an individual choice. Thus, differences in language can be readily observed among people in the same speech community.

Early sociolinguists and anthropologists thought that such variety was analogous to geographic dialects. That is, just as differences in speech could result from geographic isolation, social isolation due to **ethnicity**, nationality, or race could also create linguistic variation. Even gender could be a factor, because although women and men share the same space geographically, they might live in different social environments. For example, why don't people always choose the speech variety that would bring to them the most benefit in society? Answering such a question has to do with **language ideology**—beliefs about a language expressed by speakers as their conceptualization of the nature and function of language. In other words, language ideology is the mediating link between social form and the forms of speech.

Language, Social Class, and Identity

One of the most obvious manifestations of social class is found in language—perhaps more so than personal possessions, style, or place of residence. For our purposes, we will reduce class distinctions to differences in economics, education, familial prestige, and some other ways people might rank themselves in society. Speech differences can characterize different economic or social status. In the most extreme situations, such as the castes of India, hereditary social classes restrict the association of their members with members of other classes, and this is often reflected in language. For example, John Gumperz (1958), who spent two years in the Indian village of Khalapur, about eighty miles north of Delhi, reported that although the population at the time of his research was only about 5,000, it was divided into thirty-one endogamous castes, none of which had equal status. The linguistic differences were of several types. For instance, where the majority speech, or Standard, had a contrast between single vowels /a/, /u/, and /o/ and the corresponding diphthongs /ai/, /ui/, and /oi/ before consonants, this contrast was absent in the speech of the Sweeper caste, who had only the simple vowels. Where the speakers of the Standard had /ʊ/ before a stressed vowel in the next syllable, the speech of most of the Shoemaker caste and many of the untouchable landless laborers had /ə/. And there were also some lexical differences between the vocabularies of the different castes. The larger castes had special words for items of their subcultures, such as food, clothing, and the like.

But even in places where the class differences are less pronounced, similar kinds of linguistic stratification can be found. In the United States, William Labov conducted a well-known study of **sociolinguistic change**—linguistic change understood in the context of the society in which it occurs. Labov's pioneering work was concerned with the relationship between the social status of speakers in New York City and their pronunciation of r-sounds. The study was conducted in some of the department stores of the city in 1962. The variation of the phonetic feature under consideration ranged from the absence of (r) altogether to its presence in postvocalic position, as in the words *car, card, four,* and *fourth.*

On the basis of exploratory interviews, Labov decided to test the following hypothesis: "If any two subgroups of New York City speakers are ranked in a scale of social stratification, then they will be ranked in the same order by their differential use of (r)" (Labov 1972b:44). Rather than simply comparing the pronunciations of occupational groups representing the city's social stratification, which would be difficult to operationalize and quantify, in an elegant experiment Labov chose to try to find out to what extent stratification is identifiable within a single occupational group. The population he selected for his study consisted of salespeople in the stores of Saks Fifth Avenue, Macy's at Herald Square, and S. Klein at Union Square. These three stores represented respectively three status rankings—high, middle, and low—according to newspaper advertisements, the prices of their merchandise, the physical appearance of the store, and the socioeconomic status of their customers.

Assuming that salespeople in large department stores were likely to "borrow prestige" from their customers, Labov hypothesized that "salespeople in the highest-ranked store will have the highest values of (r); those in the middle-ranked store will have intermediate values of (r); and those in the lowest-ranked store will show the lowest values" (Labov 1972b:45). To elicit the relevant linguistic data, Labov asked a question that was best answered "[On the] fourth floor." Pretending not to understand the answer, he had the informant repeat the phrase in a more emphatic style of speech. As soon as he was out of view of his informants, Labov recorded the two words phonetically, noting not only the store in which the data were obtained but also the gender, function, race, and approximate age of the informant.

The results supported his hypothesis. At Saks, 30 percent of the salespeople interviewed always pronounced both r-sounds of the test phrase "fourth floor," whereas 32 percent pronounced them sometimes and sometimes not (as though "fourth floor" were written "fawth floah"). For Macy's, results were 20 percent and 31 percent, and for Klein's 4 percent and 17 percent. Furthermore, at Saks the difference between casual and emphatic pronunciation was insignificant, whereas at the other two stores the difference was considerable. Careful, emphatic speech appeared to call for the final (r) of *floor*, but casual speech did not.

Although prior to World War II certain r-sounds were "dropped" (except before a vowel) in the more prestigious pronunciation of New York City, in the years since then it had become one of the markers of social prestige. By the 1960s, its occurrence had increased, particularly in formal speech. In fact, some New Yorkers pronounced r-sounds even where they did not occur in spelling, as in the words *idea*, *Cuba*, and *saw* when the next word began with a vowel. Such a pronunciation or usage, which in an attempt to approach a presumed standard goes too far and produces a nonstandard form, is called **hypercorrection**. In short, as Labov's study showed, the pronunciation of r-sounds in the dialect of New York City was quite variable, depending on social factors such as status or class, and speech context such as casual versus emphatic speech.

Collecting authentic sociolinguistic data is not a simple matter because speakers are likely to adjust their manner of speaking if they are aware of being carefully observed or recorded. One way for the investigator to divert speakers' attention from their own speech is to lead informants into a relaxed dialogue. Natural speech also tends to characterize topics that help re-create emotions, as when one asks an informant, "Have you ever been in a situation where you were in serious danger of being killed? ... What happened?" The answer to such a question is likely to be spontaneous, that is, given in an unaffected manner (Labov 1972b:209–210). Tape-recording data has a great advantage over writing out a phonetic transcription of speech. Recording conversation between two or more speakers, or recording one speaker long enough or often enough for the person to become unconcerned, is preferable to recording a more or less formal interview that may well keep the informant from relaxing into the **vernacular**—the casual, normal spoken form of the language or dialect of the person's speech community.

In early sociolinguistic studies, scholars sought to identify language varieties and relate them to social differences among speakers. Since the mid-1960s, largely because of the stimulus of Labov's work, linguists have emphasized the use of the quantitative method in order to be able to describe with some accuracy the relationship between social differences and linguistic varieties. From the incidence and distribution of language variables in different social groups, scholars expect not only to learn the rate and direction of linguistic change but also to obtain valuable clues concerning the motivations that lead to such change.

In this connection, it may be appropriate to introduce the concept of **social network**. Each speaker has a social network that includes all those people with whom a speaker interacts. A high-density network refers to a group of individuals who are in frequent contact and are therefore familiar with each other. A multiplex social network is one in which interacting parties share more than one role, often reciprocal—for example, employer/employee as well as father-in-law/son-in-law. The denser and more multiplex the network, the stronger it is (perhaps the father-in-law and son-in-law are also members of a chess club and a choral society). Members of a strong network tend to make use of what is referred to as **restricted code**—informal speech lacking in stylistic range because the speakers share enough assumptions that some of the meaning of their messages is derived from context and gestures. By contrast, **elaborated code** refers to the variety of language use characteristic of relatively formal speech situations. In such situations, little if any, reliance is placed on extralinguistic context to make the message fully meaningful.

Language and Gender

J. K. Chambers in his textbook on sociolinguistic theory (1995:102) states categorically that "in virtually all sociolinguistic studies that include a sample of males and females" there is unequivocal evidence that "women use fewer stigmatized and non-standard variants than do men of the same social group in the same circumstances." Although admitting specific cultural differences, he claims this finding holds true cross-culturally as well.

First, a few general remarks about the term **gender** as it is used here. Among the several senses of this term is *sex*—meaning one of the two forms of most organisms that are characterized by differences in reproductive organs and related structures. The use of the term *gender* rather than *sex* avoids the misleading association with sexuality, but mainly it acknowledges that gender is a social construct that is likely to vary from one society to the next, or even from one social group to another within an embracing society or culture.

Here we are concerned with the concept of gender as a status ascribed to certain individuals or groups by members of a particular culture or society. Among the questions to be asked are: Do members of a society (group) differentiate gender in their speech behavior? If so, what forms does this differentiation take, under what culturally authentic circumstances does it occur, and does it have any effect on the nonverbal behavior of a society's members? To what extent is any differentiation of gender in speech the result of socialization, and more specifically, how does the expression of gender in speech relate to such aspects of social identity as ethnicity, so-called race, age, and socioeconomic class? Under what circumstances do men and women interact as equals (or nearly so), and under what circumstances do they not?

Gender and Speech in American Society. In American English, some differences have been noted in intonational patterns between male and female speakers. If one analyzes intonational contours as four relative pitch levels, then men tend to use only three, hardly ever reaching the highest one. Consider, for example, how men and women say the phrase "Oh, that's terrible!" Women's range frequently includes all four. Among the contours very rarely heard from men is the full downglide from the highest to the lowest pitch level, as when expressing surprise, excitement, concern, and the like. In general, women's speech appears to be more dynamic, making greater use of paralinguistic features and extending over a broader pitch range.

Scholars have described a variety of differences between the speech of men and women. For example, in a small sample of children in a semirural New England village studied by John L. Fischer (1958), the girls were more likely to pronounce the present-participle suffix -*ing* [ɪŋ] rather than -*in'* [ɪn], a form used more frequently among the boys. The choice between -*ing* and -*in'* appeared to be related not only to gender but also to the personality (aggressive versus cooperative) and mood (tense versus relaxed) of the speaker, the nature of the conversation (formal versus informal), the socioeconomic circumstances of the family (above versus below median), and the verb used (for example, *attending* versus *goin' to*).

The choice of words by men and women varies according to the occasion, the type of audience present, and various other circumstances. Profane or coarse speech is less likely to be heard when children or people held in respect are within earshot, and a job interview calls for a more considered vocabulary than a casual conversation between two close friends. Nevertheless, some lexical differences between the speech of men and women are fairly common and can be illustrated from American English. Certain words are used by women much more frequently than by men. Among such words are expressive adjectives that convey approval or admiration—for example, *delightful, spectacular, charming, divine, lovely, fascinating,* and *sweet*—and fashionable color names—for example, *beige, chartreuse, fuchsia, magenta,* and *mauve.*

Men are much more likely to phrase their approval or liking for something by using a neutral adjective, such as *fine, good,* or *great,* and reinforcing it, if necessary, with such an adverb as *damn,* as in "That was a damn good show." As a rule, men's color vocabulary is much less discriminating, and hence somewhat poorer, than women's. But in the United States differences between men's and women's word choices seem to be steadily growing smaller. For example, until a decade ago, *sweet* and *awesome* were slang terms exclusively used by young women, but now these adjectives are commonly used by both genders. And profanities are now casually used by many young women whose mothers and grandmothers not only would never have uttered them but would probably have been embarrassed even to hear them. Nonetheless, on the whole, as several authors have noted, in careful speech women are likely to use fewer stigmatized words than are men. An example of speech behavior differences between men and older women is illustrated in Box 13.1.

One of the characteristics of women's speech—particularly of older women—is the use of a "tag question" in certain contexts. The term refers to a question attached to an utterance to obtain the assent of the addressee, as in *"That was a silly thing for them to do, wasn't it?"* Seeking confirmation or validation of a statement may indicate the speaker's desire to avoid assertiveness. A "tag" in the form of a question may also be attached to an order or a criticism to soften it, as in *"Answer the phone, would you?"* or *"You are drinking a bit too much, don't you think?"* Another purpose of the tag question is to include the person spoken to in friendly conversation by offering the opportunity to respond, as in *"It's a beautiful day, isn't it?"* Today, younger women use tag questions much less frequently. When men use tags, they do so to obtain or confirm information, as in *"To get this work done, I would have to leave the car here until sometime tomorrow, wouldn't I?"* On the subject of tag questions, some scholars have argued that "a more sophisticated view of the complexity of both linguistic and social behaviour" is needed (Cameron, McAlinden, and O'Leary 1988:92).

BOX 13.1 TALKING LIKE A LADY

Aside from specific lexical items like color names, we find differences between the speech of women and that of men in the use of particles that grammarians often describe as "meaningless." There may be no referent for them, but they are far from meaningless: they define the social context of an utterance, indicate the relationship the speaker feels between himself and his addressee, between himself and what he is talking about.

As an experiment, one might present native speakers of standard American English with pairs of sentences, identical syntactically and in terms of referential lexical items, and differing merely in the choice of "meaningless" particle, and ask them which was spoken by a man, which a woman. Consider:

(a) Oh dear, you've put the peanut butter in the refrigerator again.

(b) Shit, you've put the peanut butter in the refrigerator again.

It is safe to predict that people would classify the first sentence as part of "women's language," the second as "men's language." It is true that many self-respecting women are becoming able to use sentences like (b) publicly without flinching, but this is a relatively recent development, and while perhaps the majority of Middle America might condone the use of (b) for men, they would still disapprove of its use by women. (It is of interest, by the way, to note that men's language is increasingly being used by women, but women's language is not being adopted by men, apart from those who reject the American masculine image [for example, homosexuals]. This is analogous to the fact that men's jobs are being sought by women, but few men are rushing to become housewives or secretaries. The language of the favored group, the group that holds the power, along with its nonlinguistic behavior, is generally adopted by the other group, not vice versa. In any event, it is a truism to state that the "stronger" expletives are reserved for men, and the "weaker" ones for women.

from Robin Lakoff, Language and Woman's Place (1975), 9–10

Another way women may try to avoid assertiveness is to use so-called **hedge words** or phrases, such as *maybe, rather, perhaps, I guess, sort of, I am wondering,* and others. A sentence using a hedge word may even be combined with tag questions, as in the first of the following examples: *"You are rather tired, aren't you?" "I have been kind of wondering if I should go," "Well,*

I guess I might have been right," and *"Maybe we could try adding some seasoning."* Once again, young American women tend to use less of this type of speech behavior, or to be free of it altogether.

To sum up, in American English there are no pronunciations, grammatical forms, words, or sentence constructions that are employed exclusively by men or by women. Rather, what differences there are between male and female speech have to do with the frequency with which some usages are employed by one sex or the other. That these differences are decreasing rather than maintaining themselves or growing is an indication that longstanding social differences between women and men are in the process of breaking down.

Other differences between the speech behavior of men and women were suggested. For example, some investigators found that when women talk with other women on a social basis, favored topics are relationships, social issues, house and family, the workplace, and personal and family finances. When men talk with other men, the favored topics have been work, recreation and sports, and women. In other studies of speech behavior, women interviewees were found more cooperative and polite, and offered more information than did men.

And with respect to any society, the following issues may be considered: what counts as a *turn* (rotation of speakers) in a discourse; how turns and interruptions are handled; to what extent culture-specific gender differences may be overridden by culture-specific socioeconomic and other hierarchies; what cues male and female speakers use to allocate turns; and so on. In short, important as the male/female distinction may be in a particular society, one should never assume that it is the only, or the main, criterion as to how the various aspects of communicative behavior are chosen and employed.

Some scholars have approached the topic of speech behavior of the genders with the view that women's language reflects men's dominance over them. They note that in many societies, American society included, men tend to control conversations. Furthermore, their talk is usually blunt (sometimes even tough), straight, and colloquial in style. Others have pointed out that women are usually better conversationalists, raising the level of discourse by striving for more harmonious relations with their face-to-face interactants. The great majority of languages, however, give *grammatical* priority to males: In deriving nouns designating females from nouns designating males—for example, *aviator-aviatrix, duke-duchess, hero-heroine,* and *waiter-waitress*; instances of derivation in the opposite direction are few; only two come readily to mind: *widow-widower* and *bride-bridegroom*.

Gender and Speech in Some Native American Societies. In Native American languages, differences in the speech of men and women are fairly common. Some are morphophonemic (that is, some morphemes of a language have a slightly different phonemic shape when used by women or by men), others are lexical (sometimes men and women use different words for the same thing or concept).

Among the languages in which certain morphemes have a different phonemic shape depending on whether women or men are speaking is Koasati, a Muskogean language spoken in southwestern Louisiana. According to Haas (1944), the speech of middle-aged and older Koasati women in the late 1930s differed from that of men in certain indicative and imperative verb forms. Because in a few instances the speech of women appeared to be older and more basic, Haas described the men's forms as derived from the women's forms. For example, verb forms ending in a nasalized vowel, such as *a·* in *lakawwą·* 'he will lift it [woman speaking]', add an *s* after the corresponding oral vowel, yielding *lakawwá·s* 'he will lift it [man speaking]'. Similarly, the women's word *lakawhól* 'lift it!' [addressed to second-person plural]' yields the men's form *lakawhós*. In other instances, a vowel is lengthened and the final *n* becomes an *s*, and in still others the men's form simply adds an *s* to the form occurring in women's speech. One may summarize the changes at the end of certain Koasati verb forms as follows: W = women's form, M = men's form, V = any vowel, V́ = high pitch, V̂ = falling pitch, Ṽ = nasalized vowel, C = any consonant, and (·) = short or long:

W	M
V̨	V(·)s
V̨(·)	V́·s
V̂l	V́·s
V̂n	V̂·s
V(·)C	V(·)Cs
V(·)CC	V(·)CCs

Haas further reported that in telling traditional narratives, Koasati women used men's forms when quoting male characters, and conversely.

For the language of the Atsina (also referred to as Gros Ventre) of Fort Belknap Reservation in north-central Montana, now spoken by a rapidly decreasing number of tribal members, we have both fairly recent information (Allan Taylor 1994) and an account from 1945 (Flannery 1946). According to Taylor, before the vowels *i*, *e*, and *a*, men often use the sound *č* (as in the word *church*) where women have a *k*-sound; for example, *ʔanáakyaaʔ* 'buffalo bull' in the speech of women would be *ʔanáačaaʔ* in men's speech. In addition to differences in pronunciation, Flannery mentioned lexical differences—the use of two completely different words, having the same meaning, depending on the sex of the speaker. Of interest are some of her findings concerning the attitudes of the Atsina toward gender differences in speech:

A much older woman said that if a member of either sex "talked like the other" he or she was considered bisexual. This she illustrated by telling of the mortification suffered by the parents of a boy who persisted in acting like a girl in every way. The boy's mother was so sensitive that "she never went about and she just bowed her head in shame when her son was heard talking like a woman." It is recognized, however, that one Gros Ventre man who at present uses woman's pronunciation and expressions does so because he had the misfortune of having been reared in a household consisting of women only. (Flannery 1946:135)

Boas, whose anthropological fieldwork was initiated among the Eskimo, reported (Boas 1911:79) that the men of some groups pronounced the final consonants *p*, *t*, *k*, and *q* (a back velar stop) quite distinctly, but that the women substituted for these four sounds the corresponding nasals *m*, *n*, *ŋ*, and *ŋ* (a back velar nasal). He added that in some dialects the men adopted the women's pronunciation, favoring the female speech forms.

A few lexical differences between male and female speech have been recorded for the Pueblo peoples of the Southwest—specifically among the Hopi of the Third Mesa, the Arizona Tewa, and the Tiwa, Laguna, and Acoma of New Mexico. With the exception of the Hopi words, some formal similarity appears to exist between the two gender forms. It is interesting that the languages listed above belong to three different language families (Uto-Aztecan, Kiowa-Tanoan, and Keresan). We may be dealing here with an areal feature. Although the number of gender-specific pairs of words is small, they occur in kinship terminology according to the sex of the ego, as well as in responses given during ceremonial observances, and they must therefore be judged as culturally significant (Kroskrity 1983; Sims and Valiquette 1990).

An interesting case was reported in 1912 by Alexander F. Chamberlain. According to him, the men's language of the Caraya, a people of eastern Brazil, differs from the women's language by the addition or change of a consonant. If the information is correct, this is another of the relatively rare cases where men's forms are derived from women's forms.

Douglas Taylor (1951) reported on a more complex situation in Central American Carib, a modern dialect of Island Carib. Two genders, masculine and feminine, are distinguished in this dialect. Gender is in part natural (assigned as a rule in accordance with the sex of a living thing), in part grammatical (for example, the words for *sun, milk, river,* and *maize* are masculine, whereas those for *star, liver, knife,* and *snake* are feminine). However, words denoting qualities, states, actions, and the equivalent of the pronoun *it* in such English sentences as "it is raining" tend to be assigned to the feminine gender by men but to masculine by women. The equivalent of "the other day," for example, is *ligíra buga* when said by women but *tugúra buga* when said by men (*buga* is a past tense particle).

Such differences as those described thus far are found the world over. For example, in North Africa, Arabs who speak French as a second language articulate the French (r) according to the speaker's gender: In men's speech it is an apical consonant (produced with the tip of the tongue serving as the active articulator); in women's speech it is a uvular consonant (made by the back of the tongue with the aid of the uvula). Because both of the (r)s occur and are phonemically distinct in the Arabic dialects native to these people, the two variants are easily pronounceable by men and women alike. According to a survey of French dialects by Henriette Walter (1988), North African men would now prefer to approach the contemporary French norm, which happens to be the uvular r, [R]. What prevents them from doing so is a fairly rigid convention, according to which the uvular articulation of r in North African French is a social characteristic of women.

Gender and Speech: Theoretical Movements. In the mid-1960s and early 1970s, when phonological differences as markers of social class were being investigated by William Labov and his students, he also suggested that gender might be marked in a similar fashion. Probably the most influential work at that time was Robin Lakoff's *Language and Women's Place* (1975). She found not only phonological differences but also subtle differences in the lexicon and syntax. Some instances of these included greater use of tag questions (" . . . , *right?*"; " . . . *don't you think?*")

greater use of polite forms (*"If you don't mind, could you . . . "*)

greater use of wh- words (*"Why don't we go to the store?"*)

greater use of hedges ("*I kinda like it*")

greater use of apologies ("*Sorry to bother you, but . . .* ")

greater use of intensifiers ("*That's so so adorable!*")

greater use of certain "women's vocabulary" (e.g., colors)

greater use of modal auxiliaries (*"We ought to/should/might . . ."*)

wider range of intonation

greater use of adjectives expressing admiration ("She wore a divine dress")

less use of swear words or profanity

In addition, Lakoff explored how language was used for different communicative purposes by men and women.

We might view current work on gender and language through three approaches: subculture theory, social power theory, and communicative strategy theory.

Subculture theory claims that the social lives of women lie in a subculture somewhat apart from the mainstream. Women and women's language are marked as different from men and men's language. As we saw in a previous section, this is why we find certain marked terms for women, such as *actress, waitress, woman, bachelorette,* and *female,* derived from the masculine forms. In other words, men's language is thought to offer the normative forms from which women's terms are derived (see Box 13.2).

The linguist Deborah Tannen is perhaps the most active proponent of the subculture theory, and advocated this notion in a series of professional and popular best-selling books such as *You Just Don't Understand: Women and Men in Conversation* (1990), *Talking from Nine to Five: Men and Women at Work* (1994b), and *That's Not What I Meant! How Conversational Style Makes or Breaks Your Relations with Others* (1986). Tannen calls gender-associated varieties of language **genderlects.** According to Tannen, each gender has different means of accomplishing conversational goals, and perhaps ultimate ends as well. The goal for men in communication is to send factual information, which Tannen calls the *report style.* On the other hand, women want to build and maintain relationships among participants of the conversations, which she calls the *rapport style.*

BOX 13.2 WHAT DOES THE WORD MAN MEAN?

It has been argued that the word *man*, as in *man is a primate*, is independent of sex, that it refers to all members of the species, and that it is just an etymological coincidence that the form for the species is the same as that for the male members of the species. Certainly, using the same form for the entire species and for half the species creates the possibility of confusion, as those colonial women discovered who rashly thought that the word *man* in the sentence "All men are created equal" included them. More confusion may come about when we use phrases like *early man*. Although this presumably refers to the species, notice how easy it is to use expressions like *early man and his wife* and how hard it is to say things like *man is the only animal that menstruates or even early woman and her husband* . . . The common theme running through these last examples is that the male is taken as the normal, that masculine forms refer both to the sex and the species, while women are the exception, usually absorbed by the masculine, but needing special terms when they become noticeable.

If the above examples have not convinced you that *man* as a generic is at best ambiguous, consider the following quote from Alma Graham . . . :

If a woman is swept off a ship into the water, the cry is "Man overboard!" If she is killed by a hit-and-run driver, the charge is "manslaughter." If she is injured on the job, the coverage is "workmen's compensation." But if she arrives at a threshold marked "Men Only," she knows the admonition is not intended to bar animals or plants or inanimate objects. It is meant for her.

from Francine Frank and Frank Anshen,
Language and the Sexes (1983), 71–72

Social power theory goes back to the 1980s when William M. O'Barr and Bowman K. Atkins (1998) studied how witnesses speak in court. In several important ways their work challenges the approaches of Lakoff's and Tannen's views of women's language. O'Barr and Atkins studied courtroom witness testimony for a two and half years, looking at the ten speech differences between men and women proposed by Lakoff and others. They concluded that speech patterns were "neither characteristic of all women nor limited only to women." Instead, they found that women who used the lowest frequency of women's language traits had unusually high social or economic status (for example, being well-educated professionals with middle-class backgrounds). A similar pattern was found for men (i.e., men with high social or economic status spoke with few women's language traits). O'Barr and Atkins argued that it was power and status, rather than gender, that accounted for these differences. A powerful position that "may derive from either social standing in the larger society and/or status accorded by the court" allowed speakers—both male and female—certain linguistic advantages. Thus, what the so-called women's speech is really manifesting is difference in power within mainstream society, where women typically are at a disadvantage.

Other studies have also examined the position of power of women in society as it is reflected in language. For example, Bonnie McElhinny did a year of fieldwork in 1992 with the Pittsburgh police department, observing the effects of gender, race, and age on police officers' language. She found that female officers tried to portray themselves as competent beyond question, and rational, efficient, and professional beyond reproach. They adopted neither the accommodating and empathetic manners typically associated with women, nor did they demonstrate the commanding physical presence and emotional aggression often associated with the police. Instead, they chose to adopt a communicative style more typical of the "middle-class masculine norm" (1995:220). Thus, although the female police officers had no intention of acting as social workers, their presence and language served as an implicit challenge to the "hegemonic masculinity" found on the police force, replacing it with a definition of policing centered around mental ability and coolness under pressure (1995:238). And Deborah Tannen (1999), too, modified some of her early ideas in her study of conversations in the workplace by incorporating some of the work of Erving Goffman (1974) on frames and the presentation of self. She showed how speakers simultaneously balance the dimensions of status and connection, and argued that gender patterns of behavior are class-linked as well as sex-linked. In other words, women's and men's subcultures are each deeply associated with social status.

Some scholars argue that women's language is also significantly shaped by the style of **communicative strategy.** For example, Jane Hill (1987) studied the social expectations, gender roles, power differences, and language in the Malinche Volcano communities near Mexico City. She found that local women changed their native language, Nahuatl, to be "more Spanish." By the mid-1970s, many Nahuatl-speaking men were earning relatively good wages in Mexico City, where Spanish was the elite language. The men saw Spanish as the language of capitalism and hegemonic power, but they used Nahuatl to maintain local social solidarity. The women remained behind to take care of the farm fields. They had the responsibility to pass the Nahuatl language on to the children. They saw the Spanish language as a modern and elite language and Nahuatl as a traditional language. Understanding the importance of maintaining the language of their ethnic group, but also wishing to show their appreciation of modern things and education, the women began to speak a form of Nahuatl highly influenced by Spanish pronunciation. Hill argues, however, that this was largely unconscious. To maintain Nahuatl, they intentionally did not use Spanish loanwords, but less obvious features such as Spanish phonology influenced the use of their native language.

Another example can be seen in the use of English and English loanwords by Japanese women. The anthropologist Karen Kelsky (2001) claims that English (and other foreign languages) are thought to be the most valuable weapon (*buki*) in the women's war for equality in the Japanese workplace. The feminist critic Matsubara Junko says that "business comes first for men and English only second, but for women English is always first. . . if you cannot speak English, you have no chance of even getting your foot into the business world" (Kelsky 2001:101). For example, more than 90 percent of interpreters for the Japanese national broadcasting corporation—and 90 percent of all other interpreters—are women (Kelsky 2001:101). Monopolizing fields such as interpreting, translating, or bilingual guiding gives women powerful—though often unacknowledged—clout in many domains. The various Japanese male attacks on the current worldwide hegemony of English—for example, *eigo byō* ["English mania"] as Tsuda (1994, 1996, 1997) calls it—might be caused by their inadequacy in the language. To be fair, many of these scholars speak very good academic English, and their theoretical and political criticisms of English should be taken seriously. But articles in popular magazines with titles such as *Nihonjin no Eikaiwa Shijō-shugi no Gu* ["The Stupidity of the Japanese Worship of English"] do give one pause.

However, English can be more than a mere tool for career advancement: Foreign languages might be the "means by which women enter bodily into alternative systems of thought and value" (Kelsky 2001:101). As Matsubara says, "English is not just a language . . . it is something that has the power even to transform women's lives." As one of her interviewees argues, "In my case, if you took away my English, there would be nothing left. I can't imagine myself existing without English." Another, even more plainly, stated, "I had so many opinions I wanted to express. I felt I couldn't possibly say them in Japanese. I wanted to learn this new vocabulary to express myself better. So I worked really hard. The average Japanese doesn't have any opinion! Even in Japanese! But I had loads of opinions, and because of that I learned English fast" (Kelsky 2001:101–102).

English **loanwords** also offer the Japanese a chance to avoid some of the constraints imposed upon them by the gender requirements of speaking the Japanese language. Not only does the use of English loanwords help them change their images of themselves, English allows Japanese women to speak about social issues or problems in ways they otherwise might not be able to do so comfortably. For example, the Japanese term *gōkan* ("rape") carries some social stigma because it suggests an act of physical intercourse instead of a crime. As a result, victims of *gōkan* in Japan are often thought to be less desirable marriage partners, and the women and their families often hide such incidents. However, because the modern English loanword *rēpu* focuses on the crime and on being a victim of a crime—rather than being considered as complicit—more women are now reporting *rēpus* to the police. Women are often making an effort to effect social change by using English loanwords that do not carry the traditional "linguistic baggage" associated with native Japanese terms (Stanlaw 2004a, Hogan 2003).

Language, "Race," and Ethnicity

African-American English. A good example of an ethnic language variety is African-American English (AAE) in the United States. To begin with, we should say that such terms as "African-American English" or "Black English" are open to some criticism because they imply that all people of African ancestry in America speak the same way. Thus, these labels should be used with some degree of caution.

AAE is characterized by pronunciations, syntactic structures, and vocabulary associated with and used by a fairly large number of African-Americans. Some of those who speak AAE use it habitually; others use it in certain situations, Standard English in others. As the speech of a sizable portion of a population living in a continent-sized area, AAE is no more uniform than the English spoken by other Americans. It exhibits a wide range of pronunciations and forms varying as to the degree in which they differ from each other and from Standard English. Some AAE pronunciations characterize Southern speech in general, black and white, although they are likely to occur in AAE with greater frequency or to a larger degree.

Spoken rather than written (with the exception of those writers who try to represent faithfully the AAE of their characters), AAE is used to great effect by African-Americans ranging from religious and civil rights leaders to school dropouts spending most of their time in the streets of black ghettos. Studies made of their speech have repeatedly established the importance assigned to verbal skills at all levels. Far from being limited to ordinary communicative functions, AAE ranges from the rhyming narrative poetry of so-called toasts to the accommodating style of "shucking (it)" and "jiving" on the one hand and the more aggressive needling or goading referred to as "signifying" on the other.

Because of the dialectal variation that exists in AAE, only some of its most prominent and common characteristics are discussed here. These features are not found in the speech of all African-Americans, particularly some of those who have lived in the North for several generations. For the most part, these features characterize the nonstandard variety of English spoken by African-Americans in urban ghettos of the United States, a variety referred to as **African-American Vernacular English (AAVE)**.

In pronunciation, the vowels of AAVE tend to be much more variable than consonants. The most common vowel contrasts of Standard English that are likely to be lost are in such word pairs as *pride* and *prod* or *find* and *fond* as well as *pride* and *proud* or *find* and *found*, which in AAVE tend to be pronounced alike. The loss of contrast in these and similar word pairs is usually limited to the position before the consonants *b, d, g, m, n, r,* and *l*. The words *oil* and *all* and similar word pairs also frequently sound alike in AAVE, in particular when vowels are followed by the consonant *l*. Finally, such word pairs as *fear* and *fair* and *sure* and *shore* may be pronounced alike; in terms such as these, the loss of vowel contrast is conditioned by the consonant *r* that follows the vowels.

The least stable consonants of AAVE are those found at the end of words. The sound written as *th* may be heard in the final position as *f*, making the words *both* and *with* rhyme with *loaf* and *sniff,* respectively. The consonants *r* and *l* tend to be weakened or are completely lost. After a vowel, the weakened *r* makes such words as *sure, shoe,* and *show* or *your* and *you* sound alike or nearly so; *r* between vowels may be lost completely, leading to such pronunciations as *intèestin', pass,* and *tess* for *interesting, Paris,* and *terrace,* respectively. A weakened *l* before a consonant may be heard in such words as *help* or *wolf;* when it is completely lost, such word pairs as *fooled* and *food, toll* and *toe,* or *bolt* and *boat* come to sound alike.

The stops *t* and *d* are quite commonly lost or modified after another consonant: Thus *last* may come to sound like *lass, mend* like *men, rift* like *riff,* and *told* like *toll.* Other final consonant clusters are frequently subject to similar simplification, resulting in the pronunciation *dess* for *desk* or *liss* for *lisp.* Other differences from Standard English are less generalizable.

Grammatical differences are usually more noticeable than differences in pronunciation or vocabulary. This is so because it is the use of "proper" grammar that is associated with a style of speaking considered prestigious and worthy of imitating. From the perspective of linguistic anthropology, the grammar used by native speakers of any language variety cannot be termed incorrect, even when it differs from other dialects or the standard itself. Some of the features that differentiate the grammar of AAVE from Standard English are to be found in the speech of non-African-Americans as well.

When compared to other European languages, English has few inflectional suffixes; the tendency in AAVE is for even these few to be weakened or lost. The *-s* of the third person singular is frequently lacking in AAVE verbs, as in "Johnny run" or "He eat meat." The *-s* marking the possessive (spelled *'s*) may be lost, as in "Hand me that man coat." The *-s* in the plural of nouns is retained, as in *desses* for *desks* after the simplification of the word-final consonant cluster *-sk* in the singular, but there is a tendency toward making irregular plurals regular, that is, making use of such forms as *foots, mens,* and *childrens* for *feet, men,* and *children.*

The past tense of verbs is either retained as in *gave,* weakened as in *kep* (instead of *kept*) or *toll* (instead of *told*), or lost altogether as in "He pay me yesterday." When there is an option in Standard English to use a contraction, for example, "He is going" to "He's going," AAVE offers the additional option of full deletion of the form of *be,* resulting in "He going." When the option to contract does *not* exist in Standard English, as in the latter part of the sentence "That's the way it is here" (one would never say "That's the way it's here"), the option to delete the form of *be* likewise does not occur in AAVE, which would use "That the way it is [*or* be] here." The phrase *there is* that introduces a sentence or clause is replaced in AAVE by *it is* or the contractions *it's* or simply *'s.*

In comparison with Standard English, AAVE is characterized by multiple negation, as in the following sentences that are to be understood as statements rather than questions: "Didn't nobody see it," "Wasn't nobody home," "Ain't nobody complainin' but you, man," and "I don't got none."

The verb form *be*, as in "She be busy," contrasts in AAVE with its absence, as in the corresponding "She busy." The latter, "She busy," means that the person referred to is busy at the time the statement is made. "She be busy" denotes a habitual or repeated state of busyness, what in Standard English would be expressed as "She is always busy," "She keeps busy," or "She is often busy."

As for optional tenses, the situation of one particular variety of AAVE has been described as follows:

I do see him is just anterior to the present and intrudes upon it, and is therefore the *past inceptive tense*. I *did see him* is slightly longer ago, or the *pre-present tense*. I *done seen him* is still further ago, or the *recent past*. I *been seen him* is even farther ago and designated as the *pre-recent past*. Moving ahead from the present, if someone says *I'm a-do it*, he will do it in approximately 30 seconds, or in the *immediate future*. If someone says *I'm a-gonna do it*, he will do it soon, that is, in the *post-immediate future*. If he says *I gonna do it*, however, the execution may be indefinitely delayed. (Fickett 1972:19)

AAVE further differs from Standard English in specialized vocabulary, variant stress patterns on certain words, and the like. Despite these and other features that set the two Englishes apart, however, the adjustment a nonspeaker of AAVE has to make to comprehend it is no more than the effort needed to understand cockney.

Scholars disagree on the current developmental tendencies in AAVE. Some believe that the long-standing but slow decreolization is continuing, that is, that the speech of African-Americans is converging with the English spoken by non-African-Americans. Others, including Labov, have reported that as a result of the increasing segregation and isolation of urban African-Americans from the rest of the society, and despite the homogenizing influence of the media on language, AAVE appears to be steadily diverging not only from Standard English but from regional and local white dialects as well. If this is so, children who speak it will encounter even more difficulties when at age six they enter an environment that uses a strikingly different code.

How Did African-American English Come About. This question is closely tied to the question, How do varieties of AAE relate to American English in general? Scholarly opinions on the subject vary. Some have argued that AAE is just another dialect of American English. They attempt to justify this interpretation by pointing out that none of the features of AAE departs significantly from those found in other dialects of English or from the historical development of English as a whole. For example, multiple negation, commonly referred to as the double negative, which is frowned upon as one of the main sins against "good English grammar," was widely used in Elizabethan times; its retention in AAE can be interpreted as a conservative feature. By contrast, the loss of *-s* in the third person singular can be viewed as the continuation of a tendency toward simplification that has characterized the English verb throughout its history. What AAE has done is to eliminate the last remaining suffix of the present tense verb paradigm, something that may well happen in Standard English in the next few hundred years. (Simplification of Standard English continues unabated, as can be seen from the ever more frequent substitution of *I* for the object form of this pronoun, *me*, as in "between you and I," that can now be heard even from major network television anchors and members of the U.S. Congress.)

Opposed to the dialectal interpretation is the contention that AAE is sufficiently distinct from and independent of Standard English to merit assignment to English-based creoles, where it would join company with Jamaican Creole and **Gullah,** the creole surviving in the Sea Islands off the coasts of South Carolina and Georgia. Although AAE is today less divergent from Standard English than either Jamaican Creole or Gullah, a number of similarities between it and the two creoles are worth noting, for example, certain patterns of pronunciation, the loss of the third person singular *-s* and the possessive *'s*, multiple negation, the zero copula (loss of forms of *be*, as in "He rich"), and some residual Africanisms. Consequently, a real possibility exists that the process of creolization contributed to the formation of AAE.

The making of AAE dates back to the seventeenth century, when slave ships carrying cheap goods sailed from Bristol, Liverpool, and other English ports; the cargoes were exchanged along the West African coast for captured Africans who, in turn, were sold as slaves in the Caribbean and the North American South for work on plantations. The ships would then return to England loaded with sugar, tobacco, cotton, and other commodities, and the cycle would be repeated. To minimize the risk of organized uprisings, the cargoes of future slaves were assembled from a variety of tribes speaking different languages. According to the revealing testimony of one Capt. William Smith in 1744,

As for the Languages of *Gambia*, they are so many and so different, that the Natives, on either Side the River, cannot understand each other; which, if rightly consider'd, is no small Happiness to the *Europeans* who go thither to trade for Slaves; . . . the safest Way is to trade with the different Nations, . . . and having some of every Sort on board, there will be no more Likelihood of their succeeding in a Plot, than of finishing the Tower of *Babel*. (1744:28)

It is understandable that need for a pidgin, or pidgins, had developed even before the ships left the African coast; The captives had to find a means of communicating, at least about the most vital matters, not only with each other but with their captors and overseers as well. Even after the captives had been sold into slavery in the New World, the need for pidgins continued for reasons similar to those that gave rise to them in the first place. In the Louisiana area, the pidgin was French-based; elsewhere in the South, it was English-based. According to J. L. Dillard, one of the exponents of the creole hypothesis, "When new generations grew up which used only the pidgin, the pidgin became creolized . . . [to] Plantation Creole" (1972:22).

Which of the two interpretations is the more plausible, the dialectal or the creolist? According to Burling (1973), the evidence appears to support both in that AAE shares some features with Standard English and others with creoles such as Gullah and Jamaican. Figure 13.1 below shows the complex interrelationships that Burling believes existed among the various forms of speech that likely contributed to AAE.

African-American English: Myths and Facts. Without question, AAE is a much-stigmatized language variety. A great many people, regardless of ethnic background, consider it a badly corrupted, deficient form of English. If the various dialects of English are accorded different degrees of social prestige, Standard English ranks highest, and AAE is among those least esteemed. The negative attitude toward AAE in U.S. society is in part reinforced by the low socioeconomic status of many African-Americans resulting from a long-standing pattern of racial discrimination.

Many people believe, and even some educators and educational psychologists have claimed, that African-American children from urban ghettos in

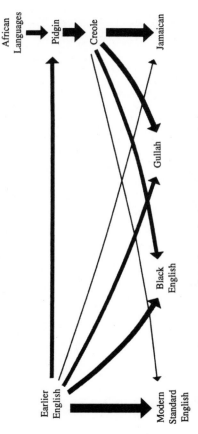

FIGURE 13.1 Languages That Shaped African-American (Black) English

In this diagram the four degrees of thickness of the arrows suggest the differential weight of influences that earlier forms of various languages have had upon later ones.

Source: From Robbins Burling, *English in Black and White*, 122. Copyright © 1973 by Holt, Rinehart and Winston, Inc. Reprinted by permission of Holt, Rinehart and Winston.

particular are verbally deprived. These children are said to mispronounce words, slur endings, and mumble; to answer in monosyllables or incomplete sentences replete with grammatical errors; to make use of a very limited vocabulary; and in general to use English sloppily and illogically. There is further a widespread belief that the use of the nonstandard vernacular is a serious obstacle to learning, a few members of the academic profession going so far as to use the verbal performance of ghetto pupils in testing situations as evidence of genetic inferiority. But is there anything wrong with AAE? Let us briefly review the evidence.

Rather than simply a random and corrupted version of Standard English, AAE is just as rule-governed as other forms of English, but the rules that characterize its usage are, as may be expected, somewhat different. We have already seen that, for example, it uses multiple negatives and dispenses with the third person singular marker -*s* in verbs, and yet the meaning of what is being said is never in question. The absence of a linking verb between subject and predicate, as in "He tired," is not a sign of corrupted speech or laziness on the part of AAE speakers; the same grammatical construction is found in many other languages of the world, Russian among them.

Careless diction and slurring of word endings are not, of course, limited to speakers of any particular dialect or language but are largely a function of speech tempo and sociocultural setting. Similarly, to fault children for answering such questions as "Where is the squirrel?" with "In the tree" rather than the full "The squirrel is in the tree" is nothing short of pedantry (Labov 1970:5). The vocabulary of a habitual speaker of AAE cannot be expected to coincide with that of a speaker of Standard English, but not to acknowledge the expressiveness that characterizes African-American verbal performances is to display prejudice or ignorance.

In a widely known and frequently reprinted article, Labov (1970) convincingly identified the main sources of misconceptions concerning the nature of AAE. African-American children indeed respond defensively to a strange white interviewer (even when he or she is friendly), and they give monosyllabic answers if they find the setting or experience unfamiliar or intimidating. Once the sociolinguistic factors operating in this inherently asymmetrical situation have been removed, these same children produce a steady stream of speech, effectively using the various stylistic devices AAE has to offer.

In the same article, Labov quoted an interview conducted with Larry H., at the time a fifteen-year-old African-American youth from Harlem. For someone who was put back from the eleventh grade to the ninth and who was also threatened with disciplinary action, Larry displayed a remarkable ability to think acutely and argue logically (see Box 13.3).

It is one thing to say that AAE enjoys little prestige among the great majority of Americans and that under certain circumstances those who use it are at a disadvantage compared with those who use a dialect of English that is socially more acceptable. It is another thing, however, to claim that AAE is a form of speech deficient in structure as well as lexically and stylistically impoverished. That is simply not true.

Nevertheless, the social and educational implications of the existence and use of AAE will be receiving national as well as local attention for years to come, and these implications are likely to generate controversies. One case in point was the Oakland (California) School Board resolution unanimously passed on December 18, 1996.

The "whereases" of the resolution included statements that "numerous validated scholarly studies demonstrate that African-American students as a part of their culture and history [as] an African people possess and utilize a language described in various scholarly approaches as 'Ebonics' (literally 'Black sounds')" and that "these studies have also demonstrated that African Language Systems are genetically based and not a dialect of English"; and it

BOX 13.3 AFRICAN-AMERICAN ENGLISH IN ACTION: A FIFTEEN-YEAR-OLD SPEAKS

INTERVIEWER: What happens to you after you die? Do you know?

LARRY: Yeah, I know.

I: What?

LARRY: After they put you in the ground, your body turns into—ah—bones, an' shit.

I: What happens to your spirit?

LARRY: Your spirit—soon as you die, your spirit leaves you.

I: And where does the spirit go?

LARRY: Well, it all depends . . .

I: On what?

LARRY: You know, like some people say if you're good an' shit, your spirit goin' t'heaven . . . 'n' if you bad, your spirit goin' to hell. Well, bullshit! Your spirit goin' to hell anyway, good or bad.

I: Why?

LARRY: Why? I'll tell you why. 'Cause, you see, doesn' nobody really know that it's a God, y'know, 'cause I mean I have seen black gods, pink gods, white gods, all color gods, and don't nobody know it's really a God. An' when they be sayin' if you good, you goin' t'heaven, tha's bullshit, 'cause you ain't goin' to no heaven, 'cause it ain't no heaven for you to go to.

I: Well, if there's no heaven, how could there be a hell?

LARRY: I mean—ye-eah. Well, let me tell you, it ain't no hell, 'cause this is hell right here, y'know!

I: This is hell?

LARRY: Yeah, this is hell right here!

I: . . . But, just say that there is a God, what color is he? White or black?

LARRY: Well, if it is a God . . . I wouldn' know what color, I couldn' say,—couldn' nobody say what color he is or really *would* be.

I: But now, jus' suppose there was a God—

LARRY: Unless'n they say . . .

I: No, I was jus' sayin' jus' suppose there is a God, would he be white or black?

LARRY: . . . He'd be white, man.

I: Why?

LARRY: Why? I'll tell you why. 'Cause the average whitey out here got every-thing, you dig? And the nigger ain't got shit, y'know? Y'understan'? So—um—for—in order for *that* to happen, you know it ain't no black God that's doin' that bullshit.

from William Labov, "The Logic of Nonstandard English" (1970), 12–15 was therefore resolved (among other things) that "the Superintendent in conjunction with her staff shall immediately devise and implement the best possible academic program for imparting instruction to African-American students in their primary language for the combined purposes of maintaining the legitimacy and richness of such language whether it is known as 'Ebonics' [or] 'African Language Systems' . . . and to facilitate their acquisition and mastery of English language skills."

Some of the phrasing of the resolution was false (that language systems are genetically based), and some could easily be misunderstood (that the schools of the Oakland Unified School District could [or should?] implement a program of instructing African-American students in various subjects that would use Ebonics as the language of instruction). The dean of the Graduate School of Arts and Sciences at Howard University, himself an African American, was quoted as saying that "it is criminal to graduate African-American students who cannot speak and write standard English."

Presentation of the Ebonics controversy is of necessity greatly abbreviated here, but at least the following points would seem to merit emphasizing: (1) There is no question that so-called Ebonics is one among many variations of English and, more specifically, of AAE; (2) not helping African-American students to become proficient in Standard American English will do them so socioeconomic disservice; (3) it might be helpful to use Ebonics in some manner with students who speak it if doing so would aid them in learning Standard English; and (4) competence in more than one language or dialect is an asset.

Language and Nationality

In the last decades of the twentieth century, many scholars argued that "ethnicity is not always the survival of cultural diversity born of geographical and social isolation, but may be the outcome of intensive interaction, a constellation of practices that evolve to channel complex social relations" (Woolard 1989:3). Following this approach, Susan Gal (1979:3) studied language shift in Oberwart, a bilingual area in eastern Austria. After 400 years of Hungarian-German bilingualism, German began replacing Hungarian in everyday conversation as well as in local business. She asked:

By what intervening processes does industrialization, or any other social change, effect changes in the uses to which speakers put their languages in everyday interactions? How does the social change affect the communicative economy of the group? How does it change the evaluations of languages and the social statuses and meanings associated with them? How does it affect the communicative strategies of speakers so that individuals are motivated to change their choice of language in different contexts of social interaction—to reallocate their linguistic resources radically so that eventually they abandon one of their languages altogether?

We might ask these questions even more broadly. Is speaking the same language sufficient grounds for people to establish a nation? Should all people in the same nation speak the same language? If the answer to both questions is no—and probably most people in the twenty-first century would agree—what should be the status of "minority" languages in multilingual societies? Because of the symbolic value of language—especially with regards to group solidarity and the ethnic identity of its speakers—language choice, maintenance, and shift are some of the most important personal and political social issues of any community.

In this section we will focus on language and the nation-state. We will look at how the symbolic value of languages is used by the people to pursue political power and ends, and foster consciousness among members of the group. We will look at four case studies: India, the Czech Republic, Canada, and Spain.

India. Occupying an area only one-third as large as the United States but with the second largest population in the world (of more than a billion people), India is one of the most multilingual countries in the world. What makes India one of the world's most linguistically diversified nations is that more than 400 languages are spoken there (Gordon 2005: 353); they span at least four language families (Indo-European, Dravidian, Austroasiatic, and Tibeto-Burman), as well as some isolates. There are twenty-two official "scheduled" languages recognized in the Constitution. Although English is not a legally sanctioned language, the Presidential Order of 1960 states that it "should be the principal official language and Hindi the subsidiary Official Language till 1965. After 1965, when Hindi becomes the principal official language of the Union, English should continue as the subsidiary official language."

How does India, a federal republic, deal administratively with such a vast collection of languages? On a regional basis, eastern India is dominated by three Indo-European languages (Bengali, Oriya, and Assamese), western India by two (Marathi and Gujarati), northern India by four (Hindi and Urdu, Panjabi and Kashmiri), and southern India by four languages of the Dravidian language family (Telugu, Tamil, Kannada, and Malayalam). The principal official language in six of the twenty-five states of the republic as well as of the country at the federal level is Hindi. However, as long as many non-Hindi-speaking citizens are reluctant to accept Hindi, English—the language of those who governed most of India as a British crown colony for nearly a century—serves as the associate national language and as a lingua franca acceptable in both the Hindi-speaking north and the Dravidian-speaking south.

In a country where many languages are spoken but do not all enjoy the same degree of prestige, bilingualism, multilingualism, and diglossia are of common occurrence. For interethnic oral communication of an informal nature, Hindi or Urdu is used to a varying degree throughout the country (the two are very similar in their colloquial forms, but Hindi is written in the Devanagari script, Urdu in a modified form of Arabic script). For reasons of cultural prestige, there has been some resistance to the use of Hindi as a contact language in the Dravidian-speaking part of the country and in Bengal. For formal and written communication, English (its South Asian variety) is used to a great extent. The importance of English can readily be seen: In 1977, although newspapers and periodicals in India were available in about seventy languages, Hindi- and English-language newspapers and periodicals accounted for, respectively, 26 and 20 percent of the total published, and those in English had the highest circulation. When India became independent in 1947, the official use of English was intended to be only temporary. But the need for English continues and in some respects has even increased. For example, to translate technical and scientific works into Hindi would be a nearly impossible task. Today, more than a half century after India gained independence, knowledge of English is still considered indispensable for high government positions, and although only a very small percentage of the population speaks and reads English, Indians with a knowledge of English tend to be the cultural, economic, and political leaders.

Such a large linguistic variety (in both languages and dialects) as exists in India poses a number of questions. Although it might be expected that one official language would tend to promote unity in a multiethnic nation, such unity would be achieved at a considerable loss of prestige to other native languages spoken by many millions of people. This is why the most widely used second language in India, Hindi, has encountered resistance in many parts of the country. And this is also why a nonindigenous and formerly colonial language, English, has maintained itself surprisingly well as an associate official language since India's independence and will undoubtedly continue to do so in the future. A second language for many Indians, English does not give an advantage to speakers of one particular native language, as does Hindi. Another question has to do with determining the languages to be taught and used for instruction in Indian schools. What eventually became known as the three-language formula has resulted in secondary students being taught the regional language, Hindi, and English (and in many instances their mother tongue is yet a fourth language or local dialect).

Throughout much of the world, dialectal differences have tended to diminish rapidly in recent decades as a result of the mass media, education, and mobility. This has not happened in India, where caste differences are effectively symbolized by speech differences. As long as the old and well-established social hierarchy persists, linguistic differences serve a useful function and are likely to be retained.

The Czech Republic. The Bohemian kingdom of the Czech people goes back to the end of the eleventh century, but the first Czechs settled in the area and made it their homeland no later than the sixth century. The development of a Czech national culture came to a temporary (though long) halt in 1620, when the Czechs possessing political rights and power were defeated in the battle of Bílá hora (White Mountain). The Bohemian kingdom lost its independence, and its provinces were declared the hereditary property of the Hapsburgs. The area of the former kingdom had a fairly large proportion of German-speaking people, the descendants of German colonists who had been invited during the thirteenth and fourteenth centuries to settle in Bohemian cities and rural areas.

During the four censuses conducted between 1880 and 1910 in the western part of the multilingual Hapsburg Austro-Hungarian Empire, the Austrian census administration used the concept of *Umgangssprache* (language of use) rather than *Muttersprache* (mother tongue). The Czechs, who at the time were still citizens of the empire, resented this terminological practice because it underrepresented their numbers among the empire's nationalities, yielding a larger proportion of speakers of the higher-status German than was warranted.

How did this happen? For example, Czechs who were employed in German-speaking households or business enterprises were listed as users of German even though Czech was their mother tongue and the language they spoke with members of their own families.

Using language to establish ethnic identity continued a little over a decade later, but with a different goal. The people of some of the border areas of Czechoslovakia, an independent country established in 1918 at the end of World War I, belonged to two or even three different language groups. One such area was that of Teschen (*Těšín* in Czech and *Cieszyn* in Polish) along the Czechoslovak-Polish border. According to the final Austrian census of 1910, based on the concept of language of use, speakers of Polish accounted for 48.5 percent, of Czech for 39.5 percent, and of German for 12 percent. Percentages from the next census, in 1921, then conducted by Czechoslovak authorities, were quite different: The Czech-speaking population of the area was now given as 65.1 percent. Apparently, the Czech administrators of the census assigned ethnic identity on the basis of mother tongue rather than language of use, and this they undoubtedly did to legitimize the hold of the new republic on at least a good part of an ethnically mixed border area.

Canada. As in India and the United States, there is great linguistic diversity in Canada—some eighty-five languages being spoken (Gordon 2005:235)—but the biggest issue is the tension between the two official languages, French and English. Problems of bilingualism have always been the central issue in the nation's politics even before the Confederation of 1867. Jacques Cartier landed in current Quebec in 1534 and claimed the territory for King Francis I, eventually calling it New France. A century and a half later, British entrepreneurs, incorporated by royal charter, started fur trading in the Hudson Bay area in northern Canada. After that, animosity between France and Britain gradually increased, and as a result of the Seven Years' War (1756–1763), the British government took over lower Canada and New France (which was renamed Quebec). The differences between these two colonial populations were significant. French colonists spoke French, practiced Catholicism, and followed the French civil code; British colonists spoke English, practiced Protestantism, and followed traditional English common law. To avert further local conflict, the British passed the Quebec Act of 1774; this guaranteed the residents the use of the French language, Catholicism, and French civil law. This practice was reified several times, and in 1969 the Official Languages Act made English and French

Canada's two official languages. According to 2007 government figures, about 60 percent of Canadians claim English as their native language, as do about 23 percent for French. The majority of these French speakers—about 85 percent—live in Quebec. More than 17 percent of the population is bilingual in French and English.

In spite of the unique characteristics and background of the original British and French settlers, Anglophone Canadians began to control most elite positions in business and industry, even in Quebec. By the 1960s, many Francophone residents began to feel that the French language was being overwhelmed by English. To maintain Canada's professed bilingualism, the federal and local governments created various departments and institutions to oversee the use of the languages in the province. For some Canadians, one of these—the Quebec Board of the French Language—has sometimes been draconian in its enforcement of language policies. For example, the Board's "language police" (as labeled by some nationalist newspapers) gave tickets to shop owners who neglected to provide signs in French. However, by the end of the twentieth century, such extreme policies were rescinded, and the laws modified to make French just markedly predominant on exterior business signs, as suggested by the Supreme Court of Canada.

For the most part, the promotion of personal bilingualism in English and French is an important objective of the Canadian government (though one not always easily obtained or consistently supported). For example, in 2003, the federal government announced a ten-year goal to double bilingualism among Canadian college graduates from 24 percent to 50 percent by 2013. In 1970, the federal government launched the official languages in education program and supported French-language immersion education in many Anglophone public school districts. However, the influence of English still remains strong. According to Monica Heller (1988), because of the social and economic tensions between Francophone and Anglophone speakers in Quebec, how bilingual speakers of French and English see these two languages is highly charged. An awareness of the social value of the two languages reflects how they are used in daily conversations.

These language issues have important political implications. Some believe that the only way to protect the French language and Francophone rights is for Quebec to split off from the rest of Canada. This has been an issue in almost every election since the 1980s. Although it is unlikely that Canada will divide, the cultural and linguistic tensions remain.

Spain. Although the official language of Spain is Castilian Spanish, some dozen other languages are spoken in the country. Catalan and Basque are two of the most important minority languages, and they are spoken by 15 percent and 1.4 percent of the population respectively (Gordon 2005:559–560). Both are important because of the issues of nationalism and ethnic pride associated with each.

Euskara (Euskera), or Basque, is the language of the Basque people who inhabitant northeast Spain and southwest France. There are about 650,000 Basque speakers in Spain and some 100,000 in France. The language is an isolate, with only disputed affiliations with other languages. It has five major dialects. Under the language policy of the Franco Regime (1939–1975), from 1937 until the mid-1950s, it was prohibited to use the Basque language in public. After the Basques regained some political sovereignty, they were once again allowed to use their language in public (including church services, education, and in the mass media). The Royal Academy of the Basque Language created a standard form of Basque in 1964—called Euskara Batua—and established a standard orthography. Although many Basque speakers were reluctant to accept such standards at first, Euskara Batua gradually became accepted and is now used by the Basques at all levels of education.

Unlike Basque, Catalan is a Romance language of the Indo-European family, and shares an 85 percent lexical similarity with Spanish. Its history goes back to the third century B.C.E., when the Catalonia area was ruled by Rome. Because of close contact with Rome, Catalan developed from a more modern and more popular form of Latin than did Castilian. Currently about 7 million people in Spain speak Catalan as their first language. It is also spoken in small areas in southwest France, and Sardinia in Italy.

Right after World War II, the Franco government took severe repressive measures against Catalan language and culture, partly because of the resistance put up by Catalonia during the Spanish Civil War. Barcelona, its capital, was then a center of revolutionary leftist activity. Much of Catalonia's prewar autonomy was lost and the public use of the *Catalan language* was prohibited. During the latter days of the Franco regime, some folk celebrations and religious observances in Catalan came to be tolerated. But because of the institutionalized language discrimination, and its similarity to Spanish, today there are few, if any, monolingual Catalan speakers.

Summary and Conclusions

Although we often think that language variation is largely due to geographically based dialects, much of the time the differences in language use we hear around us are due to other reasons. Many languages exhibit differences according to whether they are spoken by women or men. In some languages, these differences are limited to a few sounds; in others they are lexical as, for example, in American English, where certain words are heard primarily from women rather than men, and vice versa. Gender is not the only source of this kind of variation—some differences are correlated with class and ethnicity.

For example, one distinctive variety of English spoken in the United States is African-American Vernacular English used primarily by African-Americans in concentrated urban centers. Far from being deficient and its speakers verbally deprived, AAVE has its own structure, related to but distinct from other varieties of American English, as well as a range of expressive styles. The stigma often attached to it is undeserved because it confuses the lower socioeconomic status of the many African-Americans who use it with their speech—a good example of ignorance breeding prejudice.

Language reflects personal identity, but sometimes this conflicts with social expectation. For example, at a formal business meeting, the use of AAVE would be thought inappropriate. Likewise, if a woman is using "men's language" among a group of female speakers, she would be crossing a linguistic and social boundary.

Language is also an important marker at a another level. Although not every language has a country, and few countries have only one language, for many people there is an almost visceral connection between a nation-state and some of the languages used within it borders. Should one language be privileged over the others, and if so, for what reasons? What does this mean for those who are its native speakers, and for those who are not? These are by no means trivial questions, as the world's many language wars have demonstrated. And as the world becomes more globalized and the borders of countries more porous, issues of language and nationality can only become more complex.

14

Linguistic Anthropology in a Globalized World

Linguistic anthropology is generally thought to be a field of research understood and practiced by only a relatively few specialists. Although the applications of anthropology to contemporary problems are generally seen as coming from the subfield of cultural rather than linguistic anthropology, many practical uses have been found for socially oriented linguistics, and linguistic expertise is being applied with increasing frequency to problems having their roots in language use.

The most commonly used and best developed form of applied linguistics (and linguistic anthropology) is language planning. Language planning may be called for when the presence of several competing languages in a country has become divisive or when a particular language or dialect is to be elevated to serve as the official or national language of a multilingual or multidialectal society. The initial step in language planning is to define the nature of the problem. Linguists or linguistic anthropologists are best qualified to assume this task. Because the recommendation that a particular language or dialect be made the official language of a society affects everyone in that society, from elders down to elementary school pupils, such advice must be carefully considered. Once the society's leaders reach a decision, projects to facilitate the implementation of the new language policy must be initiated—for example, preparation of textbooks, grammars, and dictionaries and the development of a teacher training program.

Linguistic expertise is most frequently and extensively applied in the field of education (for example, to enhance literacy), but it also can and does contribute to more effective communication in the fields of law, medicine, and business, and it plays an important role in language maintenance and language disorders. This chapter includes some specific examples of the application of linguistics and linguistic anthropology.

Language Planning

The most common form of applied sociolinguistics is language planning. The term refers to a deliberate attempt, usually at the level of the state, to affect language use to prevent or solve some problem of communication. The need for language planning and the formulation of language policies rapidly increased during the twentieth century and is continuing in the twenty-first. The two main reasons are the dislocation of millions of people as a result of wars and political persecution and the emergence of many new multiethnic states when colonial empires were dissolved after World War II.

In a very broad sense, language planning encompasses even the invention of artificial international languages such as Esperanto or Interlingua. Supra-national languages such as these are expected to promote understanding and peaceful coexistence among people of different ethnic and linguistic backgrounds. More narrowly, language planning usually takes one of two forms. One form involves a change in the status of a language or a dialect—in other words, a change in language use. The other involves changes in the structure of a language—changes affecting its pronunciation, spelling, grammar, or vocabulary. Frequently, however, the two forms are combined. The following examples illustrate both forms of language planning in practice.

The nationalization of Swahili in Kenya is primarily an example of change in status. In 1974, the first president of independent Kenya, Jomo Kenyatta, decided that the country's national assembly should conduct its business in Swahili. When the members strongly objected, Kenyatta closed the assembly and announced: "Whether some people will like my decision or not KiSwahili will be spoken in our *Bunge* [Parliament], because it is the language of the *wananchi* [citizens, people]. English is not our language and the time will come when we will do everything in Swahili. I know many people will be annoyed but let them" (Hinnebusch 1979:290). Several dozen languages are spoken in Kenya, at least eight of them by more than 1 million speakers each. Kikuyu, the native language of more than 5 million people, is the language most frequently heard, whereas Swahili is a native language spoken by very few Kenyans and therefore is relatively neutral. To have selected one of the main languages of Kenya (for example, Kikuyu, Luo, Luhya, or Kamba) would have incited ethnic rivalry, and to have chosen English would have given preference to the non-African language of those who ruled Kenya from 1895 until 1963. At present, Swahili and English both serve as official languages, but Swahili is the national language. To promote and institutionalize Swahili as the national language of Kenya, a variety of government policies were called for; these ranged from the preparation of instructional materials to making sure that the Swahili used in official dealings is "good" Kenyan Swahili. The great variety of languages spoken in Kenya, the use of Swahili as a lingua franca and also as an important instrument of the country's detribalization, and the prestige that English still enjoys all indicate that language planning in Kenya will need to continue into the future.

Language planning of the second type has been fairly common, but usually not with the speed and to the extent carried out in Turkey after that country became a republic in 1923. When the Seljuk Turks became Islamized during the ninth and tenth centuries, they adopted Arabic script and borrowed many Arabic words, especially those having to do with religion, law, administration, and commerce. Later, when Persia (now Iran) became a part of the Ottoman (Turkish) Empire, the Turks also adopted Persian loanwords. Arabic and Persian influences affected not only the Turkish vocabulary but phonology and grammar as well. Often, then, three words—a native Turkish word and two loanwords, one each from Arabic and Persian—were available for a single referent. To make matters even more complex, the three words were not always subject to the same grammatical rules. Casual spoken Turkish and the literary language (Ottoman Turkish) were in a diglossic relationship, each with a distinct range of social functions. Ottoman Turkish (the high form), with its many loanwords, was virtually unintelligible to peasants and ordinary people, who spoke the low form.

To simplify and modernize written Turkish, Kemal Atatürk (1881–1938), the first president of Turkey, appointed a commission in 1928 to recommend a new system to replace the Arabic script that had been used for centuries even though it had never suited the structure of Turkish. The new writing system—the Latin alphabet with several diacritics—was ready within six weeks and its use became law before the end of the year. The introduction of the Latin alphabet was later followed by a reform designed to rid Turkish of

Arabic and Persian loanwords by substituting Turkish words taken from the popular language and the old Turkish texts, or coining new ones; to accomplish this demanding task, in 1932 Atatürk founded the Turkish Linguistic Society. The changing of the writing system and the simplification of Turkish grammar and lexicon helped to modernize and Westernize Turkish society, but these measures also made much of classical Turkish literature, unintelligible to modern Turks in its original form.

Literacy, Writing, and Education

There is no doubt that there are significant social and cultural differences between literate and nonliterate peoples. Having a writing system, of course, expands the collective and historical memory of the group. In theory, in a literate community accurate historical records can be kept, scientific information accrued, and religious traditions maintained. Ideally, literacy allows for knowledge to be disseminated to everyone, not just held by a select few. But things are not so simple. For one thing, we must ask, who controls the writing? What script or spelling or style is acceptable? It is commonly said that the pen is mightier than the sword, but is writing really power?

Members of complex industrial societies often underestimate the intellectual prowess and aesthetic sensibilities of nonliterates who do not make use of written language. The findings of anthropologists have demonstrated time and again how false such an assumption is. For example, there is startling imagery and intricate structure of interlocking repetitions in Navajo chants that invite comparison with the best in Western poetry, and many of the origin myths of Native Americans possess the terseness and dramatic quality characteristic of the Book of Genesis. Just as one expects the style of recognized writers in literate societies to rise above the level of everyday speech, it is common to find that demanding standards govern the performances of traditional narratives. And a reminder: Oral folklore is also alive and well in Western societies such as the United States, where it takes the form of tall tales, ballads, jokes, counting-out rhymes, and riddles—to mention only a few genres—and varies from region to region according to occupation, ethnic background, and other characteristics.

Today, literacy is no longer considered simply the ability to read and write, but is "increasingly conceived as a process of interpretation. Literacy is part of one's orientation to a lived reality made meaningful through the interpretation of text, that is, to written and oral descriptions and explanations of events that are endowed with sociohistorial value" (Baquedano-López 2006:246). In this sense, literacy allows us to reformulate existing knowledge to understand new knowledge: Literacy is less a set of acquired skills than the acquisition of a new way of thinking—one that allows us to negotiate with the world in new ways. Literacy is learning to become competent in one's community.

Even though the term *communication* also includes writing, accounts of how writing is used in a particular society appear only rarely in ethnographic literature. This is because anthropologists traditionally have been interested in nonliterate societies (that is, societies without written language) and also because anthropological studies of complex industrial societies in which writing is important and widely used tend to concentrate on face-to-face interaction rather than the relatively remote contact established and maintained by writing. Anthropologists have always recognized the invention of true writing about 5,000 years ago as the starting point of a major cultural revolution in human history, and correspondingly their focus has been on the origins and diffusion of writing rather than on the functions of written language in particular societies. This is changing, however. And Keith Basso (1974:426) reminds us that "the ethnographic study of writing should not be conceived of as an autonomous enterprise . . . but as one element in a more encompassing field of inquiry which embraces the totality of human communication skills."

The same units and components that are employed in the ethnography of speaking might also apply to writing. Several related acts of writing (writing a letter, for example) combine to form a writing event (an exchange of letters on a particular subject or for a particular purpose). The sender(s) and the receiver(s) of letters are participants, and the circumstances under which a letter is sent or letters are exchanged provide a setting for an act of writing or a writing event (for example, the exchange of holiday greetings and New Year's wishes in December). The reasons for writing a letter vary greatly: Personal letters range from bread-and-butter letters (to thank someone for hospitality) to love letters to letters of condolence; formal letters from letters of commendation to those threatening court action. The channel for writing is optical, but the codes vary: Different languages make use of different writing systems, and preschool children sometimes "write" to their grandparents by drawing pictures.

The purpose and message content commonly determine the form of a letter: For example, on the one hand, a letter of application for a position is considered a formal letter and therefore would be carefully composed and typewritten or laser-printed on paper of good quality. On the other hand, a letter to a close friend is usually casual in style, and can even be carelessly written, with the possible inclusion of slang or even an obscenity or two. To send someone who has just experienced a death in the family a card expressing wishes for a "Merry Christmas and a Happy New Year," or to type a letter of condolence rather than write it by hand, would be considered wholly inappropriate. Spoken utterances judged to be humorous even though somewhat risqué could well be considered insulting when committed to writing. In short, just as speaking is governed by rules of interaction and norms of interpretation, so is writing.

If we extend the term *writing* from true writing to any visual communication accomplished by the use of enduring marks or signs, we can then talk about various genres—road signs, pictorial advertisements, graffiti of various kinds, and many other forms. If studies in the ethnography of writing are to be complete and insightful, they need to include the sociocultural context in which they occur. Again, Basso posed some of the questions to be answered, among them,

How . . . is the ability to write distributed among the members of a community, and how does the incidence of this ability vary with factors such as age, sex, socioeconomic class and the like? . . . What kinds of information are considered appropriate for transmission through written channels? . . . Who sends written messages to whom, when, and for what reasons? . . . In short, what position does writing occupy in the total communicative economy of the society under study and what is the range of its cultural meanings? (Basso 1974:431–432)

These questions have not yet been seriously addressed for more than a very few of the world's societies, though there has been some work in this vein. For example, Niko Besnier (1995) studied literacy, gender, and authority in Nukulaelae atoll in Polynesia. The Nukulaelae are now fundamentalist Christians. Sunday sermons are carefully scripted and circulated, often like a set of handouts of lecture notes, indicating the verses of the Bible to be studied, the remarks to be made about them, and various introductions and conclusions. Particular linguistic features characterize these sermons, including elaborate poetic alteration, special pronoun use, and other kinds of formal features. Women do not write sermons, and give few, claiming they do not have the aptitude for them. Besnier argues that this is a situation in which reading and writing are directly involved in the reproduction of inequality, and control over women's access to reading and writing contributes to their lower social position. On the other hand, women are allowed more freedom of emotional expression in the reading and exchange of letters, a primary means by which the Nukulaelae stay in contact with other islands or kinfolk who have moved away. Men are allowed to appear "feminine" (i.e., showing love or expressing vulnerability) in letter writing, but only within strict limits.

Where literacy comes directly in contact with culture is in education. But being "literate" is something not always easily defined. For example, among the Vai in Africa, one can be literate in three areas: in English for science, technology, and Western education; in Arabic for religious studies and the Koran; and in Vai for local government and social affairs (Scribner and Cole 1981). No one is equally literate in all three, and not all three are equally taught in school. Schools do much more than make their students literate, though writing is the medium through which most of this enculturation takes place. Schools impart values, attitudes, and standards, and a social awareness of one's place in society. Some radical critics argue (e.g., Bourdieu 1987, 1999) that learning one's social class, and how to make appropriate class distinctions, is introduced, reinforced, and reified through language and literacy in the classroom. It is well documented, for instance, that some ethnic groups in the United States do better in formal schooling because of their exposure at home to things that would most likely help them succeed in the classroom (for example, middle-class European-American values, and language and literacy skills that are close to school practices).

The Life and Death of Languages

A look at a source book such as *Ethnologue* (Gordon 2005) shows that there is great linguistic diversity all around us: The world's 6.8 billion people speak some six thousand languages. However, 96 percent of them are spoken by only 4 percent of the population. More than half the world's population speak just twenty languages. But languages are dying at an alarming rate.

David Crystal (2004:47) claims that on average one language dies out every two weeks. At that rate, half the world's languages will become extinct within this century. We are witnessing language death at rates unprecedented in human history. In this section we will look at why so many languages are dying, and what—if anything—can be done about it.

Endangered Languages. According to the U.S. Fish and Wildlife service, in 2010 almost 2,000 species of plants and animals worldwide were considered threatened with extinction or seriously endangered, and citizens of the United States and other countries are frequently reminded of this fact by the media. On the other hand, very few people are being made aware that some of the world's languages are facing a similar threat at an ever-increasing rate. According to David Crystal (2000:14–15), about 500 languages have fewer than 100 speakers, and more than 1,500 languages have only 1,000 speakers at the most. Of the six or seven thousand languages used in the world today (keeping in mind that by the time you are reading this book the number will have been reduced by as many as several dozen), only about 600 can be considered "safe," meaning that the number of their speakers will have become larger, or at least have remained at "critical mass." (In theory, very small societies could maintain their languages if they were both viable and isolated from large societies around them; but such isolation is less and less possible, and if there still are such societies in New Guinea or near the Amazon, their isolation will not last much longer.)

Why do languages die? A fairly common reason in the past could be that very small societies did not survive epidemic diseases against which they had no resistance, or they perished in warfare or in such natural disasters as earthquakes, floods, volcanic eruptions, and drought. The most common reason during the twentieth century was the economic and cultural influence of large nation-states that encompass small tribal societies within their borders. Unable to provide for themselves by their traditional means of subsistence, they become dependent on the dominant society and must learn to communicate with that larger society in its own language. Quite frequently there is a phase of bilingualism during which members of the small society have command of both languages; but this phase usually does not last long because the next generation becomes monolingual in the language of the larger society.

This has happened with many of the Native American languages spoken in the United States. For example, toward the end of the nineteenth century and in the early years of the twentieth, an aggressive effort was made on the part of public schools and mission schools on western reservations to teach young Native American students English. School administrators used such punishments as not allowing pupils in residential schools to spend weekends with their families if they forgot themselves and spoke to each other in their native language. Less than a hundred years later, the situation has been practically reversed: The United States government has financed efforts to preserve languages on the verge of disappearing. Unfortunately, for most languages the demise can be postponed only for a generation, if that long.

Language Death. "Why should we care [if a language dies]?" asked Crystal. He devoted a full chapter of his book (2000:27–67) to discussing five reasons why we should care: because we need diversity in order to preserve our traditional cultural wealth; because a language constitutes the primary symbol of ethnic identity; because languages, whether written or unwritten, are repositories of history; because languages contribute to the sum of human knowledge; and because languages are fascinating in themselves. As one field-worker observed, "To fight to preserve the smaller cultures and languages may turn out to be the struggle to preserve the most precious things that make us human before we end up in the land fill of history" (cited in Crystal 2000:67). And as Kenneth Hale, a linguist at MIT who devoted himself to preserving languages of small tribal societies, once said, "When you lose a language, it's like dropping a bomb on a museum."

This situation poses important questions: Should anthropological or linguistic field-workers make special efforts to maintain or revitalize an endangered language? Should they try to persuade the remaining speakers of such an endangered language to make sure that the youngest members learn it as their mother tongue (along with the language of the dominant society as their second language)? And should linguistic anthropologists wonder whether they have a moral obligation to try to save a language even if its speakers are ambivalent about its practical value and future usefulness? Answers to such questions are not easy to come by. Not only has very little debate taken place on this subject, but the resources for the study of endangered languages are still far from adequate. In the meantime, languages are dying out at a faster pace every year.

Language Maintenance and Reinforcement. Since the mid-1960s, increasing efforts by linguists and Native American tribal leaders have been devoted to language maintenance and reinforcement in communities where the traditional transmission of oral skills from parents to children is no longer functioning effectively. Although perhaps as many as 200 Native American languages are still spoken at least to some extent in the United States and Canada, ever-increasing numbers of them are in danger of being completely replaced by English. Only a relatively few Native American languages (for example, Navajo, some of the Siouan languages of the northern Plains, and Eskimo) continue to play a vital role in Indian community life; they are the languages serving larger populations in the less densely inhabited parts of North America. Language maintenance and reinforcement typically include linguistic analysis (on all levels—phonological, morphological, syntactic, and lexical), a writing system (usually the Latin alphabet with a few additional symbols and diacritics if necessary), and the production of instructional materials for the use of Native American pupils.

For the Northern Arapaho of the Wind River Reservation in Wyoming, who are eager to maintain, and even reinforce, their ethnic identity and cultural heritage, the present situation is nothing short of critical. Several factors contribute to the gloomy outlook:

1. With few exceptions, the only individuals who have full command of Arapaho—even if they no longer use it habitually and even if English has come to influence it—are members of the oldest generation.
2. Parents no longer teach Arapaho to their children in the home.
3. The numbers of active speakers and of those who have at least some passive knowledge of Arapaho are declining rapidly.
4. The bulk of the population is for all practical purposes monolingual; English is preferred in essentially all situations, including even some traditional ceremonial contexts.
5. Arapaho is losing its communicative viability—its capability to adapt successfully to new situations.

It is sad that young Arapaho parents can no longer be expected to pass along to their children the rich cultural heritage of the tribe, the Arapaho language in particular. As a result, the task has fallen to the reservation schools.

The most significant step taken to arrest the language decay was to formalize the teaching of spoken Arapaho to the youngest pupils. Thanks to the foresight and energy of the administrators of one of the schools, two weeklong workshops were organized in March and September 1984 to experiment with videotaping lessons in spoken Arapaho for use in reservation classrooms. So much was learned from the work of those two weeks that at a January workshop the following year it was possible to approach the task with a greater degree of professional skill and, aided by the administrators of another school, to produce the first formal set of lessons in spoken Arapaho. The Spoken Arapaho Curriculum Development Project team set its goal for the two weeks rather ambitiously at forty lessons, but the enthusiasm of the participants was such that forty-two were completed and are still in classroom use. To spare young pupils from having to learn how to write two languages (Arapaho spelling happens to be much simpler than English spelling because it is phonemic), Arapaho-speaking classroom aides teach the students spoken Arapaho with the help of the videotapes. Forty-odd lessons will not reverse the declining fortunes of the Arapaho language on the reservation, but their completion and use in the lower grades have the great symbolic value of a last-ditch stand and a hope for things to come.

The end of 1983 also saw the completion of the *Dictionary of Contemporary Arapaho Usage*, made possible by a grant from the National Endowment for the Humanities. It was a source of great satisfaction to the Arapaho that the very same government that only a few generations ago prohibited the use of Native American languages in schools has become seriously concerned with their preservation.

While the work on the dictionary and the videotaped lessons was taking place, one of the schools continued to add to the growing series of booklets designed to aid the teaching of Arapaho language and culture in the upper grades. Overall, the body of instructional materials produced under various auspices for use with Arapaho students in the reservation schools is quite impressive—more than a hundred items, not counting the videotaped lessons. Not to be outdone by the other schools, staff members of a third school came up with an idea to further help revitalize the efforts made on behalf of Arapaho: an annual Arapaho language bowl for the most accomplished students of the reservation schools, with prizes and diplomas to be awarded.

Since the first edition of this book came out in 1993, further developments have occurred. Stephen Greymorning, director for several years of the Arapaho Language and Culture Project among the Northern Arapaho of Wyoming, began an Arapaho-language immersion project for kindergarten children and then expanded it by the addition of a preschool program. For use with the children, Greymorning arranged for the Disney film *Bambi* to be dubbed in Arapaho by Disney Studios, using Greymorning's translation and with Arapaho elders and children from the immersion program speaking the roles. The dubbed film became available in several thousand copies, and young children were said to watch it repeatedly, learning the speaking parts of their favorite characters. Although these and other revitalization efforts are not likely to save the Arapaho language in the long term, they are a welcome step forward at a time when so many languages are becoming seriously endangered or extinct.

This brief account of one example of language maintenance and reinforcement would not be complete without emphasizing that many additional steps must be taken to expand the program in the future. The following steps are worth mentioning here (the list is meant to be merely suggestive, not complete): workshops designed to develop new Arapaho curricular materials and improve the existing ones; in-service training of current Arapaho studies teachers and teacher aides; an internship program for future teachers of Arapaho studies; tribal scholarships for Arapaho high school students who have shown exceptional intellectual capacity as well as interest and skill in learning Arapaho to allow them to study linguistics and anthropology at the college level; adult education programs featuring elders narrating, in Arapaho or English, traditional tales or life histories and other reminiscences; and an Arapaho-language summer camp for preschoolers and elementary pupils, staffed in part by those Arapaho elders, women and men, who have command of the language and a willingness to share it with the young members of the tribe.

In the initial stages of any language maintenance programs, linguistic anthropologists provide useful advice and help, but it is preferable and important that, as far as possible, such programs and activities be further developed, organized, and administered by members of the societies concerned. Box 14.1 provides an example of elaborate plans for revitalizing the threatened language of a New Mexican pueblo.

Intercultural Communication and Translation

Today, when so many people frequently travel far away from home and encounter members of different ethnic groups and societies, interethnic and intercultural relations are continually being put to the test. Whether such

BOX 14.1 PLANS FOR THE REVITALIZATION OF KERES, THE DIALECT OF RIO GRANDE KERESAN, SPOKEN IN THE PUEBLO OF COCHITI, NEW MEXICO

As of this writing, the plans for the fall [2000] include (1) an all-Keres room where Head Start and preschool children can spend from half an hour to two hours daily, depending on their parents' preferences; (2) Keres language classes for tribal employees, to be given three times a week; (3) after-school arts and crafts and recreational activities for school-age children; and (4) arts and crafts and Keres classes for adults in the evenings. In addition, CIEC [Cochiti Indian Education Committee] and CETF [Cochiti Education Task Force] committee members have committed themselves to providing mentoring to less fluent speakers and to revitalizing the practice of visiting each other and maintaining Keres during these visits. Several community projects such as ditch cleaning, weeding, and painting are planned in which fluent adults are matched with learning adolescents.

All of these efforts will be undertaken either with volunteers or with tribal funds. This allows the tribe to maintain control and to remain faithful to its own values. Moreover, drawing in the different segments of the community—for example, the elders, the tribal council, tribal employees, parents, and children—underscores the fact that the language revitalization project belongs to everyone and therefore all have a responsibility to its continuation.

Future plans include a language nest, where babies and very young children can be cared for by fluent Keres-speaking "grandmothers"; an all-Keres preschool program; a healthy after-school recreational program; more community projects; adolescent-elder pairings; and consistent Keres class offerings after school and in the evenings for adults. These plans for the future will necessarily mean that more fluent speakers will be needed to teach and to lead in the various initiatives that are to come.

The CIEC, the task force, and the leaders of the community understand the commitment required to make all of this a reality. However, they also understand the power of these initiatives for the language learning of their future leaders. Much of the success that the Pueblo de Cochiti has enjoyed is owed to the fact that the leaders have moved slowly and planned carefully. Above all, they have made certain that every step taken has been consonant with Cochiti traditional culture and values.

from Regis Pecos and Rebecca Blum-Martinez, "The Key to Cultural Survival" (2001), 81–82 relations are amicable or hostile, straightforward or confused, depends primarily on how individuals or groups with differing cultural backgrounds are able to communicate with each other. Even in languages or dialects that are closely similar or considered to be alike, specific words may have different senses or carry a different emphasis from one language to the other, resulting in occasional misunderstandings. A good illustration of a lack of equivalence between American and British English was provided by Margaret Mead when she pointed out that

in Britain, the word "compromise" is a good word, and one may speak approvingly of any arrangement which has been a compromise, including, very often, one in which the other side has gained more than fifty per cent of the points at issue. On the other hand, in the United States, the minority position is still the position from which everyone speaks. . . . This is congruent with the American doctrine of checks and balances, but it does not permit the word "compromise" to gain the same ethical halo which it has in Britain. Where, in Britain, to compromise means to work out a good solution, in America it usually means to work out a bad one, a solution in which all the points of importance (to both sides) are lost. [Mead quoted in Kluckhohn 1949:158]

Not always given sufficient attention but frequently of some consequence are differences in communicative styles among ethnic groups of a particular society. A number of research projects have been undertaken to determine the extent of such differences between Anglo-Americans on the one side and Latinos, African-Americans, and members of other ethnic groups that make up the population of the United States on the other. For example, according to one study, the ten- to fifteen-year-old recently arrived Latino pupils of several samples were found to be more interpersonally oriented and more inclined to attribute the feeling of shame to themselves or to others when compared with their Anglo-American peers. If teachers are aware of differences between members of differing ethnic groups that find expression in communicative behavior, they can better understand why under certain circumstances some pupils react differently from others (Albert 1986).

According to another study, black and white students at an eastern college differed in their handling of oral disagreements. The African-American students tended to argue more persistently with each other for their positions and to take more control of the interaction than did white students, who appeared to prefer compromise or solution-oriented strategies in resolving their conflicts. Furthermore, all males in this sample, regardless of ethnicity, were more likely to engage in indirect, nonconfrontational strategies (for example, silence) than females, who tended to use more active strategies (Ting-Toomey 1986).

It is, of course, necessary to keep in mind that it would be inappropriate to extend the findings pertaining to a sample to an entire ethnic group. Any of a number of circumstances may invalidate such an extension—for example, setting (urban as against rural), the length of interethnic contact (a few years as opposed to decades as opposed to generations), amount of education, geographic location, socioeconomic status, and so on.

Ronald and Suzanne B. K. Scollon (1981) published an informative account of the nature of interethnic communication between members of some of the Athabaskan tribes living in Alaska and northwestern Canada, and Americans or Canadians having reason to interact with them. Most communication takes place in English because good speaking knowledge of Athabaskan languages among Americans and Canadians is quite rare, and many Athabaskans (especially the younger ones) now speak only English. However, even those Athabaskans speaking only English have learned from their families and communities to use the communicative behavior characteristic of their ethnic background.

The Scollons analyzed several aspects of communicative behavior between Americans/Canadians and Athabaskans. In the presentation of self, the contrast between the two groups takes a diametrically opposite form: In a conversation between strangers concerning business, medical, legal, educational, or other matters, the Americans/Canadians talk freely and a great deal, hoping to learn from the exchange what is on the minds of the Athabaskans; they, on the other hand, say very little because they greatly respect each person's individuality and right to privacy, and they carefully guard their own as well. The Athabaskans gain the impression that their opposites are too talkative, and even boastful, whereas the Americans/Canadians tend to think of the Athabaskans as uncommunicative, unsure of themselves, and probably incompetent.

When two Americans/Canadians talk, they usually take turns speaking unless the relationship between them is so asymmetrical that one of them monopolizes the conversation. Several incongruities occur in turn-taking between Americans/Canadians and Athabaskans. One has to do with the length of pauses between turns. Athabaskan pauses may be somewhat longer, causing American or Canadian speakers to feel free to resume talking. The result is a conversation that is almost a monologue. Typically, a conversation is initiated by Americans/Canadians and is terminated by them with some such formula as "I'll see you later (tomorrow, soon)." But the Athabaskans consider it bad luck to make predictions about future events and do not reciprocate with a similar phrase. This lack of closure is interpreted by the Americans/Canadians as a failure of the communicative event.

Still other sources of misunderstanding have to do with the way information is coded. If Americans/Canadians want to emphasize certain aspects of their utterances, they usually do so by such means as stress, sentence intonation, and the like. In Athabaskan languages emphasis is marked by special morphemes—for example, in Chipewyan the morpheme $k'\varepsilon'$, which expresses surprise. When Athabaskans use English, they do not mark emphasis by means of prosodic features. As a result, they may be only partly understood or, at worst, completely misunderstood.

This abbreviated account of the Scollons' research describes the confusion that is likely to occur in interethnic communication between Athabaskans and Americans/Canadians, but there are data to suggest that a similar situation exists whenever Americans communicate with other Native Americans. The differences in interethnic communicative behavior just described are easy to understand. The dangers these differences lead to is ethnic stereotyping that may have as a consequence less than friendly and cooperative coexistence. The sources of problems in communication between Athabaskans and Americans/Canadians are summarized in Box 14.2. The table is culture-specific, but it applies to a great extent to communication between Anglo-Americans and Native Americans of other tribes as well (but keep in mind that the table lists *typical* behaviors).

Translations can also be troublesome, as anyone who has ever studied a foreign language knows. The scholarly literature and personal anecdotes offer hundreds of examples of mistranslated words, phrases, or whole pieces of discourse. However, in our earlier discussions of the Sapir-Whorf hypothesis, we said that one of its refutations (at least of the strong version) was that anything in every language could be translated into any other. Although this is true, some caveats need to be made, as sometimes translations do not go smoothly. Often, the problem is not just differences in grammar or

BOX 14.2　COMMUNICATION PROBLEMS BETWEEN
ENGLISH SPEAKERS AND ATHABASKANS

What's Confusing to English Speakers About Athabaskans	*What's Confusing to Athabaskan Speakers About English Speakers*
They do not speak.	They talk too much.
They keep silent.	They always talk first.
They avoid situations of talking.	They talk to strangers or people they don't know.
They only want to talk to close acquaintances.	They think they can predict the future.
They play down their own abilities.	They brag about themselves.
They act as if they expect things to be given to them.	They don't help people even when they can.
They deny planning.	They always talk about what's going to happen later.
They avoid direct questions.	They ask too many questions.
They never start a conversation.	They always interrupt.
They talk off the topic.	They only talk about what they are interested in.
They never say anything about themselves.	They don't give others a chance to talk.
They are slow to take a turn in talking.	They are always getting excited when they talk.
They ask questions in unusual places.	They aren't careful when they talk about things or people.
They talk with a flat tone of voice.	
They are too indirect, inexplicit.	
They don't make sense.	
They just leave without saying anything.	

from Ronald Scollon and Suzanne Wong-Scollon,
"Athabaskan-English Interethnic Communication" (1990), 284

vocabulary, even though the meaning and connotations of no pair of words in two languages are ever going to be precisely the same. Included in the whole package are also matters of context, cultural expectations, stylistic features, and personal interpretation.

As an example, consider a collision between a U.S. spy plane and a Chinese fighter in spring of 2001 that almost caused an international incident. The contact occurred near the island of Hainan, a contested area, when two PRC jets scrambled to meet an American surveillance aircraft. The larger U.S. plane and smaller Chinese jet collided (killing its pilot), and forcing the damaged U.S. plane to land in China, where the twenty-four-person flight crew was taken prisoner and held for eleven days, being released after a formal apology was made by the U.S. Ambassador to the Chinese Foreign Minister at the American Embassy. What the apology said, and meant, almost immediately came under scrutiny.

Hang Zhang (2001:384) claims there are six levels of apology in Chinese, ranging from terms conveying a simple "sorry" to "feel regret" to "admit one's error and ask for punishment and humbly apologize." When the U.S. letter was delivered, it was "carefully constructed in such a way that it said the most 'sincere' words possible without assuming any responsibility. At the lexical level it avoided the word *apologize*" (Zhang 2001:385):

Dear Mr. Minister,

On behalf of the United States Government, I now outline steps to resolve this issue.

Both President Bush and Secretary of State Powell have expressed their sincere regret over your missing pilot and aircraft. Please convey to the Chinese people and to the family of the pilot Wang Wei that we are very sorry for their loss.

Although the full picture of what transpired is still unclear, according to our information, our severely crippled aircraft made an emergency landing after following international emergency procedures. We are very sorry for the entering of China's airspace and the landing did not have verbal clearance, but very pleased the crew landed safely.

We appreciate China's efforts to see to the well-being of our crew. In view of the tragic incident and based on my discussions with your representative, we have agreed to the following actions:

Both sides agree to hold a meeting to discuss the incident. My government understands and expects that our aircrew will be permitted to depart China as soon as possible.

The meeting would start April 18, 2001.

The meeting agenda would include discussion of the cause of the incident, possible recommendations whereby such collisions could be avoided in the future, development of a plan for prompt return of the EP-3 aircraft, and other related issues. We acknowledge your government's intention to raise U.S. reconnaissance missions near China in the meeting.

Sincerely,

Joseph W. Prueher [U.S. Ambassador]

The media on both sides of the Pacific began interpreting the letter immediately—the Chinese literally and the Americans figuratively. The two instances of "sorry" in the English text were much discussed and analyzed, as well as the various back-translations. The translation from English to Chinese offered a translator a choice of at least six alternatives. In its own Chinese version, however, the U.S. chose the word *wanxi* (Zhang 2001:390), a word not normally used in Chinese when involving death (and not one of the typical six terms).

Zhang argues that this apology should be viewed not only as a simple speech act but also as a discourse event, extending beyond individual behavior to national behavior—one highly ideologically invested for both sides. Language became a field of combat of competing ideologies. It was not only an outcome of such negotiations but also the means to them.

Language and the Law

According to Frake, "The Yakan legal system is manifest almost exclusively through one kind of behavior: talk. Consequently the ethnographer's record of observations of litigation is largely a linguistic record, and the legal system is a code for talking, a linguistic code" (Frake 1969:147; the Yakan are Philippine Muslims inhabiting the island of Basilan southwest of Mindanao). By contrast, the laws of the United States are written down, and legal interpretations and decisions have been recorded in scores of volumes. But the language of the law is just as much spoken as it is read, and its nature may be a source of problems for individuals engaged in litigation. One such problem concerns the understanding of legal terms on the part of those American citizens whose native language is not English; another has to do with comprehending the specialized language of the legal profession, difficult even for native English speakers. Not a few commonly used legal terms are foreign, overly formal, jargonistic, or absent from common speech to such an extent that litigants frequently find it difficult to follow court proceedings. For example, how many college-educated people know the meanings of such legal terms and expressions as *venire, tort, eminent domain, pursuant to, know all men by these presents,* and *(in) flagrante delicto?* Although most citizens may never become litigants, they do encounter legal language in insurance policies and other contractual documents. A humorous quotation from *The Tulsa Tribune,* October 6, 1959, illustrates just how wordy, pompous, and repetitious legal language can appear to lay people: The simple offer expressed by the sentence "Have an orange" might read in legalese as "I hereby give and convey to you, all and singular, my estate and interest, right, title, claim and advantages of and in said orange, together with its rind, skin, juice, pulp, and pips and all rights and advantages therein and full power to bite, suck, or otherwise eat the same or give the same away with or without the rind, skin, juice, pulp and pips" (quoted in Hager 1959:74–75).

The specific phrasing of questions can influence the answers of witnesses. An experiment revealed that the use of the word *smashed* in an inquiry concerning the collision of two cars tended to elicit estimates of higher speed than the use of such words as *collided, bumped, hit,* or *contacted* (in descending order). Further, subjects shown a film of two cars colliding responded to the question "Did you see any broken glass?" more often with a yes if the questioner used the word *smashed* rather than the milder word *hit,* even though the film had shown no broken glass at all (Loftus and Palmer 1974).

In general, *how* things are said in a courtroom—the speech behavior of the prosecuting attorney, the legal counsel for the defendant, the defendant, and witnesses—may carry more weight than what is actually being said. For example, what has been characterized as a "powerless" and therefore unconvincing mode of speech includes the use of hedges ("Perhaps . . . ," "Possibly . . . ," or "If I'm not mistaken . . . ") on the part of the defendant or a witness. And when lawyers try to manipulate and control witnesses too tightly (by interrupting them, not letting them testify as fully as they would like to), the impression may be created that the lawyers have little confidence in the testimony being given. A juror's negative impression of a lawyer as a result of his or her speech behavior with witnesses may well be transferred to the person the lawyer is representing, with possible consequences for the case (O'Barr and Conley 1996).

If a questioner's use of particular words or constructions can influence the answers without the respondent or jurors being aware of it, or if the highly specialized language used is not fully intelligible to the person concerned, some remedy is indicated. In recent years many insurance policies have, in fact, been written in more understandable language or included definitions of the legal terms used. Stylistic changes made to eliminate, or at least alleviate, incomprehensible legal formulations are examples of applied linguistics.

A concrete example of the application of linguistic findings to social issues is the case of the "Black English trial" in Ann Arbor, so referred to and described by William Labov (1982), one of the most distinguished sociolinguists in the United States. In the 1960s, the city of Ann Arbor, Michigan, decided to distribute low-income housing in various neighborhoods rather than concentrate it in the downtown area. One of the results of scattered-site housing was that African-American children from the project built on Green Road began attending the Martin Luther King Elementary School, which then came to serve 80 percent white, 13 percent African-American, and 7 percent Asian and Latino pupils.

Several years later, the mothers of the African-American pupils from the project became upset that their children were doing quite poorly in school. According to the school staff, the students were either emotionally disturbed or had learning disabilities, and in general exhibited behavior problems. Believing their children to be normal, four of the mothers sought out legal assistance, and on July 28, 1977, on behalf of fifteen African-American pupils, charged the King school with failure to take into consideration the cultural and socioeconomic factors that had affected these pupils' progress. The plaintiffs argued that the failure of the school to take appropriate action to overcome the linguistic barrier encountered by the Green Road children—namely, that they spoke a vernacular then referred to as Black English that was quite different from the language spoken by the majority of the pupils—impeded their children's equal participation in the school's instructional program. Witnesses at the trial included linguists known for their work in sociolinguistics, Labov among them. The judge ruled in favor of the plaintiffs on July 12, 1979, and incorporated into his decision a statement that summarized the results of some twenty years of linguistic research concerning the nature of African-American English. The relevant passage reads as follows:

All of the distinguished researchers and professionals testified as to the existence of a language system, which is a part of the English language but different in significant respects from the standard English used in the school setting, the commercial world, the world of the arts and science, among the professions, and in government. It is and has been used at some time by 80 percent of the black people of this country and has as its genesis the transactional or pidgin language of the slaves, which after a generation or two became a Creole language. Since then it has constantly been refined and brought closer to the mainstream of society. It still flourishes in areas where there are concentrations of black people. It contains aspects of Southern dialect and is used largely by black people in their casual conversation and informal talk. [Quoted in Labov 1982:194]

In the conclusion of his article, Labov stressed the need for both scientific objectivity and commitment to social action. He further pointed out that the trial not only took place on the initiative of African-American people but was instrumental in bringing African-American linguists into the field of research concerning African-American English. (Because African-American English is discussed in some detail in Chapter 13, Labov's account of the trial in Ann Arbor is greatly abbreviated here.)

To mention an application of a different type (Gumperz 1982): In 1978, a U.S. Navy doctor of Filipino origin attended an emergency room case. A sixteen-month-old girl was brought to the hospital with burns that her mother and stepfather claimed had been caused by overexposure to the sun. The child was treated and released in the parents' care. Six hours later, the child was brought back to the emergency room and examined by another physician then on duty, but she died later that day. It was found that the burns had been intentionally inflicted by her stepfather, who was convicted of second-degree manslaughter and sentenced to a prison term.

Sometime later, the first examining doctor was accused of perjury for statements made when he testified for the prosecution at the stepfather's trial, although his testimony had been supported by the hospital personnel who had assisted him in the emergency room. According to a report by the FBI agent charged with investigating the case, the doctor should have suspected child abuse and kept the child in the hospital instead of releasing her to the parents. During the court proceedings, one of the defense attorneys pointed out that on several occasions the doctor had used pronouns in a "funny" way even though his English was good. The doctor's native language was Aklanon, but he was fluent in Tagalog and English, the two official languages of the Philippines. A linguist was brought in as an expert to determine whether a cross-cultural misunderstanding could have occurred. The linguist was able to establish that several passages in the doctor's testimony were ambiguous because he had carried over into English the syntax of his native language, syntax that in Aklanon or Tagalog would not have been ambiguous. To quote from Gumperz's conclusion:

We have demonstrated that many aspects of [the doctor's] behavior can be explained by his linguistic and cultural background. The features in question are automatic and not readily subject to conscious control. They do not affect his written performance, yet they are likely to recur whenever he is faced with complex oral communicative tasks, so that, in spite of the fact that he speaks English well, he is more likely than native speakers of English to be misunderstood in such situations. (Gumperz 1982:195)

The miscommunication argument was accepted by most of the jurors, and the perjury charges against the doctor were dismissed.

Others who have studied how the use of language can affect legal proceedings have pointed out several instances in which the services of someone with linguistic expertise would be helpful. Such a situation could occur when legal jargon combined with certain features of grammar (for example, passive constructions or the excessive use of nouns where verbs would be clearer or more direct) keeps jurors from understanding the instructions the judge gives to them. Linguistic expertise may also be needed to counter possible listener "contamination," a danger when jurors are left to their own resources to interpret recorded conversations between the defendant and others. The linguist may be able, for example, to indicate that the defendant's silence could have been due to boredom, politeness, or some other factor rather than to tacit agreement with what other speakers may have been saying, or to identify, by their dialectal or idiolectal characteristics, the defendant's utterances among a confusing variety of voices. Another type of situation could occur if statements or questions containing a presupposition create the assumption of truth when such an assumption is not warranted. Such misleading use of language is related to the well-known question "Have you stopped beating your wife?" to which the person questioned is expected to answer yes or no. Regardless of the choice of answer, the clear implication is that such a misdeed did in fact take place. On a broader scale, the linguist may be of assistance to the court by analyzing recordings for clues relating to the intentions and the conversational strategies of speakers.

The many aspects to communicative behavior in court deserve attention if all relevant information is to be available to the judge and the jurors. Among the factors to be considered are the cultural background and communicative competence of the defendant, the plaintiff, and the witnesses; the types of questions asked during a trial (for example, the use of leading questions) and the context in which they are asked; the relative value of narrative testimony as against testimony limited to specific brief answers; the use of interruptions; the nature of the instructions given by the judge to the jurors; and others. It is clear that linguistic expertise in court proceedings can be of value.

English as an International Language

People whose mother tongue is English have a great advantage over speakers of other languages. Not only is English the official or unofficial language in some eighty countries, but it is also favored as the language of international congresses, commercial negotiations, science journals, popular music, sports, civil aviation, diplomacy, technology and industry, and other undertakings or activities involving worldwide participation. Americans traveling abroad have become so accustomed to having foreigners communicate with them in English that they are surprised and even annoyed (unjustifiably) when these expectations are not met. In short, English has become the world's number-one second language, even though resistance to it is growing in some parts of the Third World.

The primacy of English is of relatively recent date, deriving from the political, economic, scientific, and technological role the United States has come to play in the decades following World War II. During the Middle Ages, Latin served as the language of intellectual discourse in most countries of Europe even though it was no longer the first language of any speech community. French functioned as the "universal" language from the seventeenth through the nineteenth centuries by virtue of French political and intellectual influence, and it remained the preferred language of diplomacy until World War II.

Americans find it both flattering and convenient that so many people the world over have at least a working knowledge of English, but give the matter little further thought—after all, they are used to traveling for thousands of miles in their own country and throughout much of Canada without a change in language. But in Europe, the situation is strikingly different; there, traveling a mere 100 miles may involve crossing two or even three language boundaries. It is therefore not surprising that many young Europeans begin serious study of foreign languages, including English, in primary or secondary schools. (It should be noted that German is regaining some of the prestige it lost after World War II.)

According to a well-known Czech proverb, the number of languages a person knows, that many times is he or she a human being. Significant benefit indeed accrues to those who learn to speak more than just their mother tongue. They not only are made more aware of the workings of their own language but also are far better able to appreciate and understand other cultures. The lack of skills in other languages on the part of young English-speaking Americans was recognized by the President's Commission on Foreign Language and International Studies, which in its final report stated that "Americans' scandalous incompetence in foreign languages also explains our dangerously inadequate understanding of world affairs" (1979:7).

As for cultural and linguistic anthropologists, any attempt on their part to conduct serious fieldwork in a foreign setting would be inconceivable without at least some knowledge of the language of those whom they study.

Always On: New Literacies and Language
in an Online Global World

It is likely that if you are a typical student reading this book, you will probably have some other task going on at the moment. Maybe you are watching television or checking your Facebook page. Maybe you are also instant messaging. Maybe you are checking some fact you have just read on your iPad. Perhaps you are listening to music. Undoubtedly your smart phone is charged, sitting on your desk. And when you use that cell phone it is just as likely that you will send a text message as press the dial button. An obvious question is, "What are we, as speakers and writers, doing to our language by virtue of our new communication technologies, and how, in turn, do our linguistic practices impact the way we think and the way we relate to other people?" (Baron 2008:x). In other words, what is our linguistic life like now that we are "always on?" There are many ways to examine language and digital communication, but we will address the four most important in this section: We will look at sociolinguistic changes, formal syntactical and grammatical changes, changes in orthography, and possible cognitive impacts of these new literacies. Connecting with our discussions of English in the last section, we will also address the language of the international Internet.

Sociolinguistic changes. As we have already said, the use of language is perhaps the most important reflection of one's personal and social identity. Simply put, language is who you are. Some fifty years ago, the well-known sociologist Erving Goffman (1959) introduced the theoretical construct of the "presentation of self in everyday life": Though anticipated by Shakespeare four centuries earlier—all the world is a stage—Goffman argued that much of social life—our face time—is spent managing how we want others to see us. And because we are in many ways what we pretend to be, as Kurt Vonnegut said, this has important psychological implications as well.

In nondigital environments, our speech and dress are the most conspicuous presentations of ourselves. However, in day-to-day, face-to-face real life we are constrained in many ways. No matter how cool he talks and how baggy his pants are, a fifty-year-old male college professor still remains *that*, even if his ball cap is on backwards. But on the Internet these restrictions are diluted or nonexistent. On the Web, not only can we be anonymous, we can be anybody. All bets are off. Where previously the implicit rules of social politeness may have kept my language judicious, in a comment to a blog or an online news story, I literally can say whatever I please without fear of social consequences.

Likewise, in face-to-face communication, I am compelled to interact with people and conversations as they come up. You have to deal with meeting that old boyfriend on the quad; I have to deal with that problem student who comes to the office for hand-holding everyday. We cannot avoid these encounters. But in the world of digital communications, we are all "language Czars," as Naomi Baron argues (2008). That is, we control whom we want to talk to and when, and on what terms. Though in the past, letters and telephones allowed some degree of management of whom we would communicate with, this complete control of accessibility we now have in the twenty-first century is unprecedented.

The types of communications have also radically changed. To take just one example, the anthropologist Bronislaw Malinowski (1923) proposed that some speech is **phatic communication,** small talk for its own sake rather than for conveying information. All people do it, everywhere, because it is both a bonding ritual and a way of regulating discourse. For instance, two negotiators may "get down to business" after they exchange pleasantries for a while, even though each may care little about the other's family or last night's ball game. But how these pleasantries are exchanged may set the stage for how the rest of the meeting will go. Digital communication offers both faster and more distant phatic communication. As any professor can tell you, the moment class ends, out come the cell phones. Invariably, the conversation is brief and very phatic: "It's me. How you doing? I'm fine. Just got out of class. Yeah. Catch you later. Bye." But there is also an alternative. Twitter and texting offer another way of sending phatic signals, but these are "away-messages" (Baron 2008:73) waiting to be read at the receiver's convenience. The 140-character limit makes Twitter almost intentionally designed for phatic communication. Combined with social network sites, we are never at a loss to know what our friends had for lunch or the latest cute thing Grandma's cat did.

Are Instant Messages Speech? Formal Linguistic Changes. We must remember that no matter how superficially it may appear to be the same as face-to-face interactions, digital communication is *not* speech. David Crystal (2004) suggests that there are at least three major differences. First, for the most part, there is the lack of simultaneous feedback found in an actual conversation. All the proxemic and paralinguistic features are missing. The feeling that the other person is not "getting" what we are saying would allow us to alter our conversational strategy in a face-to-face encounter. Second (unlike, say, at a party where we ourselves have to decide which of the many subconversations to attend to), in a chatroom or Facebook encounter, all messages are created equal. This is both a plus and a minus. "It has never been possible before in the history of human communication, to participate simultaneously in multiple conversations." Actually, you can now "contribute to as many as your mental powers and typing speed permit" (Crystal 2004:71). Third, the rhythm of communication is different. The lag between sending a message and getting a response in digital communication is very different in telephone or face-to-face encounters. This can cause a fair degree of ambiguity: Did Jane read my tweet yet? Did Professor Smith get my e-mail, or is he just not going to give me an extension? Did I get back to Joe when he friended me, or did I forget?

Changes in Orthography. Converting spoken language into writing has never been easy, even though the school system tries to give us prescriptive rules and teach that they are absolute and unalterable. But even today there is not complete agreement about "correct" spelling and punctuation. Writing changes over time as fashions and opinions change. For example, what do you call that small permeable container that holds tea leaves (Baron 2008:177)? The *Oxford English Dictionary* cites *tea bag* in 1898, *tea-bag* in 1936, and *teabag* in 1977. And Shakespeare, the icon of all English courses, spelled his name a half-dozen different ways. That orthographic conventions are flexible is particularly true regarding digital communication. Is it *on-line* or *online*, or *e-mail* or *email*? Is the *internet* supposed to be capitalized? What do we do about all those *-s's* that are now *-z's*, as in *Dawgz*, pirated soft *warez*, and shared *filez*? Is it OK or *okay*? Is it acceptable to use *btw* for "by the way" in an e-mail message—to anyone (even a professor)? Does *lol* mean "laugh out loud" or "lots of luck"?

Another question is, should we encourage or stifle creativity in digital communication orthography and style? Constance Hale and Jesse Scanlon in *Wired Style* (1999) argue that "no one reads email with red pen in hand" so we should "celebrate subjectivity" and "write the way people talk" (Baron 2008:172). Others feel that allowing such digital anarchy is a recipe for social and linguistic disaster. As Baron (2008:171) says, "Modern linguistic theory eschews passing judgment on any linguistic variant, and I am not about to do so now. Rather, I'm suggesting that should linguistic entropy snowball, we may discover that personally expressive, culturally accommodating, and clock-driven language users will find it increasingly difficult to understand one another's nuances." (One such example can be seen in Box 14.3 below). Crystal argues that so far, at least, the pedagogical and "moral panic" surrounding e-mail and texting is overblown. The belief that the "highly deviant character" of digital communication is fostering poor literacy results has been shown by psychologists and educators to be largely an "urban myth" (2010:417).

Digital Communication, Literacy, and Cognition. One other area where it has been suggested that digital communication literacy is changing modern life is in education and cognition. Donald Leu and others (Leu et al., 2007:41) argue that there are four defining characteristics of these new literacies. First,

BOX 14.3   1337 5P34K: 4N 31337 13350N F0R 4N O1D F4RT

In a class on Japanese linguistics I was teaching, I was describing some of the new orthographic games Japanese teenage girls play on their cell phones when they text-message using symbols, emoticons, and scripts from various foreign languages. "Oh, that's just like leet!" said a student. Seeing the puzzled look on my face, he went to the board and wrote *31337 sp34k*, as if this explained everything. It didn't. After a pregnant pause, with me unsuccessfully finding a way to appear both knowledgeable and cool, he said, "You really are a *newb*—a *newbie*—aren't you?" while writing *n00b* in big letters. It dawned on me that this was some kind of code. *0* replaced the letter o, *7* replaced t, *1* replaced l, *4* replaced A, *5* replaced S, and so on. So, *31337* was supposed to be "elite"—spelled *eleet*, and shortened to *leet*, in this strange argot. But this was not what cryptologists call a transposition cipher, where numbers simply encoded letters. Instead, what was going on was a kind orthographic running joke. For example, *ph* was often used for any f-sounds, and words could be transcribed in several ways: "fear" might be rendered *ph34r, ph33r,* or *phear*. Phonetic and orthographic puns saturate *leet-speek*, and sometimes the uninitiated might miss the joke. I never would have guessed that *b7* is "banned," and the logic, such as it is, is something like this: The ampersand (&) is pronounced *"and,"* and the number 7 and the character & share the same key on the keyboard. Thus, *b* and 7 (i.e., and) make "banned." "Surely, even you . . . you who are . . . "—he wrote *4n o1d F4rt* on the board, as the class broke out into giggles—"can see this, right?" "But of course," I lied, trying to keep my composure. Later on, after class, I figured it out. I could console myself, however, that at least I was not an *über g33k* like my student.

Jim Stanlaw

new information and communication technologies involving novel literacy tasks require new skills and strategies if they are to be used effectively. Second—though this is often resisted "overtly, by deliberate educational policies . . . or covertly, by educators who sometimes are not nearly as literate with the Internet as the students they teach (p. 38)"—new literacies are now a critical component for full participation in civic, economic, and social life in a global world. Third, these new literacies are deictic—that is, they change as new technologies emerge. Of course, literacy has always changed with technology (e.g., consider the intellectual and social revolutions brought about with the advent of moveable type and the printing press). What is different about digital communication is its immediacy. It took centuries for the full impact of the Gutenberg press to be felt, but the Internet allows for the immediate and universal exchange of new ideas and technologies. Fourth, new literacies are "multiple, multimodal, and multifaceted," thus making them more complex to apprehend and understand. How this will be integrated into the twenty-first century educational system remains to be seen.

Some also wonder how new digital communication literacy is changing human cognition and patterns of thought—and not just in ways of learning or how people socially relate to one another. The rise of book culture, of course, inexorably altered the way people conceived of the world and their place in it. The collective pool of human knowledge exponentially multiplied, and people could travel vicariously to the far ends of the earth and time in travelogues or history books. However, as with anything, there were costs. Scholars at the start of the Renaissance lamented, for example, the decline of the power of human memory, and the reluctance of younger people to engage in daunting tasks of memorization. They were probably right, just as the spread of the hand calculator has impacted our ability to do even simple arithmetic in our heads. Already, for example, we see university libraries becoming places to network, or centers for collaborative learning. Few go there to consult a journal article because often these are available in students' dorm rooms on computers. What kind of world will it be in the (very near) future when all the world's knowledge, music, and art are instantly accessible to everyone? With remarkable improvements in Web translations taking place daily, even problems in cross-cultural communication due to people speaking different languages might gradually become less important.

The Language of the Internet. If you ask most people what the language of the Internet is, they would probably say it is English. Even in places where English is not natively spoken, tweets and twitters often are sent out in English. English appears to be the default language of almost any site you hit. Even though operating systems now come in different language interfaces, many people still use an English version of Windows or a Mac operating system to more easily interact with the English-using computer sites.

In his book *Language and the Internet* (2001), the noted linguist David Crystal wondered whether the English-dominated Internet would contribute to the demise of other languages, at least on the Web. Perhaps he was being pessimistic. It appears that the use of English has gone down significantly, from 82 percent in 1997 to less than 57 percent in 2002 (Stanlaw 2005). German, French, and Japanese each now make up between 5 and 8 percent of all Web pages. If we look at PDF (portable document format) pages, these differences are even more pronounced. Chinese, Korean, Russian, and Dutch all went from almost nothing in 1997 to a noticeable presence ten years later A similar trend appears if we look at the languages used to access the Google search engine. English went down 10 percent from June 2001 to May 2004.

However, we should not predict the waning of English as the dominant language on the Web yet because statistical data suggest that the drop of English is leveling off. For example, language access on Google from September 2003 to now remained essentially the same for all languages. Also, if we look at the "penetration" levels—the percentage of the speakers of a given language that have access to the Web—we see that a great majority of speakers of many European languages (such as German, French, and Dutch) already use the Internet, so the number of these speakers going online might not be expected to grow very much. In contrast, only 59 percent of English speakers use the Web, so these numbers could increase (Stanlaw 2005).

But there is another, perhaps more significant, reason why English will still be a dominant presence in the digital world for some time to come. Political unrest, and international and economic affairs will likely continue to be highly contentious in the near future, and digital communications will no doubt play an important role. For example, few could forget the vivid pictures and messages being sent out of Iran during the "Green Revolution" election protests in the summer of 2009. Because the Iranian government strictly monitors and censors such conventional media as radio, television, and newspapers, it was social networking sites, blogs, Twitter, and YouTube that became the primary source of information for the outside world (which even news organizations such as CNN, BBC, and the major print news agencies used when their personnel on the ground were quarantined). Not only were Western governments getting word of unrest taking place that they were not getting by the usual diplomatic means, the whole world's attention was drawn to these dramatic events. Reuters reported that these channels were so important that the Obama administration asked Twitter to postpone a scheduled network upgrade because it would have taken them temporarily offline. According to Twitter's own blog, they agreed to the State Department's request "because events in Iran were tied directly to the growing significance of Twitter as an important communication and information network."

Ethical Questions and Standards of Conduct

In the introductory chapter we pointed out that "native" consultants make an essential contribution to studies in linguistics, cultural anthropology, and linguistic anthropology, and that every effort should be made to enable promising members of small ethnic groups to receive training in these fields. The insight into their cultures such individuals possess would be invaluable. One must realize, however, that it will take some years before members of small societies are reasonably well represented in the fields of linguistics and anthropology, both of which are dominated at present by white males.

Doing fieldwork in a foreign culture almost invariably gives rise to an asymmetrical relationship: On the one hand there is the researcher (the word is used here to mean anyone who is an attentive and systematic observer and makes a study of something) and on the other hand the subjects (that is, those who are being studied) or natives (those who are connected to a particular community or region by birth). The researcher, typically a cultural and linguistic outsider, lives for a number of months with those who are being studied, observes them and asks numerous questions, and now and then accompanies them when they do their chores, or even helps with their daily tasks. Because much of the native consultants' time is taken up by the researcher's questions and requests for data concerning language and culture, it is customary to offer them modest but fair compensation (consultant fees usually come out of the grant the researcher has received for fieldwork).

Doing fieldwork in another country or in a foreign culture under physical conditions that are usually less comfortable than those at home, living among and depending on people who at least initially are complete strangers, having to eat unfamiliar foods, and trying to communicate with others who speak a different language require both the will and the ability to make profound adaptations. For these reasons, a few anthropologists find fieldwork too taxing, and after their initial experience engage in it only occasionally or not at all. But most anthropologists, linguistic and cultural alike, enjoy being in the field and return to fieldwork again and again.

And what about the people who are studied? An extended visit by an anthropologist is bound to have some effect on them, as every researcher needs to be aware. According to the code of professional ethics adopted by the American Anthropological Association, the responsibility of anthropologists to those they study is paramount. The aims of the anthropologists' activities should be communicated as clearly as possible to those among whom they work; consultants (informants) have the right to remain anonymous if they choose to, and their rights, interests, safety, and sensitivities must be safeguarded; consultants are not to be exploited but should receive a fair return for their services; the results of research should be made available to the general public—clandestine research can potentially be used by others against the population under study. In short, prior to commencing research the anthropologist should give serious thought to the possibility that the study of a group or community could at some future time negatively affect the people studied. If such an outcome seems possible, then the research project should be substantively redesigned, or abandoned.

A comment should also be made concerning the comportment of researchers in the field. Their expertise, educational background, and material advantages in no way entitle them to any feelings of superiority to those they study, who may live in conditions unaffected by modern technology and may be nonliterate. As guests in a foreign society, community, or home, field-workers should exercise even more sensitivity than they would be expected to use in their home environment. Asking for advice does not necessarily mean accepting it, but there are many instances when advice can be of great value and may even help determine whether a project succeeds or fails. Let us consider, for example, a group's need for educational materials designed to help pupils learn their own language and something about their culture in Western-style schools (such a situation can be encountered in schools in the United States serving primarily Native American students). If there are several adequate ways of writing down a language that has previously only been spoken, which method would be preferable to the potential users? And if an anthology of traditional narratives is to be compiled for the use of students, which of the many stories should be selected?

It occasionally happens, of course, that members of a tribe, a nomadic group, or a peasant village do not want their daily lives, religious beliefs, and traditional customs scrutinized by someone they do not know, who comes from another country, and whose intentions they cannot fully comprehend. Reverse the situation: Think of what the attitudes of members of a small community somewhere in the United States might be toward a foreigner of a different skin color, who has different religious beliefs and speaks a foreign language, announcing that he or she will live in the community for half a year or so to study the habits of the "natives."

In a world in which human communities and nations have become interdependent and in which respect for cultural diversity is essential, understanding other cultures is ever more important. This understanding is what anthropologists are committed to promote, and their behavior in societies other than their own must set an example.

Summary and Conclusions

There are many different ways of applying expertise in socially oriented linguistics to the problems of the contemporary world. Knowledge gained from studying the ethnography of communication can be quite useful when individuals or groups of differing cultural and linguistic backgrounds are attempting to communicate. The informality of Americans (the ease with which they move to a first-name basis, for example) may be regarded by other societies as ill-mannered or even presumptuous; Americans, for their part, are likely to consider the formal behavior characteristic of some other societies as stuffy and inflexible. If individuals or groups involved in intercultural contact know how to interpret each other's behavior, communication will proceed more smoothly.

Another area where linguistic applications have been found useful is in legal proceedings. Here the contributions of applied linguistics range from making the technical language of legal documents intelligible to the layperson to helping the judge, jury, witnesses, or litigants resolve problems resulting from misunderstandings caused by differing cultural and linguistic backgrounds. The recent policy adopted by the United States in 1990 (see

Box 14.4 below) encourages anthropologists to continue what they have been doing for some time now, namely, helping to preserve the languages and other cultural traditions of Native Americans.

Language problems in a pluralistic society are commonly due to the uneven status of competing languages or dialects. The question to be answered is not only which language (or languages) is to become the national or official language but what the consequences of a particular choice are likely to be for the entire society. And if an unwritten language spoken by a small population in a pluralistic society is to be maintained by introducing it into the schools as a second language, the linguist may be called upon to devise a writing system and then to help in developing teaching materials.

With cultural differences around the world becoming less distinct as a result of communications media, modernization, and the volume of international travel, the language of a minority population may be the only prominent badge of its ethnic identity and pride. It goes without saying that the language concerns of such a group need to be handled not only with expert knowledge but also with understanding and tact.

In this chapter we have looked at three major trends in what David Crystal calls the world's linguistic ecology. First, simply put, most of the world's languages are dying out—quickly—and our linguistic diversity, for better or worse, is rapidly disappearing. As a consequence, more and more people are speaking fewer and fewer languages. Second, one language—English—appears to have become the de facto international lingua franca—the world's first global language. Third, the revolution in digital technology has been inescapable, and language has been tremendously affected. But even the name of this new kind of communication is uncertain. "What do we call the language which results when people communicate using computers, mobile phones, BlackBerries, personal digital assistants, answerphones, satnavs, and all the other devices which have become a routine part of our lives? Various technical and popular suggestions have been made, such as *cyberspeak, electronic discourse, Netlish, Weblish,* and *Netspeak.* None of these is satisfactory" (Crystal 2010:414). But no matter what its name, will this new method of "talking" break down barriers to communication, as many hope, or will it erect new unforeseen gates that obstruct international tolerance and cooperation even more? Regardless, the tools of linguistic anthropology will help us analyze and understand the language problems involved, whatever the outcome.

BOX 14.4. WHAT LINGUISTIC ANTHROPOLOGISTS HELPED ACCOMPLISH

It is the policy of the United States to—

(1) preserve, protect, and promote the rights and freedom of Native Americans to use, practice, and develop Native American languages; . . .

(3) encourage and support the use of Native American languages as a medium of instruction in order to encourage and support—

(A) Native American language survival,

(B) educational opportunity,

(C) increased student success and performance,

(D) increased student awareness and knowledge of their culture and history, and

(E) increased student and community pride;

(4) encourage State and local education programs to work with Native American parents, educators, Indian tribes, and other Native American governing bodies in the implementation of programs to put this policy into effect;

(5) recognize the right of Indian tribes and other Native American governing bodies to use the Native American languages as a medium of instruction in all schools funded by the Secretary of the Interior; . . .

(7) support the granting of comparable proficiency achieved through course work in a Native American language the same academic credit as comparable proficiency achieved through course work in a foreign language . . .

Public Law 101-477 Title I—Native American Languages Act [1990]

RESOURCE MANUAL AND STUDY GUIDE

Below are some key terms and questions related to each chapter. For the true-false questions, circle T or F, as applicable, to the left of each statement. For each multiple-choice question select the most easily defensible complement or choice and indicate your answer by entering the appropriate capital letter in the space to the left of the question number. For the completions, complete each statement using the most suitable word(s). The number of words is given parenthetically. For certain chapters there are problems asking the student to apply the methods of analysis just presented to actual linguistic data. Solutions to the problems and answers to all objective questions are given in the answer section. For each chapter there are questions for discussion and sometimes also some projects. Because these are open-ended questions, we have not provided answers.

Chapter 1

Key Terms

anthropology
archaeology
biological anthropology
cultural anthropology
holistic
linguistic anthropology
language myths

Questions for Discussion

1. If you've seen *The Day the Earth Stood Still, Independence Day, Mars Attacks*, or other such science fiction films, how was communication with aliens depicted? How about in the various *Star Trek* shows and movies? Do they seem realistic to you? If an alien ship did land on the University Quad, how would we talk with its crew?

2. Imagine people growing up without language? Can they still "think" the same as someone *with* language? That is, can we think without language? What about visual artists or musicians? Do they think in language? What personal experiences might you have had yourself to use as evidence for your claims?

3. You've seen it many times: You are watching a movie about World War II and the scene takes you behind the German lines to the headquarters bunker; two German

generals are discussing plans for battle. What kind of speech are they using (if it is not one of those "authentic" films that use subtitles)? Why do you suppose the director has the actors "speak English but with supposedly German accents? What if they spoke "normal" English to each other and you were told, or supposed to assume, that they were speaking in German? Would it be a more, or less, effective cinematic technique? What if you were told that this is just a Hollywood convention (that is, in German war movies the actors do not portray Americans by using fake English accents)?

4. A professor-colleague of ours whose first language is not English sometimes uses sentences like "Oh, you've lost your weight! That exercise program must be working well." or "The vet says I have to put my dog on a diet; Max needs to lose his weight as he is just too fat!" Probably you could understand these sentences, and though you may not have phrased them in exactly that way, you might not think of them as technically "incorrect." However, according to a book on English grammar for non-native speakers, such sentences are wrong. What reasons do you think the book might have given for these sentences being wrong? How would you change them, and (if so) why?

5. One of the authors of this book has just been made King of America, and the first decree is that everyone must study a foreign language in school for at least six years, starting in the first grade. Will this act start a revolution? Would you be one of the rebels? Is this un-American? What do you think the King has in mind with this decree, and does it make any sense? What if we told you that this actually happens in numerous countries in the world?

6. Enrollments nationwide for Arabic language classes in institutions of higher education rose well over 100 percent in recent years, and the number of colleges offering Arabic instruction nearly doubled. Why do you think that is?

7. At the time of the Iran hostage crisis in 1980, Illinois senator Paul Simon said there were only a few speakers of Farsi (or Persian, the majority language of Iran) on staff at the embassy in Teheran. What does this say about the conduct of American diplomacy? What does this say about Americans' attitudes toward foreign languages and foreign-language learning? Some have said that because of our linguistic poverty in Iran, we knew only the Shah's "party line" and had no idea of how the average Iranian felt about the government, the new leader Ayatollah Khomeini, or the United States. What effect (if any) do you think this linguistic situation had on the hostage crisis and revolution in Iran?

Objective Study Questions

True-False Test

T F 1. For the most part, the terms "linguistic anthropology" and "anthropological linguistics" mean exactly the same thing, and neither is to be preferred over the other.

T F 2. Natural language itself is not ambiguous; it is people who misinterpret things that cause problems.

T F 3. According to Boas, there is no intrinsic connection between race, language, and culture.

T F 4. Almost everywhere in the world everyone is monolingual or monodialectal, just as in America.

T F 5. No language is really more complex or simpler or easier than any other; no language is harder or easier to learn than any other.

T F 6. While *linguists* are primarily interested in the structure of languages, *linguistic anthropologists* study the relationship between language on the one hand and culture and society on the other.

Multiple-Choice Questions

____ 1. The person who is said to be the "founding father" of American anthropology is (A) Edward Sapir. (B) Dell Hymes. (C) Franz Boas. (D) Karl V. Teeter.

____ 2. Anthropology as a recognized science began in which century: (A) seventeenth. (B) eighteenth century. (C) nineteenth century. (D) twentieth century. (E) twenty-first century.

____ 3. According to Edward Sapir it is the (A) syntax, (B) vocabulary, (C) grammar that more or less faithfully reflects the culture whose purposes it serves.

____ 4. During the last seventy years, the percentage of monolingual and bilingual Mexican Indians has been steadily declining in favor of Spanish by about what percent? (A) From 16 percent in 1930 to about 7 percent in 2005. (B) From 10 percent in 1930 to 1 percent in 2005. (C) There actually has been not much change. (D) Spanish has for the most part replaced almost all indigenous languages.

____ 5. Lexical specialization, that is, a large inventory of words pertaining to a particular domain, is found in which of the following instances? (A) The Agta of the Philippines have over thirty different verbs referring to types of fishing. (B) The natives of the German city of Munich are said to have over seventy terms referring to the local varieties of beer. (C) Americans have a hundred or so different names for makes and types of automobiles. (D) Only two of the preceding three choices are true. (E) All three choices, A–C, are true.

Completions

1. In the nineteenth century, one of the main intellectual and scientific tasks was to try to explain the great diversity of _____, _____, and _____, past and present (three words).

2. Sapir's description of the morphology of the _____ language demonstrated that non-Western languages can be as complex as any found in Europe.

3. A very brief and simple definition of anthropology might be "the _____ study of humankind (one word)."

Notes and Suggestions for Further Reading

There are a number of books on linguistic anthropology for beginning students, including Ottenheimer 2008 and Bonvillain 2007. Duranti 1997 and Hanks 1995 are more advanced. Duranti 2001 is a convenient encyclopedic dictionary of key terms for studying language and culture and Duranti 2006 is an edited overview of articles on topics covering the whole field of linguistic anthropology. Edward Sapir's *Language* has been in print in various editions since it first appeared in 1921 for good reason. The greatest expert in Native American languages before World War II, Sapir could also write in an entertaining manner. The most accessible of Franz Boas's linguistic work is his "Introduction" to the *Handbook of American Indian Languages* (1911).

Chapter 2

Key Terms

consultant
corpus
elicitation
fieldwork
informant
linguistics
participant observation

Questions for Discussion

1. People who are not well informed sometimes have strange ideas about the languages spoken by members of small tribal societies. Analyze the following statement critically point by point: Unwritten languages, such as those spoken by American Indians, lack well-defined sounds, orderly grammars, and extensive vocabularies. Not having been subjected to the unrelenting demands of complex industrial civilizations, these languages are inherently incapable of assuming the functions of well-established languages.

2. Suppose you were to engage in your first fieldwork experience in linguistic anthropology. How would you select your informant(s) and why would you choose certain types of individuals over others?

3. Suppose a field-worker discovered and then was making a study of a language spoken by the members of a village society in the jungle of the Amazon basin. What would be the benefits of having studied cultural anthropology?

Objective Study Questions

True-False Test

T F   1. The reason all anthropologists enjoy fieldwork is that living in the field places no demands on them that they must adjust to.

T F   2. The native speaker from whom the researcher collects linguistic (or cultural) data is referred to as an informer.

T F   3. One characteristic that sets anthropology apart from other social sciences is a strong fieldwork component.

T F   4. In the initial phases of fieldwork, the anthropologist prefers to use people who have had extended experience in the anthropologist's own society.

T F   5. In the initial phases of linguistic fieldwork, anthropologists endeavor to use informants who speak different dialects of the language studied.

T F   6. Unwritten languages of small tribal societies are primitive because these languages have little or no grammar.

T F   7. Vocabularies of the languages of some small tribal societies may not be as extensive as the vocabulary of, say, English, but are sufficient to serve the needs of the groups using them.

Multiple-Choice Questions

1. There are still hundreds of languages about which linguists and anthropologists know relatively little or nothing at all. For the most part such languages are found in (A) Irian Jaya. (B) Papua New Guinea. (C) the Amazon basin in South America. (D) only two of the areas mentioned. (E) all three of the areas mentioned.

2. For initial fieldwork in linguistic anthropology concerning, for example, Native American languages, experienced anthropologists tend to choose a native informant (consultant) who (A) is of the opposite sex. (B) has had good exposure to the larger society surrounding the tribal society being studied. (C) is young and easily approachable. (D) None of the preceding three choices is fully satisfactory.

3. The immersion of anthropological field-workers for an extended period of time in the day-to-day life of the people whom they study is referred to as (A) going native. (B) participant observation. (C) giving up one's ethnic identity.

4. Which of the following statements having to do with obtaining data for a little-known language is *least* acceptable? (A) The informant should be an older person who is an active participant in his or her culture. (B) Recording a spontaneous conversation between two native speakers yields good material during the initial stages of fieldwork. (C) Tape recordings of linguistic data (with the permission of the informant) are extremely helpful. (D) In the advanced stages of fieldwork, using informants of several age groups and both genders is highly advisable.

Completions

1. A collection of language data used as a basis for an analysis or description is referred to as a _____ (one word).

2. _____ (one word) is the drawing out of information or response from informants.

3. To emphasize the interconnection between culture and society, anthropologists use the compound adjective _____ (one word).

Notes and Suggestions for Further Reading

For a book-sized guide to linguistic fieldwork, see Samarin 1967. Quite possibly the earliest article discussing the training of linguistic anthropologists is Voegelin and Harris 1952. Useful although somewhat dated comments on obtaining a linguistic sample and a guide for transcribing unwritten languages may be found in Voegelin and Voegelin 1954 and 1959. Eliciting and recording techniques are discussed in Hayes 1954 and Yegerlehner 1955. For a practical guide to how to learn a field language, consult Burling 1984.

For contributions to the history of linguistic anthropology, see Hymes 1963, somewhat revised in Hymes 1983; Hallowell 1960; and Darnell 1992. Readers on language in culture and society and on language in the social context are Hymes 1964 and Giglioli 1972. For a detailed account of Puerto Rican experiences with language, race, and class in the United States, see Urciuoli 1996. Duranti 2001 (largely based on Volume 9 of the *Journal of Linguistic Anthropology*) contains seventy-five essays of two to four pages by specialists on "language matters in anthropology." The topics range from acquisition of language to writing. Any reader will find something of interest as well as short bibliographies of the most salient works on each topic. For a reader in linguistic anthropology, see Duranti 2009; the twenty one contributions to this work include articles on speech community and communicative competence, utterances as acts, language socialization and literacy practices, and the power of language.

Chapter 3

Key Terms

accent
allomotif
allophone
consonant
emic(s)
etic(s)
motif
motifeme
phone
phoneme
phonemic (transcription)
phonetic (transcription)
phonology
prosodic features
speech apparatus
syllable
voiced sound
voiceless sound
vowel

Questions for Discussion

1. *Emic* and *etic* approaches have their origin in linguistics but eventually have been applied in several branches of anthropology, including oral folklore. In cultural (social) anthropology the value of these two approaches has now been generally recognized. Discuss first the difference between the two approaches (phonetic versus phonemic) in linguistic analysis and description, and then how they complement each other in ethnography (description of a culture).

2. The English words *by, high, thigh, why, rye,* and *lie* (and one could list others that rhyme) belong to the same minimal set. Explain what is meant by this statement and comment on the relation between the pronunciation of English words and their spelling.

3. Morris Halle wrote that "the sounds . . . we emit when speaking are produced by complex gymnastics." Considering that people speak effortlessly and sometimes too fast, why did Halle make that statement?

4. Consider ten or so sounds of English and attempt to describe (at least roughly) where in the vocal tract, that is, between the lips and the larynx (marked in the neck by the so-called Adam's apple), each sound is produced and by what means.

Objective Study Questions

True-False Test

T F 1. American English has more vowel phonemes than consonant phonemes.

T F 2. English spelling and spoken English are well correlated; the writing system of English is therefore particularly suitable for careful linguistic work with unwritten languages.

T F 3. In the production of vowels, the air that escapes through the mouth (and the nose in the case of nasalized vowels) is relatively unimpeded.

T F 4. Pitch in a variety of intonational patterns is used in English—for example, in questions.

T F 5. The syllable written as *ma* has four different meanings in Mandarin Chinese depending on the type of pitch contour the speaker employs.

T F 6. The English words *guy* and *thigh* represent a minimal pair, that is, they vary from each other in one sound only.

T F 7. The term *emic* refers to an analytical approach based on data received from native informants, that is, it is a culture-specific (language-specific) approach.

T F 8. English as spoken in Great Britain, the United States, and Canada differs somewhat from one dialect to the next with regard to vowel pronunciation.

T F 9. Articulation of all the sounds in the languages of the world takes place between the glottis (the elongated space between the vocal cords) and the lips.

T F 10. In an analysis of an unwritten language, phonemic transcription precedes phonetic transcription.

Multiple-Choice Questions

____ 1. When the vocal cords are drawn together and made to vibrate, they produce (A) voiced sounds. (B) voiceless sounds. (C) the glottal stop [?].

____ 2. The *p*-sounds in the English words *peak* and *speak* are (A) two allophones of one phoneme. (B) two different phonemes. (C) in complementary distribution. (D) Of the three choices above only two are acceptable. (E) Of the three choices above only one is acceptable.

____ 3. The contrast between the emic and etic perspectives in linguistics and linguistic anthropology has been extended also to (A) folklore. (B) archaeology. (C) cultural anthropology. (D) This approach has been extended to all three subfields listed here.

____ 4. The sound written as [b] is (A) uvular. (B) dental. (C) bilabial. (D) None of these three choices applies.

____ 5. Which among the following statements is *indefensible?* (A) Each language has a characteristic phonemic system. (B) The grammars of unwritten languages of small tribal societies are invariably simpler than grammars of languages of large established societies. (C) The production of speech sounds is an exceedingly complex process involving some one hundred muscles as well as other tissues. (D) Native speakers of a language use it efficiently even though they may know nothing about its structure.

Completions

1. Languages that make use of distinctive pitch levels (Mandarin Chinese, for example) are referred to as _____ languages (one word).

2. The smallest perceptible discrete segment of speech is a _____ (one word); the contrastive sound units of a language are _____ (plural of one word); and the varieties of a contrastive sound are its _____ (plural of one word).

Problems

Problem 1

Based on Wonderly 1951a and 1951b, this problem is taken from Zoque, a language spoken in southern Mexico that belongs to the Mixe-Zoque group of languages. Among the sounds of Zoque are [c], a voiceless alveolar affricate (similar to the consonants in the word *tsetse* [fly]), and [ʒ], a voiced alveolar affricate. From the data given here—to be taken as representative of the language—are [c] and [ʒ] allophones of one phoneme (that is, are they in complementary distribution), or are they assignable to two different phonemes (that is, do they contrast)? Support your conclusion.

1. ʔakaʔŋʒʌhk-	'to be round'	7. nʒʌhku	'I did it'		
2. ʔaŋʒoŋu	'he answered'	8. nʒima	'my calabash'		
3. canʒamnayu	'he chatted'	9. nʒin	'my pine'		
4. cap	'sky'	10. pac	'skunk'		
5. caʔ	'stone'	11. puci	'trash'		
6. cima	'calabash'	12. wanʒʌʔyu	'he quit singing'		

Problem 2

Czech is a West Slavic language of the Indo-European language family, spoken in the Czech Republic. In Czech, among the various stops (plosives) are two alveodental stops, [t] and [d], articulated by the tongue tip against the boundary between the upper incisors and the alveolar ridge behind them, and two palatal stops, [tʲ] and [dʲ]. To how many phonemes are these four sounds assignable? Consider the following data and support your conclusion.

1. dej	'give!'	9. tʲelo	'body'
2. dʲedʲit	'to inherit'	10. teta	'aunt'
3. dʲej	'action'	11. tikat	'to be on a first-name basis'
4. dʲelo	'cannon'	12. titul	'title'
5. kotel	'kettle'	13. tʲikat	'to tick (clock)'
6. kotʲe	'kitten'	14. vada	'flaw'
7. tedi	'hence'	15. vana	'bathtub'
8. tele	'calf (animal)'	16. vata	'absorbent cotton'

Problem 3

Based on Echeverría and Contreras 1965, this problem is taken from Araucanian, a language spoken by Native Americans of Argentina and Chile. Is the main stress, marked by [ˊ], distinctive, or is it predictable by rule? Support your conclusion.

1. elúmuyu	'give us!'	4. nawél	'tiger'
2. kimfáluwulay	'he pretended not	5. putún	'to drink'
	to know'	6. θuŋúlan	'I do not speak'
3. kurám	'egg'	7. wuyá	'yesterday'

Problem 4

Based on Postal 1969, this problem is from Mohawk, the Iroquoian language of a Native American people who live mainly in southern Ontario and extreme northern New York. On the basis of the following data, what is the status of vowel length—is it predictable or is it distinctive? Length is indicated by doubling a symbol—that is, *èë* is a long *e*; [ʔ] is the glottal stop; [´] marks stress; [ʌ] is an unrounded back lower mid vowel, as in the English word *bud*; and [ɔ] is a rounded back lower mid vowel.

1. ranahéezʌs	'he trusts her'	7. wahrehyáara?ne?	'he remembered'
2. ragéédas	'he scrapes'	8. ɔwaduniza?áshege?	'it will be ripening repeatedly'
3. rayʌ́thos	'he plants'		
4. waháágede?	'he scraped'	9. yékreks	'I push it'
5. wísk	'five'	10. royó?de?	'he works'
6. rehyáara?s	'he remembers'		

Problem 5

Based on Fromkin and Rodman 1988, this problem is from Korean, a language whose af-filiation is disputed. The sounds [l] and [r] are in complementary distribution. On the basis of the following data, what is the form of the suffix meaning 'of (the)'? What change do noun stems undergo when the suffix is attached, and under what circumstances does the change occur? What are the two mutually exclusive environments (complementary distri-bution) in which the sounds [l] and [r] occur?

1. pal	'foot'	5. rupi	'ruby'	9. saram	'person'
2. paruy	'of the foot'	6. ratio	'radio'	10. saramuy	'of the person'
3. kul	'oyster'	7. mul	'water'	11. multok	'water jug'
4. il	'day'	8. muruy	'of the water'	12. ipalsa	'barber'

Problem 6

Based on Fromkin and Rodman 1988, this problem is taken from a Bantu language spo-ken in Angola, Africa. This language is a member of the Niger-Congo language family. The alveolar segments [t, s, z] in complementary distribution with their palatal counter-parts [č, š, ž] are assignable to three phonemes. What is the distribution of each of the cor-responding pairs of allophones, that is, [t] and [č], [s] and [š], and [z] and [ž]? Which of the phonetic symbols from the first pair, [t, č], would you choose to represent the phoneme, and why?

1. tobola	'to bore a hole'	8. nselele	'termite'
2. tanu	'five'	9. čina	'to cut'
3. kesoka	'to be cut'	10. čiba	'banana'
4. kasu	'emaciation'	11. nkoši	'lion'
5. kunezulu	'heaven'	12. ažimola	'alms'
6. zevo	'then'	13. lolonži	'to wash the house'
7. zenga	'to cut'	14. žima	'to stretch'

Problem 7

Desperanto is spoken in an as yet unexplored tropical forest. Among the Desperanto words are the following nouns and noun phrases (long vowels are represented by double letters, short vowels by single letters).

1. muumu	'home fried potatoes'	4. kakaa	'used bicycle'
2. kaka	'scrambled eggs'	5. mumu	'garlic ice cream'
3. wowo	'bikini swimsuit'	6. woowoo	'banana split'

Is vowel length phonemic? ___yes ___ no.

In your answer (one sentence should suffice), justify your choice:

Problem 8

Among the sounds of Czech are [k] and [x] ([x] is the sound written *ch* in the name of the composer J. S. Bach). On the basis of the Czech words listed below, are these two sounds two separate phonemes or two allophones of one phoneme?

1. [prak]   'slingshot'   5. [prax]   'dust'
2. [puk]   'puck'   6. [xroust]   'June bug'
3. [xrxel]   'spittle'   7. [kras]   'limestone region with caverns'
4. [krkoun]   'cheapskate'   8. [pux]   'stench'

__ 2 separate phonemes __ 2 allophones of one phoneme. Justify your decision:

Notes and Suggestions for Further Reading

Textbooks of linguistics are numerous, and most carry some explanations of phonology and phonemics, often along with exercises. The two classics are Sapir 1921 and Bloomfield 1933. Two excellent postwar but pre-Chomskyan introductions to linguistics are Hockett 1958 and Gleason 1961. Some representative contemporary standard texts are Akmajian, Demers, Farmer, and Harnish 2010, and O'Grady, Archibald, Aronoff, and Rees-Miller 2004. An eclectic set of problems can be found in Bergmann, Hall, and Ross 2007. For general reference, one may wish to consult Crystal 1997 and especially the excellent Crystal 2010. For more specialized topics, see Ladefoged and Johnson 2010 on phonetics, Hayes 2008 on phonology, and Chomsky and Halle 1968 on the phonology of English. Bright's four-volume encyclopedia (1992) is an excellent and reliable source on all aspects of linguistics.

Some linguists distinguish between vocoids and vowels on the one hand and contoids and consonants on the other. When this distinction is made, vocoids and contoids refer to speech sounds defined in phonetic terms and considered as phonetic entities, whereas vowels and consonants refer to segments defined in terms of the sound structure of a particular language, that is, considered as phonological entities.

By no means is there agreement as to how best to analyze the system of English vowel phonemes. In one widely accepted analysis, for example, the vowels of *pit* and *peat* are phonemically represented as /i/ and /iy/, respectively; in another, they are interpreted as /ɪ/ and /i/; and in still another as /i/ and a long /i:/. For our purposes, however, it is enough to note that alternative interpretations exist.

Key Terms

affix
allomorph
aspect
bound morpheme

Chapter 4

case
derivation
discourse
free morpheme
gender
generative grammar
infix
inflection
morpheme
morphology
morphophonemics
prefix
process morpheme
reduplication
stem
suffix
suppletion
syntax
transformation
transformational grammar
transformational rule
vowel harmony
word order

Questions for Discussion

1. The relationship between phonemes and morphemes of a language could be likened to the relationship between the atoms of naturally occurring elements and the molecules of compounds formed by their chemical union. Explain the nature of the similarity.

2. English has become the language of the world not only because it is the native or official language of many millions of people, but for structural reasons as well. Explain this assertion.

3. In comparison with English, why for example are Russian, French, German, and Spanish difficult to learn for most native speakers of English? Make references to grammatical features not found in English but characterizing any of these four languages that you happen to know.

4. Explain the basic differences between the descriptive and generative approaches to analyzing languages.

Objective Study Questions

True-False Test

T F 1. Native speakers who do not observe the proper grammatical rules (they may say, for example, "I ain't" or "he don't know nothing") are not used as informants by linguists and linguistic anthropologists.

T F 2. The study of phonemic differences between various forms of a morpheme is termed *morphophonemics*.

T F 3. Morphology is the study of the origin of words.

T F 4. Linguistic units that have a meaning but contain no smaller meaningful parts are called morphemes.

T F 5. The requirement that vowels within a word have a certain similarity results in what is termed *vowel harmony*.

Multiple-Choice Questions

_____ 1. How many *different* morphemes (not how *many* morphemes) are there in the following sentence: "She cooks tasty soups and stews."? (A) 7 (B) 8 (C) 9 (D) 10.

_____ 2. What is the *total* number of morphemes in the preceding sentence? (A) 7 (B) 8 (C) 9 (D) 10.

_____ 3. The English word *undesirable* contains (A) one prefix. (B) one suffix. (C) two affixes. (D) three affixes. (E) Two of the above choices apply. (F) Three of the above choices, A–D, apply.

_____ 4. Which of the English words listed below has a zero allomorph of the plural morpheme? (A) syllabus. (B) mouse. (C) ox. (D) sheep. (E) zero.

_____ 5. The sentence "Dogs bite thieves" contains (A) three free morphemes. (B) one bound morpheme. (C) two bound morphemes. (D) Only one of the three choices above applies. (E) Two of the three choices above, A–C, apply.

Completions

1. What kind of morpheme (allomorph) is exemplified by a change rather than an addition, as in the pluralization of *mouse* to *mice*? It is a _____ morpheme (one word).

2. In Latin, the arrangement of words in a sentence does not indicate which noun is the subject and which is the object, but rather is used to show _____.

Problems

Problem 1

Based on Langacker 1972, this problem is taken from Luiseño, a Uto-Aztecan language spoken in southwestern California. [ʔ] is the glottal stop; [q] is a postvelar voiceless stop (similar to [k] but articulated farther back in the mouth); long vowels are written as a sequence of two vowel symbols; the stress, [´], is marked only on the first of two adjacent vowels. From the following data—to be taken as representative of the language—isolate Luiseño morphemes and provide each with an English gloss (a brief translation to indicate meaning).

1. nóo wukálaq	'I am walking'
2. nóo páaʔiq	'I am drinking'
3. nóo páaʔin	'I will drink'
4. temét čáami páaʔivičunin	'The sun will make us want to drink'
5. nóo póy wukálavičuniq	'I am making him want to walk'
6. nóo páaʔivičuq	'I want to drink'
7. temét póy wukálavičuniq	'The sun is making him want to walk'

Problem 2

Based on Zepeda 1983, this problem is from Tohono Oʼodham (formerly referred to as Papago), a Uto-Aztecan language spoken in southern Arizona and northwestern Mexico. [ʔ]

is the glottal stop and [ñ] is pronounced like the ñ in the English word piñon, also spelled pinyon. On the basis of the third person singular verb forms in Column A and the plural forms in Column B, how would you describe in general terms the process of pluralization of the verb forms in Column A?

A		B
1. ñeok	'speaks'	ñeñeok
2. ʔul	'sticks out'	ʔuʔul
3. helwuin	'is sliding'	hehelwuin
4. him	'walks'	hihim
5. dagkon	'wipes'	dadagkon

Problem 3

The regular English past tense morpheme has three allomorphs: /-d/ as in *begged*, /-t/ as in *chirped*, and /-əd/ as in *guided*. The third person singular morpheme also has three allomorphs: /-z/ as in *goes* or *begs*, /-s/ as in *chirps*, and /-əz/ as in *houses*. Describe the environments in which the allomorphs of each of the two morphemes occur.

Problem 4

Based on Merrifield and others 1967, this problem is taken from Sierra Popoluca, a Mixe-Zoque language spoken in about two dozen villages and settlements in the state of Veracruz, Mexico. The raised dot [·] after a vowel marks vowel length; [ʔ] is the glottal stop; [ŋ] is a velar nasal (similar to ng in *sing* or *king*); [ʌ] is a central unrounded vowel; and [ɤ], [č], [š], [ñ], and [y] are palato-alveolars—a voiceless stop, an affricate, a fricative, a nasal, and a semivowel, respectively. From the following data, list the allomorphs of the morpheme marking what corresponds to the English gloss "my" and then state the rules that govern the morphophonemics of this prefix.

1. co·goy	'liver'	21. anco·goy	'my liver'
2. čikši	'itch'	22. añčikši	'my itch'
3. ha·ya	'husband'	23. anha·ya	'my husband'
4. he·pe	'cup'	24. anhe·pe	'my cup'
5. kawah	'horse'	25. aŋkawah	'my horse'
6. kʌpi	'firewood'	26. aŋkʌpi	'my firewood'
7. me·me	'butterfly'	27. amme·me	'my butterfly'
8. me·sah	'table'	28. amme·sah	'my table'
9. nʌc	'armadillo'	29. annʌc	'my armadillo'
10. nʌyi	'name'	30. annʌyi	'my name'
11. petkuy	'broom'	31. ampetkuy	'my broom'
12. piyu	'hen'	32. ampiyu	'my hen'
13. suskuy	'whistle'	33. ansuskuy	'my whistle'
14. suuŋ	'cooking pot'	34. ansuuŋ	'my cooking pot'
15. šapun	'soap'	35. añšapun	'my soap'
16. ši·ʔmpa	'bamboo'	36. añši·ʔmpa	'my bamboo'
17. tʌk	'house'	37. antʌk	'my house'
18. tʸaka	'chick'	38. añtʸaka	'my chick'
19. wʌčo·mo	'wife'	39. aŋwʌčo·mo	'my wife'
20. yemkuy	'fan'	40. añyemkuy	'my fan'

Problem 5

Based on Fromkin and Rodman 1988, this problem is taken from Samoan. Samoan is a member of the Austronesian language family.

1. manao	'he wishes'	8. mananao	'they wish'
2. matua	'he is old'	9. matutua	'they are old'
3. malosi	'he is strong'	10. malolosi	'they are strong'
4. punou	'he bends'	11. punonou	'they bend'
5. atamaki	'he is wise'	12. atamamaki	'they are wise'
6. savali	'he travels'	13. pepese	'they sing'
7. laga	'he weaves'		

Given the preceding data, what Samoan words would you expect for the following:
he sings _____, they weave _____, they travel _____?

Problem 6

The following data are from the Aztec dialect heard in Veracruz, Mexico:

1. ničoka	'I cry'	5. timayana	'you (sing.) are hungry'
2. ničoka?	'I cried'	6. nimayanas	'I will be hungry'
3. nimayana	'I am hungry'	7. tičoka	'you (sing.) cry'
4. nimayana?	'I was hungry'	8. ničokas	'I will cry'

Consider the morpheme marking the first person singular: Is it a prefix? _____ or a suffix? _____ What is its form? _____ What is the form of the morpheme marking the present tense? _____ the past tense? _____ the future tense? _____ What is the form of the stem meaning 'cry'? _____ Consider the morpheme marking the second person singular: What is its form? _____

Problem 7

Here are ten English words written in traditional orthography:

1. rewriting	3. tasteless	5. illegally	7. carefully	9. immobile
2. fearfully	4. carelessly	6. hopelessly	8. irretrievable	10. immorally

How many *different* (not how *many*) prefixes do these ten words display? _____ (give the number) How many allomorphs of one particular prefix are shown? _____ (give the number) How many *different* suffixes are shown? _____ (give the number) How many *different* stems are shown? _____ (give the number)

Notes and Suggestions for Further Reading

References to textbooks of linguistics may be found in the Notes to Chapter 3. An excellent sample of problems and exercises is found in Merrifield, Naish, Rensch, and Story 2003.

The Chontal examples are from Waterhouse 1962, the Isthmus Nahuat examples from Law 1958, the Samoan examples from Fromkin and Rodman 1988, and the summary of the rules of Turkish vowel harmony from Gleason 1961.

The publication by Chomsky that proved to be a turning point in modern linguistics is *Syntactic Structures* (1957). Other writings by Chomsky include *Aspects of the Theory of Syntax* (1965), *Language and Mind* (1972), and *Lectures on Government and Binding* (1993). A good introduction to Chomsky's contributions to linguistics and transformational grammar is Lyons 1978, as are Radford 1988, 1997, and 2006. Carnie 2011, Adger 2003, Cook and

Newson 2007 discuss some of the newer directions Chomsky has taken in his syntactical analysis.

Chapter 5

Key Terms

alternate sign language
American Sign Language (or Ameslan)
braille
kinesics
nonverbal communication
paralanguage
paralinguistics
proxemics
semiotics
sign language
whistle "language" (or whistle speech)

Questions for Discussion

1. Speech is the most common and effective means of communication, but various systems of nonverbal communication are also important. To what extent and under what circumstances do the latter substitute for speech, and to what extent do they complement speech?

2. Some nonverbal systems of communication derive from spoken language. Which particular features of spoken language might these be?

3. Why do Morse code and braille depend on the written form of languages? Use the English language to justify your conclusion.

4. Can paralinguistic features be represented in writing, for example, in novels, and if so, how?

5. Observe another person at close range—a teacher, a visiting neighbor, or shop clerk—for a period of several minutes in order to learn how he or she has strengthened what he or she is saying by body motions (hand gestures, facial expressions, and the like).

6. Why was the sign language of the Plains Indian tribes important in the past, and why has its importance so diminished by now that few Native Americans still know it and practically none ever use it?

7. Contrast speech behavior with some of the types of nonverbal communication. Discuss the advantages and disadvantages of each.

Objective Study Questions
True-False Test

T F 1. Ameslan (American Sign Language) has two signing systems that complement each other.

T F 2. All existing instances of whistle speech are based on languages that have distinctive tones.

T F 3. In theory, proxemic behavior varies from society (culture) to society; however, the proxemic behaviors of some societies do not appreciably differ.

T F   4. Plains Indian sign language developed to supplement the relatively poor vocabularies of languages of the tribes in this culture area.

T F   5. What is being said, and the kinesic behavior accompanying it, can be in conflict.

T F   6. The so-called whistle speech of the Mazateco people of Mexico is so efficient that the subject matter of their communicative whistling can easily be identified out of context.

T F   7. The four zones of interpersonal space discussed by Edward T. Hall in his study of proxemics are universal.

Multiple-Choice Questions

____ 1. The use of gestures to accompany speech is referred to as (A) kinesics. (B) proxemics. (C) paralinguistics.

____ 2. Which of the following nonverbal systems of communication is derived from spoken language rather than from its written form? (A) Morse code. (B) Braille. (C) Mazateco whistle speech.

____ 3. Ordinary business transactions are customarily performed at what proxemic distance? (A) Personal. (B) Public. (C) Social-consultative.

____ 4. Finger spelling is employed in (A) Plains Indian sign language. (B) American Sign Language. (C) kinesic behavior.

____ 5. During an exchange between two people, the use of silence by one of them may turn out (A) to be threatening. (B) to be a means of relaxing potential tension. (C) to mean "no." (D) Depending on the circumstances, it may serve any of the three functions.

____ 6. The channel(s) used in kinesic behavior is (are) (A) olfactory. (B) acoustic. (C) optical. (D) Two of the preceding choices are applicable.

Completions

1. The study of the cultural patterning of the spatial separation individuals maintain in face-to-face encounters is called _____ (one word).

2. Features of vocal communication that are considered marginal or optional, such as tempo or intensity, are referred to as _____ (one word).

3. The study of the properties of signs and symbols and their functions—for example, the social symbolism of certain foods—is referred to as _____ (one word).

Notes and Suggestions for Further Reading

For a discussion of paralanguage and paralinguistics, see Trager 1958 and Crystal 1974; the latter source has an extensive bibliography appended. For a selection of essays concerning kinesics, see Birdwhistell 1970. A very readable introduction to proxemics is Hall 1966; a much shorter account, with comments by a number of scholars and Hall's reply to them, is in Hall 1968. For a discussion of gestures and cultural differences in gestures, see Kendon 1997.

For those interested, the talking drums of Africa are the subject of a nontechnical article by Carrington (1971). An excellent introduction to American Sign Language can be found in Klima and Bellugi 1979. A nontechnical but reliable source for Plains Indian sign language is Tomkins 1969.

A book of readings concerning nonverbal communication, with commentary, has been edited by Weitz (1974); the topics in the anthology include facial expression, paralanguage, body movements and gestures, and spatial behavior. A survey by specialists of paralinguistics, proxemics, sign languages, and drum and whistle "languages" is included in Sebeok 1974. For a research guide and bibliography concerning nonverbal communication, see Key 1977.

Chapter 6

Key Terms

acoustic channel
australopithecines
channel
communication
Cro-Magnons
design features of language
discontinuity theory of language evolution
display
hominids
hominoids
Homo erectus
Homo habilis
Homo sapiens
Homo sapiens sapiens
iconic
innatist theory of language acquisition
monogenesis (of language)
Neanderthals
Neolithic period
neurolinguistics
olfactory channel
optical channel
pheromone
prelanguage
polygenesis (of language)
Proto-Indo-European
protolanguage
pygmy chimpanzee
social insects
socialization
tactile channel
Upper Paleolithic period
vocal-auditory channel

Questions for Discussion

1. What kinds of evidence support the view that the gift of speech is built into all human beings? And how can this widely accepted premise—that children are genetically programmed to learn easily from their parents and other caregivers any

one of the thousands of the world's languages—be used to help refute racial or ethnic prejudice?

2. All animals communicate, that is, transmit information between organisms by means of different kinds of signs. Discuss those characteristics of human languages that are *not* found in the communicative behavior of any other species in the animal kingdom.

3. By the age of five or six, all normal children everywhere have a good command of their mother tongue (even though, of course, their vocabularies are still limited). However, college students, and adults in general, find learning a foreign language quite difficult, and most learn to speak a second language only haltingly at best. How do you explain this phenomenon?

4. Chimpanzees communicate, but their means (channels) of communication are different (as is also the scope) from those used by humans. Discuss the differences and the reasons for them.

5. There must have been reciprocal feedback during human prehistory between cultural evolution and the development of language, that is, each was continually facilitating and reinforcing the other. Try to illustrate this feedback process with some examples.

6. What is the difference between prelanguage and protolanguage? On what basis do we judge the transition from prelanguage to full-fledged language to have taken place?

Objective Study Questions
True-False Test

T　F　1. Honeybees are able to communicate the location and approximate distance of an abundant source of nectar immediately after hatching; they do not have to learn how to do it.

T　F　2. Young chimpanzees can learn to say several dozen words, but when they become adult they do not teach their young to speak.

T　F　3. The discontinuity theory of language evolution holds that human language must be recognized as unique, without evolutionary antecedents.

T　F　4. Interspecific communication—that is, transmission of signals between members of different species—is far from rare.

T　F　5. The design feature of displacement is unique only to humans and some of the higher apes.

T　F　6. One amazing thing about languages is that in each a limited number of contrastive sounds—only several dozen on the average—make up tens of thousands of individual words.

T　F　7. It is reasonable to assume that the Cro-Magnons, who lived some 30,000 years before the present and were known for their cave art, had a full-fledged language or nearly so.

T　F　8. The term *prelanguage* refers to the stage in the development of language that preceded full-fledged language; *protolanguage* refers to an assumed or reconstructed fully developed language.

T　F　9. It is safe to assume that the australopithecines had some sort of a multimodal system of communication.

T　F　10. It appears that the ability of the higher primates to communicate must have been an important evolutionary step toward the development of speech in humans.

Multiple-Choice Questions

____ 1. Of all the design features of language, the one that appears to be most distinctly and uniquely human is (A) broadcast transmission and directional reception. (B) rapid fading. (C) vocal-auditory channel. (D) openness (productivity).

____ 2. The fact that the four-legged domestic animal that barks is called *dog* in English, *Hund* in German, *pes* in Czech, and *heθ* in Arapaho is the design feature referred to as (A) duality of patterning. (B) displacement. (C) arbitrariness. (D) complete feedback.

____ 3. Which of the following statements having to do with communicative behavior among the great apes is *not* acceptable? (A) The pygmy chimpanzees of central Africa appear to be more intelligent, sociable, and eager to learn than common chimpanzees. (B) Despite the well-known experiment of the Hayeses with the female chimpanzee Viki, it appears that the ability to speak is unique to humans. (C) Sarah, a chimpanzee, had a plastic-token vocabulary of about 130 terms and used them with a surprisingly high reliability. (D) Most recent research indicates that attempts to teach gorillas to talk would meet with much greater success than has working with chimpanzees.

____ 4. We *use* language to discuss language in general. This is the design feature referred to as (A) specialization. (B) interchangeability. (C) semanticity. (D) reflexiveness.

____ 5. Braille, a writing system for the blind that uses characters made up of raised dots, is an example of the (A) acoustic. (B) tactile. (C) olfactory. (D) optical channel.

____ 6. The Neanderthals (A) were not yet of the genus *Homo*. (B) were dim-witted creatures. (C) may have believed in life after death and engaged in ritual activities. (D) None of these choices applies.

____ 7. Adaptations that made speech possible very likely coincided with the initial stages of hominization, some (A) 2 to 3 million years ago. (B) 200,000 to 300,000 years ago. (C) 20,000 to 30,000 years ago. (D) None of these three choices is defensible.

____ 8. The term *blending*, as used by C. F. Hockett in his theory of language origins, refers to (A) joining together of two early human populations. (B) blending of genes in early human populations. (C) producing a new call from two old ones (of a closed system). (D) None of these choices applies.

____ 9. Proto-Indo-European was spoken about six thousand years before the present, and one may therefore assume that it was (A) grammatically simple, if not primitive. (B) a late stage of a prelanguage. (C) a full-fledged language.

____ 10. One can only estimate the age of language and its prelanguage stage. Which of the following statements would be useful in making reasonable estimates? (A) Stone-tool assemblages that require skills and forethought correlate with the complexity of a communicative system. (B) The position of the larynx appears to be correlated with the ability of early humans to produce the three extreme vowels [i, a, u]. (C) The great variety and number of languages spoken today, as well as the complexity of some of the extinct languages, help us guess how long full-fledged languages must have been in existence. (D) All three statements apply. (E) Only one or two of the statements, A–C, is defensible.

Notes and Suggestions for Further Reading

An excellent critical evaluation of and guide to works concerning language origins was published by Hockett (1978). A detailed bibliography of books and articles on the subject was compiled by Hewes (1975).

Of the many books, book chapters, and articles dealing with the evolution of speech, the following may be of interest to readers who seek less technical treatment: Campbell 1979, Hockett and Ascher 1964, Stross 1976, and Time-Life Books 1973. More technical accounts may be found in de Grolier 1983; Harnad, Steklis, and Lancaster 1976; and Wescott 1974. New standards include Fitch 2010 and Larson, Déprez, and Yamakido 2010.

The work of Bickerton (1990) is full of stimulating ideas and interesting speculations, but reviewers tend to consider many of Bickerton's specific claims indefensible and even contradictory (see Pinker 1992 and Burling 1992). For contrary views concerning the evolution of modern humans, see Wilson and Cann 1992 and Thorne and Wolpoff 1992.

A richly illustrated and well-written series titled "The Dawn of Humans" began appearing in the January 1996 issue of *National Geographic* and continued in several subsequent issues throughout 1997.

Informative sources concerning communication among animals include Sebeok 1977, Bright 1984, and Roitblat and others 1992. The dance language of bees is described in Frisch 1967. For communication of nonhuman primates, see Schrier and Stollnitz 1971, which contains articles by Keith J. Hayes and Catherine H. Nissen, Beatrice T. Gardner and R. Allen Gardner, and David Premack, who trained Viki, Washoe, and Sarah, respectively. For an extensive and richly illustrated report on the chimpanzees of Gombe National Park in Tanzania, see Goodall 1986; and for a book-size discussion of Nim, see Terrace 1979. Savage-Rumbaugh 1986 discusses at length the various projects, including her own, to teach chimpanzees to communicate; and Susman 1984 deals with the evolutionary biology and behavior of pygmy chimpanzees. For a survey of works and bibliography concerning apes and language prior to 1978, see Hill 1978.

Chapter 7

Key Terms

angular gyrus
babbling
behaviorist theory of language acquisition
bilingualism
Broca's area (of the brain)
cerebrum
code-mixing
code-switching
critical-age hypothesis
diglossia
innatist theory of language acquisition
intonational contour
language acquisition device
lateralization (of the brain)
motor cortex
multilingualism
neurolinguistics
polyglot
reflexive noises
sequential bilingualism

trilingualism
vocal play
Wernicke's area (of the brain)

Questions for Discussion

1. What kinds of evidence support the view that the gift of speech is built into all human beings? And how can this widely accepted premise—that children are genetically programmed to learn easily from their parents and other caregivers any one of the thousands of the world's languages—be used to help refute racial or ethnic prejudice?

2. Children are taught not only how to behave but also what proper speech behavior is, that is, what to say and what not to say in various situations. Here are some examples: "Don't talk with your mouth full," "Keep your voice down," "Don't mumble," "Say 'Thank you.'" What other instructions do you remember hearing concerning acceptable speech behavior?

3. By the age of five or six, all normal children everywhere have a good command of their mother tongue (even though, of course, their vocabularies are still limited). However, college students, and adults in general, find learning a foreign language quite difficult, and most learn to speak a second language only haltingly at best. How do you explain this phenomenon?

4. Should English be chosen by law to become the official and national language of the United States? Discuss the pros and cons of such a law.

5. What are the advantages and disadvantages of the United States becoming a bilingual nation?

Objective Study Questions

True-False Test

T F   1. Most countries in the world are monolingual, like the United States.

T F   2. Usually children cannot learn to discriminate speech sounds until the age of 18 months or more.

T F   3. According to Noam Chomsky, it is unimaginable that a highly specific, abstract, and tightly organized language comes by accident into the mind of every four-year-old child.

T F   4. From what is now known, all speech impairments are traceable to lesions in one particular part of the language-dominant hemisphere of the human brain.

T F   5. The most widely accepted theory concerning language acquisition holds that all infants are born with some kind of language acquisition device that enables them to learn whatever their mother tongue happens to be.

T F   6. The use of two distinct varieties of a language for the same functions is called diglossia.

Multiple-Choice Questions

____ 1. Basic biological (reflexive) noises such as burping, crying, and coughing are produced during the first (A) eight or ten days. (B) eight or ten weeks. (C) eight or ten months.

____ 2. Intonational contours, such as those characteristic of questions, begin to appear around the end of the (A) first week. (B) first month. (C) first year. (D) second year.

3. The country with the most stable bi- or multilingualism is (A) Greece. (B) the United States. (C) Mexico. (D) Switzerland.

____ 4. The area of the brain that seems especially associated with language is (A) the spinal cord. (B) the thalamus. (C) Broca's area. (D) angular gyrus.

Completions

1 A sentence such as "Sometimes I'll start a sentence in English *y termino en español* ['and finish it in Spanish']" is an example of English/Spanish _____ (two words).

2. _____ theory argues that there is a capacity for rapid language development present in the child at birth (one word).

3. The _____ theory of language acquisition argues that humans acquire language through successive stimuli and reinforcements (one word).

4. It is _____ that more than anything else serves as the people's badge of ethnic identity and uniqueness (one word).

5. Which language is the de facto second language of the United States? _____ (one word)

Notes and Suggestions for Further Reading

Useful surveys of child language acquisition and the neurological basis of language can be found in Crystal 2007 and 2010. See Chomsky 1959 for an extensive and now classic review and critique of the book *Verbal Behavior* by the influential advocate of behaviorist psychology, B. F. Skinner. Jakobson 1968 is an English translation of Jakobson's German original published in Sweden in 1942. For a detailed account of language socialization of Kaluli children, see Schieffelin 1990. More information on language development, language disorders, and language and learning may be found in Menyuk 1988 and Gleason and Ratner 2008. For a classic (though no longer the latest) account of the biological foundations of language, see Lenneberg 1967. Later sources on biological foundations include Newmeyer 1989, Christansen and Kirby 2003, Fitch 2010, and Larson, Déprez, and Yamakido 2010. For discussion of the linguistic features of Broca's area see Grodzinsky and Amunts 2006. The procedures used to measure mutual intelligibility among Iroquoian languages are described in an article by Hickerson, Turner, and Hickerson 1952. The term *diglossia* was coined by Ferguson 1959. Wei Li's edited *The Bilingualism Reader* (2007) gives many of the classic articles in the discipline. For code switching and code mixing see Heller 1988 or Gardner-Chloros 2009. Saville-Troike 2006 is good general introduction to second language acquisition.

Key Terms

agglutinative languages
Anglo-Saxon
assimilation
Beowulf
cognates
diachronic (approach)
dissimilation

Chapter 8

genetic classification
glottochronology
historical linguistics
hypercorrection
inflecting languages
isolating languages
language family
language isolate
lexicostatistics
linguistic typology
loanword
metathesis
phylum
polysynthetic languages
protoculture
reconstructions
sound change
synchronic (approach)

Questions for Discussion

1. Vocabularies of living languages change constantly to keep up with the changes in the cultures of their speakers. Is the rate of lexical change the same in all societies, or can it be expected to be much faster in some than in others? Why?

2. Can you cite some English words that have come into use during your lifetime? (One such word, to give an example, is *staycation*—the practice of spending leisure time at home instead on vacation). In what areas (domains) of culture would such new words most likely appear?

3. Can you also cite some English words that have gone out of fashion or have disappeared? Why did they disappear? What have they been replaced with?

4. Reconstructions based on linguistic data are sometimes the only way scholars can learn something about the distant past of a particular people. Explain and illustrate.

5. It is not surprising that the several thousand languages spoken in the world today have been variously classified. Contrast the two major methods of classification—genetic and typological.

Objective Study Questions

True-False Test

T F 1. Glottochronology is a reliable method of dating absolutely the time at which two or more related languages began to undergo independent development.

T F 2. The term *language family* refers to all those languages whose speakers belong to the same culture area, that is, have similar cultures.

T F 3. Languages change, but change slowly—the Old English poem *Beowulf* is still intelligible to speakers of Modern English.

T F 4. A language isolate is a language that, although related to other languages, is spoken some distance from them.

T F 5. Dealing with linguistic phenomena as they exist at a specific point of time, without regard to historical antecedents, is referred to as the synchronic approach.

T F 6. A protolanguage (the assumed or reconstructed ancestral language of a language family) *cannot* be reconstructed unless one has good records from the distant past of some of the languages making up that language family.

T F 7. The English words *illegal*, *immoral*, and *irresponsible* illustrate assimilation.

T F 8. English has never been very hospitable to words of foreign origin.

Multiple-Choice Questions

——— 1. An exemplary case of reconstruction of the location of the ancestral homeland has been done for prehistoric speakers of which language family? (A) Siouan. (B) Uto-Aztecan. (C) Indo-European. (D) Algonquian.

——— 2. The word meaning "garlic" in language A is *mopan*, in language B *maban*, in language C *mapo*. What would likely be the reconstructed word (designated by *) in the ancestral (proto-)language of the related languages A, B, and C? (A) *mapan. (B) *maban. (C) *mapo. (D) *mopon.

——— 3. Cognate is a linguistic form related to another by virtue of (A) descent from an ancestral language. (B) borrowing from another language. (C) historical accident.

Completions

1. English is a language that belongs to the ——————— language family (one word).

2. What reconstructible Indo-European word indicates that Proto-Indo-Europeans did not live near the equator? ——————— (one word).

Problems

In order to enable readers to try their hand at some simple reconstructing, a few problems are included below. Solutions can be found following the answer section. One should keep in mind that because language reconstructions are no more than brief statements concerning an earlier or the earliest stage of a language family or one of its branches, some reconstructions may need minor changes when additional data become available. The problems offered here have been simplified; they require only the most straightforward application of the techniques of reconstructing linguistic forms. Remember that the asterisk is used to mark a reconstructed form, that is, one that has not been attested or is unattestable.

Problem 1

Based on Cowan and Rakušan (1998), this problem calls for the reconstruction of the initial Proto-Indo-European consonant on the basis of the following cognates (related words) in three Indo-European languages:

English	Latin	Ancient Greek
father	pater	patēr
foot	pēs	pous
for	per	peri
flat	plānus	platos
fathom	patēre	patanē

(The horizontal lines over certain vowels mark their length; for example, *ā* in *plānus* sounds like *a* in *father*.)

Fill in the blanks: Initial Proto-Indo-European * ____ corresponds to ____ in Modern English, ____ in Latin, and ____ in Ancient Greek.

Problem 2

Based on Langacker (1972), this problem concerns the reflexes of Proto-Cupan *[l] in three languages of Cupan, a subfamily of Uto-Aztecan. (A reflex in this case is a sound derived from a prior [older] sound.)

Cahuilla	Cupeño	Luiseño	
haal	hal	hal	'look for'
kiyul	qǝyul	kiyuul	'fish'
laʔlaʔ	laʔǝl	laʔla	'goose'
qasilʸ	qǝsilʸ	qaasil	'sagebrush'
puul	puul	puula	'doctor'
mukilʸ	mukʔilʸ	muukil	'sore'
silʸi	silʸi	ṣiili	'pour'

Proto-Cupan *[l] corresponds to ____ in _____, ____ in _____, and ____ in _____ under what circumstances?

Problem 3

Based on Cowan and Rakušan (1998), this problem calls for the reconstruction of whole Proto-Austronesian words from the following cognates of several Austronesian languages:

Sundanese	Old Javanese	Modern Javanese	Malay	Madurese	
manis	manis	manès	manes	manes	'lovely'
taman	taman	taman	taman	taman	'garden'
kuraŋ	kuraŋ	kuraŋ	kuraŋ	kòraŋ	'reduction'
damar	damar	damar	damar	dhámar	'lamp'
bantal	bantal	bantal	bantal	bhántal	'pillow'
tanjuŋ	tanjuŋ	tanjóŋ	tanjoŋ	tanjhuŋ	'flower'
qupah	qupah	upah	opah	òpa	'reward'

Example: Proto-Austronesian word for 'lovely' is reconstructible as *manis.

Problem 4

According to Watkins 1992, among the reconstructible Proto-Indo-European words are the following: *grǝno- 'grain,' *bhar(e)s- 'barley,' *yewo- 'grain,' *mel(a)- 'to grind,' *sē- 'to sow,' *yeug- 'to join, to yoke,' *gʷou- 'cow, ox,' *weik- 'village,' *owi- 'ewe, sheep,' *ekwo- 'horse,' *dem- 'house(hold),' and *dhwer- 'door(way).' What conclusions can one draw from these Proto-Indo-European words about the livelihood of members of old Indo-European society?

Notes and Suggestions for Further Reading

Crowley and Bowern 2009, Hale 2007, Miller 2007, and Schendl 2001 are standard recent texts in historical linguistics. For classic technical introductions to, and survey of, historical linguistics see Anttila 1989 or Hock 1991. Several thematic sections on the subject of this chapter are included in Crystal 2010. Most of the Japanese examples come from Inoue 1979 and hundreds of others can be found in Stanlaw 2004a.

The fascinating story of the Indo-Europeans and their spread throughout Europe and Asia is told in several well-researched and accessible accounts, including Mallory 1991 and Fortson 2010. The award-winning *The Horse, the Wheel and Language* by Anthony 2007 gives a nice blend of archeology and Proto-Indo-European linguistics. Voyles and Barrack 2009, while not for beginners, is an exhaustive look at Indo-European grammar and culture. A good Indo-European reference grammar is Quiles and López-Menchero 2009. The reconstruction of the PIE word for *cloud* is based on Jeffers and Lehiste 1979. A classic dictionary of Indo-European terms is Buck 1988. The example of the reconstruction of **snusós* has been abbreviated from the discussion by Calvert Watkins of the Indo-European lexicon and culture appended to *The American Heritage Dictionary of the English Language* (1992).

Campbell 2000 and Silver and Miller 2000 are probably the two most popular and standard texts on the history of Native American languages. Although Sapir 1916 is not easily available, the entire monograph is reprinted in Sapir 1949:389–462. The number of North American language families and isolates is based on Voegelin and Voegelin 1966. Sapir's reduction of North American Indian language families to six "major linguistic groups" was published in 1929 in the *Encyclopaedia Britannica* (14th ed.) and was reprinted in Sapir 1949:169–178.

Chapter 9

Key Terms

acrolect
artificial (auxiliary) language
basilect
creole
creolization
decreolization
dialect
idiolect
language contact
lingua franca
loanword
pidgin
pidginization
standard
style
Tok Pisin
vocal tract

Questions for Discussion

1. Do you use a different term for some of the following items when you refer to them informally at home?

baby carriage   dry streambed
cottage cheese   earthworm (fishermen's term)
doughnut   pancake
dragonfly   trough along the eaves to catch and carry off rainwater

2. Differences in pronunciation among regional dialects of American English are weakening because of the ever-greater mobility of Americans, but they still exist. Write down the following words and then ask individuals from different parts of the United States (or other English-speaking countries) to pronounce them. (Don't *say* the words, as you are likely to influence the pronunciation of your informants.)

aunt	half	soot
bird	house	third
caught	laugh	which
cot	marry	witch
envelope	Mary	with
greasy	merry	

3. It has been said that a language is dialect with an army. What do you think this means? Is there any wisdom to such a claim?

4. One of the authors was in New Guinea and heard two local pidgin speakers looking at a Land Rover with a broken headlight. One said to the other, "*Eye belong 'em bugger up pinis.*" What do you think he was trying to say? HINT: *pinis* is the pidgin form of English "finish."

Projects
Project 1
Here are some English words and their corresponding equivalents in Kamtok, Cameroon Pidgin English:

I	=	*a / mi*
he/she/it	=	*i*
you	=	*yu*
we	=	*wi*
they	=	*dem*
eat	=	*chop*
know	=	*sabi*
come	=	*kom*
go/will go	=	*go*
(past)	=	*bin*
be	=	*bi*
who	=	*hu*
many	=	*penti*
home, house	=	*haus*
for, to	=	*fo*
now	=	*nau*
tomorrow	=	*tumro*

Translate the following Cameroon Pidgin English sentences into English, and the English sentences into Cameroon Pidgin English.

(1) _____ *yestadei a bin chop*

(2) _____ *tumro a go chop*

(3) _____ *a bin chop penti*

(4) _____ *a bin chop nau nau*

(5) _____ *dem bin go fo haus*

(6) He just came. _____

(7) We will eat.

(8) I know.

(9) I will go.

(10) I know them.

Write three other sentences in Cameroon Pidgin English.

(1) _____

(2) _____

(3) _____

Project 2

Identify at least a dozen words that have been borrowed into English from other languages. Try to find out what they mean in their original language. What kind of modifications do you see taking place?

Objective Study Questions

True-False Test

T　F　1. Accent and dialect are terms that generally refer to the same linguistic phenomenon.

T　F　2. An idiolect is the speech variety of an individual.

T　F　3. A creole that has become the first language of a community is referred to as a pidgin.

T　F　4. Today more people in the world speak Indo-European languages than speak languages of any other language family.

T　F　5. There are about 3,000 known languages in the world today, and only a handful are pidgins or creoles.

T　F　6. There are a number of instances when two languages are mutually intelligible but not considered to be dialects of one language.

Multiple-Choice Questions

____ 1. Tok Pisin is spoken in which of the following countries/places (A) Papua New Guinea. (B) Australia. (C) New Zealand. (D) Tahiti.

____ 2. The differentiation between a language and a dialect is based on (A) mutual intelligibility. (B) the sociocultural relationship of the two communities (groups, peoples). (C) Both of these criteria, A and B, must be taken into account.

____ 3. Although pidgins can be based on any language, the most common—or at least the most well-known—pidgins have been based on (A) French. (B) Spanish. (C) English. (D) Japanese.

Completions

1. The process of expansion of a pidgin to other language functions is referred to as _____ (one word).

2. The linguist Martin Joos claims there are _____ clearly recognizable styles in his dialect of east-central American English (one word).

3. The theory of the linguist Derek Bickerton that tries to explain the similarities found in all pidgins and creoles is the _____ hypothesis (one word).

4. A language that people who speak different languages agree upon to use as neutral medium of communication is called a _____ (two words).

5. The best known artificial language is _____ (one word).

Notes and Suggestions for Further Reading

The literature on dialectology is vast. Chambers and Trudgill 1998 is a standard introductory text. See Wolfram and Schilling-Estes 2005 or Labov 2005 for discussions of English dialects and sound change. Labov 2010a, 2010b, and 2010c will likely be the new standards on language variation and change for some time.

The origin of the word *pidgin* is not known for certain, although it is usually considered to be a Chinese mispronunciation of the English word *business*. A recent survey (Crystal 2010: 348–349) has identified more than one hundred pidgins and creoles the world over, including some that are now extinct, but there have undoubtedly been more. For example, the 15th edition of the definitive language resource *Ethnologue* (Gordon 2005) cites about four hundred pidgins and six hundred creoles, though, of course, problems of definition abound. Any figure should be viewed as a conservative estimate, as many pidgins must have ceased to exist without any record and some of the creoles of the past are no longer identifiable as such.

An excellent recent guide to the study of pidgin and creole languages is Romaine 1988; a shorter and more popular introduction to pidgins is Hall 1959, as well as the later Todd 1990. The theory and structure of pidgins and creoles are the subject of the two volumes of Holm 1988 and 1989, though students new to the topic should start with his standard introductory text Holm 2000. The new theoretical standard, however, will likely be Siegel 2008. For a brief and more popularly written article on creole languages, see Bickerton 1983. A critical, partly negative evaluation of Bickerton's bioprogram hypothesis is to be found in Mühlhäusler 1986 and Romaine 1988.

The Tok Pisin examples are from Woolford 1979 and Murphy 1980; the short text is taken from Todd 1984:65.

The procedures used to measure mutual intelligibility among Iroquoian languages are described in an article by Hickerson, Turner, and Hickerson 1952.

Chapter 10

Key Terms

communicative competence
communicative performance
context
contextualization
ethnography of communication
frame (framing)
genre
key
linguistic competence
norms of interpretation
rules of interaction
speech act

speech area
speech community
speech event
speech situation

Questions for Discussion

1. Whenever we communicate with someone face to face, we tend to couch what we say in a style to fit the given situation. What form would your speech behavior take if you were stopped by the state police for speeding? If you were falsely accused of cheating? If you were reprimanded for not having finished an assignment on time? How and why might these forms differ?

2. Imagine yourself in conversation with a person who talks incessantly. After several minutes listening to such a person you decide to interrupt the flow of words in order to make a relevant comment. How would you handle the interruption if the other speaker were a

    person about four or five years younger
    person of the same sex and age
    person of the opposite sex and about the same age
    person much older but someone with whom you are very well acquainted
    distinguished person who is much older

3. Describing a language with emphasis on its function as the primary means of communication requires discussing a number of communicative components. Discuss these components and whenever possible, offer an illustration from your own experience.

4. Different peoples have different attitudes toward the use of speech. Support this statement with examples that show how different these attitudes can be.

Objective Study Questions
True-False Test

T F   1. The rules (not grammatical) for speech behavior in different societies are the same.

T F   2. Today, linguistic anthropologists hold that languages are different from each other, but the uses to which they are put are similar if not essentially the same.

T F   3. The purpose of speaking is not always to transmit information; sometimes it is to establish a sociable atmosphere.

T F   4. If the norms of interpreting speech behavior are shared by speakers, their relations are always harmonious.

T F   5. Among the Western Apache of Cibecue, the initial stages of courtship between young men and women is characterized by much talking, both serious and light-hearted.

Multiple-Choice Questions

_____ 1. The minimal unit of speech for purposes of an ethnographic analysis is the (A) speech situation. (B) speech act. (C) speech event.

_____ 2. All those who share specific rules for speaking and interpreting speech as well as at least one speech variety belong to a (A) speech network. (B) speech area. (C) speech community. (D) None of these three choices applies.

___ 3. The drinking of "beer" among the Subanun is an occasion to (A) relax and become heavily intoxicated. (B) honor a recently deceased person. (C) extend, define, and manipulate social relationships.

Completions

1. The study of the nature and function of communicative behavior with emphasis on linguistic interaction is called _____ (three words).

2. Recently, there has been a tendency to use the term _____ (one word) to replace the term *context*; the new term denotes a *process* rather than something that is given or fixed.

Notes and Suggestions for Further Reading

The information concerning the Ashanti has been drawn from a study by Helen Marie Hogan (n.d.), who based her account on a thorough review of published data. Because most of her sources appeared between the 1920s and 1960s, some of the information may no longer conform to the current communicative behavior of the Ashanti. The examination of the essential components of communicative behavior draws on Hymes 1972 and Saville-Troike 1982.

Boas's article on the use of metaphor in Kwakiutl was originally published in 1929 in the Netherlands; it was reprinted in Boas 1940.

The standard resource on the ethnography of communication is Saville-Troike 2002. Other articles and books dealing with the ethnography of speaking include Bauman and Sherzer 1974 (or 1989); Gumperz and Hymes 1964, and 1972; Hymes 1974 and 1989; Sherzer 1977; Kroskrity 1988; and Sherzer and Darnell 1972. For a survey of literature on the subject, see Bauman and Sherzer 1975 and 1989, and Duranti 1988; for a bibliography, see Philipsen and Carbaugh 1986.

Chapter 11

Key Terms

antonym
behaviorist theory of meaning
binary oppositions
componential analysis
concept
connotation
denotation
discourse
ethnoscience
homonym
lexeme
polysemy
referent
semantic differential
semantics
semiotic triangle
sound symbolism

symbol

synesthesia

synonym

taxonomy

Questions for Discussion

1. In this chapter we saw many sets of English terms using similar sounds that seem to share certain feelings or meanings. Why might this be the case? Could this phenomenon be universal?

2. If onomatopoeic terms are supposed to imitate sounds, why are the various onomatopoeic expressions different across languages (e.g., *bowwow* in English, *wan wan* in Japanese, or *aw aw* in Tagalog)?

Projects

Project 1

You are doing an ethnoscientific analysis of soft drinks in the United States. When presented with the elicitation frame, "Tell me the kinds of Pepsi Colas there are," your informants give you the following data:

Pepsi: the regular cola-flavored brand name soft drink

Diet Pepsi: a low calorie version of Pepsi (using the artificial sweetener aspartame)

Pepsi ONE: a diet Pepsi, with one calorie per serving

Caffeine-Free Pepsi: Pepsi with no caffeine

Caffeine-Free Diet Pepsi: a diet Pepsi with no caffeine

Crystal Pepsi: a clear version of Pepsi

Pepsi Lime: lime-flavored Pepsi

Christmas Pepsi: a nutmeg and cocoa Pepsi

Pepsi Strawberry Burst: strawberry-flavored Pepsi

Pepsi Twist: lemon-flavored Pepsi

Pepsi Light: a lemon-flavored diet Pepsi

Cherry Vanilla Pepsi: cherry-vanilla-flavored Pepsi

Wild Cherry Pepsi: a cherry-flavored Pepsi

Diet Wild Cherry Pepsi: low-calorie Wild Cherry Pepsi

Pepsi Jazz, Diet Black Cherry French Vanilla: a multiflavored diet Pepsi

Pepsi Jazz, Diet Strawberries and Cream: a multiflavored diet Pepsi

Pepsi Jazz, Diet Caramel Cream: a multiflavored diet Pepsi

Pepsi AM: Pepsi with extra caffeine

Diet Pepsi Max: Diet Pepsi with extra caffeine

Pepsi Natural: Pepsi made with only natural ingredients

Pepsi Edge: a diet Pepsi containing the artificial sweetener Splenda instead of aspartame

Try to analyze these data to find the native emic categories. Can you use the table included in this chapter? If so, does it have to be modified? How?

Project 2

Make a taxonomic analysis of American-made automobiles (Ford, Chevrolet, etc.), following the example in the chapter.

Project 3

Provide a rationale for why the following pairs might (or might not) be considered to be binary oppositions:

(1) dog/cat
(2) hen/chick
(3) heaven/hell
(4) raw/cooked
(5) black/white

Do the following words have binary oppositions? Why or why not?

(1) red
(2) animal
(3) handsome
(4) Pepsi
(5) skirt

Project 4

In the chapter we saw, besides the first row discussed in the text, two other rows of sets of English words depicting possible cases of sound symbolism. What do you think the words in each column (i.e, all the words in the *sl*- column, the words in the *pr*- column, and so on) have in common?

Objective Study Questions

True-False Test

T F   1. Edward Sapir was one of the first anthropologists to be explicitly concerned with semantics.

T F   2. The semantic differential is one device used to try to measure connotation.

T F   3. Lévi-Strauss believed that all languages have binary oppositions, and that for the most part, these binary oppositions are very much alike.

T F   4. Synesthesia refers to words that try to imitate sounds in the real world.

Multiple-Choice Questions

____ 1. We find that concepts become manifested in a language through (A) lexicalization. (B) grammaticalization. (C) socialization and discourse. (D) All of the above.

____ 2. One of the historical reasons why semantics was the last area in linguistics to receive attention was because (A) anthropologists generally cared more about social structure than meaning. (B) behavioral psychologists and structural linguists believed meaning could be reduced to stimuli and responses. (C) Chomsky and other linguists in the last half of the twentieth century dismissed meaning in favor of studying the ethnography of communication. (D) philosophy had generally solved most problems concerning meaning.

____ 3. Which of the following terms is *not* associated with a semiotic triangle? (A) Symbols, or words. (B) Thoughts, or concepts. (C) Referents. (D) Idioms.

____ 4. The emotional feeling tied to a word is referred to as (A) synonymy. (B) connotation. (C) reference. (D) denotation.

Completions

1. When we look at a word as an abstraction rather than just as spoken sounds, we often use the term _____ (one word.)
2. Words that have the opposite meaning are called _____ (one word).
3. Perception is just as much about _____ stimuli as it is about responding to stimuli (one or two words).
4. The term _____ refers to the things in the real world, while _____ is concerned with how a word contrasts with, or is related to, other words (one word each).

Notes and Suggestions for Further Reading

The study of meaning and conceptualization has a vast literature. Probably for the linguistic anthropology student almost anything by George Lakoff, Brent Berlin, William Labov, Ray Jackendoff, Leonard Talmy, Charles Fillmore, Wallace Chafe, Ronald Langacker, or John Searle would be of great interest (as well as being generally accessible). Modern formal introductions to semantics include Riemer 2010 or Hurford, Heasley, and Smith 2007. For a definitive overview of current research on sound symbolism see the edited collection by Hinton, Nichols, and Ohala 2006. For a book of readings in cognitive anthropology, see Tyler 1969. It supplements two special issues of *American Anthropologist* devoted to cognitive studies and formal semantic analysis; one was edited by Romney and D'Andrade (1964), the other by E. A. Hammel (1965). More recent books include Spradley 1972, Dougherty 1985, D'Andrade 1995, and Shore 1996. For good overviews of pragmatics see Levinson 1983 and Huang 2007; for discourse analysis, see Gee 2011 and Johnstone 2008; for conversational analysis, see Sidnell 2010, and Hutchby and Wooffitt 2008; for speech acts, see Martínez-Flor and Usó-Juan 2010. Cutting's (2008) *Pragmatics and Discourse: A Resource Book for Students* (and its accompanying Web site), while primarily intended for English language and linguistics students, offers much data—and many examples—for anthropologists to examine.

Key Terms

collateral relative
cultural determinism
ego
ethnoscience
kinship terminology
linguistic determinism
linguistic relativity
Sapir-Whorf hypothesis
universalism

Questions for Discussion

1. English kinship terminology, as used by Americans, varies somewhat from person to person. Some kin terms are used by everyone—*father, mother, son, daughter*—while other kin terms are not so well understood and therefore not so commonly used—*second cousin, third cousin, first cousin once removed*, and the like. Examine those kin

Chapter 12

terms that *you* use and determine which distinctive variables they employ (for example, age, gender, generation level, and relationship by marriage rather than by blood). A hint: The kin term *cousin* applies to both males and females, but *niece* only to females.

2. There are other English words used to designate relationships of various kinds, past or present. Among such terms are *father-in-law, stepbrother, half sister, godson, godmother, ex-husband,* and *partner* (also referred to as *significant other*). According to what criteria would you distinguish some of these terms from others? A hint: A half brother has one biological parent in common with a sibling; a stepbrother has no parent in common with his stepsibling. You may have to make use of a good dictionary to learn what some of these terms mean.

3. There are also kin terms that are extended to nonrelatives, that is, to people not related by marriage or blood. For example, the term *father* is commonly used in addressing or speaking of a priest of the regular clergy, and the term *uncle* is sometimes used by children to refer to an older male friend of the family. Account for these and other such usages.

4. Benjamin Lee Whorf's articles published at the time of World War II stimulated much interest in the relationship between language and culture, but he overstated his case and in some instances his examples were only anecdotal. Explain and illustrate.

5. Do you agree with the criteria Berlin and Kay proposed regarding basic colors? What is the status of the English term *orange* by these criteria?

Projects

Project 1

Japanese kinship and pronouns. In this chapter there were some data presented on the Japanese kinship and pronominal system. It was argued that these "reflect fine nuances of meaning or social distance." Using information given in the chapter, find three examples that show how the Japanese kinship or pronouns reflect social relations in ways other than in English (or some other language). What cultural implications, if any, might this have? How would Sapir or Whorf explain these results? How would Noam Chomsky do so?

Project 2

Relativism vs. universalism. Try to find three arguments that support or refute this statement: "I would argue that one of the most important things that cognitive science has done in recent years is show that the chasm between relativists (that is, those who focus on linguistic or cultural constraints on the mind) and universalists (those who are more concerned with innate psycho-biological constraints) has now become narrower, if not closed. To put things in other terms, it seems that human beings, and their cultures, can be quite creative and imaginative—almost limitless, it would appear at first glance—but we cannot think about anything without restraint."

How might a linguistic determinist (e.g., Whorf, Sapir, or Lucy), a universalist (e.g., Chomsky), and a cultural determinist (Witherspoon or Everett) respond to your arguments?

Objective Study Questions

True-False Test

T F 1. Every language in the world basically has the same set of color terms.

T F 2. Cultural determinists believe that environment and culture determine the structure of the human mind.

T F   3. There are no areas in the world where societies have very similar cultures but speak completely unrelated languages.

T F   4. In anthropology, the term *society* always refers to a homogeneous population, that is, a population of uniform ethnic composition.

T F   5. Because the Hopi language—according to Whorf—does not have tenses in the same sense that English does, the Hopis have no way of expressing that something took place last night, or is taking place today, or the day after.

T F   6. According to Edward Sapir, easily analyzable words (for example, words that are descriptive [*battleship, ironware*]) are more recent than words whose origin is obscure (for example, *hammer, horse*).

T F   7. There is very little correlation between the vocabulary of a language and the material culture of the society whose members speak that language.

T F   8. Arapaho kinship makes no distinction between some lineal and some collateral relatives.

T F   9. Gender is not a distinctive component of cousin terminology in English.

Multiple-Choice Questions

____ 1. Which of the following is not one of the components of the Sapir-Whorf hypothesis? (A) cultural determinism. (B) linguistic relativity. (C) linguistic determinism.

____ 2. Ego in anthropology refers to: (A) the person of reference to whom others are shown to be related. (B) any person who has an exaggerated sense of self-importance. (C) the oldest male of an extended family.

____ 3. From the point of view of a native speaker of English, a peculiar feature of the Arapaho kinship system is the fact that (A) both ego's father and mother are referred to by the same term. (B) there are no kinship terms comparable to the English *aunt* and *uncle*. (C) ego's father's brother's wife is referred to by the same kinship term as ego's mother.

____ 4. One reason English grammar is much easier to learn than the grammars of some of the other major languages spoken in Europe is that (A) the gender of nouns is natural. (B) the personal pronoun of the second person singular (with very few exceptions) has only one form. (C) the subject form of a noun is the same as the direct-object form. (D) All three choices above apply.

____ 5. Which of the following statements would be impossible to defend? (A) For technical subjects, some languages may have highly specialized vocabularies that are lacking in other languages. (B) Major sociopolitical revolutions tend to change profoundly not only the structure of the societies in which they occur but also the structure of the languages spoken by the members of such societies. (C) No correlation has yet been established between certain types of cultures and certain types of languages.

Notes and Suggestions for Further Reading

The citation from Humboldt is from *Wilhelm von Humboldts Werke* (translation by Salzmann). The references to the linguistic affiliation of the Native American languages of the Great Plains are according to Voegelin and Voegelin 1966. For representative selections from the writings of Sapir and Whorf, see Sapir 1949 and Whorf 1956. The two examples in the text referring to Hupa and Nootka words may be found in Sapir 1949:436–437 and

446–447.The Pintupi examples are from Crystal 2010 and the Arapaho examples from Salzmann 1983. The acute accent over an Arapaho vowel marks prominent stress and higher pitch; long vowels are written doubly. For additional discussion of the interrelationships of language and other aspects of culture, see Hoijer 1954, Fishman 1960, Gumperz and Levinson 1996, and Lucy 1992a, 1992b, and 1997, and Pütz and Verspoor 2000. And for a survey of works on language and worldview and the relevant bibliography, see Hill and Mannheim 1992. John Leavitt 2011 will be a new standard. Goodenough's comment made in 1957 is quoted here from Hymes's reader (1964). For work on color and color nomenclature theory see Kay, Berlin, and Merrifield 1991; Hardin and Maffi 1997; MacLaury 1997; Biggam and Kay 2006; Pitchford and Biggam 2006; MacLaury, Paramei and Dedrick 2007; and Deutscher 2010. For data from the World Color Survey see Kay, Berlin, Maffi, Merrifield, and Cook 2009.

Chapter 13

Key Terms

communicative strategy theory
elaborated code
ethnicity
genderlect
Gullah
hedge word
honorific
hypercorrection
language ideology
social power theory
restricted code
sexual bias (in language)
social network
sociolinguistic change
subculture theory
tag question
vernacular

Questions for Discussion

1. "Before his interview, each applicant for the teaching position must submit an up-to-date vita and a college transcript." This sentence exhibits sexual bias. Discuss how biases of this kind are being corrected in contemporary English writing.

2. "African-American children speaking so-called Ebonics have a marked disadvantage when they enter a typical American elementary school." Discuss this statement.

3. Explain this statement: "Gender is a status ascribed to individuals."

4. Justify the statement that African-American Vernacular English may have anticipated in some of its simplifications of English grammar the future development of English.

5. Give and discuss a few examples of the use of language for political or nationalistic purposes.

Projects

Project 1

Go though a women's magazine and a men's magazine and compare their use of language. Are there any differences in vocabulary, phrases, and/or the structure of a sentence? What about pronoun usage? What about pictures and captions? Advertisements? And how would you show that a magazine was a women's or men's magazine?

Project 2

Commercials on television are presumably as self-segregated by gender as was the case of the magazines above. Repeat the exercise above but for three primetime network television shows.

Project 3

Some words are used—or thought to be used—strictly by men, and others by women. Write down five adjectives, five adverbs, and five phrases you think are mostly used by men.

adjectives	adverbs	phrases
a.	a.	a.
b.	b.	b.
c.	c.	c.
d.	d.	d.
e.	e.	e.

Write down five adjectives, five adverbs, and five phrases you think are mostly used by women

adjectives	adverbs	phrases
a.	a.	a.
b.	b.	b.
c.	c.	c.
d.	d.	d.
e.	e.	e.

Objective Study Questions

True-False Test

T F 1. So-called tag questions characterize the speech of young American women rather than of older ones.

T F 2. Both male and female speakers of American English use the same patterns of intonation.

T F 3. African-American English is remarkably uniform in pronunciation and form throughout the United States.

T F 4. In African-American Vernacular English (AAVE) the most stable consonants are those found at the end of words.

T F 5. One particular variety of AAVE has as many as six or seven optional tenses.

T F 6. AAVE is just as rule-governed as other forms of English, but its rules of usage are somewhat different.

Multiple-Choice Questions

___ 1. The most applicable comment concerning the African-American Vernacular English (AAVE) utterance "He eat meat" is: (A) AAVE is less expressive than American English (AE). (B) AAVE is a defective variety (form) of AE. (C) AAVE has carried the development of English verb morphology farther than Standard English.

___ 2. How did African-American English (AAE) come about? Which of the following choices is most defensible? (A) AAE is one of the dialects of AE. (B) AAE is an English-based creole (similar to Jamaican Creole). (C) AAE shares some features with Standard English and others with creoles such as Gullah or Jamaican.

___ 3. In American English the differences between the speech of men and women have to do almost only with (A) morphology. (B) lexicon (choice of words). (C) phonology. (D) None of the three choices applies.

___ 4. William Labov found that some New Yorkers pronounced r-sounds in words that did not include them in spelling. Such usage is called (A) hypercorrection. (B) prescribed pronunciation. (C) proscribed pronunciation. (D) a mistake.

___ 5. Which of the following is generally not the purpose of a tag question? (A) To obtain the assent of the addressee. (B) To seek confirmation. (C) To set the stage for a disagreement. (D) To avoid assertiveness. (E) To include the listener into the conversation.

___ 6. Which of the following countries is the most linguistically diverse? (A) The United States. (B) India. (C) Spain. (D) Canada. (E) The Czech Republic.

Completions

1. Beliefs about the social world as expressed by speakers through their language is called
   _____ (one word).

2. Terms such as "maybe," "rather," and "perhaps" are called _____
   words (one word).

3. Three differences between American women's and men's speech are a greater use of
   _____ (three
   _____, _____, and
   phrases).

4. The view that women's language is a manifestation not of genderlect differences, but
   of women's traditionally weaker social position, is called _____
   theory (two words).

5. In northern Spain the _____ people have sometimes resorted to armed
   struggle for their linguistic and cultural rights (one word).

Notes and Suggestions for Further Reading

Several books and collections dealing with the topics covered in this chapter include Bergvall 1999; Kroskrity 1983, 1993, and 2000; Harris and Rampton 2003; Rampton 1995; Cheshire 2002; Macaulay 2002; Mills 1995; Tannen 1994a; Hall and Bucholtz 1992, 1996. Bucholtz 2004 is a reissue with commentary of Robin Lakoff's classic 1975 text.

Some additions and corrections pertaining to Haas's report on gender-specific speech among the Koasati are the subject of Kimball 1987. The entire example from North African French has been drawn from Walter 1988. There are a number of articles and books concerned with the speech of women and men: Noteworthy among them are Coates 1986;

Coates and Cameron 1988; Kramarae 1981; Lakoff 1975; Philips, Steele, and Tanz 1987; Silverstein 1985; and Thorne, Kramarae, and Henley 1983. The last book includes an extensive early annotated bibliography (pp. 151–342). The literature on gender differences and language is reviewed in Philips 1980, McConnell-Ginet 1988, and Eckert and McConnell-Ginet 1992.

The sections concerning African-American English draw heavily on Burling 1973. In comparing African-American Vernacular English with Standard English, linguists use such expressions as *loss of* and *weakened* in their technical linguistic senses; they are not to be construed as carrying negative connotations. Weakening and losses have characterized the history of English inflections from Old English to the present, and no one has ever claimed that Modern English is the worse for it. For a survey of literature concerning the features of African-American English, theories of its origins, and several related topics, see Morgan 1994 and Labov 1972a; and for a discussion of the Ebonics issue, see Fields 1997.

For studies on language and nationalism see Joseph 2004 and May 2008. For specific countries see India: Kachru, Kachru, and Sridhar 2008; Czech Republic: Kamusella 2009 (especially pp. 481–518); Spain: Woolard 1989 and Wright 1999; and Canada: Heller 2011 and Edwards 2010.

For useful general surveys on language ideology see Woolard and Schieffelin 1994 and Schieffelin, Woolard, and Kroskrity 1998.

Work on Japanese women's language include Takemaru 2010, Inoue 2006, Shibamoto 1985, and Itoh, Adachi, and Stanlaw 2007.

See Bucholtz 2011; Hill 2008; Kubota and Lin 2009; and Baugh 2002 for discussions of language and race.

Language statistics came from the 15th edition of *Ethnologue* (Gordon 2005).

For popular and best-selling accounts of the complexities of communication between men and women, see almost anything by Deborah Tannen (e.g., 1986 and 1990).

Chapter 14

Key Terms

digital literacy
ethics
intercultural communication
language and the law
language death
language maintenance
language planning
phatic communication
translation

Questions for Discussion

1. Counter the argument that anthropology is of little consequence to life in modern complex societies (such as the society of the United States) because anthropologists concern themselves with only "exotic" and "primitive" peoples marginal to modern civilization.

2. What ethical considerations should guide the anthropologist as a field-worker, and why?

3. Many complex societies are heterogeneous (consisting of dissimilar components) by virtue of the ethnic background and socioeconomic status of their members. How does one study the sociolinguistic aspects of such pluralistic societies? From the point of view of a linguistic anthropologist, does such ethnic and social heterogeneity offer some interesting questions that could be studied? What are some such questions?

4. An excellent example of the application of linguistic findings to social issues is the case of the "Black English trial" in Ann Arbor, Michigan. Discuss this case.

Projects

Project 1

Consider the following exchange of e-mail between two college instructors, Dr. Doe and Dr. Adachi at X University. What do you notice about style, tone, and orthography in these messages? What kind of conversation was taking place? Who wanted to do, or not do, what? How could you tell? Was a successful exchange taking place? What cues are missing? What cues *are* here? How might the conversation have been different had it taken place in person?

(first e-mail message). Quoting jdoe@x.edu:

dear dr. adachi,

i am jane doe and i teach commercial art at the school of business. i am teaching a special topics course on cultural identity in advertising this semester where students learn new research methodologies in advertising so they can create designs that are more meaningful for a multicultural audience.

i am inviting guest speakers to talk about culture and identity. i would appreciate if you would be interested to be a guest speaker in my class. the class is held at Smith Hall 14 on M. and W. from 8 to 10. please let me know if this is possible.

thanks for your time.

sincerely,
jane doe

(second e-mail message). Quoting nadachi@x.edu

Dear Dr. Doe,

Thank you very much for your invitation. I am very interested in culture and identity, as that is one of my linguistic specialties. However, I am also teaching on Mondays and Wednesdays this semester all day, so I am afraid I will not be able to be a guest speaker this Spring. Sorry. But again, thank you for your invitation.

Nobuko

(third e-mail message). Quoting jdoe@ x.edu:

dear dr. adachi,

thank you for responding. i do teach on fridays as well. please let me know if feb. 10th or 17th or 24th will work for you.

thank you,
jane

(fourth e-mail message). Quoting nadachi@x.edu:

Dear Dr. Doe,

Thank you for your offer again, but I am very sorry. This semester I need to finish a project so I will not be able to come to campus on Fridays. Perhaps I might be able to visit your class some other time. But thank you again.

Best,

Nobuko

(fifth e-mail message). Quoting jdoe@x.edu:

dear dr. adachi,

i am teaching this class again in fall please let me know when you can come then.

thank you

jane

Objective Study Questions

True-False Test

T F 1. According to the code of professional ethics adopted by the American Anthropological Association, the first responsibility of anthropologists is to their country.

T F 2. Jomo Kenyatta, the first president of Kenya, chose the language spoken by the largest number of Kenyans to be the official language of the country.

T F 3. The mother tongue of Arapaho school children today is English.

T F 4. A conversation between Americans and Athapaskan Indians tends to be very asymmetrical: The Athapaskans are quite talkative and fill any pauses that may occur with speech.

T F 5. In courts, the specific phrasing of questions can and does influence the answers of witnesses.

Multiple-Choice Question

____ 1. Which of the following statements is most easily defensible? (A) The teaching of a native language of a people can begin, with a good chance of success, in elementary school. (B) When mothers speak to infant children in a language other than the native language of that people, the native language is almost inevitably doomed to eventual extinction. (C) During the past several decades, efforts to save Native American languages from extinction have been remarkably successful.

Completion

1. An imposed change in the status of a language or a dialect, and/or imposed changes affecting the structure of a language (its pronunciation, spelling, vocabulary, etc.) are referred to as _____ (two words).

Notes and Suggestions for Further Reading

Among the publications dealing with applied linguistics are Wardhaugh and Brown 1976, Crystal 1981, and Trudgill 1984. The *Annual Review of Applied Linguistics* (ARAL), first published in 1981, surveys research and comments on new trends in the field of applied linguistics. With several hundred new citations each year, *ARAL* is a good source of bibliographical references. For a survey of the uses of linguistics in medicine, law, and education, together with an extensive bibliography, see Shuy 1984. Linguistics and education are the subject of a survey article by Heath 1984; for an overview of the language of the law, see O'Barr 1981.

For sources on intercultural communication, see Scollon and Scollon 2001, Carbaugh 1990, and Samovar and Porter 1991. Language planning is discussed in Eastman 1983 and Kennedy 1983. A survey of American Indian language maintenance efforts is to be found in Leap 1981 and a guide to issues in Indian language retention in Bauman 1980.

On language extinction see Nettle and Romaine 2000 and Crystal 2000, and the resources of *Ethnologue* (start with Gordon 2005). Of interest may be the contributions to the symposium "Endangered Languages" by Hale and others 1992; for a contrary view of endangered languages, see Ladefoged 1992; and for a response to Ladefoged, see Dorian 1993.

The discussion of language maintenance and reinforcement among the Northern Arapaho of the Wind River Reservation is based on Salzmann's personal involvement in such a project during the 1980s. For the latest report on Arapaho language maintenance efforts, see Greymorning 2001.

For discussions of languages on the internet see Baron 2000 and 2008, and Crystal 2001, 2004, and 2009.

International English (or Englishes) now has become an established and recognized subfield of linguistics with its own associations and journals. The literature is vast. Anything by Braj Kachru, Yamuna Kachru, Kingsley Bolton, Larry Smith, or Cecil Nelson would be intellectually rigorous and quite readable. A good overview of the field can be found in the six-volume collection of readings of Bolton and Kachru 2006 or the single volumes Y. Kachru and Smith 2008 or B. Kachru 1992.

The discussion of the principles of professional responsibility to those whom anthropologists study is abbreviated from the pamphlet *Professional Ethics*, published by the American Anthropological Association in 1983. Besides discussing relations with those studied, the statements on ethics also cover the anthropologists' responsibilities to the public, to the discipline, to anthropology students, to sponsors, to their own government, and to host governments.

ANSWERS TO THE OBJECTIVE STUDY
QUESTIONS AND PROBLEMS

Chapter 1

Answers to objective study questions:

True-false test: 1-F, 2-F, 3-T, 4-F, 5-T, 6-T

Multiple-choice questions: 1-C, 2-C, 3-B, 4-A, 5-E

Completions: 1. race, language, and culture; 2. Takelma; 3. holistic

Chapter 2

Answers to objective study questions:

True-false test: 1-F, 2-F, 3-T, 4-F, 5-F, 6-F, 7-T

Multiple-choice questions: 1-E, 2-D, 3-B, 4-B

Completions: 1. corpus, 2. elicitation, 3. sociocultural

Chapter 3

Answers to objective study questions:

True-false test: 1-F, 2-F, 3-T, 4-T, 5-T, 6-T, 7-T, 8-T, 9-T, 10-F

Multiple-choice questions: 1-A, 2-D, 3-D, 4-C, 5-B

Completions: 1. tone, 2. phone, phonemes, allophones

Answers to problems:

Problem 1. The sounds [c] and [ʒ] in Zoque are allophones of a phoneme because they are phonetically similar (both are affricates) and in complementary distribution: The voiced alveolar affricate [ʒ] occurs after nasal consonants ŋ, m, and n (as in 1, 2, 3, 7, 8, 9, and 12), the voiceless alveolar affricate [c] elsewhere (as in 3–6, 10, and 11). The rule could be written as follows: /c/ → [+ voiced]/N___ (where N = any nasal).

Problem 2. All of the four Czech stops, [t, d, tʲ, dʲ], are separate phonemes, /t, d, tʲ, dʲ/, because they contrast, as is evident from the existence of minimal pairs in the sample (as in 1 and 3, 4 and 9, 11 and 13, and 14 and 16).

Problem 3. The main stress in Araucanian is on the second vowel of a word and hence is predictable.

Problem 4. Vowel length in Mohawk is predictable: All vowels are short except those that are stressed and followed by a single consonant (as in 1, 2, 4, 6, and 7). Vowel length is therefore not distinctive.

Problem 5. From the word pairs 1 and 2, 7 and 8, and 9 and 10, the form of the suffix meaning "of (the)" is *-uy*. Stem-final [l] changes to [r] before the suffix (as in 1 and 2 and 7 and 8). [r] and [l] are allophones of the same phoneme: [r] occurs initially (as in 5 and 6) and intervocalically, that is, between vowels (as in 2, 8, 9, and 10), and [l] occurs finally (as in 1, 3, 4, and 7) and before a consonant (as in 11 and 12).

Problem 6. The alveolar segments [t, s, z] occur before the vowels /e, a, o, u/ (as in 1–8); the palatal segments [č, š, ž] occur before /i/, that is, before a high front vowel (as in 9–14). The phonemic symbol /t/ would be preferable to /č/ because its occurrence is less restricted. It may be expected to occur before the four vowels /e, a, o, u/; in this small sample it occurs only before /o/ and /a/ (as in 1 and 2) and therefore more frequently than the /č/ that occurs only before /i/ (as in 9 and 10). (This choice also happens to be more practical because *t* is one of the standard keys on American keyboards whereas *č* is not; if one were to choose *č*, the háček [ˇ] diacritical mark would have to be selected from a separate typeface menu, requiring extra steps, and added above the letter *c* whenever the *č* occurred.)

Problem 7. Vowel length is phonemic; there are minimal pairs that differ only by vowel length (as in 1 and 5, 2 and 4, and 3 and 6).

Problem 8. The Czech sounds [k] and [x] are two separate phonemes /k/ and /x/; two word pairs of the sample, 1 and 5, and 2 and 8, differ only by virtue of these two consonants.

Chapter 4

True-false test: 1-F, 2-T, 3-F, 4-T, 5-T

Multiple-choice questions: 1-C, 2-D, 3-F, 4-D, 5-E

Completions: 1. process, 2. emphasis

Answers to problems:

Problem 1. Morphemes are obtained by comparing words or sentences that appear to differ only by a single difference in meaning (as judged from the English glosses)—for example, 2 and 3 (they differ only in the tense—present as against future). Morphemes representing grammatical meanings (in this case present tense and future tense) are usually glossed in capital letters.

Luiseño Morphemes	*English Glosses*
nóo	I
póy	him
čáami	us
q	PRESENT
n	FUTURE
ni	make

viču	want
wukála	walk
páaʔi	drink
temét	sun

Problem 2. The Tohono Oʼodham verb forms are pluralized by adding a prefix to the singular; the form of the prefix is the initial consonant and the following vowel of the singular verb form.

Problem 3. Allomorphs of the past tense morpheme: /-əd/ if the base ends in /t, d /; /-t/ if it ends in /p, k, č, f, θ, s, š/; and /-d/ if it ends in any other sound. Allomorphs of the third-person singular morpheme: /-əz/ if the base ends in /s, z, š, ž, č, ǰ/; /-z/ if it ends in any voiced sound except /z, ž, ǰ/; and /-s / if it ends in any voiceless sound except /s, š, č/.

Problem 4. The stems or roots are listed under 1–20. The first-person singular possessive uses the prefix *an-*. The morphophonemics of this prefix may be stated as follows: The *n* of the prefix *an-* becomes *m* when the initial consonant of the stem or root that follows is *m* or *p*. Concisely written:

n→m/___ m, p (that is, *n* becomes *m* before *m* or *p* [bilabials]) (as in 27, 28, 31, and 32)

n→ñ/___ y, č, š, tʲ (palato-alveolars) (as in 22, 35, 36, 38, and 40)

n→ŋ/___ k, w (as in 25, 26, and 39)

n→n/___ t, c, s, n, h (= elsewhere) (as in 21, 23, 24, 29, 30, 33, 34, and 37)

Problem 5. The third-person singular of Samoan verbs is pluralized by a morpheme whose form is derived from the singular form by reduplication (repetition) of the penultimate (next to the last) vowel and the preceding consonant. (This may be a better way of stating the rule than using the phrase "penultimate syllable" because one should then define the term "syllable" for Samoan.) Under this rule, 'he sings' would be *pese*, 'they weave *lalaga*, and 'they travel' *savavali*.

Problem 6. By comparing words 1–4, 6, and 8, we see that they all share the prefix *ni-* that corresponds to 'I' in the English glosses. By comparing words 1 and 7, we obtain the prefix *ti-* 'you (sing)'; and by comparing words 1, 2, and 8, we obtain the suffixes *-ʔ* PAST TENSE and *-s* FUTURE TENSE; it appears that PRESENT TENSE is not marked, that is, it is marked by a zero (∅) morpheme (absence of a sound). If one detaches all prefixes and/or suffixes from words 1, 2, 7, and 8, what is left is *čoka*, the stem of the word meaning 'cry'.

Problem 7. This problem is somewhat simplified. In order not to confuse students by using phonemic transcriptions, all words are written in the traditional orthography. The ten English words display two *different* prefixes, *re-* and *iC-* (C stands for a consonant). The prefix (morpheme) *re-* means 'again' (as in 1) and the prefix *iC-* 'not' (as in 5, 8–10). The latter prefix occurs in this sample in three allomorphs (forms of a morpheme): as *-im* in 9 and 10, *ir-* in 8, and *il-* in 5. The most common allomorph of this morpheme, *in-* (as in 'indecent', 'incapable', or 'inimitable'), is not represented in this sample.

Four suffixes are shown: *-ing*, *-ly*, *-less*, and *-able*. The sample contains ten different stems: *care, fear, full, hope, taste, write, legal, mobile, moral,* and *retrieve*. (Note: *re-* in *retrieve* cannot be considered in the *synchronic* analysis of Modern English as a prefix because there is no stem *trieve*; diachronically, it comes from the Anglo-French *retrueve-* 'to find again'.)

Chapter 5

Answers to objective study questions:
True-false test: 1-T, 2-F, 3-T, 4-F, 5-T, 6-F, 7-F
Multiple-choice questions: 1-A, 2-C, 3-C, 4-B, 5-D, 6-C
Completions: 1. proxemics, 2. paralanguage, 3. semiotics

Chapter 6

Answers to objective study questions:
True-false test: 1-T, 2-F, 3-T, 4-T, 5-F, 6-T, 7-T, 8-T, 9-T, 10-F
Multiple-choice questions: 1-D, 2-C, 3-D, 4-D, 5-B, 6-C, 7-A, 8-C, 9-C, 10-D

Chapter 7

Answers to objective study questions:
True-false test: 1-F, 2-F, 3-T, 4-F, 5-T, 6-F
Multiple-choice questions: 1-B, 2-C, 3-D, 4-C
Completions: 1. code-switching, 2. innatist, 3. behaviorist, 4. language, 5. Spanish.

Chapter 8

Answers to objective study questions:
True-false test: 1-F, 2-F, 3-F, 4-F, 5-T, 6-F, 7-T, 8-F
Multiple-choice questions: 1-D, 2-A, 3-A
Completions: 1. Indo-European, 2. snow

Answers to problems:
Problem 1. On the basis of the cognates listed, the reconstructed initial Proto-Indo-European consonant would be *p; it corresponds to f in Modern English and p in both Latin and Ancient Greek.
Problem 2. After the vowel [i], Proto-Cupan *[l] is represented as [y] in Cahuilla and Cupeño and as [l] in Luiseño; in all other environments it is represented as [l] in all three languages.
Problem 3. The reconstructed Proto-Austronesian words are *manis, *taman, *kuran, *damar, *bantal, *tanjun, and *qupah.
Problem 4. This is an open-ended question; the answer should be limited to what a reasonable interpretation of the data presented would allow.

Chapter 9

Answers to objective study questions:
True-false test: 1-F, 2-T, 3-F, 4-T, 5-F, 6-T
Multiple-choice questions: 1-A, 2-C, 3-C
Completions: 1. creolization, 2. five, 3. bioprogram, 4. lingua franca, 5. Esperanto.

Answers to Project 1:
1. 1 ate yesterday.   *yestadei a bin chop*
2. 1 will eat tomorrow.   *tumro a go chop*

3. I ate a lot.   *a bin chop penti*
4. I just ate.   *a bin chop nau nau*
5. They went back home.   *dem bin go fo haus*
6. He just came.   *i bin kom nau nau*
7. We will eat.   *wi go chop*
8. I know.   *a sabi*
9. I will go.   *a go go*
10. I know them.   *a sabi dem*

Chapter 10

Answers to objective study questions:
True-false test: 1-F, 2-F, 3-T, 4-F, 5-F
Multiple-choice questions: 1-B, 2-C, 3-C
Completions: 1. ethnography of communication, 2. contextualization

Chapter 11

Answers to objective study questions:
True-false test: 1-F, 2-T, 3-T, 4-F
Multiple-choice questions: 1-A, 2-B, 3-D, 4-B
Completions: 1. lexeme, 2. antonyms, 3. filtering out/ignoring, 4. referent; sense

Chapter 12

Answers to objective study questions:
True-false test: 1-F, 2-T, 3-F, 4-F, 5-F, 6-T, 7-F, 8-T, 9-T
Multiple-choice questions: 1-C, 2-A, 3-C, 4-D, 5-B

Chapter 13

Answers to objective study questions:
True-false test: 1-F, 2-F, 3-F, 4-F, 5-T, 6-T
Multiple-choice questions: 1-C, 2-C, 3-B, 4-A, 5-C, 6-B
Completions: 1. ideology, 2. hedge, 3. any three of the following: greater use of tag questions, greater use of polite forms, greater use of wh- words, greater use of hedges, greater use of apologies, greater use of intensifiers, greater use of "women's vocabulary," greater use of modal auxiliaries, greater use of question intonations in declarative sentences, 4. social power, 5. Basque

Chapter 14

Answers to objective study questions:
True-false test: 1-F, 2-F, 3-T, 4-F, 5-T
Multiple-choice question: B
Completion: 1. language planning

GLOSSARY

Words or phrases with a particular meaning in linguistic anthropology are defined here in their simplest and most general form; in some cases a brief example is given parenthetically.

Accent Articulatory prominence given a syllable—that is, stress; sometimes a combination of stress and pitch.

Acoustic channel A means of communication utilizing sounds (for example, the human voice).

Acoustic phonetics The study of the physical properties of speech sounds.

Acrolect The language variety closest to the prestige form of a language.

Affix A meaningful element attached to the beginning or end of a word or inserted within a word to produce another word (as in the word *unspeakable*, with two affixes; or an inflected form of a word, as in mountains).

African-American Vernacular English A nonstandard but expressive variety of English spoken by many African-Americans.

Agglutinative languages Languages in which each grammatical meaning is expressed by a separate piece of structure (as in the Turkish word *yaz-maliy-miš-im* 'I should have written').

Allomorph A variant form of a particular morpheme (for example, *-en* of *oxen* and *-s* of *pets* are two allomorphs of the morpheme marking the plural of nouns in English).

Allomotif A variety of a distinctive unit in a traditional (folk) narrative (for example, one of several forms of a difficult or dangerous test a hero of a folktale must submit to).

Allophone A variant form of a phoneme (for example, the *p* sounds of *pin* and *spin* are allophones of the phoneme /p/).

Alphabetic writing A writing system in which the distinctive sounds of a language are for the most part represented by a graphic symbol (letter).

Alternate sign language A sign language used among speaker-hearers as regular or occasional substitute for speech.

American Sign Language (Ameslan) A sign language used by deaf people in the United States.

Anglo-Saxon Old English, spoken in England until the end of the eleventh century.

Angular gyrus One of the convolutions of the posterior part of the brain.

Anthropology The study of cultural and biological variations of human groups, past and contemporary.

Antonyms Words of opposite meaning (for example, *hot* and *cold*).

Archaeology The recovery and study of material remains of past human life and culture.

Articulatory phonetics The study, in some detail, of the production of speech sounds by the vocal organs, and the description, classification, and transcription of these sounds.

Artificial language A constructed international language, such as Esperanto.

Aspect The ability of verbs to express the perfective and imperfective conceptions of an action.

Assimilation The influence of one speech sound on the articulation of another so that both become similar or identical (as when in rapid speech *ten bucks* is pronounced *tem-bucks*, the *n* becoming a bilabial *m* to approximate the following bilabial *b*).

Australopithecines Several species of a genus of extinct hominids who flourished in eastern and southern Africa several million years ago; some of the species are assumed to have been ancestral to modern humans.

Auxiliary language Another term for an artificial language believed to facilitate international communication.

Babbling An early stage in children's speech development characterized by the production of basic vowels and front consonants.

Basilect The language variety most remote from the prestige form of a language.

Behaviorist theory of language acquisition A theory based on the stimulus-response-reward sequence and on repetition of what the child is hearing.

Beowulf Hero of the epic Old English poem of the same name, probably composed during the eighth century.

Bilingualism Good command of two languages.

Binary opposition The perceived opposition of two mutually exclusive contrary terms, qualities, phenomena, etc.

Biological (or physical) anthropology The subfield of anthropology concerned with the study of human evolution and physical variation.

Body language The gestures, other bodily movements, and mannerisms used in communication.

Bound morpheme A morpheme that does not occur by itself but only in combination with other morphemes (as *ir-* and *-able* in *irreproachable*, or *dis-* and *-ment* in *displacement*).

Braille A system of writing for the blind that uses characters made up of raised dots.

Broca's area A part of the brain associated with the motor control of speech.

Case Grammatical category of inflected words expressing their function in the sentence.

Cerebral cortex The convoluted surface layer of gray matter in the brain that functions primarily to coordinate sensory and motor information.

Cerebrum The largest part of the brain, consisting of two hemispheres.

Channel A path or medium through which information passes.

Chereme A suggested term for the smallest sign-language contrastive unit that combines with others to form meaningful sign units.

Code-mixing The incorporation of linguistic units from one language into another.

Code-switching Changing from one language or language variety to another in the course of a spoken interaction.

Cognates Linguistic forms related by virtue of descent from the same source (for example, the words *father* in English, *Vater* in German, and *padre* in Spanish).

Collateral relative A relative not in the direct line of descent.

Communication The transmission and exchange of information between individual organisms by means of symbols, signs, or behavior (for example, words are symbols, and a kiss expresses affection).

Communicative competence The knowledge that enables a person to communicate in any socioculturally authentic context.

Communicative performance The manner in which an individual communicates in a given context (it may or may not be appropriate).

Communicative strategy theory (concerning the language-and-gender relationship) The view that speakers tend to value their language according to its usefulness and prestige in socioeconomic situations.

Componential analysis An analysis of the terms of a well-defined cultural domain in order to discover the semantic distinctions among these terms.

Connotation Meaning, or meanings, associated with a word in addition to its literal meaning.

Consonant A speech sound during which the vocal tract is either blocked or constricted enough to produce audible friction.

Consultant A common contemporary term for informant in recognition of the intellectual contribution informants make to studies in linguistic anthropology.

Context Interrelated conditions under which communicative behavior occurs.

Contextualization The process during which communicative behavior is developing and taking place.

Corpus A collection of language data used as a basis for an analysis or description.

Creole A pidgin that has become the first language of a speech community.

Creolization The process of expansion of a pidgin to fully serve a speech community.

Critical-age hypothesis The hypothesis that language is acquired with remarkable ease during brain maturation, that is, before puberty.

Cro-Magnons Early members of the *Homo sapiens* species dating from the Upper Paleolithic period (roughly from 35,000 to 10,000 B.C.).

Cultural anthropology The subfield of anthropology that deals with the study of human culture.

Cultural determinism The theory that culture determines how language and thought become manifested.

Culture versus a culture Culture is the complex of human learned behavior, knowledge, and beliefs transmitted from one generation to the next. A culture is the pattern of learned behavior, knowledge, and beliefs transmitted from generation to generation by members of a particular society.

Decreolization The change that a creole undergoes as it moves in the direction of the standard language.

Denotation A relationship between a lexeme and that to which the lexeme refers.

Derivation The formation of new words by means of certain affixes (as in *national* from *nation* or *happiness* from *happy*).

Descriptive (approach) In linguistics, an approach that attempts to describe the units of speech and their combinations as used by speakers of a language.

Design features of language An underlying set of prominent characteristics governing the functioning of speech (for example, the ability to speak about things removed in time and place).

Diachronic (approach) Dealing with linguistic phenomena as they occur over time (that is, considering their historical development).

Dialect A regional or social variety of a language (for example, one of the several regional varieties of American English or a socially differentiated variety of American English spoken by a particular socioeconomic class).

Digital literacy The ability to make use of computerized technology in communication.

Diglossia The use of two distinct varieties of language for two different sets of functions.

Discontinuity theory of language evolution The theory that holds that human language is a unique means of communication without evolutionary antecedents in the animal kingdom.

Discourse The principal analytical unit of speech, widely varying in length, form, and content.

Display Emission of visual signals used by certain animals to communicate such types of behavior as courtship or intimidation.

Dissimilation The influence of one speech sound on the articulation of another so that they become less alike (for example, the pronunciation of *February* as *Febuary* to avoid the repetition of two *r* sounds close together).

Duality of patterning The existence of a limited set of units of speech combining to form a large number of units of a higher level (several dozen speech sounds of a language producing thousands of words).

Ebonics One of many variations of English, more specifically of African-American English.

Ego The person of reference in a kinship diagram to whom others are shown to be related.

Elaborated code Relatively formal language often used by educated people.

Elicitation The drawing out of information or response from informants (in linguistic anthropology, from native speakers concerning their speech behavior).

Emic An analytical approach or description that emphasizes aspects of culture or language held to be significant and contrastive by members of the society being studied.

Endangered language A language which by virtue of being spoken only by the elder members of a society is likely to become extinct in a generation or two.

Ethnicity A broad term referring to a "racial," national, tribal, linguistic, religious, and/or cultural affiliation.

Ethnography of communication The study of the nature and function of communicative behavior among the members of a society with emphasis on linguistic interaction.

Ethnopoetics The study and analysis of traditional (nonwritten) oral folklore from linguistic and anthropological viewpoints.

Ethnoscience The study of well-defined parts of culture on the basis of how they are named by native speakers of a particular society.

Etic An analytical approach or description based on data that are verifiable objectively and applicable cross-culturally.

Fieldwork The gathering of cultural or linguistic data by talking to and observing the activities of those being studied.

Frame (framing) A context, or frame of reference, sufficiently well defined to make it possible for a communicative event to be fully understood and adequately interpreted.

Free morpheme A morpheme that can be used without any additional elements (for example, *kiss, dance, hippopotamus*).

Gender¹ A grammatical category contrasting such characteristics as masculine, feminine, and neuter, or animate and inanimate.

Gender² A status ascribed to individuals on the basis of behavioral traits typically associated with one of the two sexes.

Genderlect The variety of speech used by a specific gender.

Generative grammar An analytical approach that uses formal rules to generate grammatical sentences in a language.

Genetic classification A classification based on common ancestry (for example, the concept of language family).

Genre A class of literary (or folk literary) composition characterized by a particular style, form, or content.

Glottochronology A method, considered to be controversial, to quantify the extent to which languages have diverged from a common source.

Gullah An English-based creole, with many features of West African languages, spoken by African-Americans on the Sea Islands and in coastal areas of the southeastern United States.

Haptic Based on the sense of touch.

Hedge word A word (or words) used to avoid sounding assertive and overly self-confident (for example, *perhaps* or *I guess*).

Historical linguistics A branch of linguistics concerned with the development over time of language and languages.

Holistic (approach) Concerned with a system as an integral whole rather than with only certain aspects of the system.

Hominids Members of the family Hominidae including all extinct and contemporary species of humans and their direct fossil ancestors.

Hominoids The subdivision of primates that includes all extinct and contemporary humans and apes (but not monkeys or prosimians).

Homo erectus The extinct species of humans immediately ancestral to modern humans.

Homo habilis The earliest member of the genus *Homo* (existing about 2.5 to 1.5 million years ago).

Homonyms Words spelled and pronounced alike but different in meaning (for example, *bear* [animal] and *bear* [carry] or *ear* [organ of hearing] and *ear* [of corn]).

Homonymy Words that have the same form but differ in meaning.

Homo sapiens The species of humans that includes all contemporary and prehistoric humans as well as, according to some anthropologists, the extinct Neanderthals.

Homo sapiens sapiens The subspecies of modern humans from the Cro-Magnons on to the present.

Honorific A form of a word or phrase used to express politeness or respect (found especially in Korean, Japanese, Tibetan, and other Asian languages).

Hypercorrection An alteration of a speech habit on the basis of a false analogy.

Iconic Pertaining to a sign that bears a physical resemblance to what it represents.

Idea (or stimulus) diffusion As a result of stimulation, the borrowing of a general idea rather than of a specific technique.

Idiolect The speech variety of a single individual (that is, one's personal dialect).

Infix An affix that is added within a root or stem of a word (for example, in Bontok Igorot, a language of the Philippines, the infix -*in*- changes *kayu* 'wood' to *kinayu* 'gathered wood').

Inflecting languages Languages that mark grammatical relationships by one or two morphemes (for example, in the Latin *amās* 'you love', the ending -*ās* represents present tense, active voice, second-person singular, and indicative mood).

Inflection The change in form that a word undergoes to mark cases, number (singular, plural), person, and other grammatical relationships.

Informant A person serving as a source of data for the analysis of a language, speech behavior, or culture—usually a native speaker (in recent years the term *consultant* has frequently been used to replace *informant*).

Innatism The theory that children are born with a capacity to acquire effortlessly the language that is spoken to them.

Innatist theory of language acquisition The theory that children are born with a capacity for rapid language development.

Intercultural communication An instance of individuals from two or more societies with differing cultures attempting to communicate with each other (such communication may result in misunderstandings).

Intonational contour The varying pitches superimposed on an utterance to indicate question or statement.

Isolating languages Languages in which relationships among words are shown primarily by word order (compare the sentences *Sharks eat people* and *People eat sharks*).

Key The tone or manner in which communication takes place (for example, a mocking, serious, or perfunctory key).

Kineme A suggested term for the smallest discriminable contrastive unit of body motion.

Kinesics The study of body motions used in communication (for example, shrugs, facial expression, winking, raising of eyebrows, pointing, and the like).

Kinship terminology The terms used to designate people related to ego by blood or marriage.

Language acquisition device An inborn capacity of children to acquire their mother tongue without any formal attempt to teach it to them.

Language contact A situation of close proximity and mutual influence between languages.

Language family All those languages that are related by virtue of having descended from a single ancestral language.

Language ideology Beliefs about a language held by its users as rationalization for their conception of the nature and function of language.

Language isolate A language unrelated to any other language.

Language maintenance The application of appropriate methods to prevent an endangered language from becoming extinct.

Language myths Unfounded or false notions concerning language(s).

Language planning A deliberate attempt by an institution to affect language use in order to prevent or to solve some problem of communication.

Lateralization The localization of certain functions (for example, language comprehension) on one side of the brain rather than the other.

Length (of a speech sound) The relative duration of a speech sound; for example, in some languages short vowels contrast with long ones, and the difference in length can distinguish the meaning of otherwise identical words.

Lexeme A vocabulary item of a language.

Lexical diffusion The spreading of sound changes throughout the words (the lexicon) of a language.

Lexical item (lexeme) Another term for word.

Lexicon (adj. lexical) The word-stock of a language, a social group, or an individual speaker.

Lexicostatistics A method of establishing the linguistic relationship on the basis of a quantitative study of lexical items.

Lingua franca A language used as a common means of communication between people speaking different native languages.

Linguistic anthropology The study of language in both its biological and sociocultural contexts.

Linguistic competence The knowledge of the grammatical rules of one's mother tongue.

Linguistic determinism The assumption that the way individuals think is determined to a significant degree by the language they speak.

Linguistic relativity The view that structural differences among languages are reflected in the worldviews held by their speakers.

Linguistic typology The study and classification of languages according to structural similarities regardless of genetic relationship.

Linguistics The scientific study of the various aspects of human speech, including its nature, structure, and changes over time.

Loanword A word borrowed from another language and at least partly naturalized by the borrowing language (for example—in English, *kindergarten, spaghetti,* and *rouge* from German, Italian, and French, respectively).

Mesolithic period A relatively short transitional technological and cultural period between the Paleolithic and Neolithic.

Metathesis Alteration in the normal sequence of linguistic elements (for example, when someone says *aks* for *ask*).

Monogenesis (of language) The theory that traits requisite for the development of language came into being just once.

Morpheme The smallest meaningful unit of speech (for example, the word *unrestful* consists of three morphemes: [in conventional spelling] *un-, rest,* and *-ful*).

Morphology The study and description of the internal structure of words and of the interrelationships of morphemes.

Morphophonemics The study and description of the phonemic differences between the various forms of a morpheme.

Motif (in oral folklore) In a tale, the smallest element that has the power to persist in tradition by virtue of having something unusual about it.

Motifeme A distinctive unit of folk narratives (for example, "the hero is subjected to a difficult or dangerous test").

Motor cortex The area of the brain where impulses from the nerve centers to muscles originate.

Multilingualism Good command of more than two languages.

Neanderthals Hominids who lived in parts of the Old World between about 200,000 and 30,000 years ago.

Neogrammarian A follower of a nineteenth-century school of comparative philology claiming that sound laws admitted no exception.

Neolithic period The latest period of the Stone Age, which saw some revolutionary developments in human culture (domestication of plants and animals).

Neurolinguistics The branch of linguistics that deals with the role the brain plays in language and speech processing.

New ethnography See ethnoscience.

Nonverbal communication Transmission of messages by means other than speech or writing (for example, by means of pictorial signs).

Norms of interpretation The acceptable boundaries within which communicative activity is to be understood or explained.

Olfactory channel A means of communication utilizing the sense of smell (for example, baking cookies or bread before people come to look at a house for possible purchase).

Optical channel A means of communication utilizing the sense of vision (for example, writing or road signs).

Paralanguage Features of vocal communication that are considered marginal or optional, such as variations in tempo, intensity, or pitch.

Paralinguistics The study of paralanguage.

Participant observation The immersion of anthropological field-workers in the day-to-day activities of the people they are studying, usually for an extended period.

Passive (receptive) bilingual A person who understands a second language but is unable to speak it.

Phatic communication A speech used for social and emotive purposes rather than for transmitting information.

Pheromone Species-specific substance secreted by animals and used as a stimulus to others of the same species.

Phone The smallest perceptible discrete segment of speech, considered as a physical event.

Phoneme The smallest distinctive sound unit of a language (for example, the initial consonants of the words *bat, pat, vat, fat,* and *sat* are five different phonemes of English).

Phonemic (transcription) The representation of distinctive speech sounds by means of phonemic symbols.

Phonetic Representing in some detail the nature of speech sounds by the special symbols of a phonetic alphabet.

Phonetic (transcription) The detailed representations of speech sounds by use of the symbols of a phonetic alphabet.

Phonology The study and description of the sound system of a language.

Phylum Language groups related more remotely than languages classified as belonging to a language family.

Physical (or biological) anthropology The subfield of anthropology concerned with the study of human evolution and physical variation.

Pidgin A form of spoken communication with a greatly reduced grammatical structure and limited vocabulary that is used by speakers of mutually unintelligible languages to communicate with each other (a pidgin is not the native language of any speaker).

Pidginization The process of grammatical and lexical reduction of a language to a pidgin.

Pitch (tone) The distinctive pitch level (tonal height) of a syllable; it is a relative feature—tones of women's voices are typically higher than men's.

Polygenesis (of a language) The theory that traits requisite for the development of language originated in separate places and at different times.

Polyglot A person who speaks several languages.

Polysemy The range of different meanings in one word (for example, the various meanings of the word *seat*).

Polysynthetic languages Languages in which words are long and morphologically complex (for example, in the aboriginal Australian language Tiwi the sentence "I kept on eating" is expressed by the word *ŋgi-rru-unthing-apu-kani* [the hyphens indicate morpheme boundaries]).

Prefix An affix that is added at the beginning of a root or stem (for example, the initial morphemes in the words *rewrite, undo,* and *disallow*).

Prelanguage Any of the stages in the development of speech that precedes full-fledged language.

Primary sign language A sign language used to the exclusion of spoken language, for example, by people born deaf.

Process morpheme A change of a sound or sounds (for example, from *goose* to the plural *geese*) rather than the addition of a morpheme (as in the plural *cats* from *cat*).

Prosodic features Features other than vowels and consonants that are essential for an utterance to sound natural and to be fully meaningful (for example, stress and intonation).

Protoculture An assumed or reconstructed prehistoric culture of a people.

Proto-Indo-European The assumed or reconstructed ancestral language of all the languages belonging to the Indo-European language family.

Protolanguage An assumed or reconstructed ancestral form of a language branch or language family.

Protoword An assumed or reconstructed ancestral word of cognate words found in the languages of a language family.

Proxemics The study of the cultural patterning of the spatial separation individuals naturally maintain in face-to-face encounters.

Proxemic zone The relative distance of interpersonal space, ranging from intimate to public, that members of societies tend to observe in face-to-face encounters.

Pygmy chimpanzee (or bonobo) An endangered species of chimpanzees that are more intelligent and sociable than the species of common chimpanzees.

Race (so-called) In modern anthropology a discredited term referring to a population that shares a number of physical traits.

Reconstruction The building up or re-creating of something on the basis of available evidence (for example, of an extinct language or culture).

Reduplication The repetition of speech sounds marking a grammatical function (for example, in the Tagalog word *dadalawá* 'only two' from *dalawá* 'two'). (English has only some reduplicative compound words, such as *goody-goody* and *wishy-washy*).

Referent Anything referred to by a word.

Reflexive noises Basic biological noises of an infant, such as burping, coughing, and crying.

Restricted code A relatively informal variety of language with a reduced stylistic and grammatical range.

Root A base form of a word that cannot be further subdivided, or a basic morpheme (for example, *teach, tree, blue, nast-* [in *nasty*], and *-ceive* [in *conceive, receive,* etc.]).

Rules of interaction The knowledge of members of a speech community as to what is and what is not appropriate in communication.

Sapir-Whorf hypothesis A theory of the relationship between language and thought; also known as the hypothesis of linguistic relativity—the belief that language determines the way speakers perceive the world around them.

Semantic differential A technique to measure the affective reaction of speakers of a language to words (lexical items).

Semantics The study of meaning in language.

Semiotics The study of the characteristics of signaling systems (that is, of signs and their use).

Sequential bilingualism The ability to speak two languages, acquired in succession.

Sexual bias (in language) Those usages in a language that favor one gender over another (for example, to use the possessive adjective *his* to include both men and women in the sentence "Each driver on public roads must carry his driver's license.").

Sign language A system of hand gestures used as an alternative to speech (for example, by the deaf).

Simultaneous bilingualism The ability to speak two languages, acquired at the same time.

Social insects Species of insects that live in colonies with others of the same species.

Socialization (in anthropology) The process by which infants are taught the aspects of their society's culture they need to know to function as adults.

Social network All those people with whom an individual regularly interacts.

Social power theory (concerning the language-and-gender relationship) The view that the differences found between men's and women's speech reflect the different degrees of power or status each gender holds in society.

Society A cooperating social group, widely ranging in size, whose members have developed over time common traditions, institutions, and broad interests.

Sociocultural Involving a combination of cultural and social factors.

Sociolinguistic change Linguistic change viewed in the context of the society or community in which it takes place.

Sociolinguistics The branch of linguistics concerned with the various aspects of the relationship between society and language; the study of ways in which an individual's speech conveys social information.

Sound change A change in the sound system of a language over a period of time (for example, the change from Old English *stān* to Modern English *stone*).

Sound law The description of a regular series of changes in a language's sound system over a period of time.

Sound symbolism An association between form (sound) and meaning in a language.

Speech act The minimum unit of speech (for example, a greeting, an apology, or a self-introduction).

Speech apparatus The various parts of the human body between the larynx and the lips where speech sounds are produced; also referred to as vocal organs or organs of speech.

Speech area An area in which speakers of different languages share speaking rules.

Speech community All those who share a language variety as well as specific rules for speaking and interpreting speech.

Speech event A basic unit of verbal interaction (for example, an interview, a telephone inquiry, or an argument with a salesperson).

Speech situation The context in which speaking takes place (for example, a fishing trip, family meal, or beer party).

Standard The prestige variety of a language used by a speech community under usually formal circumstances; a variety of a language used by the educated.

Stem A single root morpheme (*bird*) or a compound word (*blackbird*); the part of an inflected word that remains after the affix has been removed (for example, *width* is the stem of *widths*).

Stress The degree of force, or prominence, associated with a syllable of speech.

Structural (approach) In linguistics, an approach attempting to describe the units of a language and their combinations in terms of structure and system.

Style A situational distinctive use of language in writing or speech. (A number of styles are distinguished, ranging from pompous to intimate.)

Subculture theory (concerning the language-and-gender relationship) The view that the differences of women's language from that of men may be due to a distinct women's subculture in a male-dominated society.

Suffix An affix added after a root or stem of a word (for example, the final morpheme in the words *horses, swims,* or *walked*).

Suppletion The occurrence of phonemically unrelated allomorphs of a morpheme.

Suppletive form A linguistic form characterized by suppletion (as in the superlative form *best* from *good*).

Syllabary A set of graphic symbols each of which represents a syllable of a language.

Syllable A unit of speech consisting of a consonant (or consonants), and either a vowel (or vowels) or a syllabic consonant.

Symbol Something representing something else by virtue of convention, resemblance, or association.

Synchronic (approach) Dealing with linguistic phenomena as they exist at a specific point in time (that is, without regard for historical antecedents).

Synesthesia A condition in which a particular stimulation of one sense evokes the stimulation of another sense.

Synonym A word that has the same or nearly the same meaning as another word (or words) in a language.

Syntax Traditionally, the manner in which words of a language are strung together into sentences; in transformational grammar, the study of sentence structure and the relations among sentence components.

Tactile channel A means of communication utilizing the sense of touch (for example, kissing or patting).

Tag question A question attached to a statement to obtain the assent of the person spoken to (for example, "It's a beautiful morning, isn't it?").

Taxonomy A principled classification into groups and subgroups.

Tok Pisin An English-based creole serving as the national language of Papua New Guinea.

Transformation Adding, deleting, or otherwise changing elements of one linguistic structure to produce another one.

Transformational grammar A grammatical analysis using linguistic operations (transformations) that show a correspondence between two structures.

Transformational rule The general statement describing a transformation.

Trilingualism The ability to speak three languages.

Universalism The belief that general principles underlie the structure of all languages (and cultures).

Upper Paleolithic period The most recent period of the Old Stone Age characterized by an explosion of creative cultural activity (roughly from 35,000 to 10,000 B.C.).

Vernacular The casual spoken form of a language or dialect.

Vocal-auditory channel A means of communication utilizing sounds that are spoken and heard.

Vocal play The extensive production by a baby of sounds resembling the vowels and consonants of its mother tongue.

Vocal tract The area of the human body where speech sounds are produced.

Vocal (voice) segregates Extralinguistic sounds used in expressing concern, excitement, disapproval, and other attitudes or feelings.

Voice characterizers Modifications of the speaking voice that occur when one talks while laughing, yawning, crying, etc.

Voiced sound A speech sound produced while the vocal cords are vibrating (for example, *b*, *d*, *g*).

Voiceless sound A speech sound produced without vibration of the vocal cords (for example, *p*, *t*, *k*).

Voice qualifiers Such marginal features of vocal communication as tempo and intensity.

Vowel Phonetically, a speech sound articulated with no significant constriction in the breath channel.

Vowel harmony A type of assimilation in which vowels come to share certain features with other vowels elsewhere in the word or phrase.

Wernicke's area An area of the brain in the upper part of the temporal lobe associated with the comprehension of language.

Whistle "language" (or whistle speech) Communication by means of whistling.

Whorf(ian) hypothesis The assumption that structural differences among languages are reflected in the differing worldviews of their speakers.

Word order The arrangement of words in a phrase or a sentence.

Word taboo A prohibition against uttering a particular word or name.

BIBLIOGRAPHY

Adger, David
2003   Core syntax: a minimalist approach. New York: Oxford University Press

Agar, Michael
1994   Language shock: understanding the culture of conversation. New York: William Morrow.

Akmajian, Adrian, Richard A. Demers, Ann K. Farmer, and Robert M. Harnish
2010   Linguistics: an introduction to language and communication. 6th ed. Cambridge, MA: MIT Press.

Albert, Rosita Daskal
1986   Communication and attributional differences between Hispanics and Anglo-Americans. *In* Interethnic communication: current research, vol. 10. Young Yun Kim, ed, pp. 42–59. Newbury Park, CA: Sage.

American Anthropological Association
1983   Professional ethics: statements and procedures of the American Anthropological Association. Washington, DC: American Anthropological Association.
1992   American Heritage Dictionary of the English Language. 3d ed. Boston: Houghton Mifflin.

Anthony, David
2007   The horse, the wheel, and language: how Bronze-age riders from the Eurasian steppes shaped the modern world. Princeton, NJ: Princeton University Press.

Anttila, Raimo
1989   Historical and comparative linguistics. 2d ed. Philadelphia: Benjamins.

Bakhtin, Mikhail
1981   The dialogic imagination: four essays. Austin: University of Texas Press.

Baquedano-López, Patricia
2006   Literacy practices across learning contexts. *In* A companion to linguistic anthropology. Alessandro Duranti, ed., pp. 245–268. Malden, MA: Wiley-Blackwell.

Baron, Naomi
2000   Alphabet to email: how written English evolved and where it's heading. London: Routledge.
2008   Always on: language in an online mobile world. New York: Oxford University Press.

Basso, Keith H.
1970 "To give up on words": silence in Western Apache culture. Southwestern Journal of Anthropology 26:213–230.
1974 The ethnography of writing. *In* Explorations in the ethnography of speaking. Richard Bauman and Joel Sherzer, eds., pp. 425–432. London: Cambridge University Press.

Baugh, John
2002 Beyond Ebonics: linguistic pride and racial prejudice. New York: Oxford University Press.

Bauman, James J.
1980 A guide to issues in Indian language retention. Washington, DC: Center for Applied Linguistics.

Bauman, Richard, and Joel Sherzer
1974 (eds.) Explorations in the ethnography of speaking. London: Cambridge University Press.
1975 The ethnography of speaking. *In* Annual Review of Anthropology, vol. 4. Bernard J. Siegel and others, eds., pp. 95–119. Palo Alto, CA: Annual Reviews.
1989 (eds.) Explorations in the ethnography of speaking. 2d ed. Cambridge, UK: Cambridge University Press.

Bergmann, Anouschka, Kathleen Currie Hall, and Sharon Miriam Ross, eds.
2007 Language files: Materials for an introduction to language and linguistics. Columbus: Ohio State University Press.

Bergvall, Victoria L.
1999 Toward a comprehensive theory of language and gender. Language in Society 28:273–293.

Berlin, Brent
1976 The concept of rank in ethnobiological classification: some evidence from Aguaruna folk botany. American Ethnologist 3:381–399.

Berlin, Brent, Dennis Breedlove, and Peter Raven
1974 Principles of Tzeltal plant classification: an introduction to the botanical ethnography of a Mayan-speaking people of highland Chiapas. New York: Academic Press.

Berlin, Brent, and Paul Kay
1969 Basic color terms: their universality and evolution. Berkeley: University of California Press.
1991 Basic color terms: their universality and evolution. 2d ed. Berkeley: University of California Press.

Besnier, Niko
1995 Literacy, emotion and authority: reading and writing on a Polynesian atoll. Cambridge, UK: Cambridge University Press.

Bickerton, Derek
1981 Roots of language. Ann Arbor, MI: Karoma.
1983 Creole languages. Scientific American 249:1:116–122 (July).

1990   Language and species. Chicago: University of Chicago Press.
2009   Adam's tongue: how humans made language, and how language made humans. New York: Hill and Wang.

Biggam, Carole P., and Christian Kay, eds.
2006   Progress in colour studies. Volume 1: Language and culture. Amsterdam: John Benjamins.

Birdwhistell, Ray L.
1970   Kinesics and context: essays on body motion communication. Philadelphia: University of Pennsylvania Press.

Black, Max
1962   Models and metaphors: studies in language and philosophy. Ithaca, NY: Cornell University Press.

Bloomfield, Leonard
1933   Language. New York: Holt.
1946   Algonquian. *In* Linguistic structures of Native America. Cornelius Osgood, ed. Viking Fund Publications in Anthropology, no. 6, pp. 85–129. New York: Viking Fund.

Boas, Franz
1911   (ed.) Handbook of American Indian languages, part 1. Bureau of American Ethnology; bulletin 40. Washington, DC: Government Printing Office. [Republished in 1991.]
1922   (ed.) Handbook of American Indian languages, part 2. Bureau of American Ethnology; bulletin 40. Washington, DC: Government Printing Office.
1933–1938   (ed.) Handbook of American Indian languages, part 3. New York: Augustin.
1938   The mind of primitive man. Rev. ed. New York: Macmillan.
1940   Metaphorical expression in the language of the Kwakiutl Indians. *In* Race, language and culture *by* Franz Boas, pp. 232–239. New York: Macmillan.

Bokamba, Eyamba
1989   Are there syntactic constraints on code-mixing? World Englishes 8:277–292.

Bolinger, Dwight
1968   Aspects of language. New York: Harcourt, Brace and World.
1975   Aspects of language. 2d ed. New York: Harcourt Brace Jovanovich.
1978   Intonation across languages. *In* Universals of human language, vol. 2. Joseph Greenberg et al., eds., pp. 471–524. Stanford: Stanford University Press.

Bolton, Kingsley, and Braj B. Kachru, eds.
2006   World Englishes: critical concepts in linguistics. 6 volumes. London: Routledge.

Bonvillain, Nancy
2007   Language, culture, and communication: the meaning of messages. 5th ed. Upper Saddle River, NJ: Pearson Prentice-Hall.

Bourdieu, Pierre
1987   Distinction: a social critique of the judgement of taste. Cambridge, MA: Harvard University Press.
1999   Language and symbolic power. Cambridge, MA: Harvard University Press.

Bright, Michael
1984   Animal language. Ithaca, NY: Cornell University Press.

Bright, William
1960 Animals of acculturation in the California Indian languages. University of California Publications in Linguistics, vol. 4, no. 4, pp. 215–246. Berkeley: University of California Press.
1992 (ed.) International encyclopedia of linguistics. 4 vols. New York: Oxford University Press.

Brown, Cecil H.
1984 Language and living things: uniformities in folk classification and naming. Piscataway, NJ: Rutgers University Press.

Bucholtz, Mary
2004 (ed.) Language and woman's place, by Robin Tolmach Lakoff: text and commentaries. New York: Oxford University Press.
2011 White kids: language, race, and styles of youth identity. Cambridge, UK: Cambridge University Press.

Buck, Carl Darling
1988 A dictionary of selected synonyms in the principal Indo-European languages. Chicago: University of Chicago Press.

Burling, Robbins
1964 Cognition and componential analysis: God's truth or hocus pocus? American Anthropologist 66:20–28.
1973 English in black and white. New York: Holt, Rinehart and Winston.
1984 (reissued with changes in 2000) Learning a field language. Prospect Heights, IL: Waveland Press.
1992 Review of Derek Bickerton: Language and species. Journal of Linguistic Anthropology 2:81–91.

Cameron, Deborah, Fiona McAlinden, and Kathy O'Leary
1988 Lakoff in context: the social and linguistic functions of tag questions. In Women in their speech communities: new perspectives on language and sex. Jennifer Coates and Deborah Cameron, eds., pp. 74–93. New York: Longman.

Campbell, Bernard G., ed.
1979 Humankind emerging. 2d ed. Boston: Little, Brown.

Campbell, Lyle
1988 Review of Joseph H. Greenberg: Language in the Americas. Language 64:591–615.
2000 American Indian languages: the historical linguistics of Native America. New York: Oxford University Press.

Carbaugh, Donal, ed.
1990 Cultural communication and intercultural contact. Hillsdale, NJ: Erlbaum.

Carnie, Andrew
2011 Modern syntax: a coursebook. Cambridge, UK: Cambridge University Press.

Carrington, John F.
1971 The talking drums of Africa. Scientific American 225:6:90–94 (December).

Carroll, John B.
1963 Linguistic relativity, contrastive linguistics, and language learning. International Review of Applied Linguistics in Language Teaching 1:1–20.

Carroll, John B., and Joseph B. Casagrande
1958   The function of language classifications in behavior. *In* Readings in social psychology. 3d ed. Eleanor E. Maccoby, Theodore M. Newcomb, and Eugene L. Hartley, eds., pp. 18–31. New York: Holt, Rinehart and Winston.

Chamberlain, Alexander F.
1912   Women's languages. American Anthropologist 14:579–581.

Chambers, J. K.
1995   Sociolinguistic theory. Oxford, UK: Blackwell.

Chambers, J. K., and Peter Trudgill
1998   Dialectology. 2d ed. Cambridge, UK: Cambridge University Press.

Cheshire, Jenny
2002   Sex and gender in variationist research. *In* The handbook of language variation and change. J. K. Chambers, Peter Trudgill, and Natalie Schilling-Estes, eds., pp. 423–443. Malden, MA: Blackwell.

Chomsky, Noam
1957   Syntactic structures. The Hague: Mouton.
1959   Review of B. F. Skinner: Verbal behavior. Language 35:26–58.
1965   Aspects of the theory of syntax. Cambridge, MA: MIT Press.
1968   Language and the mind. Psychology Today 1:9:48, 50–51, 66–68.
1972   Language and mind. Enl. ed. New York: Harcourt Brace Jovanovich.
1980   Rules and representations. New York: Columbia University Press.
1986   Knowledge of language: its nature, origin, and use. New York: Praeger.
1993   Lectures on government and binding: the Pisa Lectures. The Hague: Mouton de Gruyter.
2010   Some simple evo devo theses: how true might they be for language? *In* The evolution of human language: biolinguistic perspectives. Richard K. Larson, Vivian Déprz, and Hiroko Yamakido, eds., pp. 45–62. Cambridge, UK: Cambridge University Press.

Chomsky, Noam, and Morris Halle
1968   The sound pattern of English. New York: Harper and Row.

Christiansen, Morten H., and Simon Kirby, eds.
2003   Language evolution. New York: Oxford University Press.

Classe, André
1957   The whistled language of La Gomera. Scientific American 196:4:111–112, 114–118, 120 (April).

Coates, Jennifer
1986   Women, men, and language: a sociolinguistic account of sex differences in language. New York: Longman.

Coates, Jennifer, and Deborah Cameron, eds.
1988   Women in their speech communities: new perspectives on language and sex. New York: Longman.

Colapinto, John
2007   The interpreter: has a remote Amazonian tribe upended our understanding of language? New Yorker, April 16th, 83:117–142.

Cowan, George M.
1948   Mazateco whistle speech. Language 24:280–286.

Cowan, William, and Jaromira Rakušan
1998   Source book for linguistics. 3d ed. Amsterdam: John Benjamins.

Cook, Vivian, and Mark Newson
2007   Chomsky's universal grammar: an introduction. 3d ed. Malden, MA: Blackwell.

Crowley, Terry, and Claire Bowern
2009   An introduction to historical linguistics. 4th ed. New York: Oxford University Press.

Cruttenden, Alan
1986   Intonation. Cambridge, UK: Cambridge University Press.

Crystal, David
1971   Linguistics. Harmondsworth, UK: Penguin.
1974   Paralinguistics. In Current trends in linguistics. Vol. 12: Linguistics and adjacent arts and sciences. Thomas A. Sebeok, ed., pp. 265–295. The Hague: Mouton.
1981   Directions in applied linguistics. New York: Academic Press.
1997   A dictionary of linguistics and phonetics. 4th ed., updated and enlarged. Oxford, UK: Blackwell.
2000   Language death. Cambridge, UK: Cambridge University Press.
2001   Language and the internet. Cambridge, UK: Cambridge University Press.
2004   The language revolution. Cambridge, UK: Polity Press.
2007   How language works: how babies babble, words change meaning, and languages live or die. New York: Penguin.
2010   (ed.) The Cambridge encyclopedia of language. 3d ed. Cambridge, UK: Cambridge University Press.

Cutting, Joan
2008   Pragmatics and discourse: a resource book for students. 2d ed. London: Routledge.

D'Andrade, Roy
1995   The development of cognitive anthropology. Cambridge, UK: Cambridge University Press.

Darnell, Regna
1992   Anthropological linguistics: early history in North America. In International encyclopedia of linguistics, vol. 1. William Bright, ed., pp. 69–71. New York: Oxford University Press.

Deetz, James
1967   Invitation to archaeology. Garden City, NY: Natural History Press.

de Grolier, Eric, ed.
1983   Glossogenetics: the origin and evolution of language. Chur, Switzerland: Harwood Academic.

de Saussure, Ferdinand
1913   [1983] Course in general linguistics. (Roy Harris, translator). Peru, IL: Open Court.

Deutscher, Guy
2010   Through the language glass: why the world looks different in other languages. New York: Metropolitan Books.

Dillard, J. L.
1972 Black English: its history and usage in the United States. New York: Random House.

Dorian, Nancy C.
1993 A response to Ladefoged's other view of endangered languages. Language 69:575–579.

Dougherty, Janet, W. D., ed.
1985 Directions in cognitive anthropology. Urbana: University of Illinois Press.

Dundes, Alan
1962 From etic to emic units in the structural study of folktales. Journal of American Folklore 75:95–105.

Duranti, Alessandro
1988 Ethnography of speaking: toward a linguistics of the praxis. In Linguistics: the Cambridge survey. Vol. 4: Language: the socio-cultural context. Frederick J. Newmeyer, ed., pp. 210–228. Cambridge, UK: Cambridge University Press.
1997 Linguistic anthropology. Cambridge, UK: Cambridge University Press.
2001 (ed.) Key terms in language and culture. Malden, MA: Blackwell.
2006 (ed.) A companion to linguistic anthropology: Malden, MA: Wiley-Blackwell.
2009 (ed.) Linguistic anthropology: a reader. 2d ed. Malden, MA: Blackwell

Eastman, Carol M.
1983 Language planning: an introduction. San Francisco: Chandler and Sharp.

Echeverría, Max S., and Heles Contreras
1965 Araucanian phonemics. International Journal of American Linguistics 31:132–135.

Eckert, Penelope, and Sally McConnell-Ginet
1992 Think practically and look locally: language and gender as community-based practice. In Annual Review of Anthropology, vol. 21. Bernard J. Siegel and others, eds., pp. 461–490. Palo Alto, CA: Annual Reviews.

Edwards, John, ed.
2010 Language in Canada. Cambridge, UK: Cambridge University Press.

Ehret, Christopher
1982 Linguistic inferences about early Bantu history. In The archaeological and linguistic reconstruction of African history. Christopher Ehret and Merrick Posnansky, eds., pp. 57–65. Berkeley: University of California Press.

Everett, Daniel
2005 Cultural constraints on grammar and cognition in Pirahã: another look at the design features of human language. Current Anthropology 46:621–646.
2008 Don't sleep, there are snakes: life and language in the Amazonian jungle. New York: Vintage.

Ferguson, Charles A.
1959 Diglossia. Word 15:325–340.

Fickett, Joan G.
1972 Tense and aspect in Black English. Journal of English Linguistics 6:17–19.

Fields, Cheryl D.
1997 Ebonics 101: what have we learned? Black Issues in Higher Education 13:24:18–21, 24–28 (January 23, 1997).

Fischer, John L.
1958   Social influences on the choice of a linguistic variant. Word 14:47–56.

Fishman, Joshua A.
1960   A systematization of the Whorfian hypothesis. Behavioral Science 5:323–339.

Fitch, W. Tecumseh
2010   The evolution of language. Cambridge, UK: Cambridge University Press.

Flannery, Regina
1946   Men's and women's speech in Gros Ventre. International Journal of American Linguistics 12:133–135.

Fortson, Benjamin
2010   Indo-European language and culture: an introduction. 2d ed. Malden, MA: Blackwell.

Fouts, Roger S., and Deborah H. Fouts
1989   Loulis in conversation with the cross-fostered chimpanzees. In Teaching sign language to chimpanzees. R. Allen Gardner, Beatrix T. Gardner, and Thomas E. Van Cantford, eds., pp. 293–307. New York: State University of New York Press.

Fouts, Roger S., Deborah H. Fouts, and Thomas E. Van Cantford
1989   The infant Loulis learns signs from cross-fostered chimpanzees. In Teaching sign language to chimpanzees. R. Allen Gardner, Beatrix T. Gardner, and Thomas E. Van Cantford, eds., pp. 280–292. New York: State University of New York Press.

Frake, Charles O.
1961   The diagnosis of disease among the Subanun of Mindanao. American Anthropologist 63:113–132.
1964   How to ask for a drink in Subanun. American Anthropologist 66:6(part 2):127–132.
1969   Struck by speech: the Yakan concept of litigation. In Law in culture and society. Laura Nader, ed., pp. 147–167. Chicago: Aldine.

Frank, Francine, and Frank Anshen
1983   Language and the sexes. Albany: State University of New York Press.

Frisch, Karl von
1967   The dance language and orientation of bees. C. E. Chadwick, trans. Cambridge, MA: Belknap.

Fromkin, Victoria, and Robert Rodman
1988   An introduction to language. 4th ed. New York: Holt, Rinehart and Winston.

Gal, Susan
1979   Language shift: social determinants of linguistic change in bilingual Austria. New York: Academic Press.

Gardner-Chloros, Penelope
2009   Code-switching. Cambridge, UK: Cambridge University Press.

Gee, James Paul
2011   How to do discourse analysis: a toolkit. Abingdon, UK: Routledge.

George, Don
1981   Sweet man: the real Duke Ellington. New York: G. P. Putnam's Sons.

Giglioli, Pier Paolo, ed.
1972   Language and social context: selected readings. Baltimore: Penguin Books.

Givón, Talmy
2002   Bio-linguistics: the Santa Barbara lectures. Amsterdam: John Benjamins.

Gleason, H. A., Jr.
1961   An introduction to descriptive linguistics. Rev. ed. New York: Holt, Rinehart and Winston.

Gleason, Jean Berko, and Nan Bernstein Ratner, eds.
2008   The development of language. 7th ed. Needham Heights, MA: Allyn & Bacon.

Goffman, Erving
1959   The presentation of self in everyday life. New York: Anchor/Doubleday.
1974   Frame analysis: an essay on the organization of experience. New York: Harper and Row.

Goodall, Jane
1986   The chimpanzees of Gombe: patterns of behavior. Cambridge, MA: Belknap.

Goodenough, Ward H.
1957   Cultural anthropology and linguistics. In Report of the Seventh Annual Round Table Meeting on Linguistics and Language Study. Monograph Series on Languages and Linguistics, no. 9, pp. 167–173. Washington, DC: Georgetown University Press.
1964   Cultural anthropology and linguistics. In Language in culture and society: a reader in linguistics and anthropology. Dell Hymes, ed., pp. 36–39. New York: Harper and Row.

Gordon, Raymond
2005   Ethnologue: languages of the world. 15th ed. Dallas, TX: SIL International.

Gould, Stephen Jay
2002   The structure of evolutionary theory. Cambridge: Harvard University Press.

Gould, Stephen Jay, and Richard Lewontin
1979   The spandrels of San Marco and the panglossian paradigm: a critique of the adaptationist programme. Proceedings of the Royal Society of London B: Biological Sciences 205:581–598.

Greenberg, Joseph H.
1960   The general classification of Central and South American languages. In Men and cultures: selected papers of the Fifth International Congress of Anthropological and Ethnological Sciences. Anthony F. C. Wallace, ed., pp. 791–794. Philadelphia: University of Pennsylvania Press.
1987   Language in the Americas. Stanford, CA: Stanford University Press.

Greenberg, Joseph, et al., eds.
1978   Intonation across languages. In Joseph H. Greenberg, Charles A. Ferguson, and Edith A. Moravcsik, eds, Universals of human language. vol. 2, phonology. Stanford: Stanford University Press, pp. 471–524.

Greymorning, Stephen
2001   Reflections on the Arapaho language project, or when Bambi spoke Arapaho and other tales of Arapaho language revitalization efforts. In The green book of language revitalization in practice. Leanne Hinton and Ken Hale, eds., pp. 287–297. San Diego, CA: Academic Press.

Grodzinsky, Yosef, and Katrin Amunts, eds.
2006   Broca's region. New York: Oxford University Press.

Gumperz, John J.
1958   Dialect differences and social stratification in a North Indian village. American Anthropologist 60:668–682.
1982   Fact and inference in courtroom testimony. *In* Language and social identity, John J. Gumperz, ed., pp. 163–195. Cambridge, UK: Cambridge University Press.

Gumperz, John J., and Dell Hymes, eds.
1964   The ethnography of communication. American Anthropologist 66:6 (part 2):1–186 (special publication).
1972   Directions in sociolinguistics: the ethnography of communication. New York: Holt, Rinehart and Winston (1972) and Blackwell (rev. ed., 1986).

Gumperz, John J., and Stephen C. Levinson, eds.
1996   Rethinking linguistic relativity. Cambridge, UK: Cambridge University Press.

Gumperz, John J., and Robert Wilson
1971   Convergence and creolization: a case from the Indo-Aryan/Dravidian border in India. *In* Pidginization and creolization of languages. Dell Hymes, ed., pp. 151–167. Cambridge, UK: Cambridge University Press.

Haas, Mary R.
1941   Tunica. *In* Handbook of American Indian languages, part 4, pp. 1–143. New York: Augustin.
1944   Men's and women's speech in Koasati. Language 20:142–149.

Hage, Per
1972   Münchner beer categories. *In* Culture and cognition: rules, maps, and plans, James P. Spradley, ed., pp. 263–278. San Francisco, CA: Chandler.

Hager, John W.
1959   Let's simplify legal language. Rocky Mountain Law Review 32:74–86.

Hale, Constance, and Jesse Scanlon
1999   Wired style: principles of English usage in the digital age, revised and updated. New York: Broadway Books.

Hale, Kenneth
1974   Some questions about anthropological linguistics: the role of native knowledge. *In* Reinventing anthropology. Dell Hymes, ed., pp. 382–397. New York: Random House.

Hale, Ken, and others
1992   Endangered languages. Language 68:1–42.

Hale, Mark
2007   Historical linguistics: theory and method. Malden, MA: Blackwell.

Hall, Edward T.
1959   The silent language. Garden City, NY: Doubleday.
1966   The hidden dimension. Garden City, NY: Doubleday.
1968   Proxemics. Current Anthropology 9:83–108.

Hall, Kira, and Mary Bucholtz, eds.
1992   Locating power. Proceedings of the Second Berkeley Women and Language Conference. vol. 2, Berkeley: Berkeley Women and Language Group, University of California.

1996   Gender articulated: language and the socially constructed self. New York: Routledge.

Hall, Robert A., Jr.
1959   Pidgin languages. Scientific American 200:2:124–132, 134 (February).

Halle, Morris
1980   The rules of language. Technology Review 82:54–62 (June–July).

Hallowell, A. Irving
1960   The beginnings of anthropology in America. *In* Selected papers from the American Anthropologist, 1888–1920. Frederica de Laguna, ed., pp. 1–90. Evanston, IL: Row, Peterson.

Hammel, E. A., ed.
1965   Formal semantic analysis. American Anthropologist 67:5 (part 2) (special publication).

Hammond, George P., and Agapito Rey, eds.
1940   Narratives of the Coronado expedition, 1540–1542. Coronado Cuarto Centennial Publications, 1540–1940, vol. 2. Albuquerque: University of New Mexico Press.

Hanks, William
1995   Language and communicative practices. Boulder, CO: Westview.

Hardin, C. L., and Luissa Maffi, eds.
1997   Color categories in thought and language. Cambridge, UK: Cambridge University Press.

Harnad, Stevan R., Horst D. Steklis, and Jane Lancaster, eds.
1976   Origins and evolution of language and speech. Annals of the New York Academy of Sciences, vol. 280. New York: New York Academy of Sciences.

Harris, Marvin
1979   Cultural materialism: the struggle for a science of culture. New York: Random House.
1989   Our kind: who we are, where we came from, where we are going. New York: Harper and Row.
1990   Emics and etics revisited. *In* Emics and etics: the insider/outsider debate. Thomas N. Headland, Kenneth L. Pike, and Marvin Harris, eds., pp. 48–61. Newbury Park, CA: Sage.

Harris, Roxy, and Ben Rampton, eds.
2003   The language, ethnicity and race reader. New York: Routledge.

Haugen, Einar
1956   Bilingualism in the Americas: a bibliography and research guide. Tuscaloosa: American Dialect Society, University of Alabama.

Hauser, Mark, Noam Chomsky, and W. Tecumseh Fitch
2010   The faculty of language: what is it, who has it, and how did it evolve? *In* The evolution of human language: biolinguistic perspectives. Richard K. Larson, Vivian Déprez, and Hiroko Yamakido, eds., pp. 14–42. Cambridge, UK: Cambridge University Press.

Hayes, Alfred S.
1954   Field procedures while working with Diegueño. International Journal of American Linguistics 20:185–194.

Hayes, Bruce
2008   Introductory phonology. Malden, MA: Wiley-Blackwell.

Hayes, Keith J., and Catherine Hayes
1952   Imitation in a home-raised chimpanzee. Journal of Comparative and Physiological Psychology 45:450–459.

Headland, Thomas N., Kenneth L. Pike, and Marvin Harris, eds.
1990   Emics and etics: the insider/outsider debate. Newbury Park, CA: Sage.

Heath, Jeffrey
1985   Discourse in the field: clause structure in Ngandi. In Grammar inside and outside the clause: some approaches to theory from the field. Johanna Nichols and Anthony C. Woodbury, eds., pp. 89–110. Cambridge, UK: Cambridge University Press.

Heath, Shirley Brice
1984   Linguistics and education. In Annual Review of Anthropology, vol. 13. Bernard J. Siegel and others, eds., pp. 251–274. Palo Alto, CA: Annual Reviews.

Heise, David
2010   Surveying cultures: discovering shared conceptions and sentiments. Hoboken, NJ: John Wiley.

Heller, Monica
1988   (ed.) Codeswitching: anthropological and sociolinguistic perspectives. Berlin: Mouton de Gruyter.
2011   Paths to post-nationalism: a critical ethnography of language and identity. New York: Oxford University Press.

Hewes, Gordon W.
1975   (comp.) Language origins: a bibliography, 2d rev. and enl. ed. The Hague: Mouton.

Hickerson, Harold, Glen D. Turner, and Nancy P. Hickerson
1952   Testing procedures for estimating transfer of information among Iroquois dialects and languages. International Journal of American Linguistics 18:1–8.

Hilger, Sister M. Inez
1957   Araucanian child life and its cultural background. Smithsonian Miscellaneous Collections, vol. 133. Washington, DC: Smithsonian Institution.

Hill, Jane H.
1978   Apes and language. In Annual Review of Anthropology, vol. 7. Bernard J. Siegel and others, eds., pp. 89–112. Palo Alto, CA: Annual Reviews.
1987   Women's speech in modern Mexicano. In Language, gender, and sex in comparative perspective. Susan Philips, Susan Steele, and Christine Tanz, eds., pp. 121–162. Cambridge, UK: Cambridge University Press.
2008   The everyday language of white racism. Malden, MA: Wiley-Blackwell.

Hill, Jane, and Bruce Mannheim
1992   Language and world view. In Annual Review of Anthropology, vol. 21. Bernard J. Siegel and others, eds., pp. 381–406. Palo Alto, CA: Annual Reviews.

Hill, W. W.
1936   Navaho warfare. Yale University Publications in Anthropology, vol. 5. New Haven, CT: Yale University Press.

Hinnebusch, Thomas J.
1979   Swahili. *In* Languages and their status. Timothy Shopen, ed., pp. 209–293. Cambridge, MA: Winthrop.

Hinton, Leanne, Johanna Nichols, and John J. Ohala, eds.
2006   Sound symbolism. Cambridge, UK: Cambridge University Press.

Hock, Hans Henrich
1991   Principles of historical linguistics, second edition, revised and expanded. Berlin: Mouton de Gruyter.

Hockett, Charles F.
1958   A course in modern linguistics. New York: Macmillan.
1960   The origin of speech. Scientific American 203:3:88–96 (September).
1973   Man's place in nature. New York: McGraw-Hill.
1978   In search of Jove's brow. American Speech 53:243–313.

Hockett, Charles F., and Stuart A. Altmann
1968   A note on design features. *In* Animal communication: techniques of study and results of research. Thomas A. Sebeok, ed., pp. 61–72. Bloomington: Indiana University Press.

Hockett, Charles F., and Robert Ascher
1964   The human revolution. Current Anthropology 5:135–168 [with comments by others and the authors' reply].

Hogan, Jackie
2003   The social significance of English loanwords in Japan. Japanese Studies 23(1):43–59.

Hogan, Helen Marie
n.d.   An ethnography of communication among the Ashanti. Penn-Texas Working Papers in Sociolinguistics, no. 1. [Austin.]

Hoijer, Harry
1954   (ed.) Language in culture: proceedings of a conference on the interrelations of language and other aspects of culture. American Anthropological Association Memoir, no. 79. Menasha, WI: American Anthropological Association.
1956   Lexicostatistics: a critique. Language 32:49–60.

Holm, John A.
1988–1989   Pidgins and creoles, 2 vols. Cambridge, UK: Cambridge University Press.
2000   An introduction to pidgins and creoles. Cambridge, UK: Cambridge University Press.

Huang, Yan
2007   Pragmatics. New York: Oxford University Press.

Humboldt, Wilhelm von
1907   Wilhelm von Humboldts Werke, vol. 7. Albert Leitzmann, ed. Berlin: Behrs Verlag.

Hurford, James, Brendan Heasley, and Michael Smith
2007   Semantics: a coursebook. Cambridge, UK: Cambridge University Press.

Hutchby, Ian, and Robin Wooffitt
2008   Conversational analysis. 2d ed. Cambridge, UK: Polity Press.

Hymes, Dell H.
1958   Linguistic features peculiar to Chinookan myths. International Journal of American Linguistics 24:253–257.
1961   Functions of speech: an evolutionary approach. *In* Anthropology and education. Frederick C. Gruber, ed., pp. 55–83. Philadelphia: University of Pennsylvania Press.
1962   The ethnography of speaking. *In* Anthropology and human behavior. Thomas Gladwin and William C. Sturtevant, eds., pp. 13–53. Washington: Anthropological Society of Washington.
1963   Notes toward a history of linguistic anthropology. Anthropological Linguistics 5:1:59–103.
1964   (ed.) Language in culture and society: a reader in linguistics and anthropology. New York: Harper and Row.
1966   Two types of linguistic relativity (with examples from Amerindian ethnography). *In* Sociolinguistics. William Bright, ed., pp. 114–167. The Hague: Mouton.
1968   Linguistic problems in defining the concept of "tribe." *In* Essays on the problem of tribe. Proceedings of the 1967 Annual Spring Meeting of the American Ethnological Society, June Helm, ed., pp. 23–48. Seattle: University of Washington Press.
1972   Models of the interaction of language and social life. *In* Directions in sociolinguistics: the ethnography of communication. John J. Gumperz and Dell Hymes, eds., pp. 35–71. New York: Holt, Rinehart and Winston.
1974   Foundations in sociolinguistics: an ethnographic approach. Philadelphia: University of Pennsylvania Press.
1983   Essays in the history of linguistic anthropology: Amsterdam Studies in the Theory and History of Linguistic Science, vol. 25. Amsterdam and Philadelphia: Benjamins.
1989   Ways of speaking. *In* Explorations in the ethnography of speaking, 2d ed. Richard Bauman and Joel Sherzer, eds., pp. 433–445. Cambridge, UK: Cambridge University Press.

Inoue, Kyoko
1979   Japanese: a story of language and people. *In* Languages and their speakers. Timothy Shopen, ed., pp. 241–300. Cambridge, MA: Winthrop.

Inoue, Miyako
2006   Vicarious language: gender and linguistic modernity in Japan. Berkeley: University of California Press.

Itoh, Masako, with Nobuko Adachi and James Stanlaw
2007   "I'm married to your company!" Everyday voices of Japanese women. Lanham, MD: Rowman & Littlefield.

Jackendoff, Ray
1983   Semantics and cognition. Cambridge, MA: MIT Press.

Jackson, Howard, and Zé Amvela
2007   Words, meaning and vocabulary: an introduction to modern English lexicology, 2d ed. London: Continuum.

Jakobson, Roman
1968   Child language, aphasia and phonological universals. Allan R. Keiler, trans. The Hague: Mouton.

Jeffers, Robert J., and Ilse Lehiste
1979 Principles and methods for historical linguistics. Cambridge, MA: MIT Press.

Jefferson, Thomas
1944 The life and selected writings of Thomas Jefferson. Adrienne Koch and William Peden, eds. New York: Random House.

Jesperson, Otto
1955 Growth and structure of the English language. 9th ed. Garden City, NY: Doubleday.

Johnstone, Barbara
2008 Discourse analysis. 2d ed. Malden, MA: Blackwell.

Joos, Martin
1962 The five clocks. Indiana University Research Center in Anthropology, Folklore, and Linguistics Publications, no. 22. Bloomington.

Joseph, John
2004 Language and identity: national, ethnic, religious. New York: Palgrave.

Jourdan, C.
1991 Pidgins and creoles: the blurring of categories. In Annual Review of Anthropology, vol. 20. Bernard J. Siegel and others, eds., pp. 187–209. Palo Alto, CA: Annual Reviews.

Kachru, Braj B., ed.
1992 The other tongue: English across cultures. 2d ed. Urbana: University of Illinois Press.

Kachru, Braj B, Yamuna Kachru, and S. N. Sridhar, eds.
2008 Language in South Asia. Cambridge, UK: Cambridge University Press.

Kachru, Yamuna, and Larry Smith
2008 Cultures, contexts, and world Englishes. New York: Routledge.

Kaiser, Mark, and V. Shevoroshkin
1988 Nostratic. In Annual Review of Anthropology, vol. 17. Bernard J. Siegel and others, eds., pp. 309–329. Palo Alto, CA: Annual Reviews.

Kamusella, Tomasz
2009 The politics of language and nationalism in modern Central Europe. New York: Palgrave Macmillan.

Kay, Paul, Brent Berlin, Luisa Maffi, William R. Merrifield, and Richard Cook
2009 World color survey. Stanford: Center for the Study of Language and Information. Chicago: University of Chicago Press.

Kay, Paul, Brent Berlin, and William Merrifield
1991 Biocultural implications of systems of color naming. Journal of Linguistic Anthropology 1:12–25.

Keesing, Roger
1972 Paradigms lost: the new ethnography and the new linguistics. Southwestern Journal of Anthropology 28:299–332.

Keller, Charles, and Janet Dixon Keller
1998 Cognition and tool use: the blacksmith at work. Cambridge, UK: Cambridge University Press.

Kelsky, Karen
2001   Women on the verge: Japanese women, western dreams. Durham, NC: Duke University Press.

Kempton, Willet
1981   The folk classification of ceramics: a study of cognitive prototypes. New York: Academic Press.

Kendon, Adam
1997   Gesture. *In* Annual Review of Anthropology, vol. 26. William H. Durham and others, eds., pp. 109–128. Palo Alto, CA: Annual Reviews.

Kennedy, Chris, ed.
1983   Language planning and language education. London: Allen and Unwin.

Key, Mary Ritchie
1977   Nonverbal communication: a research guide and bibliography. Metuchen, NJ: Scarecrow Press.

Kimball, Geoffrey
1987   Men's and women's speech in Koasati: a reappraisal. International Journal of American Linguistics 53:30–38.

King, Linda
1994   Roots of identity: language and literacy in Mexico. Stanford, CA: Stanford University Press.

Kiparsky, Paul
1976   Historical linguistics and the origin of language. *In* Annals of the New York Academy of Sciences, vol. 280: Origins and evolution of language and speech. Stevan R. Harnad, Horst D. Steklis, and Jane Lancaster, eds., pp. 97–103. New York: New York Academy of Sciences.

Klima, Edward S., and Ursula Bellugi
1979   The signs of language. Cambridge, MA: Harvard University Press.

Kluckhohn, Clyde
1949   Mirror for man: the relation of anthropology to modern life. New York: McGraw-Hill.

Kluckhohn, Clyde, and Dorothea Leighton
1962   The Navaho. Rev. ed. Garden City, NY, and New York: American Museum of Natural History and Doubleday.

Kramarae, Cheris
1981   Women and men speaking: frameworks for analysis. Rowley, MA: Newbury House.

Krauss, Michael
1992   The world's languages in crisis. Language 68:4–10.

Kronenfeld, David
1996   Plastic glasses and church fathers. New York: Oxford University Press.

Kroskrity, Paul V.
1983   On male and female speech in the Pueblo Southwest. International Journal of American Linguistics 49:88–91.
1988   (ed.) On the ethnography of communication: the legacy of Sapir. Essays in honor of Harry Hoijer, 1984. Los Angeles: University of California Press.

1993   Language, history, and identity: ethnolinguistic studies of the Arizona Tewa. Tucson: University of Arizona Press.

2000   (ed.) Regimes of language: ideologies, polities, and identities. Santa Fe, NM: School of American Research Press.

Krus, David, and Yoko Ishigaki

1992   Kamikaze pilots: the Japanese vs. the American perspective. Psychological Reports 70: 599–602.

Kubota, Ryuko, and Angel Lin, eds.

2009   Race, culture, and identities in second language education: exploring critically engaged practice. New York: Routledge.

Labov, William

1963   The social motivation of a sound change. Word 19:273–309.

1966   The social stratification of English in New York City. Washington, DC: Center for Applied Linguistics.

1970   The logic of nonstandard English. In Report of the Twentieth Annual Round Table Meeting on Linguistics and Language Studies. Monograph Series on Languages and Linguistics, no. 22, pp. 1–43. Washington, DC: Georgetown University Press.

1972a   Language in the inner city: studies in the Black English vernacular. Philadelphia: University of Pennsylvania Press.

1972b   Sociolinguistic patterns. Philadelphia: University of Pennsylvania Press.

1982   Objectivity and commitment in linguistic science: the case of the Black English trial in Ann Arbor. Language in Society 11:165–201.

2005   Atlas of North American English: phonetics, phonology and sound change (with CD-ROM). The Hague: Mouton de Gruyter.

2010a   Principles of linguistic change: internal factors. Malden, MA: Wiley-Blackwell.

2010b   Principles of linguistic change: social factors. Malden, MA: Wiley-Blackwell.

2010c   Principles of linguistic change: cognitive and cultural factors. Malden, MA: Wiley-Blackwell.

Ladefoged, Peter

1992   Another view of endangered languages. Language 68:809–811.

Ladefoged, Peter, and Keith Johnson

2010   A course in phonetics (with CD-ROM). 6th ed. Florence, KY: Wadsworth/Cengage.

Laitman, Jeffrey T.

1984   The anatomy of human speech. Natural History 93:8:20, 22–24, 26–27.

Lakoff, Robin

1975   Language and woman's place. New York: Harper and Row. Revised and expanded ed. 2004, Oxford University Press.

Langacker, Ronald W.

1972   Fundamentals of linguistic analysis. New York: Harcourt Brace Jovanovich.

Larson, Richard K., Vivian Déprez, and Hiroko Yamakido, eds.

2010   The evolution of human language: biolinguistic perspectives. Cambridge, UK: Cambridge University Press.

Law, Howard W.
1958   Morphological structure of Isthmus Nahuat. International Journal of American Linguistics 24:108–129.

Leap, William L.
1981   American Indian language maintenance. *In* Annual Review of Anthropology, vol. 10. Bernard J. Siegel and others, eds., pp. 209–236. Palo Alto, CA: Annual Reviews.

Leavitt, John
2011   Linguistic relativities: language diversity and modern thought. Cambridge, UK: Cambridge University Press.

Lenneberg, Eric H.
1967   Biological foundations of language. New York: Wiley.

Lenneberg, Eric, and John Roberts
1956   The Language of experience: a study in methodology: International Journal of American Linguistics 22(2), supplemental memoir 13.

Leu, Donald J., Lisa Zawilinski, Jill Castek, Manju Banerjee, Brian Housand, Yinjie Liu, and Maureen O'Neil
2007   What is new about the new literacies of online reading comprehension. *In* Secondary school reading and writing: what research reveals for classroom practices. Leslie S. Rush, A. Jonathan Eakle, and Allen Berger, eds., pp. 37–69. Urbana, IL: National Council of Teachers of English.

Levinson, Stephen C.
1983   Pragmatics. Cambridge, UK: Cambridge University Press.
1996   Language and space. *In* Annual Review of Anthropology, vol. 25. William H. Durham and others, eds., pp. 353–382. Palo Alto, CA: Annual Reviews.

Lévi-Strauss, Claude
1963   Structural anthropology: Claire Jacobson and Brooke Grundfest Schoepf, trans. New York: Basic Books.

Lewis, Paul
2009   Statistical summaries: Ethnologue: Languages of the world, http://www.ethnologue .com/ethno_docs/distribution.asp?by=size

Li, Wei, ed.
2007   The bilingualism reader. 2d ed. London: Routledge.

Lieberman, Philip
1984   The biology and evolution of language. Cambridge, MA: Harvard University Press.

Loftus, Elizabeth F., and John C. Palmer
1974   Reconstruction of automobile destruction: an example of the interaction between language and memory. Journal of Verbal Learning and Verbal Behavior 13:585–589.

Lucy, John A.
1992a   Grammatical categories and cognition: a case study of the linguistic relativity hypothesis. Cambridge, UK: Cambridge University Press.
1992b   Language diversity and thought: a reformulation of the linguistic relativity hypothesis. Cambridge, UK: Cambridge University Press.

1997 Linguistic relativity. *In* Annual Review of Anthropology, vol. 26. William H. Durham and others, eds., pp. 291–312. Palo Alto, CA: Annual Reviews.

Lyons, John
1977 Semantics, vol. 1 and vol. 2. Cambridge, UK: Cambridge University Press.
1978 Noam Chomsky. Rev. ed. New York: Penguin Books.

Macaulay, Ronald
2002 Discourse variation. *In* The handbook of language variation and change. J. K. Chambers, Peter Trudgill, and Natalie Schilling-Estes, eds., pp. 283–305. Malden, MA: Blackwell.

MacLaury, Robert
1997 Color and cognition in Mesoamerica: constructing categories as vantages. Austin: University of Texas Press.

MacLaury, Robert, Galina Paramei, and Don Dedrick, eds.
2007 Anthropology of color: interdisciplinary multilevel modeling. Amsterdam: John Benjamins.

Macnamara, John
1982 Names for things: a study in human learning. Cambridge: MIT Press.

Maddieson, Ian
1984 Patterns of sounds. Cambridge, UK: Cambridge University Press.

Malinowski, Bronislaw
1915 The natives of Mailu: preliminary results of the Robert Mond research work in British New Guinea. Transactions and Proceedings of the Royal Society of South Australia 39:494–706. Adelaide.
1922 Argonauts of the western Pacific: an account of native enterprise and adventure in the archipelagoes of Melanesian New Guinea. London: Routledge and Kegan Paul.
1923 The problem of meaning in primitive languages. *In* The meaning of meaning. C. K. Ogdon and I. A. Richards, eds., pp. 296–336. London: Routledge.

Mallory, J. P.
1991 In search of the Indo-Europeans: language, archaeology, and myth. London: Thames & Hudson.

Martínez-Flor, Alicia, and Esther Usó-Juan, eds.
2010 Speech act performance: theoretical, empirical and methodological issues. Amsterdam: John Benjamins.

May, Stephen
2008 Language and minority rights: ethnicity, nationalism and the politics of language. New York: Routledge.

McConnell-Ginet, Sally
1988 Language and gender. *In* Linguistics: the Cambridge survey. Vol. 4: Language: the socio-cultural context. Frederick J. Newmeyer, ed., pp. 75–99. Cambridge, UK: Cambridge University Press.

McElhinny, Bonnie
1995 Challenging hegemonic masculinities: female and male police officers handling domestic violence. *In* Gender articulated: language and the socially constructed self. Kira Hall and Mary Bucholtz, eds. New York: Routledge.

Menyuk, Paula
1988 Language development: knowledge and use. Glenview, IL: Scott, Foresman.

Merrifield, William R., and others, eds.
1967 Laboratory manual for morphology and syntax. Rev. ed. Santa Ana, CA: Summer Institute of Linguistics.

Merrifield, William, Constance M. Naish, Calvin R. Rensch, and Gillian Story, eds.
2003 Laboratory manual for morphology and syntax. 7th ed. Dallas, TX: Summer Institute of Linguistics.

Millar, Robert McColl
2007 Trask's historical linguistics. 2d ed. New York: Oxford University Press.

Mills, Sara, ed.
1995 Language and gender: interdisciplinary perspectives. New York: Longman.

Montagu, Ashley
1976 Toolmaking, hunting, and the origin of language. In Annals of the New York Academy of Sciences, vol. 280: Origins and evolution of language and speech. Stevan R. Harnad, Horst D. Steklis, and Jane Lancaster, eds., pp. 266–274. New York: New York Academy of Sciences.

Morgan, Marcyliena
1994 Theories and politics in African American English. In Annual Review of Anthropology, vol. 23. William H. Durham and others, eds., pp. 325–345. Palo Alto, CA: Annual Reviews.

Mühlhäusler, Peter
1986 Pidgin and creole linguistics. Oxford, UK: Blackwell.
1987 The history of research into Tok Pisin, 1900–1975. In Pidgin and creole languages: essays in memory of John E. Reinecke. Glenn G. Gilbert, ed., pp. 177–209. Honolulu: University of Hawaii Press.

Murphy, George
2002 The big book of concepts. Cambridge: MIT Press.

Murphy, John
1980 The book of pidgin English. New York: AMS Press.

Myers-Scotton, Carol
1993 Social motivations for code switching: evidence from Africa. Cambridge, UK: Cambridge University Press.

Nettle, Daniel, and Suzanne Romaine
2000 Vanishing voices: the extinction of the world's languages. New York: Oxford University Press.

Newman, Stanley
1955 Vocabulary levels: Zuñi sacred and slang usage. Southwestern Journal of Anthropology 11:345–354.

Newmeyer, Frederick J.
1989 Linguistics: the Cambridge survey. Volume III: Language: psychological and biological aspects. Cambridge, UK: Cambridge University Press.

O'Barr, William M.

1981   The language of the law. *In* Language in the USA. Charles A. Ferguson and Shirley Brice Heath, eds., pp. 386–406. Cambridge, UK: Cambridge University Press.

O'Barr, William M., and Bowman K. Atkins

1998   'Women's language' or 'powerless language'? *In* Language and gender: a reader. Jennifer Coates, ed., pp. 377–387. Oxford, UK: Blackwell.

O'Barr, William M., and John M. Conley

1996   When a juror watches a lawyer. *In* Talking about people: readings in contemporary cultural anthropology. 2d ed. William A. Haviland and Robert J. Gordon, eds, pp. 42–45. Mountain View, CA: Mayfield Publishing.

Ochs, Elinor, and Bambi B. Schieffelin

1982   Language acquisition and socialization: three developmental stories and their implications. Working Papers in Sociolinguistics, no. 105. Austin, TX: Southwest Educational Development Laboratory.

2006   The impact of language socialization on grammatical development. *In* Language, culture, and society. Christine Jourdan and Kevin Tuite, eds., pp. 168–189. Cambridge, UK: Cambridge University Press.

Ochs, Elinor, and Carolyn Taylor

2001   The "Father Knows Best" dynamic in dinnertime narratives. *In* Linguistic anthropology: a reader. Alessandro Duranti, ed., pp. 431–449. Malden, MA: Blackwell.

Ogden, C. K., and I. A. Richards

1923   [1989] The meaning of meaning. San Diego: Harcourt Brace Jovanovich.

O'Grady, William, John Archibald, Mark Aronoff, and Janie Rees-Miller

2004   Contemporary linguistics: an introduction. 5th ed. Boston: Bedford/St. Martin's.

Ohala, John

1997   Sound symbolism. Proceedings of the 4th Seoul International Conference on Linguistics [SICOL], 11–15 August 1997, pp. 98–103.

Osgood, Charles E., and Oliver C. S. Tzeng, eds.

1990   Language, meaning, and culture: the selected papers of C. E. Osgood. New York: Praeger.

Ottenheimer, Harriet

2008   The anthropology of language: an introduction to linguistic anthropology. 2d ed. Belmont, CA: Wadsworth Cengage.

Pecos, Regis, and Rebecca Blum-Martinez

2001   The key to cultural survival: language planning and revitalization in the Pueblo de Cochiti. *In* The green book of language revitalization in practice. Leanne Hinton and Ken Hale, eds., pp. 75–82. San Diego, CA: Academic Press.

Philips, Susan U.

1980   Sex differences and language. *In* Annual Review of Anthropology, vol. 9. Bernard J. Siegel and others, eds., pp. 523–544. Palo Alto, CA: Annual Reviews.

Philips, Susan U., Susan Steele, and Christine Tanz, eds.

1987   Language, gender, and sex in comparative perspective. Studies in the Social and Cultural Foundations of Language, no. 4. Cambridge, UK: Cambridge University Press.

Philipsen, Gerry, and Donal Carbaugh
1986   A bibliography of fieldwork in the ethnography of communication. Language in Society 15:387–397.

Pike, Kenneth L.
1954   Language in relation to a unified theory of the structure of human behavior. Glendale, CA: Summer Institute of Linguistics.
1967   Language in relation to a unified theory of the structure of human behavior. 2d rev. ed. The Hague: Mouton.

Pike, Kenneth L., and Eunice Victoria Pike
1947   Immediate constituents of Mazateco syllables. International Journal of American Linguistics 13:78–91.

Pinker, Steven
1992   Review of Derek Bickerton: Language and species. Language 68:375–382.
1994   The language instinct. New York: HarperCollins.
2009   How the mind works. New York: W. W. Norton & Company.

Pinker, Steven, and Paul Bloom
1990   Natural language and natural selection. Behavioral and Brain Sciences 13:707–784.

Pi-Sunyer, Oriol, and Zdenek Salzmann
1978   Humanity and culture: an introduction to anthropology. Boston: Houghton Mifflin.

Pitchford, Nicola, and Carole P. Biggam, eds.
2006   Progress in colour studies. Volume II: Psychological aspects. Amsterdam: John Benjamins.

Plato
1961   The collected dialogues of Plato including the letters. Edith Hamilton and Huntington Cairns, eds. Princeton, NJ: Princeton University Press.

Poplack, Shana
2000   Sometimes I'll start a sentence in Spanish y termino en español. In The bilingualism reader. Wei Li, ed., pp. 221–256. London: Routledge

Postal, Paul M.
1969   Mohawk vowel doubling. International Journal of American Linguistics 35:291–298.

Powell, John Wesley
1883   Second annual report of the Bureau of Ethnology to the Secretary of the Smithsonian Institution, 1880–81. Washington, DC: Government Printing Office.

Premack, Ann James, and David Premack
1972   Teaching language to an ape. Scientific American 227:4:92–99 (October).

President's Commission on Foreign Language and International Studies
1979   Strength through wisdom: a critique of U.S. capability. Washington, DC: U.S. Department of Health, Education, and Welfare/Office of Education.

Pütz, Martin, and Marjolijn Verspoor
2000   Explorations in linguistic relativity. Amsterdam: John Benjamins.

Quiles, Carlos, with Fernando López-Menchero
2009   A grammar of modern Indo-European. 2d ed. Language and culture, writing system and phonology, morphology, syntax, texts and dictionary, ethnology. The European Union: Asociación Cultural Dnghu.

Radford, Andrew
1988 Transformational grammar: a first course. Cambridge, UK: Cambridge University Press.
1997 Syntax: a minimalist introduction. Cambridge, UK: Cambridge University Press.
2006 Syntax: a generative introduction. 2d ed. Malden, MA: Blackwell.

Rampton, Ben
1995 Crossing: language and ethnicity among adolescents. New York: Longman.

Riemer, Nick
2010 Introducing semantics. Cambridge, UK: Cambridge University Press.

Roitblat, Herbert L., Louis M. Herman, and Paul E. Nachtigall, eds.
1992 Language and communication: comparative perspectives. Hillsdale, NJ: Erlbaum.

Romaine, Suzanne
1988 Pidgin and creole languages. New York: Longman.

Romney, A. Kimball, and Roy Goodwin D'Andrade, eds.
1964 Transcultural studies in cognition. American Anthropologist 66:3 (part 2) (special publication).

Salus, Peter H., ed.
1969 On language: Plato to von Humboldt. New York: Holt, Rinehart and Winston.

Salzmann, Zdenek
1959 Arapaho kinship terms and two related ethnolinguistic observations. Anthropological Linguistics 1:9:6–10.
1983 Dictionary of contemporary Arapaho usage. Arapaho Language and Culture Instructional Materials Series, no. 4. Wind River Reservation, WY: Arapaho Language and Culture Commission.

Samarin, William J.
1967 Field linguistics: a guide to linguistic field work. New York: Holt, Rinehart and Winston.

Samovar, Larry A., and Richard E. Porter, eds.
1991 Intercultural communication: a reader. 6th ed. Belmont, CA: Wadsworth.

Sapir, Edward
1916 Time perspective in aboriginal American culture: a study in method. Canada, Department of Mines, Geological Survey, memoir 90; Anthropological Series, no. 13. Ottawa: Government Printing Bureau.
1921 Language: an introduction to the study of speech. New York: Harcourt, Brace.
1922 The Takelma language of southwestern Oregon. In Handbook of American Indian languages, part 1. Franz Boas, ed., pp. 1–296. Washington, DC: Government Printing Office.
1929a The status of linguistics as a science. Language 5:207–214.
1929b A study in phonetic symbolism. Journal of Experimental Psychology 12:225–239.
1949 Selected writings of Edward Sapir in language, culture, and personality. David G. Mandelbaum, ed. Berkeley: University of California Press.

Savage-Rumbaugh, E. Sue
1984 Pan paniscus and Pan troglodytes: contrasts in preverbal communicative competence. In The pygmy chimpanzee: evolutionary biology and behavior. Randall L. Susman, ed., pp. 395–413. New York: Plenum Press.

1986 Ape language: from conditioned response to symbol. New York: Columbia University Press.

Saville-Troike, Muriel
1982 The ethnography of communication: an introduction. Baltimore: University Park Press.
2002 The ethnography of communication: an introduction. 3d ed. Malden, MA: Blackwell.
2006 Introducing second language acquisition. Cambridge, UK: Cambridge University Press.

Schendl, Herbert
2001 Historical linguistics. New York: Oxford University Press.

Schieffelin, Bambi B.
1990 The give and take of everyday life: language socialization of Kaluli children. New York: Cambridge University Press.
2005 The give and take of everyday life: language socialization of Kaluli children. 2d ed. Tucson: Fenestra Books.

Schieffelin, Bambi B., and Elinor Ochs
1986 Language socialization. In Annual Review of Anthropology, vol. 15. Bernard J. Siegel and others, eds., pp. 163–191. Palo Alto, CA: Annual Reviews.

Schieffelin, Bambi B., Kathryn A. Woolard, and Paul V. Kroskrity, eds.
1998 Language ideologies: practice and theory. New York: Oxford University Press.

Schrier, Allan M., and Fred Stollnitz, eds.
1971 Behavior of nonhuman primates: modern research trends, vol. 4. New York: Academic Press.

Scollon, Ronald, and Suzanne B. K. Scollon
1981 Narrative, literacy and face in interethnic communication. Norwood, NJ: Ablex Publishing.
1990 Athabaskan-English interethnic communication. In Cultural communication and intercultural contact. Donal Carbaugh, ed., pp. 259–286. Hillsdale, NJ: Lawrence Erlbaum.

Scollon, Ronald, and Suzanne Wong Scollon
2001 Intercultural communication: a discourse approach. 2d ed. Oxford, UK: Blackwell.

Scribner, Sylvia, and Michael Cole
1981 The psychology of literacy. Cambridge, MA: Harvard University Press.

Sebeok, Thomas A., ed.
1974 Current trends in linguistics. Vol. 12: Linguistics and adjacent arts and sciences. The Hague: Mouton.
1977 How animals communicate. Bloomington: Indiana University Press.

Shaul, David, and Louanna Furbee
1998 Language and culture. Prospect Heights, IL: Waveland Press.

Sherzer, Joel
1977 The ethnography of speaking: a critical appraisal. In Georgetown University Round Table on Languages and Linguistics 1977, pp. 43–57. Washington, DC: Georgetown University Press.

1986   The report of a Kuna curing specialist: the poetics and rhetoric of an oral performance. *In* Native South American discourse. Joel Sherzer and Greg Urban, eds., pp. 169–212. Berlin: Mouton de Gruyter.

1987   A discourse-centered approach to language and culture. American Anthropologist 89:295–309.

1990   Verbal art in San Blas: Kuna culture through its discourse. Cambridge, UK: Cambridge University Press.

Sherzer, Joel, and Regna Darnell
1972   Outline guide for the ethnographic study of speech use. *In* Directions in sociolinguistics: the ethnography of communication. John J. Gumperz and Dell Hymes, eds., pp. 548–554. New York: Holt, Rinehart and Winston.

Shibamoto, Janet S.
1985   Japanese women's language. New York: Academic Press.

Shore, Bradd
1996   Culture in mind: cognition, culture, and the problem of meaning. New York: Oxford University Press.

Shuy, Roger W.
1984   Linguistics in other professions. *In* Annual Review of Anthropology, vol. 13. Bernard J. Siegel and others, eds., pp. 419–445. Palo Alto, CA: Annual Reviews.

Sidnell, Jack
2010   Conversation analysis: an introduction. Malden. MA: Wiley-Blackwell.

Siebert, Frank T., Jr.
1967   The original home of the Proto-Algonquian people. National Museum of Canada, bulletin 214; Anthropological Series, no. 78: Contributions to Anthropology: Linguistics I (Algonquian), pp. 13–47. Ottawa.

Siegel, Jeff
2008   The emergence of pidgin and creole languages. Oxford, UK: Oxford University Press.

Silva-Corvalán, Carmen
1994   Language contact and change: Spanish in Los Angeles. New York: Oxford University Press.

Silver, Shirley, and Wick R. Miller
2000   American Indian languages: cultural and social contexts. Tucson: University of Arizona Press.

Silverstein, Michael
1985   Language and the culture of gender: at the intersection of structure, usage, and ideology. *In* Semiotic mediation: sociocultural and psychological perspectives. Elizabeth Mertz and Richard J. Parmentier, eds., pp. 219–259. Orlando, FL: Academic Press.

Sims, Christine P., and Hilaire Valiquette
1990   More on male and female speech in (Acoma and Laguna) Keresan. International Journal of American Linguistics 56:162–166.

Skinner, B. F.
1957   Verbal behavior. New York: Appleton-Century-Crofts.

Smith, William
1744   A new voyage to Guinea. . . . London: John Nourse.

Sorensen, Arthur P., Jr.
1967   Multilingualism in the northwest Amazon. American Anthropologist 69:670–684.

Spradley, James
1972   Culture and cognition: rules, maps, and plans. San Francisco: Chandler.

Stanlaw, James
2004a   Japanese and English: language and culture contact. Hong Kong: University of Hong Kong Press.
2004b   What do cognitive scientists know, and what should linguistic anthropologists know about what they know? Teaching Anthropology SACC Notes 10(20):8–12, 33.
2005   The languages of the internet: it's not always English anymore. Anthropology News 46(4):50–51.
2010   Wasei Eigo to Nihon-jin: gengo, bunka sesshoku no dainamizumu (Japanese-English and the Japanese people: the dynamism of language and cultural contacts). Tokyo: Shinsensha.

Stanlaw, James, Robert T. Arrigo, and David L. Anderson
2006   Colors and culture: exploring colors as an anthropologist. Module for use with "The Mind Project," http://www.mind.ilstu.edu/curriculum/virtual_anthro_lab/texts/colors_and_anthro/ chap2_colors_cultures.php

Stanlaw, James, and Bencha Yoddumnern
1985   Thai spirits: a problem in the study of folk classification. In Directions in cognitive anthropology. Janet W. D. Dougherty, ed., pp. 141–160. Urbana: University of Illinois Press.

Stokoe, William C., Jr.
1960   Sign language structure: an outline of the visual communication systems of the American deaf. Studies in Linguistics, Occasional Papers, no. 8. Buffalo, NY: University of Buffalo, Department of Anthropology and Linguistics.

Stross, Brian
1974   Speaking of speaking: Tenejapa Tzeltal metalinguistics. In Explorations in the ethnography of speaking. Richard Bauman and Joel Sherzer, eds., pp. 213–239. London: Cambridge University Press.
1976   The origin and evolution of language. Dubuque, IA: Wm. C. Brown.

Sturtevant, Edgar H.
1947   An introduction to linguistic science. New Haven, CT: Yale University Press.

Susman, Randall L., ed.
1984   The pygmy chimpanzee: evolutionary biology and behavior. New York: Plenum Press.

Swadesh, Morris
1950   Salish internal relationships. International Journal of American Linguistics 16:157–167.
1955   Towards greater accuracy in lexicostatistic dating. International Journal of American Linguistics 21:121–137.
1971   The origin and diversification of language. Joel Sherzer, ed. Chicago: Aldine/Atherton.

Takemaru, Naoko
2010 Women in the language and society of Japan: the linguistic roots of bias. Jefferson, NC: McFarland.

Tannen, Deborah
1982 Ethnic style in male-female conversation. *In* Language and social identity. John J. Gumperz, ed., pp. 217–231. Cambridge, UK: Cambridge University Press.
1986 That's not what I meant! How conversational style makes or breaks relations with others. New York: Morrow.
1990 You just don't understand: women and men in conversation. New York: Morrow.
1994a Gender and discourse. New York: Oxford University Press.
1994b Talking from nine to five: men and women at work. New York: Quill.
1999 The display of (gendered) identities in talk at work. *In* Reinventing identities: the gendered self in discourse. Mary Bucholtz, A. C. Liang, Laurel A. Sutton, eds., pp. 221–240. New York: Oxford University Press.

Tanz, Christine
1971 Sound symbolism in words relating to proximity and distance. Language and Speech 14:266–276.

Taylor, Allan R.
1994 Gros Ventre dictionary. Prefinal version. Volume 1: A-L, Volume 2: M-Z, and Volume 3: Gros Ventre stem index.

Taylor, Douglas
1951 Sex gender in Central American Carib. International Journal of American Linguistics 17:102–104.

Taylor, John
2002 Near synonyms as co-extensive categories: 'high' and 'tall' revisited. Language Sciences 25:263–284.

Teeter, Karl V.
1964 "Anthropological linguistics" and linguistic anthropology. American Anthropologist 66:878–879.

Terrace, Herbert S.
1979 Nim: a chimpanzee who learned sign language. New York: Knopf.

Thorne, Alan G., and Milford H. Wolpoff
1992 The multiregional evolution of humans. Scientific American 266:4:76–79, 82–83 (April).

Thorne, Barrie, Cheris Kramarae, and Nancy Henley, eds.
1983 Language, gender and society. Rowley, MA: Newbury House.

Time-Life Books
1973 The first men. Emergence of man series. New York: Time-Life Books.

Ting-Toomey, Stella
1986 Conflict communication styles in black and white subjective cultures. *In* Interethnic communication: current research, vol. 10. Young Yun Kim, ed., pp. 75–88. Newbury Park, CA: Sage.

Todd, Loreto
1984 Modern Englishes: pidgins and creoles. Oxford, UK: Blackwell.

1990   Pidgins and creoles. London: Routledge.

Tomkins, William
1969   Indian sign language. New York: Dover. (Originally published by the author in 1926 under the title Universal [American] Indian sign language [of the Plains Indians of North America. . .].)

Trager, George L.
1958   Paralanguage: a first approximation. Studies in Linguistics 13:1–12.
1972   Language and languages. San Francisco, CA: Chandler.

Trudgill, Peter, ed.
1984   Applied sociolinguistics. Orlando, FL: Academic Press.

Tsuda, Yukio
1994   The diffusion of English: its impact on culture and communication. Keio Communication Review 16:48–61.
1996   Shinryaku-suru Eigo, hangeki-suru Nihongo (Invading English, counterattacking Japanese) Tokyo: PHP.
1997   Hegemony of English vs. ecology of language: building equality in international communication. In World Englishes 2000: selected essays. Larry Smith and Michael Forman, eds., pp. 21–31. Honolulu, HI: University of Hawaii Press/East-West Center.

Tyler, Stephen A., ed.
1969   Cognitive anthropology. New York: Holt, Rinehart and Winston.

Urciuoli, Bonnie
1996   Exposing prejudice: Puerto Rican experiences of language, race, and class. Boulder, CO: Westview Press.

Voegelin, Charles F., and Z. S. Harris
1952   Training in anthropological linguistics. American Anthropologist 54:322–327.

Voegelin, Charles F., and Florence M. Voegelin
1954   Obtaining a linguistic sample. International Journal of American Linguistics 20:89–100.
1957   Hopi domains: a lexical approach to the problem of selection. Indiana University Publications in Anthropology and Linguistics, memoir 14 of the International Journal of American Linguistics. Baltimore: Waverly Press.
1959   Guide for transcribing unwritten languages in field work. Anthropological Linguistics 1:6:1–28.
1966   (comps.) Map of North American Indian languages. American Ethnological Society.

Voegelin, Charles F., Florence M. Voegelin, and LaVerne Masayesva Jeanne
1979   Hopi semantics. In Handbook of North American Indians, vol. 9. Southwest, pp. 581–586. Washington, DC: Smithsonian Institution.

Voyles, Joseph, and Charles Barrack
2009   An introduction to Proto-Indo-European and the early Indo-European languages. Bloomington, IN: Slavica Publishers.

Walter, Henriette
1988   Le français dans tous les sens. Paris: R. Laffont.

Wardhaugh, Ronald, and H. Douglas Brown, eds.
1976   A survey of applied linguistics. Ann Arbor: University of Michigan Press.

Watanabe, Suwako
1993 Cultural differences in framing: American and Japanese group discussions. *In* Framing in discourse. Deborah Tannen, ed., pp. 176–209. New York: Oxford University Press.

Waterhouse, Viola
1962 The grammatical structure of Oaxaca Chontal. Indiana University Research Center in Anthropology, Folklore, and Linguistics Publications, no. 19. Bloomington.

Watkins, Calvert
1992 Indo-European and the Indo-Europeans. *In* The American Heritage Dictionary of the English Language. 3d ed., pp. 2081–2134. Boston: Houghton Mifflin.

Watson, O. Michael, and Theodore D. Graves
1966 Quantitative research in proxemic behavior. American Anthropologist 68:971–985.

Weinrich, Uriel
1980 On semantics. Philadelphia: University of Pennsylvania Press.

Weitz, Shirley, ed.
1974 Nonverbal communication: readings with commentary. New York: Oxford University Press.

Wescott, Roger W.
1974 The origin of speech. *In* Language origins. Roger W. Wescott, ed., pp. 103–123. Silver Spring, MD: Linstok Press.

Whorf, Benjamin Lee
1936 The punctual and segmentative aspects of verbs in Hopi. Language 12:127–131.
1940a Science and linguistics. Technology Review 42:229–231, 247–248 (April).
1940b Linguistics as an exact science. Technology Review 43:61–63, 80–83 (December).
1941a Languages and logic. Technology Review 43:250–252, 266, 268, 272 (April).
1941b The relation of habitual thought and behavior to language. *In* Language, culture, and personality: essays in memory of Edward Sapir. Leslie Spier and others, eds., pp. 75–93. Menasha, WI: Sapir Memorial Publication Fund.
1946 The Hopi language, Toreva dialect. *In* Linguistic structures of Native America. Cornelius Osgood, ed. Viking Fund Publications in Anthropology, no. 6, pp. 158–183. New York: Viking Fund.
1950 An American Indian model of the universe. International Journal of American Linguistics 16:67–72.
1956 Language, thought, and reality: selected writings of Benjamin Lee Whorf. John B. Carroll, ed. Cambridge and New York: Technology Press of MIT and John Wiley and Sons.

Wilson, Allan C., and Rebecca L. Cann
1992 The recent African genesis of humans. Scientific American 266:4:68–73 (April).

Witherspoon, Gary
1977 Language and art in the Navajo universe. Ann Arbor: University of Michigan Press.

Wolff, Hans
1967 Language, ethnic identity and social change in southern Nigeria. Anthropological Linguistics 9:1:18–25.

Wolfram, Walt, and Natalie Schilling-Estes
2005 American English: dialects and variation. 2d ed. Malden, MA: Blackwell.

Wonderly, William L.
1951a Zoque II: phonemes and morphophonemes. International Journal of American Linguistics 17:105–123.
1951b Zoque III: morphological classes, affix list, and verbs. International Journal of American Linguistics 17:137–162.

Woolard, Kathryn A.
1989 Double talk: bilingualism and the politics of ethnicity in Catalonia. Stanford, CA: Stanford University Press.

Woolard, Kathryn A., and Bambi B. Schieffelin
1994 Language ideology. *In* Annual Review of Anthropology, vol. 23. William H. Durham and others, eds., pp. 55–82. Palo Alto, CA: Annual Reviews.

Woolford, Ellen B.
1979 Aspects of Tok Pisin grammar. Pacific Linguistics, Series B—Monographs, no. 66. Canberra: Australian National University.

Wright, Sue, ed.
1999 Language, democracy and devolution in Catalonia. Clevedon, UK: Multilingual Matters.

Yegerlehner, John
1955 A note on eliciting techniques. International Journal of American Linguistics 21:286–288.

Zepeda, Ofelia
1983 A Papago grammar. Tucson: University of Arizona Press.

Zhang, Hang
2001 Culture as apology: the Hainan Island incident. World Englishes 20:383–391.

LANGUAGES MENTIONED IN THE TEXT

AND THEIR LOCATIONS

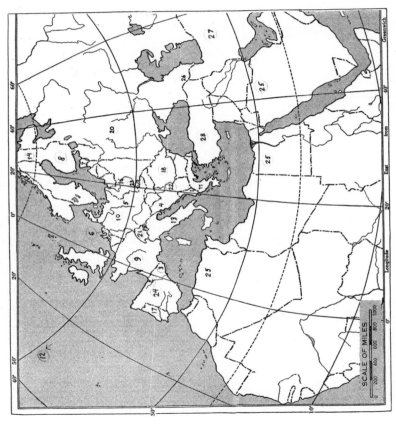

Europe

1 Albanian	9 French
2 Basque	10 German
3 Catalan	11 Greek
4 Croatian	12 Icelandic
5 Czech	13 Italian (and Latin)
6 Dutch	14 Lapp (Sami)
7 Estonian	15 Magyar (Hungarian)
8 Finnish	16 Polish
	17 Portuguese

18 Romanian
19 Romansh
20 Russian
21 Schwyzertütsch
22 Serbian
23 Slovak
24 Spanish

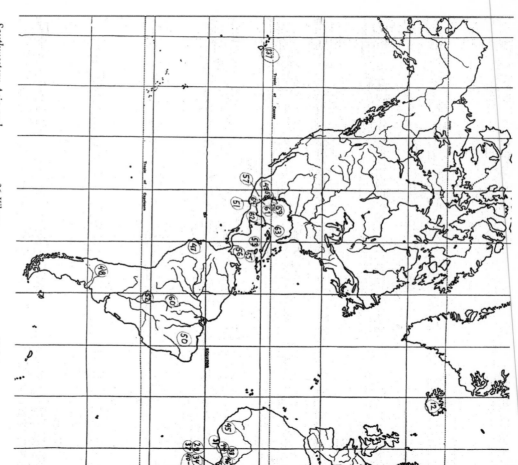

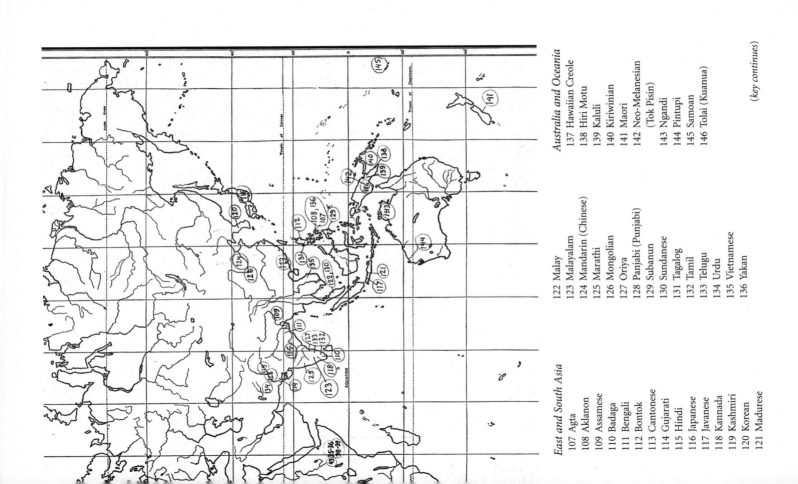

East and South Asia

107 Agta
108 Aklanon
109 Assamese
110 Badaga
111 Bengali
112 Bontok
113 Cantonese
114 Gujarati
115 Hindi
116 Japanese
117 Javanese
118 Kannada
119 Kashmiri
120 Korean
121 Madurese

122 Malay
123 Malayalam
124 Mandarin (Chinese)
125 Marathi
126 Mongolian
127 Oriya
128 Panjabi (Punjabi)
129 Subanun
130 Sundanese
131 Tagalog
132 Tamil
133 Telugu
134 Urdu
135 Vietnamese
136 Yakan

Australia and Oceania

137 Hawaiian Creole
138 Hiri Motu
139 Kaluli
140 Kiriwinian
141 Maori
142 Neo-Melanesian
 (Tok Pisin)
143 Ngandi
144 Pintupi
145 Samoan
146 Tolai (Kuanua)

(key continues)

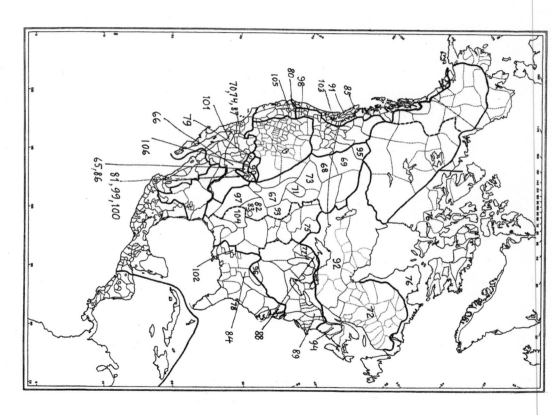

North America North of Mexico

65 Acoma
66 Apache (and Western Apache)
67 Arapaho
68 Atsina (Gros Ventre)
69 Blackfoot
70 Cahuilla
71 Cheyenne
72 Cree-Montagnais

73 Crow
74 Cupeño
75 Dakota
76 Eskimo
77 Fox
78 Gullah
79 Hupa
80 Hopi
81 Keres
82 Kiowa
83 Kiowa Apache
84 Koasati

85 Kwakiutl
86 Laguna
87 Luiseño
88 Menomini
89 Mohawk
90 Navajo
91 Nootka
92 Ojibwa
93 Pawnee
94 Penobscot-Abnaki
95 Sarcee
96 Shawnee

97 Shoshone-Comanche
98 Takelma
99 Tewa
100 Tiwa
101 Tohono O'odham (Papago)
102 Tunica
103 Upper Chinook
104 Wichita
105 Yana
106 Zuni

Note: The locations are based on the map accompanying *Comparative Studies of North American Indians* by Harold E. Driver and William C. Massey (1957).